Hungarian Flag with
Russian Insignia
Post 2nd World War

1956

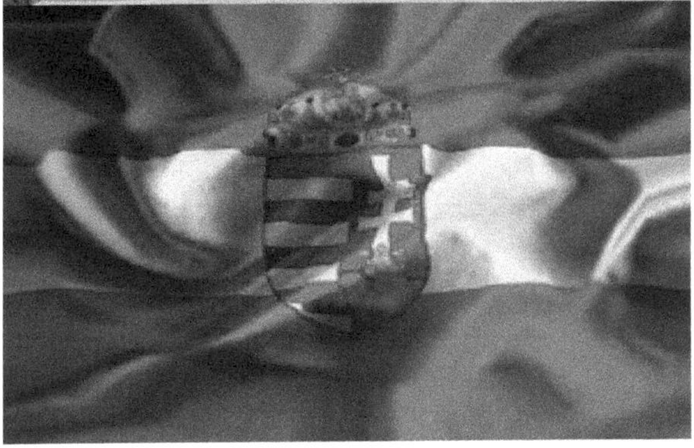

Today (Freedom)

Nandor Pekar 1956 - 1957

Abaújszántó College (Szántó)

The Last Train to Budapest

==========**==========

By
Richard Sandor Pekar

INTRODUCTION

Few people of the western world have neither experienced or understand the trauma and the fear of one nation occupying another. What is a national prisoner? What is like to be under the threat of death if a single word is uttered against your ruler?
I am an English Hungarian, born and raised in a free country. I, like many other westerners, have learned to accept freedom as intrinsic part of my life. It wasn't until 1990, three years after the death of my father, that I began to realise that I have this anomaly simply because of the suffering of others. It is through this realisation of the disturbing truth that inspired me to seek out the answers and then try to illustrate and demonstrate the life of just one person amongst hundreds of thousands, who lived through these times. My father, Nandor Pekar. Amongst a proud nation that had had its pride ripped from their soul, they united against an invincible opponent to win back their honour. They did it.
My book is based on a true story that attempts to personify a national prisoner and display the feeling of a people under the threat of death.
Driven by concern for his country, Nandi was a part of the freedom won and lost in an emotional tidal wave. In 1956 the west called it a two week blip that rocked the Kremlin. For the Hungarians, they'd been fighting the Soviets since the end of world war two in 1945.

Richard Pekar
Copyright ©)

Dedication

I spent over ten years researching and compiling evidence to eventually produce the finished article of where we Pekar's come from. I see my father as a kind of marathon runner carrying his flaming torch. The fire full of his life. He has passed the torch on to me and I have promised him that I would pass it on. Therefore, I now hand the torch to you, my daughters, Merissa, Bethany and Georgia the latest descendants of the Nandor Pekar family tree. Be proud of it.

DID1980289

#0027 - 051017 - C0 - 210/148/28 - PB - DID1980289

CHAPTER 1

MAY 13th 1987

Stoke-on-Trent (England) 9:30a.m

Nandor Pekar had taken his wife to work earlier, helped his daughter with her four-year-old twin boys and taken them to school with her before dropping Gayna (his daughter) off to his wife at Hanley market where they worked together.

He drew his old Morris Marina discoloured off-white van to a standstill outside his home in Portland Street, Hanley. For the moment, he just wrenched the handbrake as high and as hard as he could, then, just stared through the windscreen to the top of the street. He found it difficult to move for a while and almost afraid to look at his home. He knew he had to, but for the time being, he just listened to the voices echoing in his head.

Richard (his son) had left to work this morning at 8:00a.m without his keys to the house he was sure. The voices he could hear in his head were that of the conversation shared with Richard that morning.

"Are you planning to come home for your dinner today Rich?"

Richard was clipping the press-studs of his blue overall jacket and when he reached the breast pocket, which scrolled the name of the garage where he worked *TYRESERVICES*, he stopped and left the neck part open and then answered his father.

"No not today Dad I'll be staying at work, probably get some chips or something."

Nandi stared at the Tyreservices sign and flashed back to a sickening moment from over thirty years before. Just for a second he had a vision, a ghost from his forgotten past. He could see the body of a dead soldier with a woodcutters axe buried into the centre of his forehead, his shirt was ripped open and the name *"Sándor Petöfi."* had been scrolled across the dead soldiers' chest in blood.

The flashback subsided and disappeared completely after he blinked hard two or three times.

"Are you okay Dad?" Richard asked when he saw his father struggling to focus.

"Yeah, yes son. Just a bit of a headache coming on that's all. I was just checking you weren't coming home for dinner because you haven't got a key to the house and I didn't fancy leaving the house unlocked, as I won't be in. I've got a lot of work on today and I plan to have this house I'm doing fully completed by tonight. Just got the stairs and living room to wallpaper and a bit of glossing and that's it, finished. So, I wont be coming home until it's all done."

"No problem Dad. I'll see you tonight."

These last words from his son echoed a few times in his head and then he was certain that nobody had access to the house only himself.

He fumbled for the door latch and then needed to shoulder the door open before climbing out of his van and slammed the door closed. Standing on the pavement in front of his house, he stopped and admired the front view. The beautiful contours of a typical English town house that stood out against the others in the row. The outer layer painting at the top front, a brilliant diamond white, and his bedroom window, large with about 30 or 40 smaller rectangle panes to make up the whole window. The artificial shutters on either side of the bedroom window a chocolate brown gloss that added a European look to its character. And the large downstairs living room bay window that bowed outwards, that too was filled with double the amount of rectangle panes than the upstairs.

But Nandi admired the front garden, its look a minute version of his childhood home far away deep in the wilderness of the Zemplen mountains in Eastern Hungary. The crimson red rose trees, one either side of his garden, and the white roses blended together to form a beautiful array of colours brightening up the front enhanced by an ornamental cherry tree further over to the left.

He imagined it how it was, how it had looked so old and tatty when they'd first moved there in 1974. 'How much work I've done to transform it from that into this modern but somehow antique looking home.' He thought to himself, breathing deeply a sigh of satisfaction. Someone walked passed him and brushed passed his shoulder shaking him from his trance encouraging him to open the cream coloured wrought iron gate and enter his front garden onto the concrete walkway that led to the dark solid oak front door. Before he slotted the key in the lock, he smoothed his hand against the wooden door number 33, and then over his brown plastic advertisement and read it out to himself in his mind. 'First Class Painter & Decorator, Satisfaction Guaranteed.'

"How did I end up here? From Mogyoroska, Hungary to Stoke-on-Trent, England as a painter and decorator" he asked himself and then unlocked the front door and walked inside.

The living room and kitchen had been knocked into one many years ago. Before he proceeded into the kitchen to make a coffee, he put his favourite love song on the turntable of the record player next to the television, placed the stylus at the beginning and sat down on the sofa to listen to 'All the Love in The World' by Dionne Warwick.

4

Soothed by the melody, Nandi drifted off to the past many years before.

He remembered docking at Dover docks as a Hungarian refugee over 30 years ago in the winter of 1956. It was the end of a bitter fight for freedom against the Russians and their communist system. Lost and unsure, he was surrounded by other refugees he'd met on his journey from Austria. Their names had been read off a list, documents and applications filled out and stamped at customs before a further haul to the seaside resort of Blackpool.

"Blackpool." He said to himself. "Christ I was exhausted and confused by the time I got there. All as they wanted to do was check us into the hostel and all as I wanted to do was buy and write out a postcard to my parents. I did it anyway and felt a great relief when I posted it at the post office the next morning."

'All The Love in The World' faded and then stopped with a sudden swift retraction from the arm of the record player and back to its starting point, announcing its arrival by a loud click. The impetuous silence that fell across the room was, for a while, rudely disappointing, but Nandi used the interruption from his reminiscences to pour himself a strong, black coffee. He sat down with it after restarting the song again.
He whispered, reminding himself of when he first met his English wife.

" When I first saw Gwen she was barely fifteen. Even though totally English, she had the qualities of a European princess, a shapely body and a pure heart that once touched, simply melted my own .I fell in love with her at first sight. Me, a foreigner from overseas trying to take the heart of a young English girl who's father had been a sergeant major in world war two and wore his long curly military moustache and stood with a stature that demanded respect. I was up against it. He, a decorated soldier with medals for bravery pinned to his chest, recognised for it by his own government. And me, in his eyes, a rebel from other parts of the world who had fought against his own government Probably thought I was a nazi spy or something."

Nandi was correct. He was up against it in those days. But Jack Evans (Gwen's father) had not met the likes of Nandi before. Nandi's tall, broad shoulders, dark hair to go with his tanned complexion and large handsome pale green eyes were only the exterior that in itself, turned heads from every female, and even male. But Nandi, who, inside, had the heart of a lion and the nature of a butterfly, soon overwhelmed Jack.

It was 1958 when he first laid eyes on Gwen, 3 months and 3 days before his 20ᵗʰ birthday. They were married two years later and were blessed with their first baby daughter, Gayna, one year after that.

Nandi was remembering the delight and excitement, the feeling that you've created a human being. As the feeling reoccurred for a few minutes, he smiled while he sipped and swallowed his black coffee. Enjoying the unfamiliar feeling, he relaxed further back into the sofa and remembered some more.

"Gayna was beautiful, she had a fiery auburn tinge to her hair and oh my God her eyes, she had Pekar eyes like my father and me, large but more green than my own."

Then, he stopped smiling. He remembered the gut wrenching nausea. Hugging Gayna when she was one day old wandering if he would ever be allowed to enter Hungary again. He loved his Hungarian and English mixed daughter and he wanted his parents to share the love. A tear dripped from his cheek onto Gayna's chin knowing how her Hungarian grandparents would dote on her and how they would be praying at the village church to catch a glimpse of their first grandchild and praying they could hold her some day.

6

Margit and Janos (Nandi's mother and father) received his post card from Blackpool late January 1957. They had been praying for his life since November of 1956 when he was reported missing. They'd heard nothing of his whereabouts for two months, then, suddenly it arrived. Nandi could see his mother now dancing around the kitchen kissing the postcard and then onto the veranda, shouting and crying, "Thank you lord, thank you, thank you." Janos (his father) was at his Mayor's office in the village and Margit could hardly stay on balance as she ran down the snowy bank to show him that their son was alive and well living in England. His father cried for a whole week until he couldn't cry any more.

"I was the talk of every village for miles around. Everyone knew of me, I was a kind of hero. My mother invited the whole village to church for a celebration that day, then back home for chicken paprika. My father, oh my God my father, at first he was bewildered and probably angry with me, but after the initial shock he was so proud; to most people, I was a hero, to him, I was more like a God."

Nandi spent years trying to describe his forbidden home in Hungary to his English wife and daughter. A solid provider for his family he landed a secure job at the beginning of 1962 at the Michelin Tyre factory in Stoke and promised that with his increased salary that somehow he would save enough money to take his proudly found family back to his roots in Mogyoroska.

Alas, he wasn't allowed back. If he did, he would have been arrested for crimes against the state and hanged. For now, the grandparents of Gayna could only settle for the odd letter and photograph.

Once again, his song finished playing on the record player. Carrying the remnants of his coffee into the kitchen, he caught himself in the gold-framed mirror on the chimneybreast above the gas-fire and approached it with a serious composure.

"Well Nandi." He said to himself. "You are 48 years old, have a full thick, black head of hair with a few sprays of grey; are you tough enough to go through with it?" He stared himself in the eyes as if waiting for the reflection to answer. Then he smirked when he saw himself in a pub brawl back in 1961 at the Railway Inn across Vale Place.

Darts was an English pub game that Nandi enjoyed playing occasionally with Vic, Gwen's brother. His new English family of in-laws had a clear picture of the Hungarian way of life and Nandi's struggle against communism and his tough battle to escape the clutches of the Soviet Union. They were all having a family evening at the Railway Tavern when two youths interrupted and sat beside the family. Loud and foulmouthed they were asked on several occasions to relax. Nandi had clocked them and studied their body language discretely. Suddenly, the two youths split up; one dragged a chair and sat under the dartboard in front of the glowing coal fire, and the other beside Nandi's mother-in-law. Gwen hadn't seen Nandi's face change in this way before.

"Are you okay Nandi?" She asked him.

The muscles in his cheekbones pumped and then he answered,

"When I was a boy in Hungary a member of the hated communist secret police slapped my face. I learned to fight because of him."

Gwen frowned heavily and then listened to Vic talking to the man under the dartboard.

8

"C'mon mate. If you sit there you are liable to get a dart in your eye."

"And if he does." The other one interrupted. "You'll get this glass in your face."

"What did you say?" Vic raised his voice.

Then Vic's aging mother tried to diffuse the situation.

"Excuse me young man, but that's my son you're speaking to."

"Is it really? Then this glass will be for you also."

Nandi turned over the large, heavy, round; pub table full of half drank glasses of beer and whiskey onto the man's chest. Pandemonium erupted.
Trying extremely hard to remember where Gwen had gone, still looking at himself in the mirror, he decided not to bother and continue with the memories of the fight.

"I quickly began firing my best punches hoping to gain the advantage in the early going. However, at first, my best shots seemed only to have the effect of further infuriating him. Get his eyes, get his eyes, I reminded myself. My experience from my fighting in the revolution would payoff, the willingness to fight for your country, this, a pub brawl, had to be a synch. Consequently, my experience and quickness allowed me to hold my own and though I hadn't caught him with a knockout punch yet, I was stinging him with punches and kicks. And then, in his frustration that he hadn't hit me yet because I'd been dodging around, he tries to Rugby tackle me around my waste. I stepped back as he came and kicked his lowered head and, to his misfortune, I struck him with brute force in his left eye. Now, my opponent was cut and bleeding and couldn't see. My tactics from the beginning. Next, had to help my brother-in-law. The other guy was over him and Vic was on his back."

Respect from Gwen's family grew and grew for Nandi after his loyalty prevailed. Nandi rescued Vic when he immobilised the second bully with several sharp rabbit punches.
Recalling that moment, he grinned once again at himself in the mirror hearing the voices from his mother-in-law.

"Stop it Nandi, stop it! You'll kill him! You'll kill him!"

'So what?' I thought. 'I've killed before.'

And then, when the police came they asked Nandi and Vic what weapon they'd used to hit them.

"Nothing only my fists I told him."

By now, Nandi was re-enacting the fight scene in the kitchen mirror shadow boxing against his own reflected image. Then, he remembered the question he'd asked himself which triggered off the memory of his pub fight from 1961.

"Are you tough enough to go through with it?"
He paused and looked at himself again straight-laced and firm.

"Yes. I am."

He walked over to the sink and filled a small white vase full of water and left it flowerless in the kitchen window. The backdoor key had always been difficult to turn, but he unlocked it today with ease and went outside into his large back garden that started with a yellow and red flag-stoned yard with a wooden shed over in the left corner. Steps lead to the second tear, flowers, trees and shrubs to the left and to the right, a concrete base suitable for sun-beds and deck chairs on summer days. Finally, the top part was larger with cabbages and carrots in the vegetable patch and higher up, a homemade greenhouse and a beautiful rockery homing the finest of plants and flowers of all colours. It was here Nandi ventured until he cut six stems from his favourite flowers the Lilly of the Valley, that were blooming beautifully. Their white round and small bell-shaped petals stood away from the stems pert and erect. He smelled them gently before cupping them together in his right hand.

By the backdoor he didn't go inside yet, he decided to lay the flowers on the garden table and smoke a Hamlet cigar that he had retrieved from his shirt breast pocket. The time it took him to smoke the whole length hadn't gone anywhere. For him, one second he was lighting it, the next he was stubbing it out in an ashtray on the table. He remained there for ten minutes, motionless and dumb, listening to the beating of his own heart. For him those ten minutes were very long but he snapped himself away from the trance, picked the flowers up off the table, went back inside and planted them into the small white vase. Whilst he admired them turning it around in his hand, he remembered that the next day was Gwen's birthday and the conversation shared with Gayna before dropping the twins off at school.

"It's your mothers' birthday tomorrow."

"Yes I know. What have you got for her, Dad?"
"Oh, something unusual."

The sun burst through a fluffy white cloud, penetrated the thin net curtains in the kitchen window, and onto the Lilly of the Valley flowers distracting his attention away from the unusual gift he was giving his wife for her birthday the next day. He narrowed his eyes to protect them from the sun and placed the vase down beside the teapot on the worktop, and then decided it was time to restart 'All The Love in The World.' As he did, he turned up the volume so he could here it from every room of the house. The hot water was hot enough now so he began filling the bathtub and proceeding upstairs to fetch himself a clean and smart attire. He chose almost brand new underwear, pants and socks he'd only worn once before he recalled.

"Now then?" He wanted to ask himself something before he got into the bath. "How did Richard tell me, how my record player can play a record twice?" He loomed over the turntable. "Aha, I remember now. Hold the switch down on auto and do not release the switch until the needle has almost landed on the vinyl." He did it as he commentated, and now the Dionne Warwick classic would automatically start again for a second time while he bathed. The beginning of the song prompted him to run into the bathroom, strip off his clothes and soak in the hot, full bathtub where memories of his past invaded his mind once again.

It was around 1965 when he'd heard of a few Hungarians venturing back home to visit their family. Gwen and Nandi, excited at the prospect of visiting his much talked about home, began enquiring. The Soviets had agreed to a certain few going behind the iron curtain without restrictions. Leaders of the resistance from Budapest were blacklisted and their acts had been regarded as treason and death was the penalty for that crime. Letters passed to and from Mogyoroska to Stoke-on-Trent. Nandi's father knew of Nandi's active role in the revolution, but did the authorities? After a while, Janos had confirmation that Nandi hadn't been blacklisted. Nervous and uncertain, knowing his own personal involvement in the atrocities, knowing he was responsible for the death of Avu and Russian lives he thought wise to become British. To obtain a British passport, this surely would protect him against arrest or imprisonment. After all, he wouldn't be Hungarian.

"How do you feel Nandi about been naturalised as a British Citizen?" He remembered Gwen asking him.

"If being English allows me a chance to see my home, my parents, and allows me to take my daughter to see where I have come

from, then English I must be. I would call it another victory for
me. I beat them in battles, they tried to kill me but I defied them,
they tried to imprison me in my own country, I defied that too,
and now, they are trying to keep me out. I'm going to beat that
also."

"Do you know Nandi; I've never actually heard you speak in
Hungarian. I hope you can remember how to do it." Gwen was
smiling as the excitement to go and visit this dream of a country
that had never seemed possible before, the thought of Nandi
conversing in a language she wouldn't understand sent a thrilling
sensation through her body.

"Somehow, I have trained my mind to think in English. I think in
English, I talk in English. I really don't know if I could think in
Hungarian again. This has been troubling me for a while, but then
I have realised. It doesn't affect who I am, I may have an English
mind, but I have a Hungarian heart. This is the most important."

Nandi was naturalised as a citizen of the United Kingdom in
October of 1966.

As he scrubbed his neck and ears with scented soapsuds, an
occasional shiver travelled the length of his spine. In his mind, he
was travelling back to Hungary for the first time in the summer of
1967 with his wife and daughter.
Europe seemed so old then. No motorways, two-way roads only.
Dirt tracks, hills and winding lanes that pierced mainstream
Europe heading for this far away Eastern land.

He rinsed away the soap from his eyes and launched into his
memory blurting it out loud.

"Fancy driving all the way to Hungary, 1 ½ thousand miles away,
in a borrowed Mini Traveller. Christ I owed a lot to my brother-
in-law Michael that year. He leant me that car just so I could get

home to see my family that I hadn't seen for over 11 years. Even though we had 8 punctures on the way, I still owed him a lot."

The tears and the joy when Nandi reached Mogyoroska that summer. He remembered the road through the mountainous countryside. The fields surrounded them on all sides; they were of gold's, yellows and pale greens. As Mogyoroska approached, Nandi quietened and steadily forced the Mini Traveller through the tiresome jaunt, into an emotional mixture of tranquil beauty, mystery, excitement, flooding them internally with a powerful exaltation sensation, which grew as they travelled deeper and deeper into the picturesque mountainous countryside of what could be a remote and forgotten land. The roads were narrow and carried the scent of dust, twisting and turning with humps and bumps, surrounded by fields, and high mountains behind the fields, forming a sloping, green line against a cloudless, deep blue sky. The route had taken them higher and higher into the sky; closer to Nandi's childhood home. The narrow, dusty, uneven lanes were very long and would suddenly, rather rudely, twist sharply to the left, then sharply to the right, gradually getting steeper, gradually getting higher. Every few miles, the uninhabited country roads were intervened by small residential villages, easily identified by its graveyard and church, signalling a village was approaching.

But Nandi's home seemed to be at the end of the world. It was the last house in the last village, aside the last mountain. Nandi, his mother and father held each other in their front garden and sobbed, wailing aloud. In fact, Nandi remembered the soreness in his throat before he dived out of the Mini Traveller, as a consequence of holding back his tears for the final ten miles of the journey. They just couldn't release the grip on each other; they just couldn't stop their tears. Nandi's father had promised himself that he was never going to let him go and it seemed he never was. They pressed their cheeks firmly into each others letting their tears mix and become one. After a while when they thought they had control, Nandi tried to introduce them to his wife and daughter but couldn't find the words. And it didn't matter, Gwen's Mother-in-Law, Father-in-law and Gayna's grandparents didn't need and introduction, they didn't need a language. The emotion was their language, they spent almost forever it seemed, hugging them and kissing them.

This reunited moment echoed and bounced of every corner of Nandi's mind as he lay down again in the bath. The celebrations that day went well into the night and enhanced when every aunt, uncle, cousin, jammed the garden and cottage and flourished the land. They chair lifted him and drowned him with wine and questions.

An hour later, Nandi was dressed in a beige pair of cotton trousers and a blue and pale green summer shirt. He smelled fresh and clean of Brut deodorant and his clean-shaven face smarted from Aramis aftershave. He laid out some unpaid bills across the bedroom dressing table and unscrewed the lid of a whiskey bottle and poured himself a decent measure in a cut-glass tumbler. Swallowing it slowly, he decisively made up his mind to walk down to his local pub The Portland Inn at the bottom of the street and have a beer and a cigar. He checked his watch.

"Ten to twelve. Just in time."

"Hi Lou." Lou was the Landlord at The Portland Inn.

"Ay up Nand! What can I get you?"

"A pint of Skol please. Oh, and a light for my cigar, I've forgotten my lighter."

He smoked the cigar and drank the lager slowly taking a swig of it after each drag. Lou was busy doing the last minute chores before the gang came in from Century Oils, the oil company only a short distance away on Century Street. He hardly exchanged much more conversation with Nandi and after he'd prepared a few sandwiches and placed them at the end of the bar and returned to the lounge, Nandi had left leaving the froth from his lager lightly coating the inside of his empty glass on the bar.

Before he went back inside his house, he started up his Morris Marina van and parked it around the corner on Stansgate Place out of sight. He ensured the backdoors were locked as well as the front before he left it parked there. In the house, he opened the back kitchen window but pulled it to so it seemed closed.

"Right then." He started to do his security checks around the downstairs. "The backdoor and front doors are locked. Must just close the bathroom door," He closed it. "The kitchen window is closed but can be opened. Now, I will put the needle onto the beginning of my favourite song in the whole world, but switch off the record player, and then the next time it is switched on the song will just begin to play. Oh, I think it's better if I take the phone off the hook, I don't want any interruptions this afternoon."

He carried the vase with the Lilly of the Valley flowers up into his bedroom and placed them on the long dressing table at the side of their king size double bed. It was time to take his medication so he poured three tablets into his hand from the bottle and swallowed them down with a mouthful of whiskey. It stung the back of his throat and he sucked in his breath to soothe the sensation, then, dried his lips with the back of his hand. He wanted to draw the curtains and before he did he switched on the bedroom light, bolted the bedroom door, and then stood in front of the bedroom window gazing through one of the rectangular panes, waiting there motionless as a sentinel at his post. He held his arms outstretched and grabbed both curtains in his hands, he didn't close them at first he remembered the painting of Christ in his church at Mogyoroska on the wall and for the moment he

simulated the painting with his arms out and he bowed his head as
if defeated.

After dragging the curtains tightly together, he opened a gap in the
curtain with a constricted hand in order for him to peer through it.
He didn't know why or what he was looking for but found himself
straining to see if anybody was coming through the entry from the
adjacent street, Winifred Street. His daughter and mother-in-law
lived in Winifred Street and for some reason he felt compelled to
check.

He left Blackpool for Stoke-on-Trent in 1957 simply because this
English city offered potential. It had coalmines, steel works, pot
banks, the Michelin and his first rented accommodation was in
Winifred Street. What history that street possessed, this was where
he met his wife Gwen. And this was where Gwen had lived with
her parents, four sisters and one brother. Nandi remembered the
history of Winifred Street as he stared through the gap in the
curtains.

"Since then I've got married, I am the father of two children, I
have three grandsons, I've owned a pub, a chip shop, done almost
23 years for the Michelin and am now a self employed painter and
decorator."

A depressed expression still impregnated his grey façade even
after reminding himself of his relatively content and successful
outcomes. This time a full glass of whiskey may help. He poured
it, sat at the end of the bed opposite the large oval dressing table
mirror, and then, watched himself supping away at it. His mirror
image changed and he could see someone else. He knew the
person but it still took a whole lot of thought for him to realise it
was a younger look of himself. A mere replica of the past. His
mind was teasing him, constantly playing tricks. The sudden raise
of blood pressure had caused the alcohol to go straight to his head.
He saw his younger version (18 yrs old) give a military salute
followed by the sign of the cross against his chest and held in his
hand a Huzagol 35 M. rifle. Nandi watched as the reflection of

himself in the mirror held the rifle up in front of his face giving it a visual inspection and checked the integral charger and box magazine. He could see himself preparing the rifle, physically unlocking the rotating lugs on the detachable bolt head that went into the receiver.

His vision vanished when he looked away from the mirror towards the bottle of Temazepam tablets. Shaking weak hands still managed to unscrew the lid once more and empty out another three anti-depressants. He downed them with his whiskey and started to feel very relaxed and for once he was happy with the situation he'd built about him. The feeling triggered off further memories. The birth of his son Richard, on December 7th 1968. "I kept my promise to my father. He insisted I carried on our surname. My son was six months old when I took him to Mogyoroska. The closer I got to my village the more proud I became, knowing I had fathered my dad's first grandson, to carry on the family name. By the time I reached the door, I thought I was going to explode with anticipation. It was only my second time home to Hungary in the summer of 1969 and now I had my second child to brag about. My father was ecstatic, another Pekar, another Pekar, he shouted and celebrated." Nandi breathed deeply through his nostrils before taking another sip of whiskey and then decided to talk more of the past to himself. "God knows I've tried my best with him. I've tried to instil in him brains and brawn like my father had done with me in those early tough years under soviet rule in Hungary. I don't know if I've managed it. The brawn is there that's for sure. He's as tall as me, probably slightly broader. He definitely has my eyes, large, bluer though, but the same shape. Hungarian heart, I don't know? The brains to ambush an enemy in a battle for freedom, I just don't know? Jeans, denim jackets, blockhead haircut, dog chains and the willingness to fight for any reason, seems to be his way of life." Nandi smirked, chuckled, shook his head and then continued on about his son. "Girls and gangs. I shouldn't be too hard on him; he's 18 years of age. Growing up as we all have to. He thinks he's a man, well,

18

May 13th 1987

we'll see how much of a man he is. The bible, my bible, it was given to me by my father; it survived countless incursions during my fight for freedom. It protected me. Now where is it?"

Suspecting the bottom drawer, he dropped to his knees in front of it and rummaged around. He found it, and with a proud decorum, he knew exactly what he wanted to do. First, he read the words written to him by his father way back in 1956 and then, he turned over the page, picked up a pen and began writing a note to his son.

' *To Richard Sándor Pekar, from your loving Dad 13/05/1987.'*

After he'd written it, he turned back a page to the words from his father and then let his eyes blur with tears before flicking through the pages to find what he was looking for, a pressed white rose and pressed Lilly of the Valley stems. Two, once silky white flowers now charred and smeared with a hint of brown caused with age. He let a single tear drip onto them and then ran his finger along the ripped page of the bible. This page was sacred to him and his heart missed a beat recalling the reason to press the flowers on that particular torn-out page.

He closed it and placed it on the dressing table next to the vase with the fresh Lilly of the Valley.

Gwen's birthday card was large and colourful and the gold lettered words on the front stood out against the coloured bouquet of flowers ' *To my Darling Wife, Happy Birthday.'*

He spent the next hour writing on the inside page. He needed to say so much and he'd began the first paragraph the day before; but now continued to finalise the unusual gift he'd got for her. During the essay of love and devotion he'd wrote to his wife he continued to intermittently sip away at the whiskey. At the end of the birthday card he filled the glass almost to the rim once more. His hand shook but he managed not to spill any. Noticing the whiskey

May 13th 1987

bottle was down to the last third, it encouraged him to stand up and reach inside his trouser pocket and empty all of his coins onto the dressing table and added a final line to the birthday card. He read it out loud to himself as he wrote each word. "Have, a, last, drink, on, me."

Encouraged to do so by a sudden sharp pain in his forehead, Nandi took two strong paracetamol tablets and swallowed them with a mouthful of whiskey. With the birthday card in his hand, he sat back down on the bed and pushed his back against the wall behind the headboard, then read back the words he'd written to his wife.

My Dearest Gwen!

I don't even know how to start. It would have been better if I decided not to say anything just go. After all the pain I have had until now I think I can stand a bit more. The hardest thing is about all of this that I love you so much. I cannot bear to leave you alone. But, it will turn out all right for you. I feel useless in your life anymore. Physically tired and mentally exhausted. I have not gone mad, just frail. I have been called for. Sorry about your birthday present, I wish I had plenty of money I would have given you anything. I haven't the money so I offer you my life. It has been yours and only yours as long as I have been with you. Do not blame yourself or anybody else. No one can even think how I felt. It would have needed a miracle, all constant supervision on your part, which I could not ask for. I have always put you first and I am doing it now, I cannot give you anything else so I let you go free. I only ask you to remember me sometimes. I have loved you so much that I cannot say.

Nandi.

We should have kissed this morning at the market for the last time. Oh how much I love you isn't the life.
I love you
I love you
I love you
I lived for you.
If there is an after life which I think there is I will watch over all of you.
Have a last drink on me.

He shuffled across the bed back to the dressing table to pick up his pen and added a few more words at the end.

Sorry I left you no drink.

He dropped the pen back down and this time mixed a few painkillers with more Temazepam in his hand and swallowed them one at a time with his whiskey. The middle drawer contained all of his life insurance policies prepared and compiled days before. He pulled them out and laid them neatly on the dressing table at the other end. He still hadn't finished. Perfectly organised, and well thought out, his suicide plan was falling together as he had intended. The next phase was to ensure that his final thoughts were relayed to his children whom he loved dearly.

He tore out a page from his lined papered notebook, leaned on his insurance policy book and began to scribble words from his heart.

My Dear Son,

We have not had the time to get close because you have become a young man before I new it. It makes no difference I have loved you and I hope I can watch over you even longer. Please look after your mother; she is the best in the world. She will need a lot of help in the future. I am not even trying to tell you how I feel it would not make any sense to you. Just ask you to forgive me.

The bible was my father's, your grandfather's. My father died in 1977 as you well know and yours now in 1987. He made me; he gave me a soul to be proud of. This bible has been a guide for me. When you can, I will need you to find a woman name Maria Arany. Her address was 9 Jozsef Utca, Nagytarcsa. Show her the torn out page in the bible.

Sorry I cannot write anymore it's breaking my heart.

Your Loving Dad

With his recently sharpened penknife, he cut the paper to an exact size beneath the last sentence. He folded the note carefully twice so as it fitted snug inside a pale yellow envelope. He licked it and then addressed the front to: *Rich.* He made a neat pile for him. At

the bottom, the bible, on top of that, the envelope. He then
unclipped his gold watch and opened the strap to lie face up
followed by his thick gold wedding ring that slid off his finger
relatively easily due to the sweat that was running from his arms
around his wrist and onto his fingers.
He emptied his glass of whiskey and then filled it with the final
third from the bottle and let the empty bottle drop to the floor. He
hurried to prepare more paper for Gayna and set about to write her
his farewells also.

My Dear Gay,

*This is the last letter of three. I cannot even see what I writing. I must ask you to
forgive me for stepping on one side. I think it will be better for all. Even me. As I
said to Rich, you must look after your mother. She is great. Something else,
please visit my grave sometimes it will be very lonely without you all.
Your Loving Dad.*

As with Richard's note, he cut it out neatly, folded it twice and
slotted into an identical pale yellow envelope, sealed it and
addressed it: *To Gay*. The scene on the dressing room table was a
breathtaking and disturbing sight. He checked it all. Flowers in a
vase, bills, insurance policy, suicide notes, birthday card, bible,
watch and his wedding ring. He stood up and wobbled as he did,
then, with a steady stature he unhooked the clasp of his necklace
from around his neck, kissed it and dropped it in a heap on
Gayna's letter. The stage was set. He'd done it all except for one
more thing. His photograph, his favourite photograph. He tried
hard to remember its whereabouts. With his vision blurring
rapidly he threw his head from side to side searching every nook
and cranny, every shelf top and then he saw it. It was above the
fireplace on the other side of the room. He steadied his quivering
trudge across the room by leaning his left hand onto the mattress.
The picture meant the world to him so he pressed it against his
heart and then kissed it. He was sat on a wall staring into Gwen's

eyes with his left arm wrapped around her back and waste. Behind him, the River Danube and The Arpad Bridge that spanned over the river from Buda to Pest. The Arpad bridge was by far his favourite and it hadn't been intended that day in 1980 to have his photograph taken with it behind his beloved wife and him. But by an act of fate, the bridge appeared on a photograph. He knew that it was this bridge that had played a part in his decisions to fight for freedom.

He gently laid it on the pillow. He thought it best to write one note on the unpaid household bills. So he did: *Bills sorry.*
After that, there wasn't anything left to do but to fall asleep. He swallowed a further helping of Temazepam, painkillers and finished the whiskey. Peacefully, he took off his glasses and placed them on the floor. He kicked of his shoes and then pulled back the covers and the room span when he climbed into bed and pulled the covers up to his chin. He was curled and lay as a baby lies in its mother's womb.

"I'm free." He said in a voice scarcely intelligible.

His eyes closed firmly as he felt a sharp stitch in his left side; so sharp he caught his breath in half inspirations, two or three times, before venturing on a full inflation of the lungs. Then, there was nausea, and an uncomfortable tightness across his chest.

CHAPTER 2

JULY 1st 1987

A3 Motorway 50 miles from Passau (Germany)

Richard had taken over driving from his brother-in-law John since they'd stopped for a sandwich and a drink of tea at Regensburg. He was concentrating harder than usual, as the steady flowing motorway seemed to suck him into a hypnotic state. The deep end of driving for a young man of only eighteen years old, having passed his driving test only five weeks previous. Knowing the responsibility suddenly forced upon him since that dreadful day on May 13th he'd set out to undertake the impossible, passing his test in a tiny Mini Metro, to immediately train to complete his new role as a Breakdown Tyre Fitter driving an open backed transit pickup truck, then onto now, aiding to transport himself and his grieving family 1 ½ thousand miles to Eastern Europe behind the Iron Curtain, in a 12 seater Ford Transit Minibus.

He gripped the steering wheel until his knuckles turned white but then, relaxed himself by easing his foot slightly off the accelerator pedal in order to reduce his speed to less than 70mph. His mother sensed a little anxiety from her sons' sudden deceleration and so eased the tension discretely by turning around to her three grandsons at the back and began the game 'I Spy.' After a few guesses at the letter 'M', Richard called out the answer.

"Mathew!"

His mother applauded and Mathew laughed out loud, as he continued scribbling profusely in his Beano Comic book.

"It's your go now Richard." Gwen told him.

"No it's okay. I'll pass my turn onto Mathew."

Mathew was Gayna's eldest son of 8 years old. Quite tall for his age, big blue eyes, translucent skin and a fiery reddy blonde shade, thick and wiry hair massed around his lean pink cheeks. Daniel the oldest twin, who were both four years old, snatched the colouring pencil away from Mathew, seconds before his twin brother Adam did. The boyish action caused a slight ruckus before John calmed his sons down and then insisted Mathew should take his turn in the game in an attempt to diffuse the disruption. Mathew threw a dirty glare towards his younger brothers' turned his head towards his nana and continued sensibly.
"I spy with my little eye something beginning with…" he paused for a few seconds and then looked up so as not to reveal his secret.

" 'G.' Something beginning with 'G.'

Kerry, Richard's 18-year-old fiancé, had the first attempt immediately.

"Gear stick!" She called out.

"No." Mathew took an exciting pleasure to announce that she was incorrect and grinned preposterously feeling certain that he'd chose a difficult inanimate for them to guess.

Richard turned his head to look at his fiancé half grinning, half frowning and said,

"Kerry; gear stick is two words."

"I knew that." Kerry answered feigning a comical embarrassment and then waved her finger at Richard warning him,

July1st 1987

"You keep your eyes on that road." She insisted and then reminded him. "And don't forget if you have an accident, there's an extra Pekar on its way to think about."

Richard faced the traffic ahead and smiled to himself. The guessing continued but Richard deafened to it allowing a tornado of the last three months events fill his thoughts. Three months prior, he was an average everyday teenager, going through the natural motions of evolving from a boy to a man. The suicide of his father had seemed to rush him into adulthood. Responsibilities loomed over him in their droves. He was coping, driven closer to his family; they'd bonded and found comfort in each other's grief. Immediately after he'd kicked open his father's bedroom door at 7:30p.m on May 13th only to find him dead, overdosed on anti-depressants, painkillers and alcohol, the race to understand, to do what he always knew his father had wanted from him, but remained to stubborn to obey, now he had to do, he didn't even have a choice. He needed to cement his stormy relationship with Kerry and so between them an addition to the Pekar family tree was inevitable. Before their trip to see his grandmother in Hungary, Kerry announced she was two months pregnant. Maybe this was what Richard needed to ease the pain of losing his father. Maybe this was what his father would have wanted. Who knew the answer? For Richard, for the infinite future, he was determined to live the rest of his life the way his father would have been proud, and to do that, he had to learn everything about him and above all, he had to be him.

His thoughts stalled for a moment when he overtook a slow moving Mercedes towing a caravan. It was strange overtaking this way and as he glanced at the Mercedes driver when the front windscreen was adjacent with his, he wandered if he'd get too used to driving on the continent and wouldn't remember how to drive back home in England.

He slotted the minibus back into the inside lane comfortably and then began thinking about his unborn child. Comforted by the thoughts of an offspring, a continuation of Pekar's, it was still sad for him to know that the child would never see its grandfather. This magnificent man that had so much to offer and so much to teach. The grandfather to be proud of who was Hungarian born, lived life in the mountains and could kill wild animals with his bare hands. Rose up and fought against a world superpower and survived innumerable forays in enemy territory, only to scramble on his hands and knees against all odds to escape to the west, to England. Through his actions, this hired white minibus now housed his accomplishments. Gwen his wife, Gayna and Richard his children, John and Kerry, son-in-law and daughter-in-law to be, three grandsons and another grandchild on the way. All travelling back to Mogyoroska, the land, the home, the beginning where, through Nandi, they all began.

Richard sighed deeply and promised himself something and the promise was so intense he could almost hear himself think. 'If my child is a boy he will be called Nandor.'

The horizon was thick, glowing dark blue reflecting off the setting sun. Richard thought that Passau was just beyond it and then he was sure of it when he noticed two aeroplanes must have crossed each other moments earlier. He squinted his eyes in disbelief as the trail of white smoke actually scarred the blue sky with a huge cross of Christ. He shouted out.

"Granddad."

A stony silence fell across the family in the minibus for a few seconds and then Mathew smiled and without uttering a word, he pointed his finger at Richard.

"Granddad?" Kerry frowned as she looked bemused and then Mathew explained.

"Something beginning with 'G'"

"Oh very good Mathew. But you've just said it was something in the minibus." Gayna questioned.

Gwen smiled at her grandson.

"Well it is true. Mathew is correct, granddad is here with us in the minibus, now, I'm sure."

Gayna's eyes grew moist as she cuddled Mathew and then Richard changed the subject and called out to the back.

"Kerry if we have a boy, have you any objections to call him Nandor?"

"No not at all. But what if it's a girl?"

"Super, no problem." Richard reassured.

"No problem?" Kerry quizzed him.

"If it's a girl I've always loved the sweet name Merissa the only conditions that I would put on my daughter is that when she marries, she mustn't change her surname, then, her sons will carry on with Pekar. The more Pekar's in the world the better."

Kerry laughed agreeable to the name choice but then said,

"Don't you think that you are enough Pekar's in this world?"

Laughing back, he said. "Wait until you meet Feri Pekar if you think I'm bad."

John giggled and laughed in agreement as he remembered the big tough farmer from Mogyoroska whose passions were wine, women and paprika.

***

By the time they'd reached the Austrian border, they'd all nodded off to sleep at the back. The queue of traffic was fairly long and Gwen fumbled in the dashboard for the passports.
"Mum." Richard distracted her.

"Yes son." She answered and then leaned back in the seat.

"How do you think nana will react when we get there?"

"I dread to think. She must be devastated, alone in that house. Waiting for us. I suppose she will be praying that it's all a dream, some mad prank or something and praying that when we drive up to the house, that your father will be with us and he's not dead at all."

Richard imagined the moment for a while and then shook himself.

"And who is Maria? Has dad ever mentioned her to you?"

"No never. I suppose we'll find out soon enough"

"How will we find her? How will we talk to her? You know I wish dad had taught me to speak in Hungarian."

"We are going to see Andras and Erzsebet who live in Budapest. They loved your dad and Erzsebet speaks good English. I wrote to them before we came and asked them to help us."

"Tell me again mum. Who are Andras and Erzsebet?"

"Your father and I met them two years ago in Budapest. We'd needed a place for the night and all the hotels were full up. Suddenly, when we had visions of sleeping in the car for the night, Andras, who had overheard us at the reception in the hotel Metropol, approached us, spoke to us and took us in. Complete strangers who came to our rescue and became great friends. The next day we met their young daughter Adrienne and we got on so well we ended up spending a few memorable days with them. Your father talked for hours and hours with Andras about you, about Gayna and then about the revolution. He clearly had Andras entranced and you could see the admiration in his eyes."

John stirred when a border guard took the passports from Gwen through the offside window. He strolled down the side of the minibus checking each passport photograph against the passengers.

"Do you want me to take over driving Rich when we get through because we need to get off the motorway and find a campsite as soon as possible?"

Richard looked at his watch and agreed immediately.

JULY 2nd 1987

Driving into Budapest city centre, mid-evening, after a day of blistering heat is captivating to anybody for it always has something interesting, historical or just something charming to see. Hilly Buda with its stone statues, waterfalls and fountains had the children crawling across the minibus seats from one window to another, scenery to view all around. Busy, choked filled high streets decorated with rows of shiny steel tramlines, occasionally filled with long rows of yellow lumbering carriages full of Budapest workers, shoppers or tourists. Pointed churches and trees like broccoli, lined the cobblestone high street that led to the Erzsebet Bridge.

As the glossy ripples reflecting the dipping orange sun, that made the River Danube look like the surface of a huge lemon meringue pie, came into view, John, who had steered the Minibus round a curved road, gasped first, causing the rest of them to surge towards the front to get a better view of the lit up bridges leaping from Buda to Pest.

From the middle of the Erzsebet Bridge, the sight from all angles possessed a shimmering charisma. To the right, the river had moving and parked boats large and small, filling the vast water as far as could be seen, and in the distance, the Arpad Bridge began glowing its bright yellow spotlights along the steel structure. To the left, the dark orange sun seemed to be melting into the river on the horizon spilling its golden liquid onto the waters edge. The glow from it managed to change the colour of the river and the grassy bank that sloped into the water. Ahead, was the typical sight of an Eastern Bloc capital city, buildings tall, old and rough looking but containing decades of historical stories beneath their outer fabric.

"Go steady John." Gwen cautioned him. "It's a right turning somewhere. I'll let you know when I recognise the street."

That night, Andras and Erzsebet spent the evening getting to know the rest of Nandi's family. They had organised a room for them all not too far from their own flat. Over wine, palinka, plates of pork steak, garlic sauce and boiled rice, topics of conversation ranged from English and Hungarian politics, world football, decorating homes, even the odd jokes were told probably to feel out each others' sense of humour. Eventually the evening grew sullen when full and detailed explanations of

Nandi's death were explained. Andras and Erzsebet sobbed and held each other as the disbelieving tale of May 13th 1987 were unravelled.

Finally, the tears were over after they'd read the suicide note to Richard. Andras stood up out of his chair and asked Erzsebet to translate for him.

"Andras would like you to stand up Richard." Erzsike explained.

Richard stood face to face with Andras. He studied Richard's tall, broad, muscular physique and then he burned a fierce glare into Richard's large, oval, and wide vivid blue eyes. Andras saw an identical younger version of Nandi the moment he saw Richard, the hair though, short, square and spiky on top. Andras thought, if it was black instead of dark brown, this young man would be Nandi born again. But now, he was checking his soul.

"Why do you come to Hungary?" Erzsike translated.

"Because I have to see my Grandmother. I have lost a father, but she has lost her son. She needs us now, she's alone."

"And then after you have comforted her, what are your intentions?" He transfixed his stare at Richard while Erzsike slowly translated the question. Richard licked the end of his brown, thin moustache while he felt he was being interrogated. He attempted to untangle the seriousness of his question by smiling a friendly smile and looking around the room at the others. But when he looked back, Andras hadn't altered his expression. Andras's eyes still wet from crying ached for an answer from Richard.

"I intend to take good care of my grandmother for her remaining years as I expect my father would want me to do that. And as for me, I'm going to try and understand everything about the relationship my father had with Hungary. And from now on,

I will open a closed door in my heart to all that my dad stood for. That is my future now."

The room silenced. The corners of Andras's mouth twitched into a smile. A few more seconds passed before he squeezed the bones in Richard's shoulders and then embraced him kissing both his cheeks.

"We must drink a toast to that." Andras insisted, ordering Erzsebet to fill a round of palinka glasses.

He whispered in Erzsebet's ear before they threw back the palinka.

"I can't wait to see who Maria is tomorrow… I like Richard. He is a true Hungarian you can see it in his eyes and hear it in his voice. He will make Nandi proud I'm sure of it."

CHAPTER 3

JULY 3ʳᵈ 1987

Nagytarcsa

Erzsebet bought a kilo of peaches from a stall at the side of the road in the centre of Nagytarcsa town after she'd asked for directions to Josef Utca. John opened the sliding door of the minibus wide to allow Erzsike to step back in.

"Do you know where the place is?" Gayna asked her.

Before she answered, she opened the paper bag and began handing out the peaches to everyone. The juices were soft and sweet and flowed the moment they were bitten into.

John turned his peach around a few times in his hand. "Hey Rich, the furry fuzz on this peach is a bit like your moustache." He joked.

Gayna giggled aloud and prodded her younger brother in the back.

"Sod off the pair of you. At least I'm not going grey like two."

Erzsebet directed John through the town to the outskirts and then down a dirt track, alongside a railway line and then into the fields. The muddy lane narrowed and the shock absorbers on the minibus barely resisted, bouncing, juddering, throwing objects from the dashboard onto the floor. John hit the brakes and slowed to an almost gentle roll and then, in the distance, a farmhouse appeared surrounded by flat unadorned fields. It was alone. The wooden posts that fenced the property were four foot high, thin, equally spaced and held firm, in unison, with twisted cable at the top and bottom. There wasn't a road to speak of that led to it, just a dirty track that bore horses hoof prints, worn away by years of use. John yanked the minibus onto the makeshift road moving the farmhouse to front view. There was a steaming compost heap on the right of the farmhouse, a huge barn next to that and over to the far left, an open two-storey barn with a roof and no walls that sheltered piles of straw. As they got closer, the animals grew clearer, a cow and a horse tied to a post stood drinking from a wooden trough. The remains of a fire smouldered sending plumes of smoke swirling keeping the geese and hens far from it toward the back. A scythe and pitchfork leaned against the wall next to the front door.

Richard, Andras and Erzsebet approached the farmhouse while the others waited in the minibus in anticipation. A snort from the horse greeted their arrival into the farmhouse grounds. Richard knocked on the door three times against the thin, tiny planes of glass, obscured by a dark cream net curtain. Immediately, someone moved it, peered at them, and then opened the door. A shirtless, tall man, broad shouldered with a defined athletic torso blocked the doorway. He was about 30 years old, and did look about the same age as Andras, which, seemed to naturally persuade Andras to open the introductions.

"Excuse me sir, my name is Andras Sipos, this is my wife Erzsebet and my English friend Richard. I hope you don't mind but we are looking for a lady named Maria Arany, we believe that she used to live here and we hoped that you might be able to help."

The darkness of the unlit kitchen behind him made his face difficult to see, but when he switched on a light by a light switch behind the door, it lit up the room and brightened his manifestation. His natural bronze coloured skin blended well with his thick, parted jet-black hair. The eyes, large, oval and coloured a vivid dark green stared at the three of them one at a time before he answered. Grease from a cooked chicken he'd been nibbling, smeared his chin and he felt it run encouraging him to wipe it dry with the back of his right hand.

"Maria is my mother." He answered, staring at Richard as he did.

Andras continued. "Can we talk to her please?"

"She isn't home at the moment. Can I help you at all?" When he asked the question, he turned back to look at Richard. Uncomfortable by the man's automatic action to study Richard, he interrupted and asked Erzsebet to translate.

"Oh sorry. She does live here but she isn't home at the moment." Then Erzsebet turned towards the man.

"My apologies sir, but Richard doesn't speak Hungarian."

The man looked strangely familiar to Richard, which counteracted the eye-to-eye contact.

Andras carried on the conversation.

"Richard's father was Hungarian and we think Maria may have known him or maybe knows something about him."

He shook his head in disagreement and then asked the name of Richard's father.

"Nandor, Nandor Pekar." Andras informed

The man's face lit up immediately.
"Aha, Nandor Pekar. Yes, I've heard of him. He was a best friend with my second cousin Jancsi. They went to college together. So, this is his son come all the way from England?"

"Yes he has. So, does your mother know him?"

"I think so. She spoke briefly of him a few times…Come, come in, where are my manners?"

Erzsike pointed to the minibus.

"Err what about the rest of us? Is it okay if they…"

"Sure, sure fetch them over."

The man cleared away the chicken and bread off the table and blew some breadcrumbs onto the floor. He smiled, encouraged them all to sit down and poured the children fresh glasses of pure raspberry juice. When they settled, he pulled a white T-shirt over his head to cover his naked chest and then introduced himself.

"My name is Tomi Arany. Please excuse the mess. My mother won't be too long, you see it's my birthday in two days time she has been baking cakes, cooking stuffed cabbage, and now she's out picking strawberries. I am 30 years old on July 5th and my mother still insists we celebrate my birthday with a party."

Erzsike continued to interpret every word to English.

"That's a coincidence." Gwen suddenly said.

"What is?" John questioned.

"His birthday on the same day as Nandi's."

Andras raised his eyebrows at his wife and she read his feelings. The children began to get a little rowdy after they'd quenched their thirst insisting they wanted to go out on the farmyard to play. Tomi said it was okay and everyone relaxed a little more when he offered beers to them all. Amid a lot of conversations at the same time, Andras found the opportunity to whisper something to Erzsike.

"Are you thinking what I'm thinking?"

She nodded and then turned away.

Everyone stood up when a woman wearing a large straw brimmed hat, carrying a basket full of strawberries entered the kitchen. She pulled the elastic from under her chin to release the hat so as she could remove it from her head. She wore a curious smile evidently not having any idea at all who were the strangers in her kitchen. Elegantly pretty woman, definitely in her late forties, all assumed it must be Maria. Her hair showed silver stands flowing through a dark background. But it was her large eyelashes that enhanced her large eyes. Even though dark shadows marked her face beneath the lower lids and a small scar defaced her left eye, beneath that, her beauty remained.

Andras was the first to introduce himself, and then he took pleasure in revealing who the English people were. This was a moment that Andras and his wife had been waiting for even more than the Pekar's. His heart pumped hard as he studied her every expression. First, her lips quivered but she faked a smile to hide it. She looked around the room at all of Nandi's family one by one. Eventually, without any difficulty she sought out Richard. Knowing she was under scrutiny, Maria tried for every second to cloak her shock. She stepped forward to them all, shook hands and kissed their cheeks. This was enough time for her to collect her thoughts. After, she scooped a drink of water from a bucket at the side of the sofa. She passed a handful of strawberries to John and told him to hand them to the children outside.

All the time Andras hadn't stopped watching her every move since he told her this was Nandi's family. Now, he waited for her to react. She did it after bracing herself in a chair by the table. Her fingers from both hands clasped each other's as she rested them on the table.

"So, where is Nandi?"

"Oh, I'm sorry Mrs. Arany…" Andras began but Maria interrupted.

"Err… Miss Arany, I'm not married. But you can call me Maria."

"Maria." Andras smiled politely. "I'm afraid Nandi died a few months ago."

Her eyes swelled immediately.

"Died, died how?"

Erzsike continued to translate all the time.

"He tragically took his own life after a long depression. But he left his family letters and in the letter to his son, he mentioned you. So, that is why we are here."

Maria pulled out a handkerchief from her sleeve, first, wiped her nose, and then, held it to her eyes and let her tears pour into it. Tomi knelt down at her side and began rubbing the back of her shoulders.
It was five minutes before she could talk again.

"I'm sorry." Andras said kindly, "But we want to understand how and why he should mention you on his deathbed."

"I haven't any idea why he should do that." She answered unconvincingly. She looked up at Andras and knew she couldn't fool him and so tried another way.

"He called here to see my father before he escaped to England. We clothed him, gave him some food and he left. Since then, I've never heard or seen anything of him until now."

When Erzsike finished explaining what Maria had said, Richard fired in a question for her.

"Did he talk to you? Did you have any conversations that you may recall that you wouldn't mind telling us, to help us understand?"

Maria shuddered while Richard was talking and she gazed at his posture, mannerisms and face. Andras caught her doing it, she noticed that he had, their eyes transfixed and Andras carried her eyes over to Tomi three times. She moved her eyes with him towards Tomi and then, one pronounced nod to Andras and looked down at the table. Erzsike then translated the question for Richard. She answered.

"Yes we talked a lot." She decided to stand up. They watched her.

"He believed in freedom. He wanted to be free. He repeated over and over that he was fighting not only for his country but he demanded that his children and grandchildren would grow up in a free country. Fearing for his safety, I asked him many times to give it up. He was too brave though; fearless and insisted his children would be free. He told me over and over that a Pekar always kept his promise. And, it looks like he's done that. You are his children, they are his grandchildren. It's wonderful; he succeeded as he said he would."

Her eyes filled with tears once again and this time so did Gayna, Richard's and Gwen's. They thanked her and ventured outside for some air to help their troubled hearts. Andras remained inside for a while until the others left and left Andras alone with Maria.

"Is there any more to tell Maria?"

She shook her head.

"And what promise did he make to you?"

"Please don't push it Andras."

"They have a right to know. To ease their pain"

"What about my pain? He made a promise to me, he said he'd come back, he never did. What does he want from me now?"

Just then, they all walked back into the kitchen and Erzsike explained in a soft and kind voice.

"Everyone thanks you for your help and they really appreciate it. They are sorry if they've upset you but we are going to leave now."

Maria was slightly relieved but found some comfort in the hugs and kisses from them all then they left the farmhouse and embarked the minibus. Richard asked Andras and Erzsike if they wouldn't mind just nipping back to Maria for a few minutes without the rest of the family.
The three of them left the others in the minibus and went back.

Maria opened the door with a tear-wet face.

"I'm sorry but Richard has something to ask you before we go."

"Sure, come back in, sit down."

The silence fell across the table and Richard pulled out a firm but battered bible from his pocket.
Maria looked at it with a stunned disbelief. Richard was careful to flick through the pages to expose a fragile pressed rose and Lilly of the Valley stems inside the bible at the half torn page. More tears silently ran down her cheeks.

"The rose. Is it yours?"
She didn't answer for a while then, between choked breaths.

"No. Not the rose. The page, the page reads… 'Ecclesiastes 4:9-12. Two are better than one, because they have a good return for their toil. For if they fall, one will lift up his fellow; but woe to him who is alone when he falls and has not another to lift him up.' I listened to those words, and repeated them for thirty years. He who hasn't another to rely on, he who is alone is lost."

She looked at Andras, eyes glazed.

"He kept his promise to me. He came back."

There were 3 drawers in a set next to her. She looked at the top drawer, then, with a cold, shaking hand, she drew it fully open and pulled out a white handkerchief. They watched with anticipation when she carefully unfolded it into a perfect square on the table. In the centre, was a neatly folded up thin page from a book. She turned to Richard and handed it to him.

"It will fit perfectly. I've waited thirty years to see that bible again, all this time to fuse the pages back together as he promised he would."

Richard unfolded it and could barely breathe properly. The moment was somehow spiritual, the fine cool breeze that passed through Richard's body that caused his body to shudder and filled his eyes with unwanted tears. Sensational, exhilarating. Maria smiled directly into Richard's soul and for a moment, Nandi was there, massaging their pumping hearts from within.

"You are sitting exactly in the same place as your father sat with me over thirty years ago. There's more. A lot more. He told me everything about his life. Everything! I know it all. That's why he sent you here; he knows I can tell you. You see we were in love for those few short weeks. Very much in love. Being in love during wartimes is brutal yes, but also very romantic. He was wounded in the head, in a coma. In his state, he talked over and over about his life. I memorised every word, every line. I am willing to tell you what I know if you promise me two things."

After Erzsike finished translating Richard asked what the two things were.

"Please ask your family to wait out in the farmyard; it is only you I want to tell. Tomi will take them some food and drink and show them around."

"And the second thing."

"Please stop looking directly into my eyes. You remind me of Nandi and I'm liable to kiss you or something."

Erzsike laughed out loud before she translated to Richard then they all joined in which very cleverly broke the tearful atmosphere.

Maria poured everyone a large palinka while Tomi and Richard went outside to organise the family. Andras waited for Maria to sit back down before asking her a stinging question.

"And what about Tomi. Does he know he has a half brother and half sister? Will you reveal this fact to Richard?"

"My dear lord who are these people you've sent to my house to dissect my innermost secrets?" She stared at the ceiling and then responded.

"I will tell the story of Nandi as I know it. I will tell it from my heart. If Nandi chooses, he will reveal this fact to his children in his own way. But I will not point blank do it. And I will thank you to respect that, please."

"Of course!" Andras smiled and squeezed Maria's hand gently.

"Thank you."

July 3rd 1987

Richard entered closing the door firmly behind him and smiled at the large glass of palinka before he dropped his notepad and pen onto the table.

"Are you ready Maria?" Richard asked.

"No we are not." Andras insisted and then stood to attention with his glass firmly held in his right hand.

Maria, Erzsike and Richard stood up to join Andras.

With glasses in their hands they stared at each other deeply and Andras's shouted out loud in a deep stern voice.

"To Nandi."

CHAPTER 4

JANUARY 1940

KASSA: HUNGARY.

Margit and Janos had lived on the outskirts of the city of Kassa in Northern Hungary, for just a year with their two young sons Bela and Nandor. Bela was a tall good looking five year old, who looked older and Nandi was the younger of the two, a very boisterous 1 ½ year old, who possessed a large mass of thick black hair and large pale green eyes. Janos was a farmer spending most of his days tending to his cows, pigs and chickens. They all lived in a two-room cottage, which was small but cosy, and like many other families in the village they were happy but were growing a little restless with the prospect of war approaching.

Janos had been working out on the land since 5.a.m; he had finished his morning chores a little earlier than usual and was heading back towards the house a little less than two hours later. The snow beneath his feet was almost frozen making a crisp, crushing sound with every step. It was a typical January morning; the field outside the cottage was like a bed of white feathers, which seemed to stretch for miles into the distance. A long stretch of mist appeared to be hugging the peaks of distant mountaintops on the horizon; the atmosphere was fresh and cold the kind that bit into your skin.

"Come along Bela, you will be late for school," Margit shouted sharply.

Bela grabbed his coat and scarf off the stool, put them on and began lacing up his boots. Nandi scrambled eagerly towards Bela, laughing and giggling out loud, as he had noticed his older brother's big toe poking through a hole in his boot rather prominently. Nandi quickly clutched his toe with his tiny hands, which caused a shriek of laughter from Bela and his mother. Margit picked Nandi up off the floor kissing him and at the same time passing Bela a handkerchief as she noticed he had a runny nose.

Suddenly, the kitchen door flew open helped by an unexpected gust of wind and Janos stepped in with his arms full of chopped logs for the oven. The cold air followed behind him as Janos panted heavily and dropped the logs under the cast iron stove. Margit hurried to the door closing it quickly after him. Janos reached into his pocket, pulled out some loose change and passed it to his wife.

"Get some bread and salami on the way back from school."

Margit dropped the coins in a handkerchief and folded them up tight stuffing them into her coat pocket.

"Are the cows milked?" Margit asked.

Knowing the reason for the question, Janos replied

"I am just about to boil some up for Nandi right now, so run along and get Bela off to school"

Bela hugged his mother before running into the schoolyard sliding on the slippery wet ice. He turned excitedly, waved to Margit and ran to a group of boys standing just inside the school doorway.

Margit walked across the snowy road towards the village shop shaking the snow from her shoes before entering.

"Good morning Mrs. Pekar," called out a familiar voice. Margit turned her head quickly and noticed the doctor standing in the corner of the shop with a stick of salami wrapped up in greaseproof paper under his arm. Before replying, the corners of her mouth picked up,

"Good morning doctor,"

Unwrapping the woollen scarf from her neck, she proceeded towards the counter but continued a friendly conversation with the doctor.

"Nasty whether we're having,"

"Terrible, terrible," the doctor immediately answered, "And I've just heard on the wireless there's a snow storm heading this way moving rapidly from Czechoslovakia"

Margit shook her head and continued,

"That's all we need, as if we aren't suffering enough; what with pneumonia spreading our land, Germany and Russia spreading their armies and now a snow storm, what next?"

The doctor gave a silent chuckle with an agreeing nod as Margit turned to Feri and asked for her bread and salami.

"I'm sorry Mrs. Pekar, we haven't any salami left," Feri sighed as he reached for one of his last few loaves.

Without hesitation, Doctor Molnar took the salami from under his arm, unwrapped it, laid it down on the counter, took Feri's carving knife from off the scales and began cutting the stick in half insisting Margit should take it.

"Oh no Doctor, it isn't necessary," demanded Margit.

"Nonsense," the Doctor said assertively, forcing the salami into Margit's cold hands.

"Well at least let me pay for it," requested Margit, at the same time unfolding the coins from her handkerchief.
Before Margit could hand over the payment, the Doctor was heading towards the shop door, firmly repeating,

"That's not necessary, that's not necessary, any way I must dash, promised to go see Mr. Kovacs's son, young Istvan, he's running a slight temperature or something."
He paused, put on his cap, buttoned his coat and continued,

"Good day Feri, Good day Mrs. Pekar." He called out whilst turning the handle on the shop door and proceeding outside into the freezing street.

"Good day Doctor," Margit and Feri answered simultaneously, "And thank you very much," Margit added.

At home Margit began preparing for an early dinner whilst Janos shut away his two cows in the cow shed, put his pigs in the sty securing the timber gate with some copper wire and bolted the chickens in their huts. Already the sky had begun to blacken and the wind picked up slightly. Janos was interrupted from his preparation for the storm by the familiar sound of the latch on his garden gate lifting. He made his way to the front in order to greet the visitor.

"Hello son, hello Mrs. Varga." Mrs. Varga was one of Bela's schoolteacher's. They both turned towards Janos, Bela grinning impudently.

"Hello Mr. Pekar, we are closing the school this afternoon due to the snowstorm heading our way." explained the schoolteacher.

"That bad is it?" Janos asked.

"So we've heard it's leaving three metre high snow drifts in its path." Mrs. Varga informed.

Bela ran towards the house pulling off his hat and scarf as he went.

Janos shouted to his son, "Tell your mother to put some logs on the stove," He turned to Mrs. Varga, "It sounds like we going to have keep warm. Any how, thanks for bringing Bela home, you'd better be off and tuck those young kiddies of yours in."

"Oh no trouble at all, I think I'm going to indulge myself in a large glass of wine before the storm arrives," laughed the schoolteacher.

Smirking cheekily he replied, "Might just do something like that myself."

Janos stood studying the pattern of the whether as Mrs. Varga walked away. The village church bells sounding their midday melody intruded his concentration.
"Goodness 12 o'clock already," he muttered to himself.

The sky darkened ominously as they sat down to an early lunch, and the menacing roll of thunder drew nearer with every second. By the time they had eaten their thick hot goulash the storm was well in its toll. The wind howled angrily through the trees, the snow pelted hard against the windows and the irritating pounding of the garden gate seemed to soften into melody outside, as Janos had neglected to coil the copper wire tightly enough. His attempts to analyse any damage to his grape vine through his small kitchen window was in vane. It had grown too dark outside, the only thing

visible seemed to be the wind, as it twisted and turned trailing a
white mist behind it.

Margit and the boys snuggled down in their bed together pulling
the large feather filled duvet just above their noses. Nandi
squealed and kicked with excitement causing fits of laughter from
Bela and their mum as she tried to calm him down. She gently
gripped her sons in each arm and eased their pleasurable
anticipations by singing a soft Hungarian lullaby. The room was
hot, cosy, with a familiar odour of cooked paprika and pork.
Together, with a belly full of hot goulash, inevitably resulted to
the obvious… Bela and Nandi sank into a deep, uninterrupted
sleep.

Janos was tending to the stove as he poured himself a large glass
of Palinka (brandy) before piling on more logs. He quietly
pottered around the kitchen clearing away the remnants of the
dinner utensils, intermittently taking some large sips of his
Palinka. As the wind howled Janos switched off the single light
bulb which hung in the centre of the ceiling, pulled out a half
burnt candle from the drawer and lit it with a match, placing it
onto a small saucer on the table at the side of the stove. He
clumsily sat in his large wooden chair in front of the stove,
reached out to the bottle of Palinka, unscrewed the lid and once
again filled his glass. Within a few seconds, he had emptied the
glass and slowly wiped away a few drops of Palinka from his
unshaven chin with his thumb and forefinger. He stared aimlessly
into the now roaring hot stove until his eyes had firmly closed and
had fell into a deep sleep. After a few moments his load snores
could be heard by Margit in the bedroom…she chuckled to
herself, closed her eyes and fell asleep herself.

All afternoon the wind blew and the snow fell. Outside, snow
drifts were piling almost in a deliberate sequence forming what
looked like man made white hills enveloping each other, in a
various pattern stretching the garden, up against the fencing, and
continuing along the outside road, almost as far as the eye could

January 1940

see. The front garden gate had been forced off the hinges and lay in shattered piles all around. The animals had been a little restless, apart from the pigs that had buried themselves in the frozen mud and slept through the ordeal. After a few hours the storm had almost passed and what remained, was a gentle but piercing wind coupled with a slight snowfall.

The customary village church bells waked Janos suddenly. A common occurrence during a storm in order for the sound waves from the chiming steel bells to travel and break up the clouds. Janos murmured to himself before realising that they had all slept for almost four hours.

He immediately began to throw small sticks onto the fire attempting to relight the now smouldering ashes. Standing to his feet, Janos stretched his weary body letting out a long quiet yawn. Trundling across the room towards the milk urn over in the corner, he tripped carelessly over his milking stool.

"Oh shit," he called out.

With a tired groan he picked up the milk by the handle, filled a saucepan, placed it onto the stove preparing a drink for the boys who should now be almost awake. This became apparent when Janos heard a violent choking cough from the bedroom. After entering the bedroom, Janos noticed they were all arousing and that it was Bela who was coughing out loud.

"Oh dear, somebody's got a nasty cough," Janos said to Bela sympathetically. As he looked towards Bela, he smiled a reassuring smile, moved towards him and caressed his forehead. Simultaneously he turned to Margit and with a relieved tone in his voice said,

"He's cool, no fever, thank God,"

At that point Nandi jumped out of bed and scurried to the window,

"Daddy, Daddy look at the snow, Daddy, Daddy build me a snow man,"

Bela, also darted out of bed, ran to the window pushing Nandi out of the way and quickly began rubbing away the condensation from the window.

"Wow, Dad, it looks beautiful, let me go out with my sledge"

"Tomorrow you can Bela," interrupted Margit.

"Yes, tomorrow we'll build snowmen, slide on the sledge, whatever you want," their father promised. " But for now it's bread, salami and milk time."
Janos was making back towards the kitchen as he spoke, remembering he'd left the saucepan of milk on the heat. Removing it quickly, he suggested Margit should prepare the tea; he needed to inspect what the storm had left. She climbed out of bed feeling very stiff after her long afternoon nap; passing Bela on the way to the Kitchen, she double-checked her husband's diagnosis by feeling for a temperature herself. Janos was right there wasn't a fever. Extra concern was being paid, there had been a local outbreak of influenza and in a lot of cases, the virus had left the victim with pneumonia or pleurisy, often fatal.

Janos had discovered the effects from the storm, piles of snow and a broken gate was all he had to worry about. He marched around to the animals, threw the cows some hay slapping them on their backsides, threw some corn for the chickens and buried the pigs in bread crusts and potato peel. Grabbing his spade, flexing his muscles, the big farmer began shovelling away the masses of snow that had gathered beyond his front door blocking the pathway and his access to the now broken garden gate. It took Janos over one hour of continuous gruelling to get just half way to the garden entrance. Leaning on his shovel admiring his achievements so far, he wiped the sweat from his brow and noticed his friend and neighbour clambering over a snowy hill heading towards the house.

"Good day to you Tibor," Janos called out. Tibor walked a little closer before answering.

"What are you doing man? Wasting your time it'll probably snow again tonight, then you'll be back to square one in the morning."

"I'm trying to dig a pathway all the way to the pub." Janos joked.

Tibor let out a deep laugh and said "Bloody typical Hungarian, when the going gets tough, get your priorities right, and go down the pub."

"Too bloody right mate; hey it's time I took a break, there's a bottle of Palinka in the house with our names on it, fancy a quickie."

Tibor chuckled, patted Janos on the back and agreed, "Lead the way mate."

Margit had heard them talking, used her Hungarian telepathy and had already poured two large glasses of the Hungarian medicine before they entered. She was used to Janos and Tibor's regular meetings, when they would often discuss politics, the state of the world or even football. Tonight would be no different.

"Any up dates on the war?" Janos opened the conversation.

"Not really. Bloody frightening situation we're in, nazi's on one side communists on the other."

"What do y' think Hitler will do next," Janos quizzed Tibor.

"God only knows what goes through that maniacs mind."

"Well think about it," said Janos. "First he wins over Austria, then by a marvellous, crafty, acrobaticall choice of words and careful manoeuvring he barges into Czechoslovakia. Bloody obvious what was coming next, the rest of the world couldn't see it, apart from the Germans and the Poles, hey presto we're in the primary stages of another world war. It's just like 1914. What I still can't get to grips with, is what the hell were Germany doing signing a bloody armistice with Russia?"

Tibor chimed in, "Exactly, trust none of them that's what I say; only one month after the invasion with Poland what do the Russians do? Bloody invade Finland."

"Yeah, two evil powerful nations and we could get caught up between the two of them. Keep out of it, that's what we should do."

"Might not be able to." decided Tibor. Janos threw back his Palinka, frowned and said, "Why?"

"Because if we don't surrender to their demands it could be us the Germans invade next, or if they don't the bloody Russians will."

"In that case we'll end up siding with the Germans."

"Suppose that would be better than siding with Communists."

"It's all crap if you ask me, there's only one safe place to be today."

"Where's that then?" Tibor asked.

"Up Santa Clauses arse."

The two men paused for a second, looked at one another and let out a loud uncontrollable laughter. This disturbed Bela who heard them laughing, ran into the kitchen and leapt onto Tibor's knee. Tibor reacted happily by lifting Bela into the air with rough large hands.

"It's these I think about, our children, what kind of a future have these got, brought up in war and poverty, good God even our hospitals are running dry of even the simplest of surgical instruments."

They didn't talk for much longer before Tibor finally left and Janos continued his quest to dig a walkway through the thick heavy snow.

What the two men had discussed was absolutely correct and more or less showed the feeling of Hungary as a people. For the last two years since 1938 was a time of strangely mixed developments and feelings. Lavish ceremonies had been organised in the midst of ominous international events, and revisionist jubilation existed alongside grave anxiety for the future. Two years earlier in 1938 was the 900th anniversary of the death of King Stephen, the founder of the Hungarian state. While the people of Hungary commemorated St Stephen, Europe had had a more serious issue to think about, the prospect of piece was far from reassuring. As Janos and Tibor had discussed, on September 1st 1939 the German Army had invaded Poland. Luckily for Hungary at this time, absence of pressure from Berlin for Hungary to join in the attack, made it easier for the Hungarian government to keep out of the hostilities. Count Pal Teleki now Prime Minister of Hungary for a second time, refused to give assistance to Germany and the Hungarian railways were not used for transportation of German troops or supplies. At the same time, Teleki opened the border to Polish refugees; Hungary had preserved its non-belligerence.

But now, as did Tibor and Janos suspected, how long could Hungary refuse assistance to Germany?

5 o'clock the next morning was introduced by Janos's cockerel, letting out its usual, frequent cries, wakening him in an instant. He caught sight of a small crack in the ceiling as his eyes flickered open. He slowly sat up, in order for a better view of the weather outside through the window. It hadn't snowed all night but everywhere looked white and frosty. As he surveyed the conditions outside, Janos rubbed his swollen eyes and then began combing back his thick black hair with the fingers of his right hand, followed by the palm of his left. As he stretched and yawned, he noticed his breath visibly hanging in the air like a floating grey cloud. He climbed out of bed and stood up using the headboard to steady his tired body.

"Ouch," Janos yelped out as quietly as possible, snatching his right hand away from the headboard. Something had caused a rough, sharp pain, as he examined his palm he soon realised the cause; two large bubbles widely spaced across the centre of his hand.

"Bloody blisters," he complained to himself with an irritated tone in his voice.

By now Margit was stirring,

"Shut up Janos, you'll wake the boys," she whispered.

With that he turned his head swiftly towards them; they looked both sound asleep, but something disturbed Janos. He frowned as he moved nearer to their bed to observe a closer look. As he slowly approached the boys, his eyes were firmly fixed on Bela, as it became apparent his cheeks were glowing red and his hair was drenched. He gently knelt beside him to stroke his forehead. As he feared, Bela had a high temperature and felt worse as the intense heat from his forehead, seemed to scorch Janos's blistered hand. Bela slowly opened his eyes, looked at his father sympathetically, then suddenly sucked in his breath deeply and let out a violent coughing fit, which sounded like a choking dog. Shocked, Janos rose to his feet in a flash, only to be substituted by his panicking wife as she barged her way to her son's side. She sat him up quickly to allow him room to breath, trying to unblock his airwaves by fiercely rubbing and patting his back. It was a few minutes before Bela's attack ceased. She carefully laid him on his side and fearfully looked up at Janos. They faced each other in silence. In just a few moments, Janos had read his wife's concerns, her face white, even her lips had turned the same colour. As her large green eyes pierced her, husbands pale blue eyes, she decided and instructed Janos,

"Soak me a cotton blanket in some cold water, ring it out quickly and bring it to me,"

Without any hesitation he darted into the kitchen and began soaking a blanket understanding her need. Bela let out a long and grateful sigh as his parents wrapped his naked burning body in this cool relieving cover. Margit sat Bela on her knee and held him to her chest, rocking him gently forward and back. The room was silent for a moment until broken by quicker sharp coughing erupting from the chest of Bela, only this time it ended suddenly when Bela seemed to lose his temper with it and let out an angry squeal followed by a self-pitying sob. Margit tried desperately to console her son whispering in his ear, "Don't worry, mummy will make you better."

At this, Janos decided to act without delay. He leaned over the two of them placing his right hand onto Margit's shoulder. They both looked up at him as if desperate for a solution.

" I'll mix some lemon and honey with vinegar and boiling water for his cough. Then after, I'm not taking any chances, I'll go into the village and fetch Dr. Molnar."

Relieved at his decision Margit quickly answered

"Yes, please hurry Janos"

Only half an hour later Janos returned with the doctor; it had seemed like hours for Margit, but as they entered the bedroom, the doctor wore a kind and reassuring smile. By now Nandi had awoke and was sitting by one side of his brother on the bed, with Margit on the other, holding Bela's hand tightly. She carefully unclasped her fingers from his, and shuffled herself to the edge of the bed so her feet were touching the floor. Behind her shiny, glazed eyes, Doctor Molnar could sense the anxiety.

"Please doctor, please help my son."

Before the doctor answered, Janos had lifted Nandi into his arms and was making his way passed them both into the kitchen. Doctor Molnar stooped down in front of Margit and took her hands in his, gripped them gently and said,

"Don't worry, I'll do all I can; please, go into the kitchen to Janos and Nandi wait there while I examine him and, I'd love a coffee; by the look of you; you could drink one too."

She smiled nervously and after giving Bela a hug, she did exactly as he advised.

They all waited in the kitchen anxiously. Janos paced around slowly with his head pointing towards the floor concentrating on his every foot step, in deep thought, occasionally he would interrupt his regular walking sequence by combing back his hair with his thick, large rough hands. Nandi sat on the floor, unusually quiet, dropping a few coins into a large metal mug. He could sense a tense atmosphere. Margit had made some coffee but now she sat at the kitchen table with her hands together, eyes closed in deep prayer.

A short while later Janos sat down beside Margit. She looked deep into his eyes while hers filled with tears again. He took hold of her arm gave a reassuring squeeze and said,

"Be brave, everything going to be fine, I promise."

Doubtable she questioned,

"What if it's not?" At the same time biting her lower lip.

They paused for a moment, looking at each other, fearing the worse for a split second, and then embraced each other tightly. She put her head on Janos's left shoulder and let out a silent sob trying very hard to contain her silence so not to draw Nandi's attention. They comforted each other for a few minutes until Margit was the bravest to release her clasp from her husbands back. She drew in her breath, sat upright and began sipping her now luke warm coffee.

As Margit placed her empty mug down on the table the door from the bedroom opened making a long, slow creaking sound until it was wide open and the dark shadow from the doctor entered the kitchen before he did. Margit and Janos both stood up together like they were standing to attention. As they searched Doctor Molnar's face for signs of hope, Janos was the first to speak, "Well, how is he?"

Before answering he turned and closed the door quietly behind him, looked first at Margit and then towards Janos,

"He's sleeping at the moment, but I'm afraid he needs taking to Szikszo hospital, immediately."

"Oh God, so it's serious?" Margit asked sharply.

The Doctor's mannerisms were a little give away as he straightened his back, placed his leather briefcase on the table and looked at them both again.

Nandi, who was still quietly playing on the floor beside them, looked deeply at the briefcase. It was a look coupled with a 'déjà vu' experience, the kind of magical look that this briefcase was a tool, a tool of freedom, and a freedom that rescues a person from all that is evil. Only Nandi felt this, only Nandi was experiencing this weird sensation.

Before Doctor Molnar commenced, Margit caught hold of her husband's hand.

"His temperature has risen to 40 c, he has malaise, complains of a headache and aching pains in his body. His pulse is rapid, the skin is hot and dry; I'm afraid these are all signs of pneumonia."

The colour drained from their faces… Janos felt Margit's hand shake vigorously in his… Suddenly her knees went like jelly and her body limp. She began collapsing to the floor when Janos quickly grabbed her and held her upright. After an effortless attempt he gently placed her safely in the chair, he was whispering all the time words of reassurance

"C'mon Margit, try to be strong."

After a few moments slumped in the chair, she relieved the doctor and Janos's concerns by responding,

"I'll be alright, just give me a minute."

At this, Janos stood up tall, looked the doctor in the eyes and asked the inevitable crippling question,

"Is he going to die?"

There was a short pause before Margit picked her head up from her hands, looked at the doctor and awaited a possible painful answer. Cautiously he replied,

"Unfortunately there isn't much treatment for this illness, he needs concentrated oxygen and something to reduce his temperature which we have in the hospital, but as of yet there is no known cure, having said that if we act fast enough, what facilities there is in the hospital, could be enough; but with God's good will, he'll be fine."

Janos reacted quickly to the doctor's statement,

"Ok, let's get him to the hospital right now."

His decision prompted the doctor to begin organising the inevitable.

"Yes, of course, get Bela ready, pack a few clothes up for him along with anything else needed, I will fetch my car and take you there myself."

"Yeah, thanks doctor." Janos said gratefully as he walked him to the front door. As the doctor was making his way out Janos took hold of his hand and forced a sum of money in his palm firmly. "Janos, there's no need…..really…………." "Just take it." Janos interrupted, "And make my boy better again."

Doctor Molnar patted Janos on his broad back in appreciation looked at him directly and patted him again, the second pat, a pat of encouragement. He made his way out.

They quickly prepared Bela for the journey, washing him and collecting any requirements together in a small suitcase. It wasn't long before they heard the doctors car approaching.

Margit carried Bela wrapped in a small white blanket into the hospital with Janos carrying Nandi at the right side of her and Doctor Molnar the other. The corridor leading to the hospitals reception area was long narrow and unclean. The floor was cobble stoned, the walls were bare brick and there was an aroma of vermin in the air. Equally spaced on either sides of the corridor were old wooden benches, littered every so often with gypsy type people who had found refuge, some were lying, sleeping. Doctor Molnar quickened his pace to walk in front in order to open the reception area door to allow the Pekar family to enter.

As they entered, they stood just inside the reception area. The doctor made his way towards a lady sat behind a table a few feet opposite, dressed all in black wearing a black headscarf also. As they waited, they studied what lay before them. A large, square room, opposite, slightly to the left was another doorway which seemed to lead into the hospital ward. The room was dark, heavy damask curtains were drawn. There was a fire in the opposite right hand corner of the room burning a dull glow. The reception table where the doctor and the lady stood collaborating had an inkpot in one corner and the gas in a single globe turned very low in the other.

As he was talking to her, apparently explaining the situation, Margit shuffled herself across to her left in order to have a clear view of the hospital ward. In the dim light she could barely see, but could just make out it was one large room with about five or six beds down one side and about the same number, adjacent. At irregular intervals, going from patient to patient, she noticed about two or three nurses attired in an identical uniform of a black lace trimmed dress with a white cap. They moved around the ward quickly almost as though they were gliding on ice, their dresses were so long their feet were hidden, but even though they looked stressed and rushed, it was combined with gracefulness as Margit noticed one in particular, was carrying a large jug of water in one hand and a bloody towel in the other, as she hurried from one bed to another she never spilt a drop; in fact there wasn't even a splash.

Her concentration was interrupted in an instant as the old lady talking to Doctor Molnar called out loudly, directing her voice towards the ward behind her,

"Nurse…. Nurse Gizzi." as one of the nurses responded to the old lady by way of a glance then a nod, the old lady continued,

"Doctor Molnar is here from Kassa, he's brought a little boy who needs concentrated oxygen immediately, he thinks he may have Pneumonia."

By now, Nurse Gizzi had entered the reception area and was standing with the doctor. He continued the explanation of his patient's condition insisting he needed a bed and attention immediately. The nurse was listening attentively and all the time looking across at Bela giving a kind of visual examination. She gave a kind smile at the parents, then beckoned them towards the ward,

"Yes, of course, bring him this way Mrs. Pekar; we have a bed over here on the left down the bottom by the window."

She led the way with the family and the doctor followed close behind.

Bela was gently placed into his new bed, the thick quilt and pillow were old but immaculate, although the ward itself felt damp and depressing. Bela began to lash out a coughing fit; the nurses responded to Bela immediately holding him over a bucket at the side of the bed. Tenacious sputum loosened from his throat as he wrenched and with a fierce spurt, a rust coloured gob of saliva fell from Bela's mouth and covered the base of the bucket. The colour of the saliva concerned the nurses knowing the cause being blood.

Bela was treated with high concentrated oxygen to help his breathing, while another nurse injected Bela in his bottom, reassuring Margit it would reduce his temperature.

All day long Bela had full attention from the nurses and Doctor Molnar. They examined him regularly, paying particular attention to the colour of the saliva and worked all day to cool him down. Throughout the day Margit, Janos and Nandi stayed at the hospital. It was 4 o'clock in the afternoon when Dr. Molnar revealed a little good news,

"His temperature has reduced slightly, he's coughing a little less more frequent, but he still hasn't eaten anything, at the moment he is exhausted and so he sleeps; it's probably advisable for you all to go home to get some rest, especially Nandi, then come back in the morning."

Janos gave an agreeing nod but Margit looked horrified as she gazed at the doctor indignantly and said,

"There is no way I'm leaving Bela, not a chance."

Nurse Gizzi overheard Margit's anxiety and interrupted,

"I'm sorry Mrs. Pekar, but you can't stay here there's no where for you to sleep. Bela is in good hands, we can send for you if there's a need; don't worry."

Margit wore a defiant look as her eyes searched the ward and spotted over against the back wall, a small black horsehair sofa, packed with pillows and covered with shawls. She pointed to it and demanded,

"I can sleep there!"

Before Nurse Gizzi could answer Doctor Molnar turned his head sharply towards the nurse and insisted,

"Yes, ok, I don't think there will be any problem with that, will there nurse?"

Reluctantly she agreed,

"Err no; ok…..I'll make it a little more comfortable."

So, Janos and Nandi went home and would come back in the morning. Margit felt relieved that she could stay with Bela. She knew in her heart to go home would have been a mistake. For the rest of the afternoon and evening she remained knelt by his bedside holding his hand and stroking his forehead. She sang and told stories to Bela always about what they would do together in the future.

"When you get better, Daddy's going take you deep into the woods to fetch me some mushrooms and when you get back I'm going to cook a big saucepan full of fresh chicken and mushroom soup."

Bela lay still listening to his mother, the stillness occasionally interrupted by wild coughing bouts. Later he found the energy to sit up and draw a picture. Margit watched as Bela sketched a family picture of the four of them standing together holding hands on top of a mountain, He signed the bottom…. *Bela Pekar 1940.*

The next morning Janos returned to the hospital at 9 o'clock with Nandi. He had brought with him a clean shawl for Margit and some garlic sausage for her breakfast.
In a kind and concerned manner he leaned over Bela slowly, smiling all the time and prompted him to talk,

"How's my son this morning?"

Bela attempted to lift his head from the pillow but failed, so instead he just looked long and fixedly into his father's face, pleased to see him he forced half a smile and replied sympathetically,

"I'm alright Daddy."

Janos moved his face closer to his and lightly caressed his forehead with his lips. Bela could smell the familiar clean scent of soap from his Dad's now clean-shaven face. He sighed happily as he was comforted by his father's actions.

Janos noticed Bela was still very warm. He moved away from the bed to direct his attention to his wife. Stroking her cheek he said,

"You look so tired, how was your night?"

Margit didn't answer him immediately, noticing Nandi had climbed into bed with his brother producing a pleasing smile on the face of Bela. With that, she stood up and caught hold of Janos's hand and walked him over to the horsehair sofa where they sat down together in order for a private conversation,

"Inevitably I didn't sleep a wink; Bela didn't sleep either, well, he'd fall asleep for about half an hour or maybe a little more and then would wake himself with his own coughing; he hasn't eaten for over 24 hours which is obviously concerning the doctors and nurses. They say he must eat to give him strength to fight the pneumonia, but every time he tries to eat, not only does he eat very little, what he is eating, he sicks back up. They are going to try him with some breakfast in about half an hour…. Oh Janos, this is the worst time of my life, my stomach feels so tight, my throat is so sore; every time I look at our son I, I, have to fight back my tears; my poor, poor baby, he lies there so ill, so helpless, my heart cries out to him, my poor innocent little boy, he doesn't deserve this. I have prayed so hard, I couldn't bare anything happening to him. Please God, make him better."

By this time, she once again had her hands together, praying. Her eyes were closed but tears forced their way through her eyelashes. Janos said nothing. Just put his hand on to Margit's back as a sign of agreement and consoling. There was enough pain and worry in his face that spoke louder than words. They sat still for a while just staring into another dimension.

Janos was disturbed for a moment. His deep thoughts intruded by something. He looked across the ward into the doorway. A new patient was entering the ward aided by a doctor. As they came closer, Janos noticed the injured man was a Polish soldier. Still wearing his uniform, it was obvious he had a severe leg wound. A gunshot maybe. A large screen was placed around an empty bed opposite Bela before the doctor and the soldier disappeared behind it. Janos could hear their conversation, it seemed each of them could speak a little of each other's language. As Janos could make out, the soldier was explaining the horrors of the German and Russian attack on his country. The man was first in Warsaw holding off the German air raids when he had a call to retreat to the East immediately as the Russians were advancing. He cursed and swore, complaining all the time how these two countries had persecuted and tortured an innocent race of people inflicting their Nazi and Communist laws on to them. As the soldier preached more and more he boasted, how he'd personally defied logic and cheated death, thanking the Hungarians for their support. But had Hungary really supported them in their hour of need Janos thought to himself.

Nandi running and jumped on to his mother's knee suddenly disturbed this tormenting situation,

"Mummy," he said, "Want you come home."

For a brief moment Margit smiled and answered him as simply as possible.

"I can't go home yet baby, not until Bela gets better, then we'll both come home."

The next half an hour seemed like half a day while they sat waiting for his breakfast to arrive. Janos sat looking at Bela's picture of the four of them standing at the top of a mountain. Nandi climbed all over his mother as she tried to occupy him so not to torment Bela. At precisely half past nine, Nurse Gizzi entered the ward with Bela's breakfast on a wooden tray, which consisted of a small slice of cheese, bread, a cup of fresh milk and a shallow saucer of melted butter, vinegar and sugar. As the nurse approached Bela's bed, his eyes were closed but sensed someone coming toward him. His eyes opened slowly, it seemed like it was too much effort just to open them. He frowned as he looked at the wooden tray in her hands. He turned to his mother without lifting his head from the pillow, a look of anguish penetrated, as he let out a pitiful whimper.

"You must eat a little my darling." Margit said coaxingly.

She carefully sat him up packing pillows about him to support his weak, limp body. The nurse placed the tray of food on to his knee, smiling at Bela all the time persuasively. He not once acknowledged the nurse, his eyes, pointed downwards into his lap, so as the tray was gently landed onto his knee, his view of his top bed sheet was then obstructed by his unwanted breakfast. They all watched with anticipation as Bela slowly reached out for his cup of milk. He swallowed the drink quickly taking large mouthfuls at a time to soothe his sore, thirsty throat. The nurse spooned a dollop of the very warm melted butter into his mouth explaining that the concoction would loosen the infection from his chest. He swallowed it. There was a look of satisfaction on all their faces when he swilled the strange tasting cocktail down with the last drop of milk in the cup. With very little physical or mental exertion, Bela began to nibble at the piece of cheese. He took two or three bites before finally placing it back on to the tray. Exhausted, he let out a long sigh and sank back into the large feather filled pillows. Margit sat down on the bed. Concerned, she stroked his brow and tried to persuade him to eat a little more. After he refused, Bela felt the need to hold his breath.

His efforts to prevent himself from coughing suddenly failed with a terrifying jerk of his head. The spasm exploded, ejecting large amounts of blood and phlegm from his mouth. He was held over the bucket at the bedside by nurse Gizzi, as Margit assisted by rubbing and patting his back. More and more blood stained saliva loosened from his chest as he coughed and spat it into the metal bucket. For a moment, his mouth was clogged, overflowing at the corners making it difficult for him to breath. This struggle to catch his breath caused him to heave and splutter, until unavoidably, he began to vomit. The milk he had just drank, the cheese and even more, poured into the bucket. He coughed and choked until every last drop of bile from his stomach had settled into a frightful, thick greeny brown fluid almost to the rim of the bucket. His stomach was torn and empty.

Bela's head now hung silently over the full cylindrical container. Mouth half open with a string of vomit and saliva hanging from his upper and lower lips. Even though his eyes were firmly squeezed shut, tears streamed from them soaking his cheeks. Secreted mucus encumbered his nostrils hindering his ability to breath, producing a terrifying droning sound, which sounded like a deep hum from the bottom of a tomb.

After a couple of minutes, realising he had finished coughing for a while, the nurse sat his   lifeless body upright with her arm remaining behind him for support. His head fell to one side in an exhausted state; the coughing and wrenching had totally sapped the boy's strength and energy. He looked and was completely drained. With her free hand, the nurse picked up a clean, damp cloth and began gently wiping Bela's eyes, nose and mouth. She felt so sorry for him as she stared into his now pale, sick face. A choking sob rose in her throat as she gently lay him back, placing his head on the pillow behind him.

By now, Janos had taken Nandi out of the ward into the dim lit reception area. As Bela lay still and quiet for a while, Margit went to join her husband. He greeted her with a tight grip of her hands, whilst his were shaking vigorously.

"Is he alright Margit? Has he stopped coughing and sicking?"

"Yes, he's stopped for now." She answered quickly, noticing she had no control over her quivering voice.

"I couldn't let Nandi watch his brother suffering like that, it was frightening him." Janos explained.

"Oh yes, you're so right, we mustn't bring Nandi here any more, not only is it morbid, he may get a viral infection or something."

"But what should we do?"
Margit thought for a minute and then answered,

"You and Nandi go home right away. While you are there, write a letter to my sister in Fony, the address is in the bottom of my wardrobe in a shoebox, explain everything to her and tell her we need her here quickly, as soon as possible, then she can help out with Nandi."
Agreeing, he scratched his head nervously.

"Before you both head home I need us all to be together for five minutes while we say a prayer for Bela." Margit insisted. She carried Nandi back into the ward with Janos following behind. As they huddled close together on the bed, they squeezed Bela's hands. He looked so tired gazing at them all one by one until finally smiling before Margit began.

"Dear Lord my God;......... When we feel sad and lonely, we sit in your church garden and quietly think of you, we hear your voice, we see your face, the wind brushes past us and we feel your embrace. We pick a flower and see your smile, and we are with you for a while, we look around and you are there, all is quiet, all is bare. But please dear God we need you now, we need you to give us all strength to get through this sad upsetting time.

And most of all we beg you with everything that is decent and holy; to please be with Bela and whatever happens, help us to understand...   Please give him strength and love, all the remedies for a cure."

Everything went silent and still for a while as she paused, took a long deep breath through her nose never opening her eyes for a second, before continuing.

"Dear Lord, rouse thyself! Please don't sleep 'o' Lord. Awake! Don't cast us off, don't hide thy face. Don't forget our affliction and oppression. Our soul is bowed down to the dust, our body cleaves the ground. Rise up, come to our help! Deliver us for the sake of our steadfast love! Dear Lord we love you with all of our hearts and beg you to answer this prayer... Amen."
At this point, there was a slight angered tone in her voice along with the cries of a desperate, begging mother.

Before leaving the hospital Janos hugged, kissed and encouraged his sick son promising, "I'll be back later sunshine, I'm coming back." He released his embrace and without opening his eyes, he stood up and held his wife close to him never opening his eyes until disturbed by Nandi deciding to talk to his brother.

"I'm going home now Bela, but when I'm there, I'll make you a big prize, cuz I love you, when you come home you can have it; so, bye bye Bela, love you, see you later."

Bela watched Nandi walking away from his bed and out of the ward. Nandi turned around and gave a wave to Bela. Before Nandi and Janos disappeared, Bela managed to lift up his weak arm and struggled a wave back. "I love you too Nandi." Bela whispered.

Later that night, Margit's deep haunted sleep on the horsehair sofa, was tumultuously intruded upon by a bright, blinding light. Her eyelids flickered quickly as her eyeballs rolled trying to focus to make sense of the white beam. As her pupils dilated, she blocked out the light with her right hand. In a startled state, she sat up, noticing the culprit for her sleep intrusion. The curtains behind Bela's bed had blown apart at their edges only to allow a cascading light from a full moon in the nights clear skies. She tiptoed over to the curtains intending to close them but found herself gazing out into the empty sky. She saw her own face reflecting on the glass and she superimposed on the picture. Lines on her face had deepened. A stressful look stared back at her. At first she was almost unrecognisable to herself until a realisation of an older, worried looking lady stood in front of her. She studied the faint impression of herself through the smeared glass without blinking or moving her eyeballs. The still concentration ended when Bela called out;

"Mama,"

Startled for a second Margit drew the curtain shut before she answered,

"Yes dear,"

Bela looked at the silhouette of his mother in the murky hospital room and asked,

"What's heaven like?"

Shocked at her little boys question she sat beside Bela on the bed, smiled, caressed his right cheek with the back of her hand and answered,

"Well……………. Heaven is a beautiful place full of angels and all nice things; it's peaceful and a place full of content. There's no pain or illness and everyone there is happy and free from cruelty. The air smells of sweet flowers and big white horses play together in miles and miles of green meadows."

"Is everybody going there?"

"Only good and nice people go to Heaven."

There was a long pause whilst Bela searched the room in deep thought until the next question sprung into his mind and simultaneously out of his mouth,

"Am I going to Heaven? Am I good?

"You are good. You are the best and when you go to Heaven, God will know he has taken the best?"

Bela's aware thoughts led him to his next crucifying question,

"Mama; am I going to heaven soon? Am I dying?

Margit's stomach sickened, her mouth and throat were dry whilst she attempted a comforting response.

"If you do I will be holding your hand all the way 'till you get there and do not worry because I'll always be with you; no matter what, no matter what."

"And mama, how will I know when it's time to go there? And how will I find the way?"

Margit embraced her son immediately holding him against her now pounding heart,

"God will be your guide Bela, he will lift all your pain, relax all your aches and when you feel peaceful and happy, AND only if you want to, when you are ready; you will drift towards the most loving, exciting world that YOU will recognise, because you are pure and harmless and have a heart that lights up everyone's life. So, with God as your guide, you with no pain and a smile and me holding your hand, when it's time, you will drift towards the sweet, smelling meadows of God's world."

Still holding Bela against her warm heart, she lifted both legs together on to the bed and lay down, resting her head onto Bela's pillow. She took a deep breath, squeezed Bela reassuringly and continued,

"But don't fret Bela; me and your Dad will make you better."

Bela lay motionless for a few seconds as if frozen to his mother's warm body. He blinked his eyes slowly, two, three and on the fourth flutter he clasped them tight shut, gave a long wheezy sigh through his nostrils and snuggled closer into his mother's comfortable, safe grasp and sank once again into a deep, haunted sleep.

A tear rolled off Margit's right cheek and dripped onto the back of Bela's hair as she reiterated the unbelievable conversation the two of them had taken part in her mind, over and over. Margit felt overcome with emotion as she experienced a whirlwind of mixed torment connected with an unusual feeling of torrid relief. Somehow, she knew someday, she would feel a certain comfort

by what they'd shared in a conversation, that at this moment; cut
her like a knife..........

Five more days, four more nights passed. As the tension increased
in the hospital, the tension was swelling in Europe and in deed the
world. There was widespread speculation and rumour as to what
would happen next in a precarious war situation, with its nucleus
in the centre of Europe to the West of Hungary, and Russia to the
East. The red army, who had aided Germany in their invasion of
Poland, now occupied Finland. There was talk of Germany
retaliating to the West's decision to declare war on Germany, or
even a Northern invasion from the Nazi's in response to the
Russians unpredicted attack on their Finnish neighbours.

But as the hostilities in Europe grew, the Pekar family paid little
attention to it, as they had spent the last week of their lives
watching Bela deteriorate. By now his body had been tortured and
it showed; his hands, wrists, fingers and toes were so thin &
ragged they were almost transparent, lined with enlarged deep
blue veins. His chest had sunk with a rather painful looking
swollen stomach and his eyes red roar lost in a circled, grim, black
shadow. Around his mouth and chin in a kind of peppered fashion
was dried blood, covering a few small scattered open wounds
caused by the constant cleansing with a rough medical cloth, of
his own blood stained saliva.

Each day had now become routine, Janos, Margit and Bela
together through the day, followed by Janos going home late
evening to Nandi and Margit's sister after a full day of desperation
drown with tears, tears dried with anger and anger overcome with
prayer. Under nourishment, malnutrition, pneumonia, was too
much for a little boy to bear. In the eyes of the Doctor's and
Nurses showed signs they'd given up hope.

Margit sat still in a chair at his bedside with a cup of water clasped in both hands. As she sipped it intermittently, her eyes carefully rolled around the hospital in a daze like fashion, wondering why she was here and why there was so many sick and injured people surrounding her. In her dizzy state she hadn't noticed a small cockroach had crawled onto the bed and slowly onto Bela's chin, where it had decided to stop and probe at his blood smeared skin. Bela hadn't the energy to swat it or brush it away at least; it was there for a while before he found effort to only whimper quietly,

"Mama."

She looked fearfully at him for a second before realising his intentions. Holding her breath in an attempt to keep in her tears, she flicked the cockroach onto the floor by her feet and stamped on it in a silent rage. She couldn't hold back any longer and began to weep out loud; she noticed she'd caught the attention of her husband as he walked briskly over from the opposite window. She could bear no more, grabbed her son's right hand and lifted a small pillow from the end of the bed with her left hand and held it firmly to her mouth in order to drown out her uncontrollable screams. As Janos approached the bed he was sharply looking toward both of them, first Margit then Bela and back again. He stopped by the bed with a thud, as both feet seemed to have decided to halt at the same time. He thought he'd seen something but wasn't sure. Margit didn't seem to have noticed that Janos had moved away.
Nurse Gizzi had her back to Janos when he turned her around instantly by her shoulders with his large spade like hands.

"Nurse, it's, it's Bela, quick, quick."

The nurse rushed over, closely followed by Janos and two other nurses.

Bela's head had moved to one side looking away from Margit. A wave of panic rushed to the head of Janos, they stood and stared for what seemed like hours but was just a second or two. Before anyone continued their intentions, Bela gave two slightly pronounced pants and then was very still. Margit uncovered her face and stared at her son in silence. Her grip on his hand tightened as two large tears burst out from her lower eyelid. They thought he'd died but could not be sure. The silence was broken when Nurse Gizzi asked the other nurse to pass the mirror. She held it to his mouth: There did not seem to be another breath. They stayed there quietly for a few moments until Margit struggled and said,

"My God………….. His lips have gone very white."

She reacted putting her other hand over his forehead, turning him to face her gently, and closed his eyelids. First the left and then the right. She stretched her neck over to him so she could whisper into his ear. With a quiet shuddering voice, she told Bela,

"Now drift towards the sweet smelling meadows of God's world baby. You're safe now. Free. No more pain, no more hurt."

There was total stillness.

It was over.

Less than one week later, Janos, Margit, Nandi, along with a grieving community of relations, neighbours, friends, found themselves in their local churchyard encircling a short, narrow but deep hole. They watched aimlessly as two grey haired funeral directors dressed in black, slowly lowered the small coffin into the earth as the priest prayed from the bible and repeatedly made the sign of the cross to Bela sinking deeper into his tomb. The crowd were silent one minute and the next; a burst of cries could be heard from one person to another. Tears rolled, throats were choked and soar, the emotions grew when even the priest struggled to pray, lost and heartbroken through the content of the sermon. As this large crowd were disbelievingly paying their respects to a tragic moment, Tibor found the strength to take a photograph of this unforgiving moment from a suitable position beyond the grave.

"This photograph," Tibor presumed, "would show everything, in years to come when they need to remember Bela, they can see how beautiful an ugly situation has become, I know they will thank me some day for capturing this moment of grief."
The photograph would show Janos stood six foot two inches tall, his broad shoulders, now slouched forward, his thick black hair now showing a sprinkling of grey, combed in a straight flowing motion towards the back. His eyes a wide vivid blue buried into a long lean face, bearing no expression, absolutely like stone. His thirty-year-old features had aged, as crevices in his face looked grey and deep.

Margit was a little younger, age 25, no shallow girl, but a fully mature woman. Her hair was short cut above her shoulders, black, but buried beneath a thin-cottoned black head square. A lock of hair had seemed to of crept its way out of the head-square in a loose curve over her right eye. Her face, definitely east European in appearance, had high prominent cheekbones, the cheeks themselves concave. Her jaw was curved. Her eyes, wide-spaced, watery green. Her mouth was tender, sensuous and was clearly defined against her tanned but somehow, translucent skin.
She held Nandi in her arms; he was wrapped in a large, thick padded coat with just his small cute face peering through the hood. The three stood motionless staring down the hole at the box that Bela lay. The photograph showed it all. Their feelings, their stunned grief.

In the midst of the dense, deference quietness, Doctor Molnar embraced the family with a solid grip and shed his tears with them for while. He couldn't leave without offering something to them so, for reasons he couldn't understand himself, he gave Nandi his pure leather briefcase.

"This is for you. You must use it when you are older. Keep your education in it as I did. Education is the key to freedom; you can hide your freedom in the secret compartments."

Margit thanked the doctor and took it from him then looked away towards the grave.

"Nandi doesn't understand what I'm saying today Margit. But he will tomorrow."

The doctor wiped his eyes with a handkerchief and left the family to grieve.

They had stood there for hours, or so they thought. The shuffling of feet from the audience about them as they quietly filtered away interrupted the mesmerised stillness. People were holding each other for comfort as they left dragging themselves away in respect. Low muffled cries softened into melody from the dispersing crowd. As they departed the graveyard, they each in turn took a long despairing gaze at the Pekar family, still standing beside their beloved Bela's grave. Their hearts cried out to them.

As this stressful moment grew, Janos reached inside his coat pocket and pulled out a handkerchief and began wiping his now sore, red bloodshot eyes. At this, the church bells began ringing a respectful chime.

Janos moved towards Margit, took Nandi from her in his left arm and with his other, he wrapped it around Margit, squeezing her against him. Her head comfortingly rested on his chest as she sobbed and pressed her face inside his unbuttoned coat.

A short time after, the church garden was empty leaving the three of them wallowing in their own personal grief. The chimes from the church bells ceased with a jolt. All was quiet. They were very still. A gentle breeze blew through the bare frosty trees.

The sky had grown dull when Janos suggested they should make their way home.

CHAPTER 5

APRIL 1941

Over one year had passed since Bela's death. The war had developed along with the grieving and the memories of their first son.

Things had changed a little. To cope with their loss, they had occupied their daily routines with their normal household gifts, executing them to earn money from home. Janos's inherited trade as a cobbler prospered along with his regular farming duties, whilst Margit spent her days embroidering cushion covers, table mats and table cloths of fine white cotton, decorated with an array of coloured flowers, red, yellow, pink, formed with neat tiny stitches, edged and inset with the utmost of exquisite stitchery; artistically arranged against handmade lace.

Her embroidery world was an ideal time for her to lament in her own quiet method, as she would lose herself in memories of Bela.

As she pondered over her patterns, Margit remembered the picture Bela had drawn in the hospital. She recovered it from her personal drawer at the side of her sewing machine and   studied it with intent. Thoughts of her son's tragic death invaded her mind as tears flooded down her cheeks. After a few minutes she wiped her tears away, took hold of a pencil from the nearby table, turned over the page of his drawing and began to write.

"Dear Bela,

Your quiet nature was one to admire
Peace and contentment your own desire
Out of this world of suffering, you heard that gentle call

So quietly you went and left us all
I cannot get used to losing you
The pain is deep inside
My heart aches, I cry
I feel so done
Oh, how I miss you, my gentle perfect son
One day we'll meet again, and all the hurt will go
I'll put my arms around you son
And never let you go.

She folded the paper and stored it away back in her personal drawer.

***

Not only was April 1941 distressful for Janos and Margit for the loss of their son, but April 1941 was also a time for fear and distress for the whole of Hungary and its people. It was a time when Hungary could enter the war on the side of the Germans. There was a great number of anti Nazi's but also a great number of Hitler supporters. Every Hungarian spent all day long with their ears glued to the wireless, hoping and praying the inevitable wouldn't happen. It was April 3rd 1941 when all their faith was smashed.

Janos had just finished cooking stuffed cabbage when it was announced on the wireless.

" Last week under considerable pressure from Hitler, Horthy and his general staff decided to participate in the projected attack on Yugoslavia—despite the 'treaty of eternal friendship' that Hungary had concluded with Belgrade on December 12th 1940." The presenter went on to say,

"Last night Teleki (Hungary's Prime Minister) who had regarded this as a fatal step and was not prepared to endorse, <u>has committed suicide.</u>"

Janos stared at the wireless with disbelief breaking out across his face. He tried to swallow twice, but his saliva had dried. Fearfully he looked at Margit

"This is disastrous." He announced.

It had dawned on Janos as by now it was dawning on all Hungarians. Hungary would be entering the progressing worldwide war. It was now not if; but when!
Teleki had thereby acknowledged the failure of his own policy along with the responsibility of revisionism for Hungary's entry into the fighting. The news presenter explained that Teleki had sent a letter to Horthy saying: -
"We have become breakers of our word; we have sided with scoundrels….. We shall be robbers of corpses! The worst of nations."

Teleki intended his suicide as a gesture and anti– Nazi circles understood it as such. Alas, Teleki's death was unable to alter the underlying course of Hungarian policy. Laszlo Bardossy succeeded Teleki instantly and only eight days later, on April 11th 1941, on instructions from the government, Laszlo Bardossy instructed the Hungarian Army to cross the Yugoslav border. During the 1930's, Horthy's government, supported by a strong tide of nationalism, sought to have the treaty made with the allies in 1920, revised. The Horthy regime were adamant and determined to have returned to them their own parts of Czechoslovakia, Romania and Yugoslavia, which was after all, Hungarian territory. Horthy had appealed unsuccessfully to the Western Countries, after failing there; he had sought help from the Germans. He managed it, but only by making concessions to

Hitler. A clever campaign to entrap Hungary's leaders. It was now time to pay back the debt to Germany.

✱✱✱

Janos sat alone in his kitchen drinking brandy, staring at his own shadow on the wall, which quivered caused by a flickering candlelight behind him. It was early evening, April 11th 1941, Janos lost in the thoughts of the advancing Hungarian Army into Yugoslavia, Nandi and Margit were sleeping in the bedroom. Janos decided to go for a walk in the clear moonless night; he rose to his feet and smoothed out the creases from his trousers, before leaving the house, quietly closing the door behind taking care not cause a loud slam.

As he walked he took the time to pay some attention to the stars above, he halted his stride, still gazing into the black sky, took a deep breath and said to his self out loud,

"What a terrible year we've had."

His self-pitying moment remained silent for a minute or two until disturbed by the travelling brawling voices from the local pub. His concentration broke, the voices indicating a beckoning call and with that, he made his way to the pub.

As he entered the pub doorway, it was to no surprise to him the bar was full of concerned looking Hungarian farmers, dressed in their work attire, faded dungarees and work boots. Janos instantly sensed the get together had grouped an hour or two before by the dried mud that laced their pitch forks, and sickles stood up beside each table, where the men sat. As Janos walked over to his two friends Tibor and Andras, sat over the far corner near to the bar, he was picking up comments of the bar rooms identical conversations, Hitler, Stalin, war. The atmosphere was almost as thick as the cigarette smoke.

"Evening." They all said to Janos and vice versa, at the same time.

Janos continued,

"I won't say <u>Good</u> evening; because there's isn't anything good about it."

He reached out to any empty chair behind him, pulled it closer to their table and sat with them. As he dragged the chair closer with his feet Laszlo the landlord had already poured Janos a Szilva Palinka (plum brandy) and placed it on the table in front of Janos.

"Thank you; give me a bottle of beer to go with it." Janos decided.

Janos looked at Tibor to catch his attention and then pointed to his watch, sighed and said,

"Well, our army should now be entering the Bacska."
This was the triangle of territory between the Danube and the Drava Rivers.

Tibor replied,
"If it's any consolation, our country has increased in size by quite a few square kilometres and our population has risen by a few thousand."

Janos drank all of his brandy with one large mouthful, put the glass down onto the table, released it and began wiping away the remnants of the spirit from his lips with his thumb and forefinger. His eyes filled with far away thoughts before he gave his stern reply.

"Do not get disillusioned Tibor, in our governments bid to get back what is rightfully ours, we have made a deal with the devil. Since Germany made Russia an ally before the invasion of Poland, our country has been flooded with fascist and communist ideas. Everything may look rosy at the moment, but what price must we pay for democracy. A bigger country, bigger population means nothing if you can't enjoy freedom; and how can we be free if Hitler or Stalin are calling the shots. What next? Today Yugoslavia; what happens if Hitler wants to go further, where will he stop? Think about it, 1938 Austria, 1939 Czechoslovakia and Poland, last year Denmark, Norway, Belgium, Holland, Luxembourg, France….

"They failed to take Great Britain." Andras interrupted,

"Ah, Great Britain." Janos continued.

"A bloody mystery that battle. Have you asked yourself, why in heavens name did Germany pause their attacks on Great Britain; and now he moves into the Balkans."

"What are you suggesting Janos?" Tibor questioned.

"What happens if all along his plans have been for a much bigger fish."? Insinuated Janos.

"Like who?" Tibor asked intriguingly

Janos gulped his beer before answering,

"Russia."

"My God, you could get shot for even thinking It." said Andras.

Janos continued laying out his fears and suspicions,

"Look how Hitler is laying out his strategic manoeuvres, perfectly positioning himself for an attack to the East; this guy is clever, a lunatic, but nevertheless, a clever lunatic. And who is in the middle of his crazy ambitions to rule the world; we are,

Hungary. Everything seems safe at the moment; we are on the side of this purpose built German Empire, but what happens if it all goes wrong, where do we stand?"

Laszlo passed the three men another brandy that seemed to stall Janos's conversational flow, which gave him the opportunity to join in the debate,

"Talking of Great Britain, it was announced today that they have broke off diplomatic relations with us in view of the attack on Yugoslavia. I agree with Janos, bloody Germans aren't stupid you know, they have been using us all along, promising us a lot, but when it's all over, where will we end up?"

The four of them raised their glasses in approval, made a toast to their army and a quick end to the war and swigged back their brandy in unison.

Tibor sucked in his breath and clattered his teeth together as the hot sensation burnt the inner walls of his oesophagus. As the sharp tingle relaxed, he felt he must agree.

"Yeah, you're right, sneaky bastards I reckon these Germans."

"Exactly." said Janos. "Sneaky bastards and nothing else."

They talked and drank long into the night and by the time they were ready to home, they were all very drunk but they'd solved the war twenty times over and felt much better after relieving their tensions with a heavy drinking session.

Janos emptied the last drops of his beer from the bottle into his mouth, stood up, swaying slightly and shouted in his deep bellowing voice,

"C'mon you pair, I've got to take you home."

They both laughed at Janos and replied.

"Yeah, but who's going to take you home?"

Janos sniggered out loud at them and replied.

"I'll send a telegram to Hitler and say, Hey bastard, fly over here with your Luftwaffe and take me home."

Arm in arm the three of them left the pub leaning against each other in a pathetic drunken manner.

"Goodnight." Laszlo shouted to them as they wobbled away singing Hungary's National Anthem.

They first got to Janos's house who noticed Margit must be up because the kitchen light was on and felt sure the candle he'd left flickering would have burnt itself out by now.

"Shush you two, Margit's awake." He whispered.

Bela and Tibor released their grip from the arms of Janos simultaneously, causing him to stumble and side shift into his garden gate. He managed to stay upright by clinging on to the fence. As the unsteadiness passed, the three of them let out a shriek of laughter. Margit had heard them long before, but from their laughter she swung the front door open sharply,

"Janos, is that you?" she called out.
"Yes, my sweet." He called back.

"You must be drunk; you only call me sweet when you're drunk."

Concentrating on each step, he made his way to the house and the three men shouted goodnight to each other.

In the kitchen, Nandi was sitting at the table slurping away at a mug of warm milk. A half eaten stuffed cabbage was pushed to the right side of him in a small cracked dish.

"Oh, what are you doing up this late, my son?"

"He couldn't sleep." Margit informed Janos.

Janos pulled up the milking stool and sat beside Nandi.

"Are you missing your brother?" Janos quizzed Nandi.

Nandi stared deep into his father's eyes when he answered,

"Yes I am Papa."

Margit was washing a plate in a large, white enamel bowl somewhat chipped around the rim, she stopped rubbing, turned and stared at them both.

Janos cupped Nandi's cheeks with both hands gently and pulled his face a little closer to his. Their eyes transfixed together as if the sight of each other's large eyes were glued to each other. Janos's eyes were moist and he knew it, so he blinked twice before he continued,

"Me too. I want you to promise me something son, that whatever happens in your life, whatever happens in our future, you will always do the right thing, you must always follow your heart and above all, you will be free. And promise you will never leave your family. If you can promise me these things, I will make a pledge to you of my own, I'm going to teach you all I know and more, I'm going to teach you how to use your brain, how to use your hands, how to fend for yourself and to fight for freedom."

Nandi, not exactly sure at this moment what his father meant, agreed.

Janos embraced Nandi tightly kissing him on both cheeks. When they let go of each other, Margit intervened; picking Nandi up insisting it was time to go back to bed.

"Goodnight son." Janos called out.

"Goodnight Papa." Nandi called back.

JUNE 22ND 1941.

It was 6:00 p.m. There was chicken, pasta and carrots simmering on the stove, along with   walnut cakes baking in the oven part.

Nandi and his father were outside, about to feed the chickens.

"Okay, son do you stuff." Janos instructed

Nandi had a cotton bag full of seeds, which he had clasped tight in his right hand. Following his father's instructions he proceeded over to the homemade wooden hen hut where twenty chickens were clucking imprisoned behind a locked door. The hut stood on stone legs to discourage rats and Nandi began sprinkling the seeds at the doorway and further away. When the bag was empty, Nandi knew what to do next. He removed the wooden latch from the clasp, opened the door and beckoned the chickens with the familiar call.

"Bitszi, bitszi, bitszi, bitsz." He repeated.

The first chicken peered its head through the doorway as if sizing up the daylight. And then in a systematic fashion, it stepped out onto the short wooden ramp that led the way out into the garden. One behind the other, the chickens strutted with the dignity of plump matrons down the ramp, the early evening sun glinted on their brown feathers as they eventually all scurried down the ramp and began pecking at the ground.

In the house, Margit sat in the middle of the kitchen with a deep bowl full of potatoes and water, peeling them with a small knife. She hummed a soft tune to herself, to relieve her agitated and frustrated mood, not uncommon with the people of Hungary today.

Margit's soft meditation was interrupted with a jolt. It was like a rifle shot whistling passed her ear, she drew in her breath as her eyes opened wider. The announcement on the wireless from the bedroom had aroused Hungary's worst nightmares. She called out to Janos, at first her voice choked, but then she managed it.

"Janos, Janos, come quickly."

Janos hurried across the muddy path and into the house with Nandi close behind.

"What is it woman?" Janos asked impatiently.

"It's happened, there, they've announced it on the wireless."

"Announced what?"

"The Germans attack on the Soviet Union."
Janos looked at his wife in dismay. He caught the last few words of the news flash, which   explained Slovakia and Romania immediately offered to join the attack voluntarily.
With a relieved tone in her voice Margit stated.

"At least we didn't volunteer."

Janos stamped over to the Wireless, unplugged it in disgust and turned to look at Margit. He looked her directly into her frightened eyes. A muscle in his cheek jumped with emotion before he said,

"I'm afraid my dear, it will just be a matter of time."

"Time for what?" She knew the answer.

"We will be in danger here in Kassa."

"But why?"

"The Germans will come this way to Russia and Russia will try to stop them. Kassa is only Hungarian territory because Hitler gave it back to us. It will be the intent of the Russians to gain control of this city."

"How can you be sure?"

"So sure of what Margit? The fact that our country will be joining the attack on Russia, or the fact that the Germans, Hungarians and Russians will be fighting in Kassa?"

Margit looked at her son fearfully.
"What are we going to do Janos?"

Janos knelt down beside the table in the corner of the bedroom, reached under and pulled out an old box where he kept all of his private papers. He rummaged around and snatched out the letter he was looking for.
Margit looked confused until Janos began to explain.

" I've been expecting the worst, so, I've made some plans; my sister Terezia and her husband have informed me of a house for sale in their nearby village, Mogyoroska."

" Mogyoroska?" Margit answered surprisingly.

" Yes, we'll be safe there; and there's work there too."

" But it's so far."

" The bloody further away from here the better. And I haven't seen Erzsebet, Ilona, Imre or Istvan for years."

"Yes it would be nice to see all of your brothers and sisters again. They all have children now, our nieces and nephews."

" I know. Together in Mogyoroska we could take care of each other. Share land, work together and above all protect Nandi. He will be surrounded by his cousins, aunts, uncles all Pekars'. And don't forget your sister's only in the next village."

" Oh yeah, Fony, it's only about half an hour from Mogyoroska by horse and cart." Margit reminded herself.

" Exactly. So what do you think?"

There was a moment's silence until Margit convincingly answered.

" Yes, let's go… But when and how?"

" Tomorrow I will trade all our animals to Tibor for his horse and cart and some cash, then, by the time we've organised everything else, and I've wrote a few letters to my sister, we can be on our way in about a weeks time."

June 26th 1941

Three days passed by, they seemed so busy, so intense, everything had to be right. Money, Furniture, clothes, food, everything had to be sorted and everything had to be secret.

That night Janos and Margit fell into a deep sleep very early. They had drifted into a restless sleep; thinking about what they were doing, was it the right thing or was it wrong? Should they go or should they stay? Whatever the answer they were vacating Kassa no matter what.

It was long after midnight when Janos suddenly awoke from a dreamless sleep. Something had disturbed him ———————— some noise like a distant explosion, he sat up in the darkness, only a glimmer of starlight came from a broken mirror opposite the window. He listened, mouth half open checking his breath to catch the faintest murmur of sound. A few seconds passed and then Janos heard the distant buzzing sound of airplane engines. He wondered, German or Russian?
Janos threw back his quilt, bounced out of bed and made for his coat from the wooden peg on the bedroom door. He buttoned it up in an instant and reached for his cap with the long earflaps, he looked towards Margit, she hadn't heard anything. She still slept soundly.

Outside Janos scanned the area; the skies were dark but clear, he could still hear the sound of airplanes, but louder now. Then, in an instant, it happened, explosions, machine gun fire, Janos was so startled by it, without thinking he jumped to the floor covering his head. Realising it was some distance away he got up and ran towards the gate where he had a better view of the City. Above Kassa, he could see and hear explosions totally encircled the vulnerable city. He turned and ran back to the house meeting Margit at the door. She grabbed Janos about the neck screaming.

" What's happening, what's happening?"

Janos rushed Margit back into the house. He told her, " It's a bombing raid."

" On Kassa, by who, why?"

" At a guess it's Soviet aircraft, but whoever it is we must take cover; quick get Nandi."

In a complete panic, the three of them ran outside, after turning out the lights, across to the far side of the garden to the large garden shed which was well hidden under a canopy of weeping willows and obscured from view by a large walnut tree.

" We will be safe in here." Janos reassured Margit as he bolted the heavy door behind him.

Margit parked her bottom down on a wide circular sawn down tree trunk, with Nandi still sleeping in her arms.

Janos paced around the shed muttering to himself as they both listened and awaiting for the explosions to cease. The echoing blasts exploded in the distance one after another, one or two bombs appeared to be louder than the others and it was these that caused the ground beneath their feet to shudder. In an instant they thought the last bomb had been dropped. They strained their ears eagerly so that they could be sure.

They were finally certain it was over when they heard the engines from the flying war machines growing fainter and fainter by the second; an indication they'd done their duty, made their point and probably heading for their next target.

Janos struck a match and looked at his pocket watch.

" 15 minute bombing raid. Perhaps we should go to the air raid shelter." Janos thought

" Are they coming back?" Margit asked

" Good God, I hope not, but we're not waiting around to find out; a couple of days before schedule, but we are not waiting around to get killed, I'm loading up the horse and cart right now, and off to Mogyoroska we go."

Janos drew the horse and cart up outside the house close to the door. Margit began carrying what she could out of the house and laid them on the grass near to the cart. Janos ran over to Tibor's place for his planned assistance. All was ready, all had been rehearsed.

The three working tirelessly, taking only two hours to load all of their belongings onto the back of the cart.

" Okay all finished I think." Stated Tibor as he forced the last package between a stool and a small wooden box.

Janos insisted on a final check as he ran back into the house for a last minute visual search.. Not a thing was left. No furniture, no cooker. They had loaded it all. He hurried over to the windows to make sure the curtains were tightly closed. He stopped suddenly, looked around, made a grieving noise in his throat and said,

"Goodbye."

He slammed shut the front door with a thud and locked it.

Margit was already sitting at the front of the cart with Nandi in her arms still fast asleep. Tibor was caressing the horses' head, but looking at Janos walking towards him who was pulling out the pocket watch from his trousers.

"It's 3:30 a.m., by Midday we should be in Mogyoroska."

June 26th 1941

Tibor grabbed Janos's hand and pulled his arm so Janos was forced to step forward into the embrace of Tibor's other arm.

With his chin resting on Janos's left shoulder, he instructed.

" Don't forget to write, friend!"

Patting his friend across the shoulder blades answering,

"Of course, and when the war is over, come and visit; or just come and visit."

With that, Tibor climbed up to Margit, kissed her face and forced a bar of chocolate into her hand, demanding she take care of herself and the family.

Janos climbed aboard next to Margit, took the reigns in his hands, glanced over to the house, smiled to his friend and shouted,

" Yah, Yah," and gently whipped the horse twice; and off they set.

Tibor stood watching as his best friend and family road off into the distance. He watched and watched until the rear end of the clattering cart turned a corner and he could see them no more. As Tibor had vanished from sight, Margit broke the emotional silence by asking Janos if he was sure of the way,

"Oh, yes my dear, just follow the road to Szikszo and Miskolc, that will keep us occupied for a few hours; it's a long way though, but the night is warm and fresh, try to sleep now, you may not have the chance later when Nandi wakes."

Margit didn't answer, stunned and somewhat speechless at what they had been forced to do by military circumstances, she just leaned to one side and gently placed her head onto a large pillow in the corner and quickly sank into a deep sleep.

✳✳✳

It had been a quiet, hypnotic few hours for Janos, staring and steering the horse along a straight, narrow, stony road. By now a golden sunshine, coupled with early morning mist and dew on the fields, either side of the road, marked the dawn of a new day. He now had a clear view of the voyage ahead, a long hilly road, stretching as far as the eye could see, which seemed to curve upwards to meet the sky. A low hedge fenced the land either side of them and each field adorned with acres of sunflower, strawberry plants or cherry and pear trees. The tranquil silence of a beautiful day was only made more cheerful, with the background rhythm of the horses' hooves, a buzzing bee, a wood pigeon and an occasional rustle in the grass, probably a hare or a fox.

Janos checked on his wife and son before bringing the horse to a standstill.

"Still sound asleep." He whispered to himself, "Thank God too. Time to stretch the legs and give the horse some breakfast, though."

After disembarking the cart, he began scooping grain out of the gunnysack and into the canvas feedbag. The horse turned his head trying to watch his new owner, then, in an instant; abruptly the horses ears picked upward, and he turned his head toward the front, up slightly. A moment later Janos noticed it also and so did his wife and son, as their eyes flickered open. They didn't move, just listened attentively… It was an intermittent buzzing as if a mosquito were turning its shrill hum on and off. Janos straightened up and listened. Nervously running his fingers through his hair, his face clouded suddenly.

" Not fighter planes, not more bombing," called out Margit.

" I don't think so."

"Are you sure?" she asked hopefully,

"No, it sounds like a single plane,"

They both went silent again, listening harder for more evidence.

The horses' curiosity about the unfamiliar noise ended and he nickered again for his breakfast. Janos shrugged and finished filling the feedbag as the humming receded.

He was just slipping the leather strap over the horses' ears when the buzzing sound returned with a rush. Margit squeezed Nandi closer to her chest. It seemed to come from a great height, faint at first and then increasing until the sputtering hum seemed it was overhead. Then it appeared, there was a swoosh of air that swirled the dust in the road around them. Margit screamed out and Nandi held on tighter. Janos instinctively ducked his head slightly then picked it back up as it flew passed. An instant later there was a sharp crack, as if a frozen tree limb had broken off, followed by more snapping noises and the rattle of breaking glass. The plane that was about to crash land, flew across the sunflower field barely skimming the tips of the plants with a trail of smoke behind. In sheer anticipation, the three of them watched in horror as the plane tried in vain to land safely. Instead, it nose dived into the field. After a few short seconds, it exploded. Boom, boom, two loud explosions that shook the ground beneath them. Margit and Nandi were ducking, whilst Janos smothered them in an attempt to shield his family with his large physique. The horse quivered and began dragging the cart sideways. Shrapnel from the burning wreck flew towards them and only fell short by a few metres. When it had finished shredding its body parts, they opened their eyes to see the wreckage. It burned furiously and they could feel the intense heat from the burning fuel and metal.

Janos was sure there could be no more explosions so he leapt down off the cart and made his way towards what seemed to be a section of the planes wing burning on the grassy bank beside the road.

" What are you doing," Margit shouted after him.

Janos didn't answer just ran towards it, then stood and gazed at it until he realised,

" Russian! It's Russian." He revealed,

" How can you tell?"

" Here, on the wing, it's the Russian insignia."

" Janos come back, let's go before its rescuers come looking for it, I'm afraid and so is Nandi."

The horse grunted and neighed as if to agree with Margit. He ran back, removed the feedbag from the horse, climbed back into his seat and with a slight whip of the reigns, without much more persuasion the horse galloped away swiftly, without hesitation. Nandi peered over his mother's shoulder at the burning wreckage as they progressively rode away from its vicinity.

Thirty minutes later along the road, Janos turned and surveyed; thick black smoke could still be seen on the horizon rising higher and higher into the summer blue sky. Margit turned too, then turned back quickly, sighed, closed her eyes, put her hands together and prayed silently. A few minutes later, when she'd finished praying, Janos quizzed her about the prayer,

" I hope you've prayed to end this bloody war."

" Hope. Hope is what I've prayed for. I have prayed that Nandi doesn't see any more destruction and that something nice happens to us; and our home is peaceful, like heaven. And, and I've prayed for forgiveness."

" Forgiveness? Forgiveness for what?"

" Forgiveness for leaving Bela's grave unattended."

" Margit, don't say that! We've been forced to leave. It would have been suicide to stay there; any way, I don't think we are going to be disappointed with our new house in Mogyoroska, a new fresh village, with a new fresh happy start for us; I know Mogyoroska is beautiful."

Nandi broke the tension when he shouted out excitedly,

"Look, look!" pointing in the road ahead. In front, racing towards them in the centre of the road, was what seemed to be a small black ball of wool with four legs, a tail, and a large pink tongue hanging from its chops, swinging from side to side as it raced towards them.

"It's a collie dog." Janos observed.

"More like a puppy," his wife noticed.

The puppy's intentions were obvious to them all when he pounced aboard the cart onto Nandi's lap and began licking his face. Nandi was laughing so hard his mother had to calm the situation down, explaining if Nandi laughed any more he would wet himself. Janos drew the horse to a standstill.

" I think this gives us a good excuse to stop for refreshments; look there's a great spot over there in the shade under that oak tree; and Nandi can go and play in the field behind with his new friend."

June 26th 1941

Margit spread open a blanket in the field, sat down and began unwrapping the bread, ham and cakes, whilst Janos and Nandi got themselves acquainted with their uninvited guest. Clearly, Nandi loved this little puppy, who was smaller than him and seemed to love Nandi too as it ran around, over and through him, yapping and jumping like an over excited kangaroo.
"I think the first half of your prayer has been answered." Janos called out to Margit.

Margit turned her head sharply and looked at Nandi and the dog together. The corners of her mouth picked up as she happily answered when she realised,

"Yes, I haven't seen him so happy for a long time; I wonder who the puppy belongs to?"

" It's bloody ours now." Janos decided.

" We can't………………..Can we?" Margit contemplated.

" Anything that puts a smile on my sons' face like that; is his!"

Margit laughed to herself as she continued laying out their feast.

" Thank you Lord." She muttered to herself.

As they sat together eating their first meal of the day, they noticed a cyclist approaching along the road.

" Good morning." Janos called out to him.
He stopped immediately and dismounted his bike.

" Good morning to you."
He paused for a moment, pulled out a handkerchief from his inside jacket pocket and wiped away the sweat from his forehead

and around his face. Janos rose to his feet realising the man must be thirsty and offered him a mug of water.

" Thanks very much, thirsty work cycling in this heat." Janos agreed.

They talked for a while, Janos explaining he had witnessed the plane crashing when the stranger queried the smoke still visible rising over yonder.

" Heard the news this morning?" The man asked.

"No." Margit and Janos answered at the same time.

"Soviet aircraft carried out bombing raids on Kassa, Munkacs and Raho."

"Really," Janos replied. " We know about Kassa, that's why we left there early hours this morning, but I wouldn't have expected Munkacs and Raho as well."

Janos thought for a moment and then continued,

"Well our government were only waiting for a suitable pretext and now they have it; have we announced our retaliation on Russia yet?"

"No not yet." The man answered, " But it's inevitable now."

After a few more mouthfuls of water, he offered it back to Janos, mounted his bike once again, bid them good day and good luck and set off, wobbling slightly as he pushed down on the pedal.

Nandi ran towards his mother with the puppy following close behind,

"Can I keep him Mama, can I keep him?"

"You can keep him if you can think of a name for him."

Nandi though for a minute and then like a flash he knew what to call him,

"His name is Fekete (Blackie.)"

"Okay." Janos chimed in, " And you and Blackie can sit down, have a bite to eat and a drink of milk."

Later, Janos cleared a space for Blackie at the back of the cart and tied him to the seat via a long, thin rope; Nandi helped by brushing and stroking the puppy's fluffy, curly black fur with his hands; Blackie stood patiently, wagging his tail, allowing Janos to secure the leash.

After Margit had tidied the remnants of the picnic, they all returned to their seats, refreshed and prepared for the journey ahead.

The sun shone, emitting a blistering heat, causing a shimmering haze to ride into to, along this monotonous but hopefully rewarding jaunt to Mogyoroska. The road had been long, desolate and increasingly uncomfortable. The towel, which perched beside Janos up on the brake lever, was soaked in his head sweat, from his continual efforts to prevent it from running into his eyes. It seemed hours since their picnic, and was.

The deserted road now showed signs of life. Detached farmhouses with thatched roofs approached, on either side. As they trotted closer, the area of road instantaneously metamorphosised from a dry, infinite slog, to a warm, cosy estate. The lingering aroma of boiled chicken hung in the air, entwined with a gentle distant smell of charred wood. As they penetrated this inhabited section of the road, a large dog from one of the houses began barking loudly as if announcing their entrance. As they passed, a gaggle of geese from the opposite side ran from their open gateway towards the rear end of the cart with their necks stretched forward in curiosity at this unusual sight before them. Blackie caught sight of them, leapt to his feet and made his feelings known by yapping his disapproval at the feathered family, causing them to hiss their reply. To their right, the next house was surrounded by a square, high, wooden fenced boundary, with lengths of wire mesh nailed to the bottom, in order to prevent small animals from escaping between the wooden struts. Behind the fence, stood a proud cockerel momentarily strutting from side to side as if guarding the property. About him, scattered around in no set pattern, were half a dozen hens, clucking and pecking at the ground, not at all interested with the spying eyes from the horse and cart. The owner of this establishment, sat deeper back on a low wooden stool up to a wooden table, slightly out of sight obscured by a low, leafy hanging branch from an overhead grape vine. He was breaking the shells from a large heap of walnuts and dropping them into a bucket beside him. Janos decided to stop alongside the front entrance.

"Good day to you, Sir."

The man looked intently between the leaves at them…Janos continued…

"I will be following this road until, if my information is correct, I reach a left turning to a town signposted Encs. Could you tell me if I am far from there?"
Before the man answered, he stood up, brushing a few broken walnut shells from his dungarees, and walked closer to them, swiping the hanging branch to one side, not wanting to appear ignorant.

" Encs is about twenty kilometres from here, not too far with a horse, about one hour that's all. Are you staying there in Encs?"

" No, not Encs, a small village twenty five kilometres passed Encs, out into the mountains, Mogyoroska, do you know it?"

" Oh yes, sure, the mountains of Mogyoroska lead right into Czechoslovakia passed Satoraljaujhely."

"That's right and………."

"And home to the Rakoczi Castle rebuild by Rakoczi in 1700" Interrupted the man knowingly.

" Yes. Your historical facts about Mogyoroska are rather precise."

The man grinned and then asked,

" Have you come far?"

"We have; from Kassa."

" Oh, don't blame you for that, from what we heard this morning. A vicious bombing raid wasn't there, early hours this morning?"

" Mmm, bloody war driving people from their homes." Janos added

" Ah, but never mind, maybe it's for the better, as long as you are safe. Mogyoroska is enchanting." The man reassuringly stated.

"So we've heard. Anyway thanks for the directions, we'd better get on our way."

"Just wait a second," the man insisted. "I've got something for you, to help you on your journey."

With that he scurried over to his bucket of walnuts, scooped out three large handfuls, poured them into large, cotton, square table-mat, folded the corners to the centre and tied them into a knot. He hurried back to them, opened his gate and held out the gift to Margit. She looked at him, read his feelings and grinned appreciatively, accepting the mans' gift and kindness. He next fumbled into the front chest pocket of his dungarees, pulling out a small bottle of homemade brandy; he unscrewed the lid and offered a swig to Janos explaining that this was fuel for the journey. Janos took a polite mouthful, thanked him for his hospitality and with a persuasive whip of the reigns, they pressed on.

The man was correct, it was one hour later when Janos steered the horse off the main road to Miskolc, to turn left into the direction of the town Encs. Janos's estimated time of arrival to Mogyoroska had not been too accurate, it was now midday and he'd expected to be there by now. But he was only twenty-five kilometres short.

The road merging into the outskirts of Encs town began wide, but gradually narrowed the further in they got. It was coated with a thin grey layer of dust, lined with small and large pebble stones, which flirted from under the cartwheels when rode directly over them, causing an uncomfortable rock, to and fro for its passengers. There were deep ditches running alongside them, parallel to the road on both sides following them towards the town centre. The ditches lay between the road and an unpaved, dusty, walkway, which; too spanned the road into the town and was the pedestrian access to the centre. Encs was a small town, around two Kilometres Square; it was pleasant but old in appearance. The road had been a down bank slope, but now, as they were reaching the Town Centre it had levelled itself out. This is where the various shops and stalls began, a cake shop and a vegetable stall stood side by side to the left of them and a small clothes shop on the opposite side, to their right, deserted, with a closed sign taped to the front window. There were few people at this end of town, the shopping looked busier further on beyond the direct train line, which crossed the main road, indicating the Centre. They were forced to stop on this side of the track, first in a small queue of four, containing in addition, a bike, and two German made cars. A loud bell repeated in succession backed up by a sudden change of colour from the signal traffic lights. There was a train passing through. They waited patiently, the suspense building by the second, they could hear the slow chug and the screech of the train wheels, the hot smell of steam engulfed the atmosphere, when, with a sudden sharp appearance, the long clattering train crossed the road before their eyes. Helped by Margit, Nandi stood up and marvelled at the steam train, clapping his hands with excitement. By now they could see it was travelling quicker than it first sounded in the direction of Miskolc and Budapest.

Janos and Margit then noticed something, a somewhat disturbing sight. The front engine had passed, but now, crossing the line in front of them, towed by the powerful steam engine, were carriages normally used for the transportation of cattle, crammed full of people. Women and children in so many, and only men in others. Their arms hung out of the wooden cross members of the carriages, noticeable to all onlookers observing the long line of the shunting train. They stared in bewilderment, looking for some clue as to who and why these people were imprisoned in such an inhumane fashion.

As the last of a long line of train carriages passed and departed Encs, along with the noise and the smell, Margit turned to Janos and broke the silence with an inquisitive statement and question,

" There were hundreds of them, who were they? Russians? Germans? Hungarians? Certainly prisoners, I could see that how they were just uncaringly squashed together."

Janos felt a moment of chill and then shook himself before he answered,

"It's just a hunch, but I think they were Jews. Hitler has always hated the Jews, and I've heard rumours….., but for him to spread his hatred for them beyond Germany; Christ it's scary."

The traffic behind them grew impatient as they began surging forward to prompt the horse and cart to continue across the train line now the obstruction had departed.

Further on, passed the train lines, was the busiest part of the town, with a long line of shops, buildings and stalls on either side of them. They passed in succession, a café, an ice cream kiosk, a haberdashery, and two deserted shops, closed and dark, impossible to fathom out what they sold. All on their right side. On their left, in order, a shop with a large front window, with old wooden tables outside on the front pavement, shelving cooking pots, pans and large tin mugs; followed by three long open air vegetable stalls, possessing nothing more than a few yellow peppers, potatoes and carrots. After the vegetable stalls there was a gap and then a brighter, much more charming looking shop. Outside it, decorated with what looked like red streamers, however as they drew nearer, it became clear they were strings of dozens and dozens of paprika peppers, hung up to dry in the sun. Finally, a bakers shop, followed by the towns police station, easily noticeable by its high stone walls and the large iron gate where two policemen stood chatting and smoking a cigarette. Thirty or Forty metres on, a pub to the left of the road and a single pump fuel station to their right, indicated the end of Encs. From here, they could just make out where they were heading, out into the sweet fresh air of the countryside, out into the wilderness.

The journey now had shifted from a tiresome jaunt, into an emotional mixture of tranquil beauty, mystery, excitement, flooding them internally with a powerful exaltation sensation, which grew as they travelled deeper and deeper into the picturesque mountainous countryside of what could be a remote and forgotten land, which, was now to become their home.

The road become narrow and carried the scent of dust, twisting and turning with humps and bumps, surrounded by fields and high mountains behind the fields forming a sloping, green line against a cloudless, deep blue sky. After each kilometre, the horse struggled more and more, as without realising it, the route had taken them higher and higher into the sky; closer to their heaven. The narrow, dusty, uneven lanes, were very long and would suddenly, rather rudely, twist sharply to the left, then sharply to the right, gradually getting steeper, gradually getting higher. Every few kilometres, the uninhabited country roads were intervened by small residential villages, easily identified by its graveyard and church, signalling a village was approaching. As the signposts with the names of the villages became legible, Janos would check his handwritten map sent to him by his sister.

As they left each of the villages behind them and got closer to Mogyoroska, the scenery seemed to grow more pleasing to the eye. The sea of green meadows which continuously encircled them, now somehow, progressively, felt different, as though they had been swallowed up by the glory of this world, and were sitting in the nucleus of a sweet smelling pasture of paradise. As they looked about them, forests that had seemed a million miles away hours before, now were so close, they looked as if they could reach out and touch them. Staring hard at the never-ending miles of mysterious trees brought them to life evolving and rotating a feeling of adventure and intrigue.

Janos had realised the next approaching village was Fony, the home of Margit's sister. To the delight of the horse, as the road dipped down slowly whilst entering Fony, there was a large stone horse trough, full of fresh sparkling water. The trough was placed on the roadside where it forked, straight on to Mogyoroska or right leading to the houses, cottages and farmyards of the village. Without any persuasion, the horse made its way towards the water and began gratefully lapping up this God given gift. Janos jumped down to stretch his legs; he looked around, not a person in sight. Scattered in groups here and there just roaming the village, were hens, chick lets and geese, but no people. Janos helped Margit and Nandi off the cart; they also needed some exercise.

"C'mon," Janos insisted, "Let's go and see if Marta is home, it's only a short distance down there, Blackie will look after the horse and cart."

Margit and Nandi sniggered as the three of them strolled down the road towards her house. The tall, Iron Gate to Marta's perfectly square garden was unlocked so they pushed it open and walked in. Her house was a rectangular shape with the only entrance to it at the side furthest away from the gate. They walked the full length of the house, before turning the corner, twisting themselves a 180-degree turn and climbing six stone steps, which led onto the veranda and to the front door. Margit was the first to notice a note pinned to the wooden doorframe. She unattached it and read it out loud,

" Hi, hope your journey has not been too tiring, we are waiting for you at Terezia's in Mogyoroska.
Love Marta."

By the time they had got back to the horse, cart and Blackie, the horse trough was almost empty. They stood around for a while, had a drink themselves, and set off for the final stint of the journey.

The road descending Fony had to be the steepest and most gruelling up to yet. Margit thought any higher and she would be above the clouds, Janos thought this had to be the highest point in the world. The road snaked, spiralled, U-turned and climbed, but at last, the peak was in sight. Their hearts beat faster as Janos forced the horse to drag them to the summit. He knew once there, it would be like crossing into another dimension. Their horse strained and pulled until finally, with an achieved grunt, the horse stopped at the summit to allow them all to marvel at what they'd all been waiting for.

The bird's eye view from here was absolutely breathtaking, they could only imagine, this must be a sight from heaven. Behind them the miles and miles of greenery they'd just travelled which was an infinite sweet view of various shades of green. Around the sides of them, about 200 metres from their road began a thousand miles of forestry, which seemed to stretch and creep its way over the hills and mountains. Ahead, on the horizon, mountain after mountain, forming a powerful visual display of emerald green, each one standing proudly to attention, but each one rolling into the next as if hugging each other.

The road now inclined and finished in Mogyoroska. As they continued and travelled down the dry dusty track, there was no sound, only the gentle clip clop of the horse's hooves and the unsteady rattle of the cartwheels, struggling under its heavy weary load. Occasionally, the sound of a cricket interrupted the uncertain silence; birds swooped low to take a closer look at this unusual sight now in its territory. There was a hot scent floating off the fields, filling the atmosphere around them and the feathery bushes made a constant susurration in the light, warm breeze, giving off a dry, peppery scent as they passed them.

They gazed around them as they made their way slowly towards the village, and with each stride; step by step, home was becoming closer; and so the mountains became larger, seeming to be gradually enveloping this little family to its bosom, beckoning, protecting, loving. Suddenly, Nandi pointed a finger and as if in unison, the horse ground to a halt snorting its approval. The family stared wide-eyed at the sight in front of them. It was breathtakingly beautiful. Margit gasped as she held Nandi protectively to her side. There in the middle of this magnificent emerald green sea, slightly visible, was the village. Dotted here and there they could see rooftops, some thatched, some tiled red. Standing tall and erect, they could see the church steeple. But above all that, standing alone, barely touching the others, stood the tallest mountain, looking proud and stern, overlooking Mogyoroska. Looking as if balancing at the peak was the castle. It stood out against a backdrop of azure blue sky, like a jewel in a crown, it stood, watching, waiting. By a trick of perspective, it looked as though they could toss a pebble into the courtyard of the castle.

Slowly they continued, no words were spoken. Only once Janos glanced at the two people seated beside him and felt a surge of love. His heart beat faster in anticipation of what lay ahead. The fields surrounded them on all sides; they were of gold's, yellows and pale greens. The sunflowers bowed their heads slightly as if shy of the new faces entering their little world. Slowly, but surely, the trio entered the village of Mogyoroska, they passed the proud little cemetery to their right; Margit noticing the neatly kept graves, each one surrounded by beautiful arrays of flowers which shouted out their love for the deceased. She made the sign of the cross, and as she looked to her left, the tall church was upon them. Margit silently marvelled at the stained glass windows, glinting and shining like rubies, sapphires and diamonds in the fierce sunlight. An iron fence wound round the church in a protective circle and the gates stood wide open.

Janos brought the horse to a standstill once more, whilst they all admired this temple of God, the religious representation and protector of Mogyoroska.
Without a word, Margit disembarked the cart, never taking her piercing gaze away from the church, as if in a trance. She began her way into the churchyard through the open gates, heading for the church doors.
Janos called out to her

" Margit…. I will run along to Terezia's, tell her we have arrived, and get the key from her for our new house————I'll only be five minutes."

Margit turned to Janos and nodded before lifting the large metal latch and pushing open the oak door and entered. As she stepped inside her skin was overwhelmed with goose pimples from head to toe, it felt as if the love of God had rushed through her interior sole. The sight of the inside of this temple was overpowering. She walked forward a few more steps along the centre aisle, which symmetrically split the church in half. She stopped, she gazed, and she studied. She marvelled in this rapturous moment. Margit wanted to take everything in, so every couple of steps, she paused and looked around. There was a large painting of the crucifixion on the far wall to the left of her, it was eerily compelling, as

she walked further forward along the centre aisle, she was always within sight of it and the twisted body of Christ, seemed to turn towards her, forcing her eyes back to the image of pain; Christ's knotted muscles standing out from the arms, as they bore the weight of the body, the head bowed it appeared, in defeat.

Ahead was a huge alter, which was flourished with statues and symbols of Christ. Dozens and dozens of tall thick candles burned away with their gentle, flickering flame cascading a kind of religious glow, reflecting hundreds of miniature flames in the silvery ornaments around, together they lit up the whole of the alter. Above, the ceiling was dome shaped with another painting of Jesus, but this picture had Jesus smiling, wearing a white robe with his arms outstretched, overlooking the congregation as if observing from heaven. Somehow, it looked as if Jesus stood out of the plastered ceiling, almost three-dimensional.

There were archways painted in a warm gold colour and the walls were a clean, pure, unstained, silky white. Either side of Margit and the aisle that she strolled, were rows and rows of solid oak seats. The church was empty, not a soul in sight. Margit noticed the smell of incense in the air and how cool and refreshing the temperature was in comparison to the outside.

Margit by now had walked the full length of the aisle to a large brass cross on a table that indicated the end of the walkway. She knelt down beneath the cross and began to pray.

She left the church feeling overjoyed and relieved, only to be met by an excited group of family and friends. They were embracing and kissing Nandi and Janos before dragging Margit politely into the middle of this joyous whirlwind of celebration and reunion. Everyone were trying to talk at the same time, it was almost impossible to hear one sentence, before another had interrupted it, or a shout, laughter, tears or a kiss. Terezia was busy trying to explain to her brother that she too had moved to this village a few days ago. Pleased that he had his family together in one village, Janos noticed a man in a boy he once knew. Sixteen year old Ferenc Pekar; he hadn't seen him since he was seven or eight years old. This was Erzsebet's boy, Janos's nephew. Coincidently, Erzsebet had married a man with the same surname, 'Pekar.' Not a blood relation of course, but all the same to Janos_____, Pekar was important, "The more of us the better, flood the world with Pekar's." Janos had once said.

Janos looked at him with a proud stare, "A typical looking Pekar man." He said to himself before approaching the young man. He was almost as tall as Janos, a lot leaner, and wore husky, chiselled, facial features with dark brown hair almost black. Janos grabbed his right hand sharply, as if to challenge his strength. Ferenc gripped his uncle's large spade like hand firmly.

Janos let out a loud, short, sharp laugh and followed on, saying,

"You have strength in your arms boy, a typical Pekar and a Hungarian, good lad, good lad, c'mon," He let go of his nephew's hand, moved to the side of him and clenched both of shoulders with his hands and led him to a box at the back of the cart. Inside, Janos pulled out a bottle of the home-made plum palinka (Brandy), unscrewed the lid, wiped the mouth of the bottle with his shirt sleeve and offered it to young Feri,

"Taste it lad, it'll put hairs on your chest."

Feri reluctantly took half a mouthful and swallowed. He felt the sting of this firewater immediately, but knew he had to contain his inexperience to impress his uncle and at the same gain some respect from him. As the hot sensation, slowly crept away from his throat, down the middle of his chest and snowballed into a burning mass at the pit of his stomach, Janos waited in silence for this precise occurrence as if he knew the exact moment when the brandy had reached its pinnacle effect and then, he roared a deep laughter patting Feri hard on his back,

"Oh yes, oh yes, definitely a Pekar, definitely a Pekar." he said proudly.
After plenty of loving welcomes and happy discussions, it was decided the three of them and their dog, should go to their new home alone, then after an hour or so, Terezia's husband Lajos, Marta's husband Laszi and young Feri, would come and help unload the cart.

They mounted the cart for the last time to complete the final leg of their long journey. Ahead of them, the road forked off in three ways, right, left and straight ahead; Janos was to go straight ahead, passing immediately to their left, a one storey building with two adjoining rooms, one was a shop and the other was the pub which was nothing more than a small bar room, and shelves loaded with bottled beers behind a long counter. As they passed the pub, the wide road junction that had given them three options, had now narrowed into a muddy dirt track, shaded from the sun slightly by tall overhanging weeping willow trees on either side. Behind the trees to their right, they could just make out the village school, set back off the road side and surrounded by a dusty garden with patches of grass here and there, and a wooden trellis supporting a grape vine made an arbour around a window.

To their thanks, the muddy lane ahead had dried solid, as they all were imagining the difficulty to get through the mud bath if it had been raining. Stepping forward beyond the short stretch of weeping willows was like exiting a tunnel of which you have no idea what to expect on the other side. To their disbelief, directly before them, with no road to aid them, was the foot of the steepest, uneven hill they'd encountered up to now. The next fifty meters or so was almost a straight vertical climb, until the hill, as far as they could see, slowly but surely levelled itself out, but climbed higher and higher and further away into the clear blue skies. Janos and Margit laughed excitedly as they forcefully persuaded their horse to heave this eager family to its paradise. The cart creaked, squeaked, cracked and snapped as the weary horse mercilessly dragged the load through mud, stones, over grass, anthills, passed tall trees, small trees, passed farmyards, cottages with their semi-circular windows in the roofs, which peeped out under their heavy lids of rush thatch or wooden shingles, homes of their new neighbours, towards their own haven.

As they trudged on up the trackless hill, passing the village Water Well, they could see the front part of their house, just coming into view. This was like a Greek mythology story where they had travelled to the end of the world to retrieve the golden fleece, this was it, the last village, beside the last mountain, on top of the last hill was the last house, right there in front of them was their reward for travelling to the end of the world; a golden fleece for the Greeks, but a home, a sanctuary covered in a thick mass of red roses for the Hungarian Pekar's. The climbing rose had wildly grown from floor to the thatched roof-top, spanning the whole area of wall, twisting and intermingling each branch, spreading, and forming a beautiful array of crimson red, brightening up the front of the cottage. The cottage and land drew nearer, every second their home became clearer and they seemed to forget their tiredness, feeling a sense of complete satisfaction and peace. Then, it was almost as if the whole world had been put in slow motion until paused. The horse stopped at the front of the fenced off garden. The building stood on its own, about ten metres set back from the garden fence, it was a fine rambling old cottage, perched on a slight eminence with a spectacular view from whichever side or corner of the building you would choose to stand. From here, they could notice this end of the cottage was not only crawling with red roses, but a separate climbing rose was spouting, producing diamond white petals, which blended behind the reds. In the middle of the facing wall, one slightly over to the right, and another slightly over to the left, behind the branches and spines of the blooming climbing rose, were two, small, wooden framed windows. The cottage was rectangular, with the longest adjacent walls of the rectangle shape running back away from them. Half way along the long side of the cottage, to the right of them as they stood, was the front door that stepped out onto the veranda. At this side of the house, the veranda acted also as the long walkway leading to the front door half way down, and further on to the dorsal end. Directly opposite the front door, across the veranda, were three stone steps that led down from the raised building into the side garden. Janos knew from previous descriptions of this property, that the garden at the side, opposite the front door, led out around the back and out into very, very wide and long grounds, beautifully landscaped, this view was obscured for the moment.

Janos quietly climbed down from the cart to unlock the garden gate, whilst Margit and Nandi looked around to admire the view, which would be their surroundings for countless years ahead. All around the majestic mountains surrounded them. They could smell them; feel them, their presence like a protective arm around them. Margit dismounted the cart herself with Nandi sitting in her right arm. She looked at the ground around her and beneath her feet; it was flat with scars in the dry earth from tractors, hoof prints, interrupted here and there with masses of wild flowers; blues, yellows, reds. Small bushes grew wildly in patches; wild strawberries and mushrooms also littered the ground. And then, "The eight wonder of the world," Margit was sure of. Only about one hundred metres from where they stood, began the thousands of miles of forest, right opposite their home, Margit was sure this was the beginning and end of all forests, which lay on her doorstep of heaven. As her eyes followed the trees, it was certain that they grew taller and taller rolling on upwards, like waves on an emerald green sea, climbing the mountain until they reached the top where the jewel in the crown stood. The Castle. It was directly opposite their cottage, staring down at their home, it seemed to beam at them and shine a glare like a warships searchlight scanning the whole of Mogyoroska, but at the moment shining a spotlight on its new family. Margit sighed a sigh of excitement at the prospect of having this idol to see every morning and every day for the rest of their lives. As Margit looked, she felt if she reached out, she could pluck the castle off the top of the mountain and hold it in the palm of her hand.

Janos untied Blackie and began leading his tired horse into the side garden through the now open gates. Blackie sprinted off towards the back with Nandi toddling after him.

"Let's look around before we go inside," Margit suggested. She pointed a finger to the area in front of the climbing roses.

"Here, I shall fence it off and keep it especially for roses, it will be my own private rose garden. Roses are for love Janos, and that is what I feel when I look around our own private corner of the world.

They walked along the veranda passing a small window and then the front door. The end of the limestone veranda signalled the end of the cottage. In front of them was a small wooden door leading into something.

"It's a small storage room." Janos guessed.

To their left was a large wooden door, which was the entrance to the back end of the cottage. They proceeded through it into an open-air extension to the cottage, under cover by the thatched roof, held up with pillars and posts at the corners. To their left was the end wall of the building, but to their right and in front, there was no brick structure, just a few wooden frames and supports made from old chopped down tree branches. This area was attached to the cottage, with access to the loft via a homemade wooden ladder leaning against the brick wall. It also contained a hen house, an area for chopping logs easily identified by a sawn off tree trunk and an old axe left wedged in the centre. Immediately behind the door, to their left in the corner was their toilet. A purpose built long wooden boxed shape, with a hole cut out to accommodate all bottom sizes, covered at the moment with a thin plywood lid; and not visible, inside this wooden lavatory was a two metre deep man made hole, cleaned out once a month by gypsies.

"Plenty of ventilation in this bathroom, when I overdose on garlic and paprika." Janos joked.

Janos noticed another door at the end of the open-air bathrooms only wall. It was locked so Janos fumbled inside his pocket for the keys and then opened it.

" Ah, it's the cow shed." he realised.

They walked further on now away from the cottage viewing their land at the back. They both gasped simultaneously. The lawn that they'd seen at the side was like the river Danube and the land before them the Black Sea. At first the lawn fell away from the

June 26th 1941

cottage steeply and then flattened itself and flowed onto six acres of short grass cut land, perfectly square, bordered by twenty five metre vertical high trees, around the perimeter, and in front of them at the far edges, smaller ornamental, cherry, pear and plum trees scattered the land.

As they raptured; a single rain cloud floated into the clear blue skies above their land, bringing with it a spray of rain arching across the sky; a strong breeze blew the water into a curve which caused the rays of the sun to be netted by the drops, turning them into diamonds flashing through every colour of the spectrum. The sight was magically refreshing and colourful.

"Is this really all ours?" Margit asked in disbelief.

" You'd better believe it. This house and land will stand as a symbol; a symbol of the Pekar's, and will be passed down through our generations, Nandi's children, their children, and on, and on; this IS definitely a heaven; **Pekar's heaven.**"

The land was large and beautiful, it had so much potential and Janos knew it. He rubbed his hands together in excitement at the prospect of working the field. The cottage had the one entrance to the interior, which consisted of just two rooms. The first room behind the front door was to be the kitchen, and the other room, accessed by a single doorway to their left as they entered the cottage from the veranda, would be the bedroom/dining room. This room was twice the size of the kitchen and would easily accommodate their three beds and the dining room table. The floors were concrete based covered with a speckled green lino, all the walls, inside and out, were coated with limestone and painted over a clean bright white, the ceiling was the dark wood varnished side of the lofts wooden beams and wooden floor.

The cottage in an instant had somehow become acquainted to its new family, who had fallen in love with it. They revelled in the cosy luxury of their bedroom as they peered through the two bedroom windows. Beyond the red and white climbing roses, the forest outside and the single pyramid shaped mountain, with its ancient ruin perched on its peak, was a view from a painting. "We will explore that castle someday." Janos was certain.

The three men turned up as planned and they all set to work immediately unloading the furniture and belongings, closely supervised by Margit who was ensuring her home was being equipped to her liking. It wasn't too long after, when the women arrived with a large black stewing pot, full of a thick, deep paprika red, lamb goulash. It took two of them to carry it up the bank, each women holding the same handle, side by side. The smell of cooked lamb, spices, combined with boiled red wine flourished the kitchen and swept through the nostrils of its occupants as they transported in their surprise.

"Mum's, been cooking that all day, out in our garden over an open fire Uncle Janos," Feri announced.

"Yes, I think we've stripped the forest clear of its wood the amount of times she sent me away to cut down more and more firewood." Lajos continued.

Janos, Margit and Nandi were most grateful as they took the opportunity to take a break and fill their hungry stomachs, whilst the rest of them continued offloading all articles from the cart.

It wasn't long before this gruelling day was almost complete. By now everything had been transported from the cart and indoors. All of them had a final drink together when Lajos proposed a toast

"To Janos and Margit's new home,"

Before they were to neck back their palinka, Janos interrupted and lengthened the toast,

"And to Hungary's freedom."

"Here, here." They all agreed at the same time and finally drank to their new home and freedom. Margit drank it and smiled at Janos over the rim of her glass.

Janos, Margit and Nandi stood at the front gate to see them all off and to bid them goodnight. As their family walked home they felt relieved and satisfied, but tired with the healthy tiredness, that comes from a long day of vigorous, but not exhausting exercise in fresh air and sunshine. The sun had started to set, the jewel in the crown stood silent against the darkening sky, the breeze blew gently through the trees, and the mountains whispered goodnight.

CHAPTER 6

On June 27th 1941, Janos and Margit's first day in their new home, was also the day Hungary declared war on the Soviet Union. This critical step was not debated in parliament and the decision was merely announced to its members. On this day, the Hungarian army crossed the frontier.

Initially there was great success on the Eastern front, as Germany and Hungary advanced into the Soviet Union promptly. Despite this, Hitler forced all Hungarian men of fighting age, to be drafted into his armies in January 1942; some went into hiding and formed a resistance. Also, the German army demanded active support from its other allies. Italian and Romanian armies advanced to the Don, and also in January 1942, the Hungarian government committed itself to despatch the second Hungarian army to Russia. This was a total of 200,000 soldiers and was immediately placed under the command of the German military leadership.

Partisans in Hungary resisted the German occupation and clearly were against the attack on Yugoslavia and Russia. In early January 1942, Nazi army units killed around 5,000 Hungarians (mostly Jewish) in retaliation for alleged partisan activities. Partisans resisted the Nazi occupation and were executed wherever they were found. This partisan war in Hungary gave the Germans an easy excuse simply to hang or shoot anyone they didn't like the look of.

By undertaking the attack on Yugoslavia and by declaring war on the Soviet Union, Laszlo Bardossy fulfilled his fateful role, and on March 9th 1942 Miklos Kallay replaced him as Prime Minister. Initially Kallay continued the policy of his predecessor, but soon after, he began some very delicate manoeuvring. Kallay aimed to break with Germany at a suitable time and in a suitable way, to reach agreement with the Western allies, and to ensure the survival of the Horthy system for the post-war period. Approaching October 1942, the area of territory controlled by the Nazi's and their European allies had reached its peak, but Kallay wanted the German's out.

At this time, Hungary's economy was suffering more and more. Shortages of food and   commodities grew constantly and remained even after the introduction of rationing. The black market flourished.

The Hungarian economy was subordinated to German interests and demands. During 1942, 90% of Hungary's Bauxite production went to Germany, as did 50% of its oil production. Certain industries produced more for the German army than for the Hungarian army. Also, it was the same for Hungary's agriculture, most of Hungary's maize, wheat and oil seed went to Germany. Moreover, Germany never paid for what it received, nor had it ever any intentions of ever doing so, in short, Hitler's war was partly financed by Hungary.

After Hungary's entry into the war, the people of Hungary experienced special measures that had been introduced. There were rules such as the banning of political rallies, inaugurated censorship of the press, banned listening to enemy radio stations; communist activity was dealt with severely with long-term prison sentences or execution.
In spite of these extreme measures, there was still a growing army of people in Hungary opposing the regime. They rallied around various opposition organizations, they denounced the war, they called for an end to the German alliance, they acted as agents for freedom, and they would demand Hungary's withdrawal from the hostilities. These Hungarians opposing Hungary's participation in the war received encouragement in the autumn of 1942. The allied

powers made some good advances on the German armies, something that had not happened since Hitler began his crusade back in 1938/39, it was unacceptable for the German dictator, but an angle for Kallay. In November 1942, the British defeated Rommels army at El Alamein and American Units landed in North Africa. Shortly after this, Russia's Red Army victory in Stallingrad. They had eventually annihilated the German sixth army. This victory was absolutely imperative for the Russians.

In January 1943 the Hungarian second army along with Italian and Romanian soldiers suffered tremendously after Soviet troops launched a successful offensive along the River Don, in the course of this attack the Hungarian army, stationed in the Voronezh Region, was destroyed. They lost more than 150,000 men.

After this, the Kallay government vehemently refused to despatch another army to the Eastern front in spite of considerable pressure from Hitler to do so.

By October 1943, Italy turned on its former ally and declared war on Germany. With the end of the war in sight, Kallay wanted to build up combat-ready forces in Hungary and his government put out diplomatic feelers in the West in an attempt to pave the way for an armistice and the country's withdrawal from the war. It was important for the Hungarian government not to be military exhausted by the time an armistice was signed. It was also hoped that if Hungary succeeded in pulling out of the war, it would be able to retain the territories it had annexed since before the war began. Negotiations had to be carefully and secretly done with the West and Kallay had to be intelligent and patient. Kallay, importantly needed to take Hungary out of the war, but also needed to preserve the existing political structure.

The allied landing in Sicily initially raised Hungarian hopes. But, the advance of English and American forces in Italy had been ground to a halt due to German troops occupying Rome. This was an event that must not occur in Hungary. Kallay knew that the Germans must not be occupying Hungary, because on September 9th 1943 the Kallay government's representative received from the British, conditions for an armistice, to come into force when British and American forces reach the Hungarian frontier. If the Germans were occupying Hungary at this time, this would mean a repeat of what was happening in Italy, which would result in Hungary in a war it didn't want, thus ending up with Hungary at the end being bombed to a pulp, leaving it being financially and military exhausted. It was almost certain by now that Germany would lose their aggressive attempts to conquer the world. Hungary wanted to be on the right side when they finally lost altogether.

Kallay's plans were smashed when Hitler and Germany became aware of Kallay's secret negotiations with the West, thanks to Hitler's secret Nazi intelligence service. Hitler ordered "operation Margarethe" He demanded a meeting with Horthy and would use his by now, well practised bullying tactics, which had been successful in his rape of Austria in 1938, his occupation of Czechoslovakia in the same year, and with countless other leaders of the world. It was now the turn of Hungary to experience Hitler's bullying and persuasive dictating. The meeting was held at Klessheim (near Munich) on March 18th 1944, which ended inevitably in Hungary agreeing to the German occupation. Hitler yet again proved to be a master of his forceful tongue.

On March 19th 1944, the German army moved into Hungary, and, as with other invaded countries, Germany set up its own band of leaders or butchers some preferred to call them.

Although domestic political circles feared a German occupation was imminent, they were surprised and unprepared when it actually happened. The supporters of a divorce with Germany were not united. None of the groups could boast armed fighters.

The Hungarian army remained passive. No one issued orders
to resist. Officially, the occupiers had to be received as friends.

No sooner had the occupation taken place did the butchery, arrests
and the complete strip down of the anti-Nazi's begin. Politicians
were arrested, together with the leader of the opposition to
Germany within the governing circles. During March and April of
1944, some 3,000 people were apprehended including Jozsef
Mindszenty, the Hungarian Roman Catholic prelate for his
outspoken opposition to the occupying Nazi's.

Kallay resigned and took refuge in the Turkish Embassy, but by
the autumn of that year, he too was arrested by the Germans.
The war almost came to a dramatic end, when unrest and mutiny
within Hitler's main band of officers were feeling the squeeze of
the enemy and feared the worst if revenge from their former
captured countries, were to avenge their aggressors. Feeling
defeat for Germany was becoming more and more unavoidable,
as armies were advancing closer to the Fatherland, to be rid of
Hitler they could end the war and make a deal with the
advancing armies. A group of German officers concluded in
July that getting rid of Hitler offered the last remaining chance
to end the war before it swept onto German soil from two
directions. On July 20, they tried to kill him by placing a bomb
in his headquarters in East Prussia. The bomb exploded,
wounding a number of officers—several fatally—but inflicting
only minor injuries on Hitler.

The Soviet Union's push towards the West continued, on August
23rd 1944, they crossed the Romanian frontier, their government
was overthrown and Romania changed sides. To the
disappointment of the Hungarian nation that their plans to make
an armistice with the West, to be liberated by the West, they were
beginning to realise they could not count on the appearance in the
country of British or American troops, so now they were forced to
discard their anti-Soviet stance. On September 28th, a delegation
was despatched to Moscow to negotiate an armistice. On paper,

Stalin agreed to let the people of Hungary to set up their own democracy after the Nazi's had left. On October 11th, 1944, the Hungarian delegates signed the preliminary agreement in the Soviet capital. It was hoped and planned by the Hungarian government that this gesture would encourage the Germans to flee their country, thus sparing Hungary from any military action. This was regarded by some as a dilettante approach. The German army responded. They set about occupying Budapest's strategic points and installations, including Buda Castle.

In the autumn of 1944, Soviet troops crossed the Hungarian borders. Ferocious battles were encountered in most major Cities, pushing the Germans further west, demolishing the country on its way. By Christmas 1944, the Soviet army had surrounded Budapest, and, prepared to spare the City the horrors of a siege, they sent two officers in under a flag of truce to propose Budapest's surrender. To no surprise to the Russians, as with battles on the Russian mainland, the German commander rejected the offer. What followed was a two-month battle, devastating the Hungarian capital.

Hostilities in Hungary lasted a total of 194 days. After fierce street fighting, the Pest side was liberated on January 18th 1945, Buda was liberated on February 13th 1945 and eventually the last German units were expelled from the country by April 13th 1945. Hungary was now free from Nazism, but a new master was preparing a much firmer strangle hold on its old Hungarian enemy…..Josef Stalin___ Stalinism___ Communism.

As Hungary were bracing themselves for the uncertainties of what lay ahead for them as a nation occupied by another. The world saw 1945 to be the end of what seemed to be never ending. Germany had been defeated by May 1945 and Japan by September. Incredibly, the world looked upon the last six years in disbelief. Though thousands and millions observed the Germans at first hand, it is amazing how little they really knew of how they came about. The plotting's and manoeuvres, the treachery, the fateful decisions and moments of indecision, the dramatic encounters of the principal participants which shaped the course of events took place in secret beneath the surface, hidden from the prying eyes of foreign diplomats, journalists and spies.

CHAPTER 7
DECEMBER 1948

"After the Russian army had driven the Germans out, most of the Partisan groups disbanded and went home, but some Hungarians didn't trust the Russians, we stayed together, and we've been distributing and producing freedom, we want Hungary to get the same kind of post-war deal as Austria. It is clear now… Matyas Rakosi is a puppet for the Kremlin. Look what this Communist regime has imposed on Hungary, Communist propaganda in school curriculum's, compulsory courses in the Russian language, in Marxism-Leninism the imprisonment of Hungarian leaders belonging to the Roman Catholic Church, yes, there are now three classes of Hungarians in Hungary, those who are in prison, those who are going to prison and those who have been to prison. Soviet tanks first rolled into Budapest in the winter of 1944, they came as liberators but have stayed on as masters, in writing Stalin agreed to let us set up our own democracy, it has been a promise that is proving to be worthless. Now what do we have? Russian monuments in every city, town and village on our sacred historic land, big red stars in our city centres, a bloody big statue of Josef Stalin in the middle of Budapest, the Russian insignia printed slap bang in the middle of our national flag. Poland, us, Czechoslovakia, Yugoslavia, Romania etc, buffer zones, that's what we are, bloody buffer zones; he calls it the Iron Curtain, but we are buffer zones, protection from the West."

Peter broke off sipping his beer, staring at Janos and Nandi across the bar room table. Janos took the opportunity to ask a question,

"So what do you want from me?"

"Listen Janos, I had to flee Budapest earlier this year because the Avo were getting to close, we had been distributing papers."

"Papers, what kind of papers?"

Peter Csonka lowered his voice and leaned forward,

December 1948

"Papers gathering our Hungarian brothers to rise together in the name of freedom and break our chains; anyway, someone, a communist, had seen copies of it, condemning the communist regime, and calling for an uprising to set the country free. The Avo captured some of my colleagues, executed them and the betrayer got a big fat reward. But they were getting to close to me and so I am here in this remote village; but you should know Janos, we are underground, growing by the hundreds, thousands, you should think about joining us. Did you here about our Cardinal Mindszenty? He was charged with treason and illegal monetary transactions by the puppet of the Kremlin and was sentenced to life imprisonment."

Peter took another drink and Nandi asked, "Who are the Avo?"

Janos jumped to his son's protection immediately and covered his mouth with his muddy hand,

"Shush, boy; keep your voice down, you don't know who is listening."

Peter continued,

"No doubt about it you'll find out young man, these people are Moscow trained secret policemen, they are not Hungarians, they are traitors who have sold their soles to the Devil; while we can't hardly afford a loaf of bread to feed our families, these Commie gits are swanking around in a life of luxury at our expense. I saw them when I was in Budapest, I saw a workingman after he finished work, walking home, I assumed. He was threadbare but clean, with patched shoes, he was a small, stiff man with greying hair at the temples. I followed him with my eyes for some reason, as I sat on a chair outside a café sipping my coffee and smoking a cigarette. He was begging passers-by for a cigarette, he looked curiously unsettling and then I saw him lose it, he lost his self control running around shouting and screaming, bad-mouthing the

Russians, swearing about the Communist regime, 'here I am begging for a lousy cigarette, I'm working all day for a pittance, these bastard Russians, I cannot feed my family, go home you Communist pigs.' People were backing away from him and so I stood up to get a better view and within a few seconds' men with black leather jackets and guns surrounded him, he was bundled into an unmarked Skoda car and whisked away. The next day big signs went up all over Budapest, that this man had been executed for treason. This was engineered by the Avo." His words were tumbling over each other, his eyes moist.

Janos finished his bottle of beer and clutched Nandi's arm,

"C'mon son, supper is waiting." They stood up together and Peter tilted his head a little to look up at them,

"You think about what I've told you Janos."

"I will Peter, but please be cautious when you mention that word Avo, Mogyoroska is remote, but not entirely safe."

On their way home Nandi began asking his father questions about all Peter had said.

"Listen, Nandi, what Peter has said is true, but the road to freedom is education, the Avo may be able to cover up our pride and imprison the threats to them, but they can never take away a man's education, so first learn how to use your head and the rest will fall into place."

The next day when Nandi came home from school, he dropped his satchel on the kitchen table and immediately sought to find his father.

"Where's Papa? I need to ask him something."

December 1948

"He's out on the land somewhere." Margit informed.

Nandi darted out along the veranda and headed towards the back with his mother calling after him. "Tea will be an hour."

There was a fine layer of snow covering the land and a thin crescent of new moon, was casting a faint silvery light over the surface of the white sheet, making it easier for Nandi to spot his father over in the far left corner. He noticed his father's large footprints in the snow leading to him and Nandi ran along the dented snow trying to simulate his father's wide strides. As Nandi approached, Janos turned and put one finger over his lips,

"Shshshsh, I'm setting a trap."

"A trap for what?"

" You see those pine trees, a powerful sap drips from the scars and do you know what animal needs that sap, wild boar, and guess what? There are wild boar tracks here at the back and rubbing marks on my pine trees and look, over there where the soil has been turned over, they dig with their tusks looking for worms, grubs and roots from plants."

"So how can you catch it?" Nandi asked inquisitively.

Janos pointed to a square wooden enclosure; with four wooden walls about two metres high and an open doorway.

"With my homemade wild boar trap, and its almost finished."

Janos picked up a heavy wooden door, which was lying flat in the snow.

"This will fit neatly in the slides of the doorway, held open by this latch, it works like a guillotine." Janos mounted the heavy door between the slides and slid it down until it was in line with the latch.

"Quick Nandi slide the latch across."

Nandi did it and Janos released the door.

"Now I must attach this thin wire to the latch, and feed the wire across the centre of my enclosure, and when the boar kicks the wire, the latch is released and down comes the door."

"How can you get the boar to go in there?"

"Corn! Boars love corn."

As Janos finished tying up the wire Nandi laid some corn on the wall opposite the doorway.

"That should do it" Janos said satisfactory. " I've made a long, thick, sharp, wooden, spear, all we need to do now is wait and we've got boar for dinner tomorrow. This is the art of capture, ambush, like I told you yesterday, use your brain."

"So what do we do next Papa?"
Janos bent down, picked up his sharp, heavy, wooden spear with his left hand and put his other arm around the back of his son and cupped his far right shoulder with his hand and began   walking him away,

"Now son, now we wait, we hide and we be patient; I don't know about you lad, but I'm   starting to get a little Hungry, let's see what your mother's cooked us for tea."

" Mama said it wouldn't be ready for another hour." Nandi then remembered what he wanted to ask his father.

"Papa, we have began a topic today in our history lesson, about the Turks, when they ruled half the world and how they invaded

Hungary, tomorrow we have to write an essay about what we can find out about it. But, I got to thinking to myself, it seems history proves that Hungary has always been a victim of invasion, picked on and occupied by a bigger aggressor, more recent the Germans and now, we are ruled by Russia, why is this? Why can't they leave us alone? Why can't we get rid of them?"

The two of them stopped walking in the centre of the field, they turned and faced one another, Nandi looking up only slightly at his father as he was shooting up fast and it was obvious he was going to be as tall as his father, or maybe taller; Janos stared proudly at his son with a strange joy flickering at the back of his eyes; he passed the spear to Nandi and he received it with both hands.

"Nandi, you are just turned ten years old, but you have a mind of an adult, here I'm going to tell you a story to teach you something about Hungarians…."

Janos stood behind Nandi and told him to look straight ahead.

"Now imagine this, a battlefield."

Nandi stared hard and then Janos covered Nandi's eyes with his hands.

"In the year 1526 the Sultan of Turkey, emperor of all the Ottoman lands, which then extended from Spain across North Africa, to the Middle East and into Europe as far as Bulgaria, Romania and Yugoslavia, turned his attentions to our small and proud country; Hungary. The King of Hungary was called Lajos. A statue of him stands alongside a dozen or more so of our historic heroes, in a cup shaped curved high stone wall, one after another to form a whole line of gallant Hungarians, you can see these in Budapest, Heroes Square it's called, I will take you there someday; unless of course the Russians have covered it with a red

star. Anyway, Lajos was a brave young man, like you, at only 20
years old he was King of Hungary and he was an inspiring leader
of men. He knew he had to re-establish Hungary's army. Hungary
had no chance of defending itself against Turkey's greedy
intentions and the Sultan of Turkey could easily have put half a
million soldiers against Hungary's small army of only twenty
thousand. The armies of Turkey's empire were feared throughout
the world, they had reputations of ferocious bravery. King Lajos
tried everything, diplomacy with Turkey didn't work; he sent
word to his allies for help, the West, England and France, closer to
home, Poland. He was shunned, nobody was interested to go into
battle and help Hungary. ' Let Hungary look after itself.' Were the
words from the West. But still Lajos took to the field with his
small army; he was not the kind of man who would bow down to
this Turkish bully without a fight. The Turkish army invaded
Hungary on horseback and the Hungarian army confronted them
on the battlefield in Mohacs, vowing to defend their land and fight
to their death. Thousands upon thousands of Hungarians were
killed that day; they went down fighting with honour for the
freedom of Hungary against a foreign invader. King Lajos, well,
he fought to his death on that day of August 29th 1526."

Nandi gripped the spear until his knuckles turned white as he
imagined the battlefield; the small gallant force of Hungarians,
and the hoards of Turks galloping on horseback, with their wicked
curved swords sparkling as they raised them in the sun.

Janos moved his hands away from Nandi's eyes. He opened his
eyes wide and could see an invading army hurtling towards him,
in an instant; he was caught up in the emotion of the moment and
felt himself there, defending Hungary's honour. He held the spear
high with his right hand and ran towards his imagination, and with
all his patriotic might he hurled the spear into the crowd of
Turkish invaders.
Janos grinned to himself, as he knew his boy had developed a
proud Hungarian soul, he continued.

" The Turks, they may have won the battle, but they couldn't take the whole of Hungary, Lajos and his army's heroic stand against the most powerful force in the world, seemed to inspire the country and to make them even more determined. A man defending his home is more powerful than ten hired soldiers. Hungary held its own, we were the final rock by where the wave of their advance broke."

Nandi inhaled deeply before asking his father the final question.

" What about now? What would King Lajos do about the Russians?"

" That's something you will have to figure out for yourself, but I can tell you, in the clutches of the Soviet Union, you have to put Hungary first, before your family, before your friends; if you believe in freedom."

Walking around the side of the cottage, they could smell tea cooking, a strong mixture of tomato, onions and yellow pepper fragrance, clung to the cold air about them. They could hear the rhythmic swish of bristles over the limestone veranda, as Margit brushed away some light snowflakes that had blown across from the garden.
Margit heard their footsteps crushing the soft snow and looked down at them.

" Tea's not quite finished, but I've just boiled some water for a coffee. Nandi, take your shoes off before you go in and warm your toes by the stove."

Janos kicked the snow from his boots against the steps before he entered, and looked forward to a hot drink.

" Have you finished setting your trap?" Margit asked as she followed Janos into the kitchen, looking at him with a speculative interest.

" Yes it's all set, bait, trip wire, trap door and spear, equals, wild boar dinners for a month."

" I'm more concerned for Nandi; I just want it gone, they're dangerous, big ugly bugger wandering around our land."

" Don't worry about Nandi, he's a tough lad, with plenty of common sense, no bloody overgrown pig is going to scare him; will it son?"

Janos ruffled Nandi's thick black hair.

" No way Papa, I'll take to the battlefield like King Lajos and rid our land from a tyrant."

Later that night after tea, Janos strapped a churn full of milk from his cow, to his go-cart. Nandi kneeled at the back, leaned forward and held the large milk container secure with his hands, whilst Blackie squeezed at the front, sat up straight with his chest sticking out as if he was the captain of a ship. Janos picked up the rope attached to two large bent nails at the front, dug his heels into the snow and heaved the load through the snow until it picked up momentum down the bank and then he faced forward, held the rope over his right shoulder with two hands and just kept tugging intermittently when the go-cart slowed, or wedged in the snow. Nandi loved this part of the evening, delivering milk to the village shop. It was fun and a chance for Nandi to be chauffer driven down the slippery bank.

At the shop, Janos delivered the milk in exchange for salami and a few Forints.

" How's Margit?" asked Erzsike the shopkeeper's wife as she rolled up the salami in a square, thin sheet of greaseproof paper.

" She fine; been cooking and embroidering all day."

" Something nice for tea?"

" Oh yes, stuffed peppers in a tomato sauce."

Whilst Erzsike exchanged friendly small talk, Nandi had been distracted by something outside. He left his father in the shop and popped outside to investigate. A black Skoda car approached the village slowly. It wasn't often cars entered Mogyoroska. The headlights grew brighter, as it glided around the corner; the snow muffled its arrival, turned right before the shop and then appeared to stop just out of view for Nandi, but he heard a sudden screech from the brakes and the engine switch off. By now Janos was outside also,
" What's the matter Nandi? What is it?" Janos asked, intrigued.

" A black car has just pulled over around the corner."

In a sharp realisation, dawning on Janos with a snap, he realised that just around the corner was the home of Peter Csonka. Sensing trouble, he pulled Blackie over to a nearby post, pulled a short length of rope from his pocket and tied him to it. The village centre was deserted, just a low deep drone came from the pub where a couple of men could be seen through the open doorway, stood drinking and talking together.
Janos walked to the corner where he could observe the car, Nandi followed. Four men jumped out ran towards Peter's house, shouting instructions to each other in Russian and Hungarian. Two of them ran around the back of the house and the other two began pounding on the door. The dogs in nearby houses began barking frantically, Blackie snarled, barked and yanked the rope with the full force of his neck and body, the pigs next door

grunted and squealed in panic. As Janos looked harder, a light from the porch gleamed on something in the men's hands; revolvers. Janos grabbed his son's arm and stepped back into the shadows in order to ensure they could see, but could not be seen. Nandi suddenly felt sick and afraid. As they watched, Peter opened the door and spoke to the shouting men in a low voice. It was obvious they weren't there to listen or talk and after a few seconds, they grabbed him and dragged him away from the door. Still shouting, one of them struck him on the side of the face and Peter fell to his knees and covered the back of his head with his arms. One of the men began yanking his arms away from his face, until he released and then the other pressed the barrel of his gun under his chin. The two men came running from around the back to join them; one of them jumped into the driver's seat and started the engine. Nandi stared in horror as he noticed something dark running down Peter's face. Eventually they shoved Peter into the back, squeezed in themselves, one either side of Peter and one in the front; u turned the car on full lock and sped away, out of Mogyoroska.

It all happened so fast; Janos and Nandi were transfixed and motionless. Janos's stillness interrupted itself as a disturbing thought entered his mind. He hadn't moved completely out of sight when the car drove away, had they seen them? He felt a moment of chill and then shook himself.

"Quick Nandi, untie Blackie and let's go."

Nandi did it immediately, leaving the rope around Blackie's neck so he could lead him home. As they got closer to home, Janos stopped and let go of the go-cart. He was sure no-one could hear him now.

"Nandi, now listen very carefully, you must not tell anybody what you've seen tonight, you must not mention it to anybody, not a soul, for your own safety don't speak a word of it, not even to me."

"What about Mama?"

"Especially your mother. Do not say anything. She will only panic and get worried for our safety. It is imperative that not any of us panics. So this means you have to be solid, nerves of steel, you hear?"

"Yes Papa, not a word, I promise."

"Good boy. But don't you worry, in a few days, it will all be forgotten."

"Why have they taken Peter Papa?"

"Because he wanted his country to be free son, because he wanted Hungary to be free." The next morning Janos returned home at six o'clock from his early chores on the land. He sat alone in the kitchen while Margit and Nandi slept. He lingered lazily over the last of his breakfast inhaling the dark burnt chocolate smell of the coffee.
"Bloody communists." He whispered to himself.

Nandi was awake a short time afterwards, but lay staring at the window, which was fringed with frost. He decided to get up after he heard his father cough and shuffle his stool.

"Good Morning Papa." Nandi said as he closed the bedroom door behind him and entered the kitchen.

"Good Morning son." Janos studied Nandi's expressions for a second as he dragged the milking stool from the corner and sat on it.

"Got anything planned for this fine, typical, wintry, Saturday morning?" Asked Janos.

"No, not really." Nandi thought for a minute and then remembered.

"Have you checked the wild boar trap this morning Papa?"

"Yes I have, nothing yet though, but there's plenty of time. Clever beggars you know these boars, probably saw us setting the trap; they'll keep away for a while. 'Till they get hungry of course. But if you've nothing planned today son, if we catch this monster, I want to teach you how to cook Kocsonya."

"Is that pigs cheeks in jelly?"

"That's the one son; a fine Hungarians man's cuisine, for the finest Hungarian men."

"Okay papa, I'd like that."

"Right then Nandi, when you've had something to eat and got dressed, you can nip down to the shop and fetch me some garlic and some black pepper."

Nandi didn't feel like eating breakfast today so he settled for a fresh glass of milk and a few bites of bread, before throwing on his trousers, thick pullover and his woollen gloves and set off with Blackie to the shop. He decided to take advantage of the snowy bank by rolling and sliding down and making snowballs throwing them at his dog causing him to yelp as he attempted to catch the cold missiles in his mouth. As he approached in close vicinity of the shop, he remembered the night before and then, he froze to the spot. Parked outside the church was the same black Skoda from the night before. In a moment of madness, Nandi darted around the back of the shop. From here, he was directly behind the car, about twenty-five metres between them. He remembered his father's words… 'Ambush.' He knelt down in the snow and began rolling a large snowball, squeezing it tight in his hands as he added more snow, patting and shaping it until it was just large enough for one hand. He thought of King Lajos and the Turkish army as he made his way towards a telegraph pole. Standing behind it, with Blackie at his side, he did it. With a strong and impulsive swing, he lobbed his snowball grenade high into the air and; thud. The snowball pelted the rear window and exploded into a million minute white fragments, followed by post explosive snow dust that obscured the view of the car for a moment. Simultaneously, all four doors of the car flew open. Nandi's eyes grew wide with a realisation attack of what he'd done. He scampered in a flurry slipping and sliding in the snow as he tried effortlessly to stay on his feet. He thought quickly, if he went into the shop for the pepper and garlic they'd never suspect him. His plans were scuppered as the men were too quick and met him at the front entrance to the shop. Nandi stopped in his tracks and looked up at one of the men approaching him. He was tall with short, black straight hair, flattened to his head; he wore a thin, long moustache that crept long over his bulging chin. His eyes were dark and small, and his stare pierced into Nandi's face. As he walked closer, he began to unbutton his long leather coat and then removed his black leather glove from his right hand and stuffed it into his left coat pocket. Nandi's heart was pounding fast and he felt a trickle of sweat roll of his forehead. The man stopped within inches from him. Blackie growled at him, but Nandi ordered his dog home and Blackie obeyed scurrying away quickly. The man paused, said nothing and then sucked in his breath. It was as quick and as sharp as lightening and Nandi's head jolted to one side as the man swung and slapped Nandi's left cheek with the flat of his right hand. Not wanting to show any emotion, Nandi returned to his original stance and looked back at the man.

"That was you! Yes?" The man said impatiently.
Nandi didn't answer.
 "Well, speak boy, was that you?" There was a deep note of scorn in his tone.

December 1948

Nandi though for a minute and cautiously answered,
"Yes, but I was only playing. I didn't mean to offend you Sir."
"Ahh, you speak Russian, young man."

It had come to Nandi in an instant, what his father had taught him; 'use your brain, get educated and everything else will fall into place,' what Nandi had considered rubbish at school, he now had used it in a threatening situation, speak Russian and they may forgive him.

"Just a little." He reverted back to Hungarian.

"Okay boy, what do you know about Lenin?"

Nandi had been ordered at school to memorise certain communist paragraphs about the life of Lenin and Stalin. He had always hated to learn it, but now he was faced with a frightening situation. He searched his mind, he remembered the red cover of the book, he recalled the page number and then the words....

" Lenin was the creator of the Union of Soviet Socialist Republics and headed its first government. He was born in 1870 and died in 1924. In 1903 Josef Stalin joined the Bolsheviks, who were led by Lenin, and then later in 1912, Lenin promoted Stalin to a leading Bolshevik party body......"

Nandi was relieved when the man interrupted,

"Very good, boy, and do you enjoy Communist Politics?"

Nandi opened his mouth to answer but was seemingly rescued by the familiar shout from his father, from a short distance behind him.

" Nandi!"

Nandi turned his head sharply and breathed a sigh of relief as the tall proud figure of Papa strode concerningly toward them with Blackie strutting by his side. The other three men stepped forward, closer to Nandi, all four of them now stood in a line, equal distances between them, facing Nandi and his approaching father.

"Is there a problem gentlemen? This is my son, Nandi."

"No there is no problem, it seems your son has been studying what is good for him...Russian Language, Russian history….. Allow me to introduce myself, my name is Captain Nistor."

"Good morning Captain, so you are a soldier?"

"No, no, you could say I am a Police officer."

"Oh, can I help you with something in Mogyoroska."

"Yes; you can start by explaining to your son that throwing snowballs at strange cars, is not very advisable….and then you could show me some identification."
Janos adjusted his facial expression, in response, to accommodate the sudden raise in volume of the Captain's tone. His frown deepened across his forehead when his inside right pocket of his coat was empty and switched hands quickly when he realised his papers were in the left side. Janos snatched them out and passed them to the Captain. He received the papers and began unfolding them. As he opened out the identification, he began to read after he had inserted his monocle into his right eye and held it in position with his facial muscles.
He read through it quickly muttering his details out loud.

"Mr. Janos Pekar, date of birth 1910, married, blah, blah, blah, occupation farmer, oh.. Interesting.. A member of The Hungarian Communist Party the MKP?"

"Yes, that's right." Janos answered.

The Captain unobtrusively folded the information back up to its original folded state, made easy by the deep creases in the paper forged through years of folding and unfolding. He passed it all back to Janos,

"Very good; just one more question, do you know Peter Csonka?"

"Yes, he lives just around the corner." Janos pointed a finger behind them, but they didn't look.

" Has he ever offered you magazines, newspapers or talked to you about his past?"

Janos acted out a concerned thought in his eyes as though trying to recall such a moment; and then he answered,

"No not as I remember. What kind of newspaper?"

"Full of false propaganda…"

"Goodness no, I would have remembered that; and probably would of reported it to the authorities if he had, no, no, haven't heard or seen anything like that around here, never."

"Good." The Captain replied, " Then there's no need for me to keep you any longer, thanks for your time, both of you." He ruffled Nandi's hair and then walked away to the car with the three other men who had remained silent throughout the ordeal.

The tension was eased when the AVO had decided to leave Mogyoroska immediately. Nandi and Janos began to breath normally when the car of the AVO drove out of sight.

"What happened son?"

Nandi didn't look at his father when he answered,

"I bombed their car with snow...direct hit too."

"What did they say to you?"

"They didn't say too much Papa."

Janos turned Nandi's face to look at him. His left cheek was red and plump showing the imprint of four finger shapes, spread over his cheekbone towards the eye.

"Oh, I see." Janos ground his teeth in silence behind his closed lips.

"But Papa, I thought they wanted to kill me, I was so afraid, the first thing that came into my mind was to speak Russian, I did it and he left me alone, but tell me why I feel so guilty, like I have betrayed Hungary, like I have betrayed who I am."

Janos now had a clear picture of what had happened and what Nandi had been put through, and achieved. He was overwhelmed with pride as he put both hands on his son's shoulders and said, contrite...

"I'm sorry son for what you've experienced here, I'm sorry for the way you are feeling right now, but, look at me, I am a member of a communist party, I am a member of everything I detest, but the intelligence of you and me and every other God loving Hungarian in this country, is not inferior to the Russians, we are greater than them, if I or any other good Hungarian have submitted to the communists with clenched teeth, just for appearances sake, to protect ourselves and our families, then we will not pass sentence on those people, and we must not pass sentence on our selves, we must help and support all who are subject to this, the spiders web of the Soviet Union."

Nandi and Janos obtained the garlic and pepper from the shop and walked home in silence, Nandi and Blackie slightly in front of Janos. As they got closer to their cottage, Nandi had begun to understand what his father meant and the guilt was easing but the anger remained. He relieved his tension with a final sprint through the gate and head towards the land at the back whilst Janos took the pepper and garlic into the house.

Nandi ran out into the open field, slid and jumped over Blackie, rolling in the snow. Blackie leapt onto his chest and began licking his face as if he knew Nandi was injured. But he'd forgotten about the stinging sensation in his cheek as he wrestled with his trusted companion, knowing it was Blackie who had raised the alarm to his father.

Just then, Nandi heard something and so did Blackie. The dog's ears pricked up and he switched his head from side to side trying to home in on the unfamiliar sound. Nandi was sitting in the snow when he saw it, charging and squealing in the trap.

"My God we've caught the boar."

It seemed Blackie had understood and without any prompting, he ran towards the animal, barking and growling on the way. Nandi called out to him. "Wait, get back here."

But Blackie had surveyed his prey and, like any guard dog, had an obligation to protect his home from any intruder.

As Blackie sprinted boar bound, he leapt high into the air attempting to clear the high wooden walls of the prison, but only managed to scramble his paws across the crossbar, clawing and scraping the wood until finally plunging back to the snowy ground landing on all fours. The boar responded by butting the fence wildly with his tusks inviting the dog for a dual. Blackie snarled and snapped his teeth between gaps in the fence desperate to savage this wild intruder. By now Nandi had retrieved the spear that he had hurled at the invading Turkish Army the night before, but now it was for real, Turks, Germans, Russians, the Avo; all swamped his mind in a sudden rush of exhilarating fever. He seemed to know exactly what to do. Panting and running towards danger, Nandi repeated to himself between breaths, "Ambush, ambush, use my brain, think, think, defeat the enemy, defeat Communism." His father's lessons were now being put to the test. Nandi zigzagged his way around to the back of the enclosure behind the boar that was being kept busy by Blackie. He looked up and noticed a nearby tree hung its thick bare branches directly above the Boar trap. Without hesitation, Nandi secured the spear high up in a small gap between two entwined ramifications. When certain the spear wouldn't drop, he carefully began scaling the trunk jamming his toes and fingers inside scattered indentations in the bark. Eventually Nandi reached the branch, which stretched out far and long arching over the centre of the arena. He cocked his left leg over parking his bottom between the tree trunk and the branch. Sitting secure Nandi then leaned to down to the side, stretched out an arm and recovered his spear. Driven only by courage and anger from the events of the day he shuffled himself out along the branch. He found himself having a birds-eye view of his dog and the boar battling with each other through sides of the enclosure, oblivious to Nandi overhead surveying his prey like a predator. It was now for Nandi that the whole world went quiet and in slow motion. He couldn't hear the barking of his dog, the grunts from the boar, nor could he hear his approaching father, closely followed by Feri Pekar shouting, " No Nandi, no."

He had one thing in mind, defeat the enemy; it's now or never. He poised himself for attack, now sitting with both legs on the same side of the branch slightly apart, gripping the spear with both hands pointing the spike towards the ground between his feet. Waiting the auspicious moment, until it came, his heart missed a beat as his aim became perfect, the boar had galloped and stopped directly beneath the spike. Nandi could see the back of the boar's neck was exposed and vulnerable; he clenched the spear tight in his hands and leapt from the tree, he could hear the wind whistling passed his ears as he plummeted towards the animal,

" I mustn't blink." He thought. His eyes remained wide and transfixed onto the neck of the boar. With a jolt, a thud and a rough tumble, Nandi had vaulted into the corner of the enclosure somehow upside down with his legs ledged against the fence. He seemed to be in this position for ages until he came to his senses, "Where is the boar? Where is my spear?" He said to himself. "Must get up off the floor."
Now he could hear his father and Feri,

"Nandi get up, quickly, quickly, run, run,"

Nandi made himself stand up, his legs were a little shaky and his head dizzy, but after brushing himself down, he soon pulled his senses back together.

"I'm not even hurt." He reassured himself.
He looked across at his victim. The boar lay curled up with its back facing Nandi, the spear stood firm and erect clearly exposing the area of penetration, deep into the neck of the boar. Nandi smiled nervously at his cousin and father who were together holding open the trap door, still beckoning and calling to their triumphant young protégé.

"C'mon Nandi, get out of there it isn't dead." His father called out to him. He was right; seconds after Nandi had brushed himself off the boar began stirring. At first Nandi didn't move, only watched the boar struggle to his feet. It grunted, shook its head from side to side and then squealed as it broke of the spear with its right hoof. A trickle of blood oozed from the open wound and then it caught sight of the culprit. As Nandi and the wild animal made eye contact, panic and the realisation that the animal would attack, engulfed Nandi's thoughts.

"Shit, run." He told himself and he did. Run that is, as he did manage to keep control of his bodily functions...just about.

He darted in a flash towards the exit; the boar was alert and galloped towards the exit itself in an attempt to block off any escape route. Nandi knew he must get there first; the race for the door seemed a long one and as he got closer, so did the boar. Now almost side by side, both with heads down, Nandi just one or two strides ahead, the finish line was approaching. Nandi shouted out loud, as he could feel the hot breath of the pig against his ankle. He raced through the exit with such speed as he felt a sharp ripping pain cut through his shinbone which sent him hurtling head over heels landing face down in the snow. He had tripped over the trap door wire, the very thing that had caught the animal, had now hindered Nandi's escape, expecting nothing but attack from an angry pig, Nandi's life passed before his eyes. In a second he looked behind him to see his attacker, visibility was poor owing to the exploding snow dust which had erupted around him amidst the mayhem. As if in a strange dream, Nandi was looking down to earth from a cloud, he could see his country being swallowed by a huge wild animal, he could see himself hurtling spear after spear at this wild animal. Then, in an instant, caused by a swift loud crack and something squirting onto his face, Nandi snapped out of his dream and was back with reality. As the pig charged after Nandi, Janos had been ready with his axe, and with one accurate almighty swing, the boar was lying at Nandi's feet with a fifteen-centimetre long axe blade buried into its skull.

Margit screamed out loud when Feri carried Nandi into the kitchen.

"Don't worry Margit, that isn't Nandi's blood across his face, we've killed the boar and the blood has splashed over all of us."

Janos followed behind,

"Eh, eh, our son's a bloody hero, you should of seen him, fantastic, climbed the tree over the pen, jumped down, stabbed the pig with the spear, my God I'm raising one hell of a brave young man, the damndest of bravery I've ever seen. Good lad, good lad." Feri sat him down on the milking stool, beams of pride lit up Nandi's face and he forgot all about his cuts and bruises. Margit didn't though; she quickly rolled up his trouser leg to examine the deep cut that had torn through his trousers and through the flesh over his shinbone.

"I don't think he needs stitches." Said his relieved mother.

"Of course he doesn't, of course he doesn't, he's a bloody Pekar, hard as nails and as tough as old boots, that's my boy."

"I think we should celebrate," Feri decided with a jubilant tone to his voice, pulling out a silver plated flask from his dungaree trouser pocket.

"Too bloody right, pass it here lad." Janos politely snatched the full flask of Palinka form his nephew, unscrewed the lid and took a large swig before passing it back to Feri,

"To your health." Feri toasted before swallowing several small gulps of his brandy.

"Can I have a taste Papa?"

"Yes you can boy, if your strong enough to fight one on one with a wild boar, then you're strong enough to taste Hungary's strongest spirit; a strong spirit versus a strong Pekar; yeah a good contest, here boy, first smell it and then knock a mouthful straight back."

Margit looked concerned for a second as Nandi let the hot, plum flavoured liquid brandy scorch the inner walls of his oesophagus and eventually his stomach. It was when the warm sensation in his throat changed to a sharp sting that Nandi yelped and began to cough and splutter. Feri squealed out loud a high-pitched laughter, clapping his hands several times before aiding his cousin with a couple of slaps to the middle of his back. When he had finished coughing, Janos and Feri shook each other's hands vigorously, chuckling to each other victoriously.

" You bloody Pekar's, crazy men, crazy." Margit told them.

Nandi joined in the laughter.

Nandi had to stay in the house whilst his mother cleaned and dressed his wounds. Feri and Janos carried out their pig cleaning and dissecting equipment, which consisted of 2 large sharp carving knives, 3 full tin buckets of water, a large tin bath, two axes, some salt and a box of matches. And before they had left the house, they had put a large tin bowl of water on the stove for boil.

" What's this mark on your cheek?" Margit asked as she finished checking and sponging down every scratch and cut on Nandi's injured body.

"Don't know; I've got loads of war wounds haven't I mama?"

"Yes son, you look like you've been in a war too."

"I have mama, against the Turks, the Russians and the Secret Police."

"The AVO Nandi; what do you know about the AVO?"

"Oh nothing, I've just heard some people whispering."

"Saying what son."

"Just that the AVO are Moscow trained traitors."

"Listen Nandi, I don't want you to repeat these words to anyone, keep it to yourself, I mean it, you could be shot for saying such things, quiet now you hear, not another word about it."

Margit put two fingers over Nandi's lips as she said it and then pulled them away.

"I know mama, I know."

"And you be careful Nandi, that was very dangerous climbing trees, stabbing boars, you could have been killed."

"I'm always careful mama."

"I know son, but don't let it go to your head, next time you might not finish up with just a few cuts and bruises."

Nandi was clean and refreshed by the time he met up with Feri and his father around back. The air was full of smoke from a fire and he could smell and hear the sound of crackling pig hair as the two men held large joints of the boar over the roaring flames to burn away the large tufts of black hair spread over its skin. As they turned the leg and thigh of the animal, Nandi could see the hairs smouldering and singeing away and watched as they examined their work section by section and then tossed their completed piece into the large tin bath of clean water..

"He's here now, the Hungarian Gladiator." Feri announced.

"Can I do something Papa?"

"Yeah, are your hands clean?"

"Spotless, Papa."

"Then pour about five handfuls of salt into the bath and then start scrubbing the pieces of boar with your bare hands."

Nandi began.

All morning the three of them worked on the boar, dissecting, chopping, slicing, gutting, burning, washing and sterilising until finally every edible piece of the wild boar was stacked high in the large tin bath and every other piece were burning away furiously on the now sizeable bonfire.

As the three of them proudly cleared away the remnants of their makeshift slaughterhouse, neighbours Sandor and Joe returned from the fields with their cows, they could smell the fire and see from a distance they were working on something. Janos saw them peering towards them, dropped his spade and hurried over towards them inviting them in.

"Come in and have a look what we've caught; shut the gate behind you though, don't want your bloody cows in 'ere."

Sandor and Joe walked in.

"Go on, go around the back, Feri and Nandi are there, I'm just going to nip in the house for something."

Joe and Sandor laughed aloud when they saw the feast before them.

"Good God, you'll never starve with that amount of pork, you'll all be grunting in a few days."

Nandi laughed and before he could explain the rigours of his morning Janos interrupted with a bottle of village beer for each of them.

"Here boys, get that down you."

It wasn't long before Janos and Feri began explaining and boasting about Nandi's heroic combat, boy versus beast story. They drank their beer and continued for an hour exchanging conversations about the weather and the state of the country.

The fire was burning low now and as the two men congratulated Nandi on their departure   Sandor asked Janos if he'd heard any rumours about Peter Csonka.

"No, I haven't heard anything, why?"

Nandi clutched his father's arm.

"Well rumour has it, he's been arrested."

"Arrested for what?"

"Well between you and me Janos, I've heard it's for espionage activities."

"You just don't know with some people do you? And here in Mogyoroska too, in Budapest you could believe it, but in this tiny village, no way." Janos pulled his boy closer to.

"Anyway Janos, we'll have to go, can't see my cows now."
Janos turned to Nandi as they closed the gate behind them.
"C'mon son, don't worry about that. It's time for you first lesson in cooking Kacsonya"

Janos and Nandi spent most of Saturday Afternoon cooking in the kitchen, whilst Margit slept in the bedroom under her thick quilt. Janos had sent Feri home with about three kilograms of wild boar meat.
Janos instructed his nephew.

December 1948

" Go and give that to Mogdi, that should keep a smile on her face, you know how pregnant wives can get all moody when their husband is out all morning hunting."

Saturday afternoon was to be quality time with father and son.

"Before we start we must make sure we have enough wood for the stove, so if you go out back you will see the trunk of a slender silver birch, take the short handled axe from behind the hen hut and, get chopping son."

Nandi enjoyed any physical work, ever since his teacher at school had told him he had the shoulders of Hercules and Janos had reassured him that good hard manual labour would ensure a fine physic. Nandi had mastered the art of chopping up large logs into small identical sized sticks ideal for starting oven-stove fires. Chop, chop, one after another, he could spin the axe between his fingers, grab it firmly by its handle with the sharp edge facing the right way, aim, swing and split the log perfectly in half. If it happened that the axe head caught on a tough wooden knot, Nandi would lift the axe with the log attached, a few more chops and bang, log perfectly chopped in half. It was like a challenge for

Nandi, and a moment of personal pride when the mission to chop up a tree was accomplished.

After only thirty minutes of none stop woodcutting, Nandi had a pile large enough to keep the stove going for three days. As he finished the last piece, he pulled the axe from the log, looked up, aimed, imagined the Russian AVO from in the morning and threw the axe with precision accuracy. It spun through the air and struck the wooden structure's support leg. Nandi blinked and then realised it had lodged perfectly tight and wasn't going to fall out.

"Bulls eye." He shouted out. Chuffed with himself, as this was only the second time he had managed to achieve this.

In the kitchen, Janos and Nandi stoked up the cast iron stove.

"Okay son that will do. Now, there's the meat you will need, cheek and trotters."
Janos pointed to the kitchen table where a piled up pyramid shaped stack of wild boar lay.

" Take the sharp knife and cut up the cheeks into large, square pieces measuring about ten centimetres square."

Nandi followed his father's instructions all afternoon. He peeled the skin off sixteen cloves of garlic, half filled a very large saucepan with cold water from the well, fetched the water to the boil, then removed it from the heat, dropped in the cloves of garlic, then the cheeks and trotters, followed by half a packet of un-ground black pepper balls and three table spoons of salt. "Very Good." His father said. " Now, we must simmer it all very slowly for about four hours, just removing any scum with a spoon as it goes."

Whilst the meal stewed and the fresh pork soaked and absorbed garlic, salt, pepper; filling the cottage with a delicious, savoury odour, Nandi and his father continued with their regular farmyard duties. Janos repaired some holes in the fence, fed and milked the cow, Nandi fed Blackie, collected the hens laid eggs and decided to clean out their hut. First, scattered their feed across a wide area leading them away from their warm homes, then opened the hut doors and watched all the chickens descend from the hut with mincing gravity, down the sloping gangplanks.

The afternoon was busy and typical, and while the boys worked outside; Margit had done some cooking of her own, soaking some thin slices of the boar in milk, coating them in flour and paprika and then frying them in a deep saucepan of hot fat. Within a short time, Margit had prepared almost thirty individual, hot, crispy pork snacks, ideal for her men on a cold wintry Saturday afternoon.

"Come over here son and hold me this for a second."

Nandi had just about finished cleaning out the hen huts and was coaxing the birds back when his father called him.

"Coming…. what is it Papa.?"

Janos was nailing the sides back together on his cart.

"If you hold that up for me right there, that's it. Just knock a couple of nails in and that should do it."

After the repairs to the cart were completed, they sat on the back of the cart together, subconsciously deciding that they had deserved a well-earned break.

"Well son, you've had rather an exciting day, full of police, history, fighting, cooking, now then what would you like to do next? Maybe go to Africa and kill a lion or something."
Nandi laughed; thought for a minute and then said,

"Can we go to Budapest? I'd love to see Hero's Square, Buda castle and maybe go on a tram."

Janos adjusted his facial impressions to accommodate the idea.

"Yes, I'd like that too. You could have a history lesson of Hungary, yes it will be good for your mind, don't know when though Nandi, it's expensive to get to Budapest and almost six hours by train, but we'll see, we'll see."

"The kacsonya should be finished by now." Nandi reminded his father.

"Yes son should be finished by now. And here comes your mother, looks like she has got something for us to eat and just in time too; I am feeling quite hungry after a long vigorous day...... Hurry my dear, you've got two hungry workers out here." Janos called out to his approaching wife.

Margit uncovered a large plate of her tempting, hot fried pork.

"Get them while they are hot, it's freezing out here."

Hungrily they grabbed a couple each off the plate, and Janos was so hungry he almost   swallowed the first one whole.

"Mmmm, delicious and so tender. Well I suppose that's what you get when only a few hours ago Nandi was fighting it like a Spanish bullfighter." Janos laughed to himself once again a quiet proud chuckle and then continued. "C'mon then son, let's go and wrap up this strenuous day and finish off our gourmet meal."

They both dismounted the cart, Nandi still chomping away at his mother's savoury pork pieces and made their way back indoors.

"Papa says we can go to Budapest Mama."

"Oh and when is this happening?" Margit looked at Janos for an answer.

"Not until next Summer hopefully. It'll be good for Nandi's education."

"That it will and oh, the River Danube is beautiful. But don't forget, half of Budapest is still under construction, you know, all the blown up buildings and bridges. The aftermath, thanks to the Russians and Germans."

Janos nodded but didn't answer, only inhaled deeply the scent of the aromatic herbs and spices, the tenderness of simmered pork soaked in garlic. He turned on the kitchen light, vision slightly obscured by a lingering steam cloud which hung at head height, causing condensation to collect on the inside of the small rectangle window panes of the front door.

"Leave the door open." He instructed as he began scooping a brown coloured scum off the surface of his boar filled saucepan.

"Okay Nandi, lay out about twelve dishes onto the kitchen table."

Nandi did it and then waited further instructions.

"Next, using the ladle, scoop out the meat and divide it amongst the twelve dishes and then after, fill up the dishes with the juice."

Nandi began.

"But, careful not to put in any of the garlic cloves or pepper balls. They have given off enough of their flavour into the juice."

Nandi carefully did as his father told him whilst Margit watched and smiled to herself. When he had emptied the saucepan, Janos took over while Nandi watched with a speculative interest. He sprinkled a little salt and a teaspoon of paprika into each individual bowl.

"And now son we must leave each bowl overnight in a cool place, not cold, but cool. A fridge would be too cold."

"So where do you suggest Papa?"

"How about on the top shelf in the outside shed."

Between them they carried the twelve bowls of Kacsonya and after clearing off a ball of string, an old rusty key, a bag of chicken feed, a few loose nails and screws from the top shelf, they neatly placed the bowls side by side all along the overhead shelf. Janos blew out the single candle that illuminated the shed just enough in the dusky evening, locked the shed door behind him and put the key away in an old tin mug at the back of the kitchen cupboard.

Before Nandi went to bed that evening, his mother filled the tin bath with hot water in order for him to scrub away the day's grime. His hair and fingernails were clogged with tiny bits of boar skin and blood. After, he felt revitalised and was quite happy to sit up in bed in his pyjamas revising symbols of metals, entering them into a periodic table. After a couple of hours Nandi felt his eyes growing heavy and struggled to keep them open. He closed his exercise book and slid it, with his pencil, into his school satchel then tossed it under his bed. The room darkened swiftly after he blew out the two large candles that flickered on a saucer, on top of an upturned metal bucket at the side of his bed. Nandi flattened his large pillows with his hands and waited for a few moments allowing his vision to adjust to the dark before lying back. Within a few seconds, Nandi reiterated the day's events, frowning to himself on some parts, smiling at others. Even though the curtains were closed, Nandi could see the windowpanes fringed with frost, which twinkled through the thin cotton curtains that were no defence against the penetrating moonlight. The sparkling was pleasing to the eye, but eventually helped to settle off to sleep this tired young boy.
"He has endured a momentous day that will later prove to be a major significance to his life."

Janos said to himself as he peeped through the bedroom doorway.

Needless to say, the next morning Nandi ran into the kitchen, climbed onto the milking stool so as he could reach the tin mug at the back of the cupboard, retrieved the key and ran across to the shed, scampering barefooted over the thin layer of frozen snow.

As he fumbled the key into the shed door, he hopped from one foot to the other, controlling the stinging, frosty sensation piercing his feet and toes. Relieved when he flung open the door and stepped in onto the much drier shed floor. He could reach the bowls on the high shelf and so he carefully lifted down one of them. Forgetting what to expect when he looked at the outcome, he was shocked for a second when he descried his work. The salt and peppered, garlic, pork flavoured liquid had now set into a cold, soft textured, smooth jelly. The gelatine itself had a beige tinge with a scattered fiery red blotchy surface. Beneath the set translucent jelly, the deeper dark coloured chunks of meat, like a shadow of an underwater whale, hugged the bottom of the bowl and here and there pyramid shaped points of meat rose above the reddy surface like an iceberg floating across an ocean. The shed now redolent with an exquisite cooked pork vapour, Nandi inhaled through his nostrils deeply and what followed was a rumbling in his tummy with a sensation of early morning hunger.

He took three bowls back to the house, one for each of them, Janos and Margit, already sat at the table, were waiting in anticipation with bread already sliced.

"Aha, breakfast is served." Margit and Janos said at the same time, as Nandi proudly laid out his first time cooked Hungarian Cuisine.

School lessons on Monday were intense, filled with Mathematics, Hungarian and history. But the last lesson of the day had Nandi intrigued and very attentive. During science, they were studying electronics and were describing how a radio works. Mr. Nagy, the science teacher, had the inside of a radio sprawled out all over his front desk, he had diagrams chalked over the blackboard, he clearly had Nandi entranced as he lectured in detail explaining where and how the parts and components attached together and how they received and produced their sound…. " The history of radio really began in 1873, with the publication by the British physicist James Clerk Maxwell of his theory of electromagnetic waves. Maxwell's theory applied primarily to light waves. About 15 years later, the German physicist Heinrich Hertz actually generated such waves electrically. He supplied an electric charge to a capacitor, and then short-circuited the capacitor through a spark gap. In the resulting electric discharge, the current surged past the neutral point, building up an opposite charge on the capacitor, and then continued to surge back and forth, creating an oscillating electric discharge in the form of a spark. Some of the energy of this oscillation was radiated from the spark gap in the form of electromagnetic waves. Hertz measured several of the properties of these so-called Hertzian waves, including their wavelength and velocity." Mr. Nagy continued but Nandi's concentration was distracted when his classmate Jancsi nudged him and whispered,

"Nandi, what are you doing?"

"I'm making notes. Why?" Nandi whispered back.

" Because it looks like you are writing a bloody book."

"Shut up and digest it all will you. I'll explain why later."

When the final lesson was over Jancsi and Nandi collected their books and walked out from their class together.

"So, what's on your mind Nandi?"

Nandi's other friend Attila joined them suspecting a private confab, not wanting to be left out.

"Since our radio broke a couple of years ago, Papa hasn't replaced it and there isn't another radio in the village…."

Attila and Jancsi looked at each other with a puzzled frown,

"Listen to me, dumb heads. Jancsi has your Papa got some copper wire?"

"Somewhere yes."

"Okay good, I've got some Iron Pyrite here in my pocket taken from Mr. Nagy's laboratory, and I've an old headphone at home. Now all as I need is a cardboard toilet paper tube, some fine sandpaper and a small piece of metal for a connector."

"I can get them." Attila volunteered.

"What are you going to do with all that?" Jancsi asked

Nandi checked all around him that no one could hear.

"We are going to make a radio. Just a theory but I think I can do it."

"Christ Nandi; that's illegal, my God if you manage to get a signal from the West, bloody hell they'll lock us up for life."

"I know Jancsi, exciting isn't it? So, are you with me or not?"

"Yeah, too bloody right."

"Okay then I'll meet you at my house after tea, say, in about one hour's time, bring everything with you and we'll get working."

The two boys arrived on time with a bag full of Nandi's radio component suggestions.

" He's around the back." Margit shouted to them. "Just come through and close the gate behind you."

"Thanks Mrs. Pekar." The boys replied.

Nandi peered his head from out of the open loft down at his friends below.

"Psst, I'm up here."

They looked up immediately; a moment of excitement broke out across their faces as this secret mission was becoming more intense by the second.
Nandi beckoned them up to him and they casually began climbing the wooden ladder entering Nandi's straw filled loft. Above, Nandi had attached a metal coat hanger to a gap in the roof and fed some wire from it to the floor.

"Okay lads, empty what you've got on to the floor over there."

They did it and Nandi grabbed what he needed first whilst Attila punched a small hole in the thatched roof to let in some light.

Nandi took the fifteen-centimetre toilet roll and coiled the copper wire from one end to the other leaving a few centimetres overhang at each end. He took the six-inch piece of metal (shaped like a thin nail) and bent it over at a 90-degree angle and then attached one end of the copper wire to it. The other end of the copper wire was entwined around the loose wire, which hung from the coat hanger.

"Okay what's next? Let me think." He said to himself

Jancsi dragged over a small bale of hay and placed their makeshift radio onto it ensuring he didn't pull the aerial from the roof. Nandi then coupled his earphone to the free tip of the 90 degree bent piece of metal.

" We're getting there! Can one of you just lightly rub down the copper wire with the fine   sandpaper?"

Attila did it while Nandi read through his notes.

"Now here's the technical bit where the iron pyrite comes into it."

He pulled out a fairly large rock from his pocket and turned it with his fingers under the ray of light that was beaming through the hole in the roof. The crystal glinted cheerfully; Nandi narrowed his eyes and studied it for a few moments.
The iron pyrite then needed to be attached between the coil and the headphone. Nandi and Jancsi did it, not so easy at first, small and fiddly little job, fastening this to that and that to this.

"Need to be a bloody octopus to do this." Jancsi complained.

"Need to have patience." Nandi responded.

"Nandi, I don't wish to be a defeatist or anything, but how is it going to be powered? You know batteries or something." Attila asked sarcastically.

"Well if my theory is correct my friends, according to my calculations, it should be powered by the static electricity in the air."

"Oh right." Attila answered. " So, it is finished?"

"Yeah, I think so." Nandi answered, but still going over the set up of his contraption in his mind.

"Well have a listen then."

Nandi picked up the headphone and held it to his right ear. He listened hard for a minute.

"Shit. Bugger all. Here you listen while I check everything is connected up correctly."

Attila and Jancsi shared the earpiece but alas, there was nothing. After a while the three of them sat in the hay, pondering, talking and chewing strips of straw until Jancsi said,

"It doesn't half make you feel alone on the earth does it?"

"What did you say?" Attila asked.

"I said it doesn't half make you feel alone on the earth does it?"

Attila was silent for a few seconds and then he jumped up and ran towards their radio, picked up some wire and began searching for a suitable area on their radio.

"What the hell are you doing?" Nandi called across to him

"You haven't earthed it have you, you dick head."

Attila earthed it while Nandi and Jancsi crowded him in an impatient but apprehensive, anxious state of mind.

"Okay Nandi, it's your toy, go for it."

Nandi hesitated slightly, opened his mouth to offer the glory to someone else and then thought better of it. As he picked up the earpiece and slowly lifted it towards his right ear, a surging aggrandizing moment enveloped his hesitancy, until proudly and confidently, he pushed the

tiny speaker into his ear hole. The loft fell into an eerie silence
while the two boys held their breath.
Nandi raised an eyebrow and looked at Jancsi, then Attila, then
back at Jancsi and said,

"When the nazi's left Budapest at the end of the Second World
War they blew up Radio Budapest as they were retreating. But by
May 1, 1945, Radio Budapest was back on the air and now the
Hungarian Standard Factory has almost completed building a new
135 kilowatt transmitter."

"How do you know that Nandi?"

"Because it's just been announced on Radio Budapest."

"**YAHOOOO**" They all cheered together.

"We did it, we did it." Nandi stared at Attila with a question mark
across his expression.

"Well I mean you did it Nandi. But I earthed it."

The boys laughed and danced around the loft. They spent the rest
of the evening sharing the headphones, discussing the news
between them on every half hour, discussing sport, and revelling
at Hungarian violin players that harmonized the zest of the
evening.

Nandi went to bed that night feeling like a scientific genius. As he
examined his thoughts, the rectangle of the bedroom window
grew pale with the rising moon. Before he sank into a restful
sleep, he was listening to a conversation outside with his father
and Mr. Sipos the Agricultural teacher from his school,

"I hear Nandi has been fighting with wild boars then Janos."
"Oh, my son been bragging then has he?"

"Nandi brag? Not ever. He's a fine young lad with a good clean head on his shoulders; he's growing up to be a gentleman. No, some of the blokes down the pub have been talking about it, they said he jumped on it with a spear."

"That's right, he did."

Nandi didn't hear much more, just smiled to himself before drifting off to sleep.

***

The summer of 1949 in Mogyoroska and Hungary was unsurprisingly hot. Janos had almost fifty chickens, a cockerel, two cows and a pig roving his land. He had spent most of spring constructing partitioning wooden fences and gates, sectioning off an area for the cows, an area for the pig, separate from the chickens and all without access to the vegetable patch and grape vine at the back; and Margit's rose garden at the front.

Nandi and his father were a few miles from home deep in a thick dense part of the forest, where it was quiet, dim and cool, protected from the intense heat from the outside weather.

"How much further is Papa?"

"Not far now son… Look over there Nandi, beyond those trees, we've made it to the foot of the mountain."

Nandi and Janos had decided to spend this hot summer's day hiking and climbing to the top of the mountain to explore the mysteries of the Rakoczi castle. The mountain, on which Rakoczi castle perched, was covered in a thick dense forest. The trees acted as climbing aids for them as they clung to each tree pulling themselves on to the next, as the ratio of the mountain grew more vertical with each step.

Janos and Nandi leaned with their backs firmly pressed against a wide tree trunk and gazed upwards through a neat mass of trees, wild bushes, nettles, low hanging branches. Nandi carefully looked around the tree trunk behind him in order to check out the distance they had climbed. It looked so steep and Nandi thought if he stepped out, he would slide back to the bottom.

"Tell you something Nandi, an invading army would have a hell of a task trying to conquer this castle. Can you imagine trying to get to the castle, carrying weapons and things, as well being attacked from above by the defending Hungarian army?"

"Was Rakoczi the king of Hungary Papa?"

"Not exactly son. He was a leader and he wanted free of the Austro Hungarian Alliance, yes another leader that wanted Hungary to be free and independent. And this amongst many other Rakoczi castles was where he and the Hungarian army kept watch from all surrounding enemies and would attack them at first sign of invasion. You see from up here you can see beyond all the Zemplen mountains into Czechoslovakia. It's a brilliant view, ideal for an army defending its country."

"So is that why Rakoczi built this castle?"

"Well, Rakoczi didn't build it. It was already here, Rakoczi just actually restored it. The date of birth of this castle is unknown, though it was already here by the Tatar invasion in 1285 that is known; then after that we know Rakoczi, found it, restored it and used it and that was around 1700."

"So how long as it been unused for now Papa."

"Oh my lord, almost two hundred years. C'mon son grab this rope and tie it tight around the trunk of this tree, or it will be another two hundred years before we get to it."

Nandi wrapped the rope around the trunk twice and tied a tight knot whilst his father scrambled on up on his hands and knees with his long coil of rope looped over his right shoulder. Janos dug his toes deep into the leafy soil with each long stride and uncoiled the rope as he climbed further away from Nandi. The rope was fifty metres long and when it had ran out, Janos found a suitable tree, climbed it so far with rope in hand and when the rope lifted just about chest height from the earth, Janos wrapped it and tied it securely up and around three strong branches.

"Okay Nandi, pull yourself up." Janos shouted to his son. His voice bounced off the surrounding mountains, repeating the instruction four or five times before fading and absorbing into the distance.

Nandi gripped the rope and pulled himself up. He slipped a few times at first but then got the hang of the rhythmic pull in time with his stride. Nandi kept his teeth tightly clenched as his biceps and shoulders flexed hard with every heave. First his right arm pulled, followed by his left. The rope burnt his palms when he struggled to the end of his fifty-metre stint.

"Two hundred years since this castle was inhabited. No wonder." Said Nandi catching his breath. "It would take four days just to nip to the village well for a bucket of water."

After a few more similar climbing struggles, nettle stings, sore hands and knees, they finally made it to the pinnacle. It was a glorious moment; they were both speechless whilst examining the castle ruins. It was difficult to imagine that this was a castle. From here at the nucleus of this six hundred year old stone building, it just looked like a few high, crumbling stonewalls. They could just make out the four corners of the square shaped castle, with its round holes that must have been a window or lookout point. The main structure of the castle and its central courtyard must of collapsed over the years because it was non existent and probably lay beneath the trees and forest plants that had now overran this area of the castle like a spreading cancerous growth. This beautiful, historical doorway to the past was rampant with neglect and demanded some attention. Nevertheless, it seemed the sheer abandonment of this forgotten castle, added to the excitement of the adventure, a feeling that two explorers had uncovered the mysteries of a lost world. Nandi thought they were the first to be there since Rakoczi left in the early eighteenth century.

They scrambled to the highest point onto a stone oval platform and marvelled at the breathtaking sight all around them. Could they view the whole world from here? The dark blue sky met the dark green earth at the horizon. They both stood and swivelled their feet and heads slowly 360 degrees, following the blue and green skyline, which outlined the shapes of the scenery around them. The Zemplen Mountains that surrounded their house and village and were normally viewed from below were now been looked at from a different angle exposing new venturesome exhibitions. Nandi and Janos searched for their house and it was a while before they found it standing out slightly by its unique looking frontal view, of the climbing red rose bush which covered the front from floor to roof-top.

"Aha good, you're mothers started the chicken and mushroom soup. Can you see the smoke from the chimney rising into the sky?"

"Yes, but how can she cook it without any mushrooms?"

"It's okay she'll cook the chicken first and add the mushrooms later."

Janos had worked out what he thought to be the positions of the castle.

"This is the Mogyoroska side of the castle of course, but over there on the East side of the castle is the village of Regec. Those two rather awkward shaped stonewalls would have been the look out points and although there isn't a wall now connecting the two lookout points, there would have been in 1700. The East side also overlooks Czechoslovakia so any invading army from the East could have been spotted from thousands of kilometres away. Who knows maybe the Ukraine's came that way in 1285. But in 1700, Rakoczi was fighting the Austrians and he had castles like this on all borders of Hungary. Legend has it Nandi, that there is a secret tunnel somewhere up here leading to the castle near Szanto."

" Shall we find it Papa?"

"No, no, it's only a legend."

"Can we go to the Regec side?"

"No son, we wouldn't be able to get across there. Look, the castle has definitely subsided in the middle leaving only its four corners. To get across to the East side we would probably have to begin our climb in Regec."

They decided to take a seat on the rocky cliff that perched firmly facing Mogyoroska and eat their bread and salami. Nandi let his feet dangle over the side feeling very brave, defying the 100-metre drop below him. He looked down and tried to comprehend how high he was knowing he was 100 metres higher, than the 50 metre tall pyramidal, coniferous trees with their needle-like leaves and erect cones.

"To imagine I am actually higher than the massive forest trees that mass all the Zemplen Mountains. Amazing."

"How are you doing with sports at school, are you still training for your competition?" Janos changed the subject.

"Yeah. I won the hammer throwing contest the other day and I scored a goal in a football match yesterday."

"Oh, that's good son."

"Eh Papa what do you think of Ferenc Puskas?"

"Sounds like a great footballer doesn't he? The year you were born Nandi, we should have won the World Cup that year. Bloody Italians beat us 4 - 2 in the final."

"I think we have a great National team coming through Papa, Gyula Grosics the goal-keeper he's like a big black panther, he can spread himself across the goal, nobody can score passed him. Puskas scored fifty goals last year, but I like Hidegkuti the best."

"Why, is he so skilful or something?"

"No because is first name is Nandor."

Janos laughed and patted Nandi on his back.

"C'mon son let's head back, your mother will be needing our mushrooms soon."
Nandi decided to inscribe his initials on a lonely tree that was quite young and growing beside them at a slight angle. He buried the blade of his penknife into the bark as deep as possible ensuring he cut into the main body of the trunk. It read **" N.P 1949"**

Getting down the mountain was so much easier than coming up. They decided to leave their rope attached to the two trees.

"You never know Nandi; we will probably use it again the next time we come."

"If it's still here."

"Hopefully it will still be here when you bring your son up eh? Don't forget now! You've got to have a son so as the Pekar family tree continues."

At the foot of the mountain, Janos decided to take a different route back through the forest on the pretext that he was sure there were plenty of wild mushrooms in this other direction. Janos definitely knew his country for as they entered the undergrowth, peppered for miles deep into the heart of the forest, was a carpet of mushrooms of all different shapes, sizes and colours.

"Just look at all this food growing wildly from the ground. But they are dangerous, some are edible some are not. So listen to me carefully before you go off just picking anything, there is an art to this."

Janos knelt down by a cluster of them growing in a circle. "You see these; remember it's always better to dig them out not pluck it out of the ground. That is because some of the most deadly poisonous mushrooms have a bit of a cup that grows at the base of the mushroom but underground. So watch."

Janos took his knife and began scooping down around the base and sure enough, the cup shape was lying underground.

"You see that Nandi. Now these mushrooms are poisonous. Aha, those over there that look like a lumpy white football."

They rushed over to the spot.

"Now these are easily identifiable because if Puskas was here he would probably kick them. But we won't because these are called Puffballs; they are edible and tasty. The only thing you have to check for with these is that they are pure white inside, if they are anything but white, then we do not eat them."

Nandi broke a couple open and could see they were fresh, ripe and very, very white. Together they dug out around twenty of them

Summer 1949

and popped them into the empty carrier bag, which was carrying the rope, bread and salami earlier that day.

They trekked further on, scanning the floor as they went, until Nandi noticed about thirty mushrooms growing from a dead tree stump.

" What about these peculiar ones Papa?" Janos showed immediate interest in this kind and jogged back over to Nandi.

"Oh, these are great mushrooms, very interesting because what they do is send out black rhizomes to attack other trees, which will then die. And the rhizomes, on a moonless night, actually glow in the dark."

"Are they edible?"

"Yes they are. Put them in the bag, no problem."

"Look at these Nandi, now these are perfect for soups." Janos pointed to a muddy bank only a few metres away from them. He stooped down beside and studied them while he waited for Nandi to load up the bag. It was only a few minutes before Nandi joined him in his mushroom studying trance.

"This one is called the Saffron Milk Cap and grows near to pine trees. Look pine trees surround us. If we cut the stem like this, it will bleed a carrot coloured milk. It's a very sensitive mushroom and you will notice the cap and gills will bruise green when you touch them. Anyway son, they're great for soups, your mother will be chuffed to bits."

The density of the forest began to thin out the closer to home they got. Large patches of strong sunlight seemed to force its way through large openings between the spaced out trees and branches. Nandi was sweating and so removed his T-Shirt and tied it around

Summer 1949

178

his waist. He soldiered on through overgrown grassy fields,
wild raspberry bushes and swarms of forest horse flies that buzzed
around his head and ears and seemed to be drawn by Nandi's
sweaty skin. By now he had broken a long, flexible stick from a
tree and was using it to cut down thorns, nettles or any plant that
blocked his way making a flattened pathway through the
overgrown fields and woods. He couldn't see his father anymore
but that was fine because he knew his way home from here and
seized the lonesome moment to escape into a make believe world.
As he crossed the small brook Nandi picked up several small
rocks from under the water and stuffed them into his pocket. He
had his stick that was now a rifle and the rocks were grenades.
Nandi crawled through an area of tall, yellow, dried grass and
peeped through it. He crawled on all fours a little further, paying
attention not to disturb the enemy. A large fallen down tree had
become a tank and six younger, thinner trees surrounding the tank
were Russian soldiers walking along side the tank. Nandi took out
his grenades. "Only six left." He said to himself.
"Okay, I have a plan."
Nandi lobbed the grenades one after another hitting five Russian
soldiers; he saved one grenade but charged at the remaining
soldier shooting his rifle. He shot the soldier in the leg disabling
him but he wasn't dead, now the tank was turning its long barrel
towards Nandi, he had to be quick. His rifle was now out of
bullets causing him to swipe the soldier with the but of his gun
killing him instantly. Nandi then leaped onto the roof of the tank
opened the lid, dropped the grenade into the middle of the tank
where the driver was operating and dived into the bushes.
"BOOM." Nandi imagined. "Commander Nandor Pekar saves the
King of Hungary. The Hungarian royal family know they can
sleep safe while this Commander defends their Rakoczi Castle."

Nandi clambered on through what was left of his journey. He
brushed away the final overhang of a large leafy tree only to
reveal his beautiful home. Nandi breathed in a satisfactory intake

Summer 1949

of breath and then he saw his mother carrying two buckets of fresh well water up the bank towards their front gate.

"Oh great, I'm so thirsty."

Nandi shouted to his mother and then ran to her.

"I must remember to ask Mr. Nagy how to blow up a tank, he should know, he was at war only a few years ago." Nandi said to himself as he gazed at the water splashing over the sides of his mother's metal buckets.

"Don't spill any Mama, I'm dying of thirst." He called out to her.

The next day at school Nandi didn't forget to ask Mr. Nagy and it was easy as his first lesson was science and even before Mr. Nagy had time to light his Bunsen burner Nandi rushed over to the front desk and asked him,

"Mr. Nagy, have you ever put a tank out of action, and if you have, how did you manage it?"

He cocked an eye at Nandi in a stunned disbelief.

"What an earth do you want to know that for?"

"It's just a game I'm playing and to know how to do it would be beneficial."

"Okay Nandi sit down with the rest of the class and I'll explain."

Mr. Nagy continued after Nandi took his seat.

Summer 1949

"Nandi has just asked me an interesting question and as it happens we could use the answer in science. Nandi wants to know how to disable a tank or put it out of action in a war. There are two ways of which I used in the Second World War. One is a Molotov cocktail, which is basically petrol in a bottle, stuffing a rag into the neck for the fuse; light the fuse and throw it at the tank but aim for the grill, because the grill will suck the burning fuel into the room thus engulfing the inside with flames. The second way is a little trickier. I was caught in a crossfire by the banks of the River Don at the end of 1942. Russian tanks raced through the shallow waters of the river and once out, crushed trees like paper. Anyway, a few others and I hid inside a trench we'd dug. After a while six tanks parked, but left their engines running, only a few metres from our hideout. We decided to pay them a visit. We took off our woollen socks, crammed them full with some demolition, some TNT and composition B. Rigged up a long fuse and spread axle grease all over the wool. At the right moment we lit the fuse, sneaked up at the sides of the tanks and splat our homemade bombs between the wheel and their tracks.

Hit them in the tracks, we were ordered. Anyway, as sure as eggs were eggs, they blew the tracks right off the wheels thus immobilising the tank… This brings us nicely into our lesson today, which will be the contents of the explosives just mentioned. Please make notes. Trinitrotoluene is commonly known as TNT. TNT is a constituent of many explosives, such as amatol, pentolite, tetrytol, torpex, tritonal, picratol and composition B. In a refined form, TNT is one of the most stable of high explosives and can be stored over long periods of time. It is relatively insensitive to blows or friction. It is non-hygroscopic and does not form sensitive compounds with metals, but is readily acted upon by alkali's to form unstable compounds that are very sensitive to heat and impact. TNT can be used as a booster or as a bursting charge for high-explosive shells and bombs. Any questions so far?"

Attila raised his hand sharply.

Summer 1949

"Yes sir just one. What does non-hygroscopic mean and; do we have to remember all these constituents of TNT?"

"That's two questions boy. The answer to your first question non-hygroscopic means it doesn't get damp. And do you need to remember pentolite, tetrytol, torpex, tritonal, picratol and composition B? Indeed you do and by the time we have finished all the theory, followed by the practical, you <u>will</u> know the contents of TNT off by heart."

Mr. Nagy paused before noticing Nandi had his hand raised also. "Nandi?"

"Why did you need to cover your socks with axle grease, was it something to do with ignition?"

"No boy, it was to ensure the bomb would stick to your intended target. Slap it onto the side of a tank, it stuck, stayed in position, while we took cover, ensuring the tank was put out of action."

"Aha." Nandi realised, made a quick note of it and listened attentively as Mr. Nagy continued with his science lesson.

November 1949
Despite the long, cramped journey to Budapest, Nandi and his father had enjoyed the adventure. But in spite of Janos being elected Mayor of Mogyoroska in the autumn of 1949, it still didn't improve their poor livelihood enough to allow them a first class travel to Budapest. Far from it; they had hitchhiked most of the 400-kilometre journey and had spent the previous night in an old barn somewhere between Gyongyos and Hatvan while they awaited the early 5:25A.M bus into Budapest City centre. This had been their first payment towards their travel to the country's

November 1949

capital and so Janos was pleased that although the journey was physically tiring, it would be achieved at a low rate.

Margit had spent weeks before their journey stitching up some thick, material, patching them together to make them both a long, black overcoat each. They were now thankful for her concerned efforts as a cold November draft swirled the interior of the old rickety bus each time it came to a halt at a bus stop and passengers were let on. Although tired, the cobblestone roads and the excitement of the trip kept them alert, as they remained silent for a while just taking in the scenery of the Budapest outskirts.

The City seemed to grow all around them the closer to the centre they got. Tall storey buildings on either sides of the road had wrought-iron railings on every floor, stone balustrades, uneven bricks, some with broken corners.

Janos kept thinking of the political troubles, the workers of Budapest, who were being pushed to the limit of endurance by their existence under Communism. He had to keep reminding himself that Budapest would not be the glorious City it once was. He was checking and concentrating at every turn and every street, knowing and looking out for signs of, a once proud Hungarian City that had now been carved up by barbarians who had called themselves nazi's, but now changed their names to Communists. The rumours were now becoming more apparent the deeper into the heart of the City they went. Janos intended to seek answers in the streets and stones of the City.

They descended the bus at the corner of a traffic and pedestrian choked road called Kiss Jozsef Street. The Chain Bridge was there next destination and they could almost smell the water. The walk was littered with views that would be remembered forever. Grand buildings from the turn of the century (the City's most glorious period) were not yet being restored; most were still black with grime, and many ornate facades in sculpted stucco were

November 1949

crumbling. Nandi and Janos stood for many a while looking over one certain building, made interesting by a long row of bullet holes, like a dotted line underscoring one of the first floor windows. Its colour was admired too, painted many years before a warm cinnamon that had bleached in the sun not unpleasantly, so that the colour looked like faded autumn leaves.

They turned into a wide road graced with trams, men on horseback, tractors and Czech or Russian cars. It was obvious now that this was probably the main shopping centre, with rows of buildings on either side that soared high into the November blue sky. They stretched long and far in a straight line and they couldn't help noticing Hungarian flags perched out of every top floor window, leading away from them towards the bridges of Budapest. Janos sighed when he scowled at the hammer and sickle that the Russians had placed in the centre of their national red, white and green flag.

The clear waters of the Danube stretched away into the distance under the sun. The edges of the river were frozen but were thawing slowly as the busy traffic was causing continuous hypnotic ripples making their own way to the shore. Huge lumbering barges, small boats and large boats were moving in both directions. As the two of them walked alongside the Danube towards the Chain Bridge, Nandi could see a girl on one boat with a bright red skirt washing down the deck with a bucket and mop. Large, yellow trams clanked up and down at the side of them between the promenade and the river. Across the river, the cliffs of Buda rose high above the flat plane of Pest. To the right, high up, the peak of the cliffs, were crowned by a castle and by aspire, Janos said it was the Matyas Church. To the left of the Cliffs was a statue of a women holding aloft a plume in both hands dominating the skyline. Further on, groups of small rowing boats were tied to a landing stage beneath them.

November 1949

Janos's hairs on his arms stood to attention as he gently pulled Nandi near to the front of swelling crowd of about a thousand proud Hungarians encircling the re-opening of The Chain Bridge. A tall man with a clean-shaven face and a flat cap stood on a high wooden box and spoke to the crowd.

"Welcome to this historical event. In 1820, Count Ferenc Szechenyi died and his son Istvan, who was a hussar captain at the time, travelled to the funeral and wanted to cross the River Danube at Pest. He had to wait for a week because of stormy weather. He wrote in his diary "I would offer my total annual income if a bridge was built between Pest and Buda." From that time on Count Istvan Szechenyi worked to build the first bridge to link up the two cities, studying bridge architect in England. The Chain bridge was eventually designed and built by the Englishman Adam Clarke and the opening ceremony was on November 20th 1849. How history evolves! Ladies and Gentlemen, as you are all well aware, some of you may have witnessed it, the Chain Bridge was blown up by the retreating German Army in 1945. Now, I can proudly announce, exactly 100 years to the day since this famous bridge was first opened the reconstruction and the re-opening of our very first bridge of Budapest. Ladies and Gentlemen I give you, The Chain Bridge."

With that the man cut through a long ribbon that prevented any access to the road leading over the Danube, pulled a cord to release two white covers that hid away two statues of large lions. The crowd applauded and cheered and felt fulfilled as their famous city was slowly and surely being restored of its historical beauty. Janos mingled with the people for a long time, talking and questioning them with genuine concern.

The day was far from over with a purpose visit to the Parliament Buildings which now balanced a huge red star on its roof, which, somehow sickened a marvellous sight. However, they patriotically admired the building that was even more impressive than a picture

November 1949

or photograph, with its reflected dome and perfect symmetry's reflecting upside down in the river at its feet.

They continued their tour of Budapest from here with only one other intended destination; Heroes Square. But as the midday sun shone on this cold wintry day, bringing to life the surface of the Danube as it sparkled and reflected the sunrays, it didn't seem to matter how long it took to reach this famous, legendary plaza. They would continue with no rush or eagerness, just accepting and absorbing whatever Budapest decided to reveal.

They hadn't yet left the banks of the Danube when Nandi noticed more construction work on another bridge. Nandi pointed to it and quizzed the rebuild wondering if it was another casualty of the war and what was its name. Janos couldn't make out what was happening at first, but after a few minutes he could see more clearly now that he wasn't looking directly at the sun, but his vision was still sway with stars and explosions of light. He was intrigued and needed to ask a passer-by what was going on. The man stopped and studied Janos hard before explaining that the bridge had began being built in 1939, but that had been interrupted in 1943 because of the war. The building works had been re-launched last year and were expected to be finished next year. When Janos asked the name of the bridge he looked uncomfortable. He fidgeted, wouldn't look Janos in the eye and whispered that in 1943 it was going to be named The Arpad Bridge. The man was walking away when Nandi asked him what was its name today. Both Nandi and Janos gasped in horror to learn the new name for this bridge was to be; The Stalin Bridge. They hurried away shoulder to shoulder with their fists clenched tight in their overcoat pockets, mumbling to each other and reciting the well known history of Arpad, probably the greatest Hungarian ever lived, the founder of Hungary, the man who led the Magyars into Hungary as early as 870 A.D to give them their home now in the middle of the 20th century. Who was to be replaced by an evil communist Russian tyrant.

November 1949

They tried to ease their torment by window shopping and checking out a few market stalls in the streets or small supermarkets. There were shops with windows displaying dusty jumbles of ribbon, hairbrushes, children's shoes, men's shirts and women's stockings. Nandi observed the shop with the cluster of ribbons noticing that amongst the different colours, entwined together, was his favourite colours red, white and green. Generally, they just blended in with the hustle and bustle of the Budapest City dwellers.

Eventually they found themselves walking along a much quieter road and Janos knew he was close to Heroes Square when he checked out the street name Dozsa Gyorgy Street. He was explaining to Nandi who the street was named after, Gyorgy Dozsa the Hungarian revolutionist, a soldier of fortune, who won such a reputation for valour in the Turkish wars, when with another vile shock they saw what they'd hoped to avoid. A twenty-five feet tall metal statue of Jozsef Stalin. Stood not far from Heroes Square in a newly named area; Stalin Square. They promised each other they wouldn't acknowledge or look at it as they scurried past, but Nandi stared at Stalin's boots and tried to reach it with a mouthful spit. Janos saw Nandi and cringed but avoided a scene; afraid if he scolded Nandi it may draw attention to what he'd done.

When they thought it was safe to do so, they turned around and stared at the Jozsef Stalin statue in disgust. A symbol of everything they hated, stood proud in the heart of Hungary, watching, glaring, spying. Like a spider waiting for its victim to move.

Entering Heroes Square instantly changed their mood. They stood still and soaked up the emotion. Before their very eyes was a sight so huge they felt like pawns on a chessboard. It seemed they had shrunk to three centimetres high and all around them were Giant Hungarian Gods who had sucked them into a secret doorway to

November 1949

the past. A vast and grandiose symbol of 19th-century Hungarian nationalism. In the centre of a huge Greek replicate coliseum looking arena, was an enormous, imposing, 36-metre high column that supported the winged figure of the Archangel Gabriel. Gyorgy Zala on a pedestal, encircled by statues of the seven conquering Magyar tribal chiefs on horseback. Behind them, two semi-circular colonnades housing the statues of the most famous Hungarian rulers in Hungarian history. Nandi and Janos gracefully entered deeper into the womb of Heroes Square reading every plaque under every monument. They particularly noticed the commemorative words carved into a stone tablet in front of the main column that was also being admired by a group of Hungarian soldiers smoking cigarettes. The words paid tribute to those who died for national freedom and independence.

Nandi read it and then tried to examine the feelings of the soldiers. One of them noticed Nandi was studying his face. The soldier looked back at Nandi and then at the tablet. Nandi simulated the soldier's eyes. First looked at the soldier and then at the tablet. The soldier nodded once, took a long drag of his cigarette, inhaled and then blew out his smoke slowly through the corner of his lips. Nandi remembered something the man had said at Chain Bridge. 'How history evolves!'
Finally, they admired the statues of the ancient leaders of Hungary from as early as 997 A.D through to the 16th century. King Istvan (The Saint) 997-1038, King Ladislas 1077-95, King Coloman 1095-1116, King Bela IV 1235-1270, King Ladislas IV 1270-1290, King Charles 1308-1342, King Lajos I 1342-1382 and many more. Each had an incredible crusade in Hungary's history. All passionate, all patriots, all were symbols of status and truth. Janos explained everything around them was mere stone. All the words were only words carved in stone. "When the words are carved into your heart that is what will make you a true Hungarian. Faithful towards your country's honour, to the bitter end."

November 1949

The more he looked, read and walked the paths of history over in his mind, the more that his sub-conscious questions were being answered. Nandi had never sought to find any answers to his personal concerns, as he was beginning to accept his vexations as an intrinsic part of his own being. The queries that a child growing up in a world of corruption may have were being dealt with today. The whys, the hows, and the wherefores. What am I doing in this world? What do I represent? Who am I? All these questions were being answered around Budapest and Heroes Square.

Gratification and satisfaction loomed over Nandi's fulfilled heart. His father finalised a unique hour of blinding zeal, when he suggested there was a spare place for another hero in the colonnades. Nandi grinned cheerfully and suggested that it would be himself.

✳ ✳ ✳

The journey home seemed to be easier and shorter aided by a bus journey out of Budapest followed by a hitched ride on a tractor pulling a cart half full of straw. Luckily, the farmer driving the tractor was going as far as Szikszo, which would leave behind two thirds of the journey. The two of them huddled together and covered themselves with thick layers of straw at the back of the cart. Nandi fell asleep first and a few minutes' later Janos's snores were being drowned out by the diesel chugging engine and the spluttering exhaust funnel from the tractor.

They were just beginning to feel the sting of huge blisters erupting about their heels and toes when Janos called in to see his friend in Encs. After explaining the huge journey that they had endured in the name of education and history, Communist supporter Imre Davids, was more than happy to borrow them his elegant white Lipizzaner stallion. Janos remarked that this was Hungary's horse of royalty until the fall of the Austro-Hungarian Empire at the end of World War I.

A beautiful, expensive animal one that could only be afforded by a Communist. Once again, Janos found himself politically bluffing a renegade that were increasing in all districts of Hungary. But, Janos could use his status as Mayor of Mogyoroska to ease this tiring journey home.

Nandi sat behind his father, gripped his waste and rested his left cheek up against his back. The rhythmic strides from the stallions' hooves would send Nandi off again into a restful sleep, but not before he had realized that his father had had to praise the look of the Stalin statue to Imre Davids just to keep in with these dangerous, spying local Communists.

It was approaching midnight when they finally got home. Margit had a hot meal waiting and Feri, Mogdi (Feri's wife) and their newborn son, Feri Pekar junior, were also there awaiting a report, an account of their voyage to Budapest.

It was after 2:a.m when all the excitement had simmered down. Nandi was tucked under his quilt with his mother lying by his side still discussing all the Budapest events. Mogdi and Feri Junior were on their way home but Feri and Janos sat talking in the kitchen and enjoying their now 5th glass of white wine and soda.

" So what did you find out in Budapest?"

" It's sad… I eavesdropped avidly on shoppers in supermarkets, families strolling in avenues, commuters crowding in the subway. Amongst much fear, I have discovered they have now stopped granting exit visas out of the country. The fear is apparent; we are now officially prisoners in our own country. I saw hundreds maybe thousands of homeless beggars on every street corner; sleeping on the pavements, in alleyways, trying to keep warm. I saw many shoppers, but I did not see them actually buy anything, they were just looking, picking up goods, turning them around in their hands, but not actually purchasing them. I had a sense of nervousness amongst a people, like everyone were not actually freely talking to each other or not actually freely strolling down a street, but a feeling of being made to talk in a certain way or being made to walk in a certain way. The people of Budapest seemed as if they needed to check who was watching or who was standing close to them before they could open their mouths. It was an eerie, spine chilling atmosphere and for the first time in my life, I felt alone, I felt like a stranger amid my own people, I was lost and realized in a panic that my inner thoughts, my own voice had to remain silent. We **are** prisoners and there isn't anybody who is willing to listen."

✳✳✳

From the end of World War 2, Moscow had dispatched to Hungary its specialists, its deeply trained Communists, to manipulate, to instil its Communists laws and beliefs. It was the process that slowly and surely, brought pain, suffering, misery and poverty to the Hungarian people. Bit by bit, under the watchful eye of the West, the grip from the Kremlin tightened, knowing all the time if this national prisoner bled or screamed out to the West, they would have to answer for it. The people of Hungary were living in hope believing the West would not surrender Eastern Europe, giving one hundred million souls to the Soviets.

The Communists were operating cautiously with a stopwatch. They opened up the nation's body, joint by joint, like a surgeon dissecting parts of a body for an anatomy demonstration. They still spared the more vital organs for the moment. They still didn't sever the more essential nerves, but they were already carving up the viscera with scalpels and forceps.

For now, the Kremlin had spun a giant web around all corners and across the main body of Hungary and when its victims moved, it felt the web vibrate, and what followed would be a ruthless, rough justice.

As time went on, it was evident that little or no objections at all came from the West. And so, the web thickened, and so the gates of hell that surrounded Hungary became permanently bolted.

A decree on public works, control of private lives, the workplace, the garbage disposer, family life, an idea, all controlled or annihilated.

In comparison to how the Nazi's treated their victims, they would force their victims to work themselves to death. Torture them. Humiliate them. They prided themselves with a physical destruction of their victims.
The Communists were much more brutal. They demanded that their victims remain alive and celebrate a system that destroys human sensibility and self esteem, sucking from the victim his pride, honour; twisting and brainwashing their minds and souls with acts of inhuman barbarity.

Where could Hungary turn? For a thousand years, the people of Hungary dwelled in Eastern Europe and sought someone it could confide with. It never found anyone. In an amazing flash of reality, after being squeezed until its face turned blue, the realization that Hungary was alone and being bullied to death, was now beginning to dawn on the Hungarian people.

192

CHAPTER 8
MARCH 4th 1953

SZANTO BOARDING COLLEGE (*20 Kilometres from Mogyoroska.*)

It was Professor Horvath's first day as a Physics lecturer and Physical Education instructor at Abaujszanto Boarding College. He spent his morning with fellow mathematics lecturer Professor Szeman who had given him a grand tour of the splendid college ten-storey building consisting of forty classrooms, science laboratories, libraries and sports fields. The college was set on ten acres of land and faced Szanto train station all surrounded by the Zemplen Mountains. Szanto town centre was only two kilometres away and the opposite direction would find the crossroads, left to Encs or straight on towards the mountainous climb to Mogyoroska. Professor Horvath had seen the enrolment figures and had met a majority of his students.

Whilst Professor Szeman tried to briefly explain the college daily routine from registration, early morning assembly etc.. The new lecturer had noticed someone across the pathway on the opposite playing fields. He was the tallest of a group of teenagers looking as if they were organising a 5 aside football match. Interested, the new Professor moved closer where he could observe them, Professor Szeman walked towards them too still explaining the colleges' daily activities and strict rotas. The shirtless boy was tall, broad shouldered with a defined torso the kind of physic you'd see on an athlete of some kind like a swimmer or a rower. His natural bronze coloured skin blended well with his thick, parted on one side jet-black hair. Professor Horvath watched with his arms folded as the two teams were organised by the boy and kicked off. Within sixty seconds a low cross was fired towards goal, the tall boy sharply received the heavy leather Casey on his chest, directed it to the ground, swivelled on his left foot, shot with his right to perfectly place the ball in the corner leaving a helpless goalkeeper stranded. His team cheered and Professor Horvath interrupted his guide,

"Who's the tall lad with black hair placing the ball on the centre spot right now?"

The Professor looked across and answered,

"That's Nandor Pekar. He's fourteen years old. One of our brightest students, passed all his examinations last year with good grades and nothing suggests he won't do the same this year. He's very fit as you can see, likes to be involved in everything down to debates, in lessons and any outdoor activities too. His father is the Mayor of his home village and a farmer and Nandi holds some very rare personal self-disciplined gifts learnt from living off the fat of the land I suppose. Yes he is a very practical lad and modest with it."

" Is he one of mine?"

The Professor turned over a few pages on his clipboard, searched through the alphabetical list with his finger and found his name.

" Yes, for Physics and Physical Education. I haven't got a copy of the timetable but you are his new lecturer. Do you want me to introduce you?"

" Please do." He said gratefully.

" **NANDI**." The Professor called and beckoned him over.

Nandi responded immediately and jogged over to the teachers at the side of the pitch. His hot body steamed in the March cool air and a single tear of sweat rolled off his right eyebrow made its way along a thin crevice above his large eyelid, dripped onto his unusually very long, black eyelashes and eventually splashed into tiny particles, ran and dripped down his lean cheeks and high cheekbones. Nandi wiped his face dry with the back of his hand as Mr. Szeman launched into his introduction.

Nandi's large watery green eyes weighed up his new Physics and sports teacher with interest and after Mr. Szeman had finished with the formalities, he shook his hand,

" I'm very pleased to meet you sir."

Mr. Szeman interrupted,

" Is that bubble gum in your mouth Nandi?"

" Yes, why?"

"Go and spit it in the bin young man and use your manners."

Nandi apologised and obliged his Maths teacher.

"Thinks he's bloody Elvis Presley." Mr Szeman remarked as Nandi spat a lump of gum into a nearby bin.

Mr. Horvath began to make a short conversation with Nandi.

" Like football do you Nandi?"

"Yes sir. But I like throwing the hammer competition best."

"Oh I see. That was a half decent goal you have just scored. Who's your favourite footballer, Ferenc Puskas?"

"He's great, but I like to play like Nandor Hidegkuti."
" And why is that then?"

"Oh because Puskas is left footed and I'm right footed."

"Fair enough lad. What do you think of Hungary's chances in next year's world cup?"

"We will beat the Russians, the Germans, the Brazilians, the English everyone and we will be the world champions."

"Yes we will, yes we will. One final question Nandi before you run off to finish your game. What career are you aiming for?"

"I want to be the King of Hungary sir…No seriously I want to be a Doctor or maybe a lawyer."

"Good occupations lad. Any particular reasons?"

"Nothing specific. Only, education is the key to freedom and ruthless leaders may take away possessions or even your livelihood, but they cannot take away your knowledge, therefore they cannot take away your key; the key to freedom."

"Mmm, interesting theory. Okay Nandi get on with your game and I'll see you later."

Nandi ran back to his match and the rest of the lads were inquisitive.

"Is that our new Physics Lecturer Nandi?"

"Yes. He seems okay. But let's wait until they've pissed off back in then we'll go and have a fag behind the trees." Nandi decided.

A few of his classmates stayed and continued knocking the ball about while Nandi, Laszi, Attila and Jancsi ventured behind the nearby cluster of trees and shared their last cigarette between them. They puffed hard and passed the cigarette around to each other checking that no one had noticed their disappearance.

" It's all clear." Laszi revealed.

"Eh Nandi are you seeing Irinka tomorrow night?" Attila asked smirking as he took a drag of the cigarette.

" Should be if I can get out of here."

"Have you asked the Janitor to leave the ladders by our window again?" Jancsi reminded Nandi.

"No not yet but I'll tell the old fart later."

 "How much money have we managed to save up?" Nandi asked Laszi who had been given the job to pool their funds together.

"Well I've sold a few fags yesterday and my penknife, put that together with all your donations over the last few weeks, we should have enough for quite a few bottles of beer each. But I hope you don't think you are using it to buy your gypsy girlfriend any beer"

They all laughed at Nandi and remarked,

"Fancy falling for a bloody gypsy."

"Eh dick heads, you're only jealous. She's bloody gorgeous, gypsy or not."

Nandi sucked in the final drag of the cigarette, pushed into the damp soil with his foot and led the way out from behind the trees and continued with their football.

****

The first lesson in the afternoon of the next day was Nandi's class's first lesson with their new Physics lecturer. He began with his introductory rigmarole explaining who he was, what he expected from his class and introduced himself as a fair but determined teacher who was willing to teach students who were willing to be taught. After that he handed out copies of literature explaining chromosomes and mitosis, sat down behind his desk and began reading out loud the first paragraph,

"Mitosis. Process in which a cell with a nucleus, known as a eukaryotic cell, divides into two identical daughter cells. As a cell grows to full size, it makes an exact copy of its genetic material, or deoxyribonucleic acid (DNA), and then divides into two cells that each has one copy of the DNA. Mitosis permits single-celled organisms to reproduce. The process also allows animals and plants that begin life as single cells to develop into complex organisms containing billions of cells. Mitosis continues in full-grown organisms as a means of replacing dying cells and facilitating new growth. In the cells of the human body, for example, mitosis occurs about 25 million times per second."

He stopped reading all of a sudden. Nandi looked up from his text and noticed something had distracted the teacher. He was looking towards the classroom door and by then the rest of the class was trying to see what he was looking at. After this brief pause Mr. Horvath had realized the class had been silent long enough to arouse their inquisitiveness and responded by excusing himself from the lesson.

As he pulled open the classroom door Nandi could see the Principal of the college was standing behind the door almost out of sight in the dark windowless corridor. As he closed the door behind him Nandi noticed there was another person standing in the corridor reflecting against the glass from the door and at first glimpse, the other person seemed to be wearing some kind of an emergency service uniform like a policeman or fireman. The rest of the class mustn't have noticed the man in uniform as they didn't show any concern, just sat back in their chair aloof and instantly began chatting to each other the most inappropriate of conversations. Jancsi, who was sitting in front of Nandi, leaned back in his chair and asked. " Nandi. Ladders arranged yet or what?"

Nandi didn't answer him. He just stared at the classroom door.

" What's the matter?" Jancsi was suddenly intrigued with his trance.

Nandi whispered his answer back to Jancsi.

" Did you see the policeman outside the classroom door?"

Jancsi tried to look through the smeared small, square panes of glass in the upper half of the classroom door, in vain. He turned and leaned back again towards Nandi.

" No I didn't see a policeman. What's the matter, worried Irinka's gypsy parents have called the police."

"Oh shut up you prick." Nandi said to Jancsi and flicked a blob of ink at his friend, which landed in Jancsi's ear.

Jancsi was about to retaliate but thought better of it when Mr. Horvath re-entered the classroom with an enigmatic look in his eye.

The class silenced suddenly awaiting some kind of explanation.

Mr. Horvath hesitated and then announced.

"Class. I have some 'g' news. A news bulletin has just revealed that Joseph Stalin has died of complications from a stroke."

The class fell into an eerie silence. Nobody moved. No one uttered a word. It was probably a minute later or maybe longer when low sighs could be heard around the room. It seemed to echo and sounded like it was droning from the bottom of a tomb. Nandi felt a moment of joy but decided to contain his excitement behind his cool façade. ' Could this be the beginning of a free Hungary?' Nandi thought to himself and then decided to burst the membrane of tension that had stretched around the teacher and students.

" Sir. During your announcement, you stumbled your words but I'm sure you said I have some 'good' news?"

Mr. Horvath grinned inanely and then adjusted his mouth trying to conceal his happiness. He frowned before he answered.

"No, no Nandi, I was trying to find the correct word for such an announcement, I was going to say, I have some gory news."

" Yeah right." Nandi responded, which was quickly followed by a succession of sniggers about him.

Mr. Horvath showed his approval by dismissing the class for the rest of the afternoon 'to allow them time to grieve' as he sarcastically put it to the Principal and the Policeman. Nandi was the last to leave the classroom and as Mr. Horvath straightened his papers on the desk, he called out to Nandi.

" This may help you towards that key you were talking about yesterday."

"I certainly hope so." Nandi said optimistically.

That afternoon the boys remained in their second floor dormitories discussing the possibilities of an ameliorative country. An opportunity for Hungary had certainly presented itself and the country was aware of negotiations taking place between Russia, USA, Great Britain and France with regard to their occupation of Austria.

" Eh perhaps now the Russians will leave Austria and if they do that, they may even leave Hungary too." Attila remarked hopefully.

Attila, Laszi, Jancsi and Nandi lay on top of their beds facing the ceiling. Their beds were in that order side by side with equal distances of about two meters between them.

" A bloody great prospect we've got now. Can you imagine freedom? Being able to talk to each other in public, being able to criticize our country's leaders without the fear of being arrested or shot. I don't even know how that would feel. Just think what Stalin has been doing in secret, I bet western Europe know nothing of it. Bloody arresting and executing bourgeois politicians, intellectuals, clergymen, just because they threaten his loopy communist ideas." Nandi said with a patriotic passion.

Jancsi remembered their communist leader and reminded the others.

" Tell you what we should now. Fuck that Matyas Rakosi off. Bloody bastard sold his soul to Stalin he has."

" Yeah almost forgot about that wanker. And my dad reckons Imre Nagy is the best prime minister for us." Laszi said.

" Can you hear what we are saying?" Nandi interrupted.

"What?" They all said simultaneously.

"If the authorities could hear us we'd be arrested ourselves. Good God the bastard's only been dead for a few hours and we are talking like free men already. We must keep our wits about us and keep praying. Celebrate his death in silence."

Nandi's statement made them fall into a short stillness whilst they considered what he'd said until Laszi remembered something else.

"And before we all get too excited.. Who is going to replace Stalin?"

The question wasn't answered or even thought about as their political conversation was disturbed by a noise from below their window ledge. They jumped to their feet together and leaned out of the window that was behind Nandi's headboard slightly to the left. Four heads peered out and below, as planned, four o'clock in the afternoon Miklos the janitor had began wiping clean the dormitory's windows.

"Great stuff." Nandi said with a satisfied tone. He followed his clockwork, rehearsed plan and stuck a packet of twenty Fecske cigarettes to the inside of the windowsill with a gob of chewing gum pulled from his mouth. "And there's his wages. C'mon lads let's go down for tea, we don't want anyone to get suspicious."

After tea the four of them roamed the grounds killing time waiting for it to fall dark. They synchronized their plans and at just turned six o'clock they retired back to the dormitory. They checked that their escape ladder was in position and then lingered around their beds scattering homework and textbooks around the bedside tables. Half an hour later, right on time, two lecturers paroled the dormitory checking and talking to the students and when they were satisfied nothing was amiss, they left and continued on to the next rooms. When the boys were sure they'd vacated their block, they changed into their evening attire and waited for the seven seventeen train to Budapest.

The steam train tooted its arrival three minutes late and filled the air and train station with its dry, hot steam as it screeched to a halt. This was the signal for the first of the boys to begin his climb down and out of the college grounds. The ladder leaned firmly against the side of the building, inclined towards a large bush that was outside the surrounding low wall. The bottom of the ladder disappeared into the bush and signalled the outside world out of the college grounds. Attila went first, followed by Laszi, then Jancsi, Nandi kept watch and would climb out last. He checked his pockets whilst he stood on the tenth rung from the top, just high enough in order for him to push the windows to and hold them closed with a purpose made wooden wedge. " Okay." He whispered to himself. He began to slowly step down the ladder when in an instant the steam train went silent and concurrently the ladder creaked followed by a snapping sound on the ground below. Nandi stopped dead in his tracks. His stomach boiled as he looked all around him taking care not to move his head, just his eyes. To the right of him, Professor Szeman had stepped onto a twig as he watched the steam train opposite and lit a cigarette. "Oh shit." Nandi thought to himself. " I must keep absolutely still. Now how long does it take to smoke a cigarette? I've timed it before, less than ten minutes. Just got to keep still for ten minutes, then maybe he'll piss off back inside. I hope the others have seen him. I should think so, they're very quiet."

Nandi could just see the Professor in the corner of his eye. He concentrated on his movements, hoping he would keep his back to Nandi. He side shifted and shuffled his feet, intermittently dragging his cigarette taking his time with it and appeared to be enjoying the tender moment of this fresh evening. After a couple of minutes, the temporary silence from the train ceased with a loud and long scream indicating its departure. Nandi could breath again. He panted, puffed and blew knowing in a few seconds the train would be gone and there wouldn't be anything to drown out the sounds. It chugged away into the distance slow chugs at first. As the train speeded, the volume decreased as if someone was regulating and diminishing the loudness of a radio until it faded completely leaving no sound just a cool, slow desolate breeze swirling the dusty road between the college and the train station.

Nandi clung on to the ladder tight with both hands hoping the dark colour of the ladder; his black hair and clothes were enough to camouflage his figure. He tilted his head upwards slightly checking and appreciated the cloudy night, as the full moon would of certainly lit up the evening enough to reveal Nandi's whereabouts. The ten minutes felt more like ten hours as Nandi took every movement, every sound and every smell in attentively. The charred burning smell of his tobacco became irritating the longer he was savouring his evening wind down. Nandi felt a cramp growing in his right calf and began to wonder how much longer he could remain still. At last, he heard the Professor scraping his shoe on the grit below and Nandi correctly assumed he was extinguishing the cigarette. It wasn't over, he could hear the Professors footsteps beneath him striding back indoors and Nandi knew if he looked up slightly to his left, the game was over and Nandi would be facing expulsion. He held his breath.

"Nandi!" A low voice came from behind the bush. He answered after letting out a gust of air from his mouth.

"What?"

"He's gone inside now."

"I know that."

"Well come on then."

" I can't."

"What do you mean you can't?"

"I've got cramp in my calf."

"The three boys sniggered together."

"Shut up you bastards, it hurts." Suddenly the pain eased at the same time as Nandi began to see the funny side and joined in with the laughter.

"Christ." He said to himself. "I'll get them." He thought and then turned himself around 180 degrees so that he was facing the train station with his back resting against the wooden rungs. He couldn't see his friends behind the bush; only hear their uncontrollable chuckles. Nandi bent his knees so that he was almost fully stooped holding on to the sides of the ladder with both hands. Using his knees and elbows as springs he jumped from the ladder crashing through the bush landing with awkward grace but downed the three boys grabbing two of them in a headlock and neutralizing Jancsi with his foot on his chest.

The shock had paused their laughter.

"Now then my friends if you were Russian soldiers I have just ambushed you and killed you."

The three boys laughed and wrestled Nandi to the floor.

The friendly banter didn't continue for much longer as they knew they had to vacate the college vicinity before another unsuspecting teacher decided to stroll outside for a smoke.

The four lads stood in a semicircle outside a bar in Szanto town centre supping a bottle of beer each. The town was rampant with neglect and displayed a population of gypsy folk and peasants. The road into the centre was a wide spacious cobblestone and split two ways around a church and met with itself again at the back but then separated again, as if making way for a giant red star that marked the centre of Szanto. This large red ornament was perched on top of a stone mantle and towered twenty foot high protected by an iron fence that wound around it. Five Russian soldiers stood leaning against the fence at the moment in sombre mood it seemed probably discussing the death of their leader.

Nandi and his friends had decided not to smile in case it drew attention to them realizing the presence of the Russians had cast a paranoid mood on the town. Relatively noisy gypsies were unusually quiet, scattered around the square in groups of two's and three's either slumped on a bench or leaning against a wall. Nandi had noticed that beyond the star from where they stood, the spare ground on which outside vegetable stalls were in place in the day and where young teenagers and gypsies normally congregated at night; was deserted.

An hour later, the spirit of the young men had improved owing to the disappearance of the soldiers and the increasing quantity of beer consumed. At last, they could relax and begin to enjoy their absence without leave. The town had also begun a pleasant tempo boost. People were talking much louder, old people shared conversation in the street, a rare violinist played from the inside of another nearby bar filling the air with old Hungarian Folk songs adding to the stimulation of the evening. The numbers were swelling. Other circles of men had grouped together outside the same bar as Nandi and his friends; and suddenly there was an added zest to the evening and everyone were conspicuously celebrating. The groups of men were slowly forging into one big group when conversations between them were being open and shared.

"I can't ever remember people of Hungary uniting like this before." Jancsi suddenly shared with the others. Everyone agreed and decided to continue enjoying it.

Nandi was laughing at a joke when he spotted what he'd been waiting for far across the other end of the street. She had noticed him too, gently waved and began to walk towards Nandi. Without a word to the others, he put down his bottle of beer on a nearby table and stepped out from the crowd. Before hurrying towards her, he stood and stared at her approaching. Nandi stood tall and broad wearing black trousers, an open necked black shirt and a pair of bright polished black shoes. His left hand remained in his trouser pocket while he finished the last few drags of his cigarette, flicked it to the floor, combed the back of his hair flat with the palm of his right hand and then set out to meet Irinka in the middle of the square.

She was petite, at least ten inches shorter than Nandi. His heart turned to molten lava as he got closer. She had the face of an angel, fragile, mystical. Her long dark hair flowed like a river and kinked at the ends just below her shoulders. She wore a tight, yellow bodice that clung to her shapely bosom leaving her neck and tops of her shoulders exposed. Her skirt was a matching, paler yellow, long dirndl skirt. A large white rose attached below her parted hair complimented her thick, dark red, sensuous lips that beamed across her dark tanned skin unveiling her bright white teeth. An exotic, sensual, beautiful creature whose obvious passion for Nandi was barely contained beneath her cool façade.

At last, they stood toe to toe beside the red star. They gazed at each other for a while, smiles of joy breaking out across their faces and then Nandi cupped her delicate cheek with his right hand catching a finger in her large circular gold coloured earring. She closed her large, round, twinkling brown eyes as he touched her and then opened them innocently only to find her tall handsome boyfriend had leaned forward to greet her with a soft but long lingering kiss on her mouth. She responded romantically pulling him a little closer. They released their embrace but Irinka clung to Nandi's right arm when a shout from across the way called out to them.

"**Oy you two**! Wait there I'm coming over." A stiff man of average height, with a spray of grey hair emerged from another crowd from an opposite pub.

"It's my uncle." Irinka whispered tightening her grip on Nandi's arm.

Nandi looked down to the right of him at Irinka and gave her a reassuring smile.

Her uncle possessed a round face and wore a stern look with threadbare attire. Nandi noticed that before her uncle had reached talking distance, his march over to them had attracted other members of Irinka's gypsy family and they too followed the uncle, six abreast across the square.

"So you are the young college boy who has been dating our Irinka then eh?"

"Yes sir."

"Ooh sir, I like that."

"I've been brought up to use my manners. My name is Nandor Pekar."

"I know your name lad. And I am Irinka's Uncle Joe."

"Pleased to meet you." Nandi greeted him

"Yeah me also." Joe replied.

By now a sizeable crowd of gypsies had gathered opposite Nandi and Irinka and Nandi's friends had seen the disruption and were making their way over to join them.

"So young Nandi how old are you?"

Nandi swallowed before he answered.

"I am sixteen." Nandi had lied about his age to Irinka knowing she was too old for him.

"Oh so you are one year younger than my niece then eh?"

Joe steadily circled Nandi looking him up and down as he strutted.

"Tall handsome lad I can see that. Probably the son of rich parents; been counting money all your life?"

"Not at all I am…." Joe interrupted before Nandi could answer

"A rich college student with all brains and no muscle. Let me see your hands."

Nandi held his arms outstretched, Irinka still holding his arm by the bicep.

Joe grabbed his hands and inspected them.

"You see spotless, with clean fingernails." Joe had failed to notice Nandi's scars and an axe wound on his right thumb.

"So my hands are clean, what does that mean?"

The crowd of gypsies laughed out loud and Irinka intervened.

"Leave him alone you lot and go back to your drinking."

Joe settled her down and said, "It's okay my dear, I promised your father while he was gone I would look out for you, I don't mean any harm to Nandi I'm just checking him over that's all. Come over there with us and have a beer."

Irinka smiled when Nandi agreed and they all proceeded over together to the spare ground where the vegetable stalls stood during the daytime.

The crowd dispersed and broke up into many smaller groups around the ground giving Nandi a chance to talk with his girlfriend. He sat on a wide sawn off tree trunk and invited Irinka to sit on his knee. It wasn't long before the gypsy games began and was being organised by Uncle Joe. He scarred the earth with a sharp stick drawing out several squares about two metres wide. After, he was shouting and calling over to the merry gypsy boozers and set about organising their competition. Nandi watched with interest as two men stood inside two separate two metre square boxes. The first man was passed a large, black laced up army boot.

"When you are ready!" Uncle Joe called out.

The man held the boot in his hands, concentrated for a few moments, drew in his breath and tossed the boot high and far across the ground. It landed some distance away and the crowd applauded and cheered whilst an older cousin of Irinka ran to it and hammered a wooden peg into the ground precisely where the boot had landed to mark his performance. The boot was returned to the other man who attempted the same throw obviously intending to throw it further. This went on through the now drunken crowd until, slowly but surely, the ground was full of pegs marking the competition. Eventually the sport had become the background entertainment for Nandi and his friends as they amused themselves in their own social circle, laughing and exchanging their teenage banter. Nandi had bought Irinka an ice cream and when Laszi scowled at Nandi for doing so, Nandi grinned and said,

"You said I couldn't buy her any beer."

Laszi didn't care really. The five of them were enjoying themselves and that was their intention.

"Your lips feel cold." Nandi said to Irinka after a long kiss

"It's that ice cream…My lips are cold but my heart is warm."

"Leave each other alone you soppy pair." Jancsi joked.

"No way she's all mine." Nandi said pulling her closer too across the wide tree stump.

The crowd silenced slightly causing the five of them to look over at the boot throwers.

"Oh no." Irinka groaned as she had realised why.

"What the matter…. Oh no." Nandi had realised something also.

Joe was bowling over towards them carrying the large boot.

"Come on Nandi, you have a go, let's see if you are just a rich college boy."

"No thank you Joe. A test of a mans strength is in his mind not in his muscle." Nandi declined.

"Yes lad, but brain **and** brawn will win you a war."

Nandi stared at the boot.

"Come on Nandi have a go." All his friends encouraged and tempted Nandi.

"You bastards." Nandi said to them grabbing the boot from Joes' hand causing a huge applause from the crowd.

"Okay Joe, it's time to go to war."

Nandi strolled over to the marked out crease tossing the boot from one hand to the other as he went testing and getting used to its weight. He sized up his test of manhood competition checking the launch pad, seeking the furthest away peg in the ground obviously the leader of the competition at present. When he had thought out his throwing technique he looked over to Irinka and give her a thumbs up. Irinka blew him a kiss. Then, he stood to the back of the drawn out square with his face turned away from his intended landing point. Laszi, Attila and Jancsi had turned over an old rusty, empty metal drum that was lying at the side of the road and decided to intensify the atmosphere by banging a slow beat drum roll. Szanto town centre silenced and even old ladies in the street stopped and watched with anticipation. A man pulled his horse and cart to a standstill climbed quickly on the top of his hay so as he had a better view. Somehow, all eyes were on Nandi as if everybody knew the importance of this friendly competition and an outsider being encouraged to compete. Nandi gripped the boot tight in his right fist and grit his teeth tight until he felt his jaw crack. The muscles in his lean cheeks pumped and flexed hard until, like someone had released the top off a shaken up bottle of pop, Nandi turned sharply ran to the front of the box, swung his right arm with all of his might and felt his shoulder jolt as he released and hurled the boot.

"Ahhhhhh" He shouted out as he watched the boot climb higher. The Szanto gypsies sucked in their breath and watched in amazement as the boot cleared the first set of pegs, then the next, until finally gravity got the better of it and the boot came hurtling to the ground, knocked out the furthest away peg and rolled over a few turns to be the current leader of the competition.

Nandi was the last to realise he had beaten everybody. Once again, the crowd silenced. Nandi stared at the wide-eyed mob not knowing what reaction to expect. At first, he suspected hostility until the silence was broken when Irinka applauded first. **"Yahooo"** Joe cheered. "Rich college boy my arse." And with that, as if the gypsies were awaiting Joes's approval, they all chanted and cheered and ran towards Nandi and lifted him up above the crowd congratulated the hero of the day. He was passed over a sea of hands and dropped to the ground in front of Irinka who embraced her boyfriend.

"You did it. You did it." She said proudly and excitedly to him.

What a moment for Nandi it was when the crowd began chanting his name.

"Nandi, Nandi, Nandi, Nandi, Nandi."

"Now I know how Nandor Hidegkuti feels when he scores a crucial goal for Hungary."

"Hidegkuti hasn't got a patch on you. I think I love you."

"What?" Nandi said unable to hear Irinka above the noisy fans.

"I said I love you."

Nandi paused and stared Irinka in the eyes in the middle of this noisy audience.

"And I love you too."

Nandi's boot throwing had created more interest in the game. More hordes of people congregated onto the sporting arena attempting to beat Nandi's distance. That was the moment Irinka and Nandi had taken advantage of the opportunity and slipped away out of the town centre down the grassy hill to the side of the deep, slow flowing river. They sat huddled together by the narrow river talking and soaking up the romantic flowing sounds of the water running and rippling over the rocks and stones. They both looked up simultaneously when as if by magic, the clouds cleared and a bright full moon cascaded its bright light onto the surface of the river through the trees. Nandi had a sudden impulse to stand up, strip down to his underwear and bathe in the river. Irinka squealed with excitement as Nandi stiffened his body when the cold water reached his stomach.

"C'mon Irinka, join me."

Without much more enticing Irinka removed her clothes down to her bra and knickers and waded in across to Nandi clutching her arms around his broad shoulders when she reached him in the centre. An erotic sexual moment invaded their thoughts but

Nandi restrained, in an attempt to prolong the temptation to enhance the moment. He released his gentle grasp, took her by the hand and continued walking up stream.

"So, how about you Irinka? Did you think I was a rich college boy?"

"Well when I first saw you at Szanto train station with your father and you were standing there with your expensive leather briefcase, even though you looked incredibly handsome, you did look shall I say, posh, a cut above the rest."

"Ah my briefcase. We didn't buy that briefcase; it was given to me many years ago by our family doctor when I lived in Kassa. Dr. Molnar was by our side at my older brother's funeral after he'd died of pneumonia, and he thought it correct to give me a present to comfort me and for some reason, I have always treasured it, like a child feels comfort with their favourite teddy bear, I feel comfort with my briefcase. It reminds me of Bela and for some reason helps me to feel free. Strange I know, but true."

"Oh I didn't know you had a brother."

"I don't remember him really, but the briefcase reminds me of him."

Further upstream Irinka pointed out her house that backed onto the river.

"Nobody is home Nandi. Let's go in and get dry."

They climbed through an open window and didn't turn on any lights. Irinka pulled out two large cotton sheets from their ottoman and passed one to Nandi and then closed the door behind her after she entered another room. Nandi wrapped it around himself and noticed wet stains forming onto it enhanced by the moonlight that shone through the kitchen window. Nandi sat on the floor outside the room in the shadows of the windowless hallway awaiting Irinka; she emerged from the room only a few moments later with her hair freshly combed. Nandi stood up immediately. Their eyes firmly transfixed onto each other's. They stood gazing at each other for a few moments and then let their cotton sheets drop to the floor; his eyes explored her glistening wet body and she him. She must have removed her bra and knickers when she was in the other room. He took her in his arms her body firmly pressed against him. They kissed. Irinka almost passed out from the rapture of the moment, Nandi gathered her in his arms as her body went limp and carried her into her bedroom.

✷✷✷

Nandi awoke suddenly when Irinka nudged him.

"What's the matter?" Nandi whispered and then realised where he was. "Oh my God what time is it?"

"Somebody is tapping on my bedroom window." Irinka told Nandi.

Startled, Nandi jumped from her bed and looked over at the bedroom door. It had been wedged shut with a chair to his relief.

" Nandi, it's six o'clock in the morning but someone has just knocked on the window."

"Jesus, where are my trousers?"

"They're down by the river, don't you remember?"

"Oh my lord, where are my pants?"

Irinka laughed as she leaned out of bed and grabbed Nandi's pants off the bedroom floor and threw them over to him.

"Here. For God sake check outside, someone has just knocked on my window."

"I know, I know but my first lesson is in two hours time and I haven't got any clothes."

Nandi pulled up his pants and then looked over to the window noticing a breeze from the river was stirring the curtains.

"Are you sure you weren't dreaming because the window must be slightly open. Can you see the curtains blowing?"

Just then, the silhouette of a person emerged at the window and tapped again softly.

"Shit, who the hell is it." Nandi said in a panic.

"Well go and have a look and you'll see."

"What if it's your uncle?"

"It isn't; he's snoring his head off in the other room I heard him come home hours ago."

Nandi shook himself and then bravely peered through the curtains.

"Your trousers, shirt and shoes are here son."

Nandi closed the curtains tightly shut and then jumped back onto the bed.

"Who is it?" Irinka asked.

Nandi paused and then revealed.

"It's my father."

"Oh no, he can't see me like this." Irinka panicked

Nandi leaned across to Irinka and kissed her on the lips.

"I love you sweetheart. Sorry I must dash, but, I think I'm in trouble. I'll see you soon."

Irinka pulled her quilt above her nose and pressed it against her mouth to hold in her laughter as Nandi opened the window and bounced out wearing nothing but his underpants.

"Hi father. What brings you here?" Nandi asked shivering in the open air.

Janos threw Nandi's trousers to him.

"Get dressed lad. Now!"

Janos had his horse and cart waiting out on the open road and they didn't speak a word until they were on their way back towards the college.

"How did you know I was here papa? Am I in trouble at the college?"

"The college knows nothing about this, I hope. I know what's been happening because you don't think you are out here all alone do you? Everything you do son I will know about. I was young once you know. Now listen. I know you have made a name for your self by winning that boot throwing competition and you feel good. But I tell you; your education must not suffer. Now you get back in that college the same way as you came out, freshen yourself up and focus on your education.

It's Saturday tomorrow and you will be coming home for the weekend and then we'll talk."

"Does Mama know anything about it?"

"No she doesn't, and she won't find out either."

Janos pulled the horse to a stop opposite the ladder.

"Go on son, off you go and I'll see you tonight."

March 1953

Nandi kissed his father on the cheek thanked him, disembarked the cart, waved and scrambled up the ladder to his room.

July 6th 1953

Examinations had been completed at the college and the end of another school year was approaching. Results were to be announced on July 18th the day before the beginning of a long summer holiday through until the first Monday of September. The final two weeks of the year were been spent with students participating in various voluntary activities such as hiking, sports, gardening or reading. Nandi had volunteered to train to box in the gymnasium and to take part in a twenty-four hour survival course that involved four teams of five being assessed based on their teamwork and survival skills. It was the day after Nandi's 15th birthday and excluding yesterday, when he had been home to celebrate his birthday with his parents, Nandi had been working out in the gym for months preparing for this day when he was about to fight his first fight in the ring against an older student, in front of the whole college. He could now skip, jog ten kilometres, do sixty press ups, one hundred sit ups, work the heavy boxing bag and he completed all this every day, in less than four hours. Determined as ever to succeed Nandi had been drinking six raw eggs every morning before his energetic day began.

But now he sat in the changing room wearing a vest, a pair of long baggy shorts, plastic lace up boots and an old mustard coloured robe over the top. He had already been told that the hall was filling rapidly which didn't do anything to ease the tension. Mr. Horvath was tying the lace in his heavy boxing gloves and preaching words of encouragement. Nandi's tactical instructions were to keep his gloves up high and go for the solar plexus.

"Use your height and your long reach, when you see the opening, explode all over him."

Nandi's heartbeat raced and he felt a little sick when three other lecturers entered the changing room to inform him it was time and that they had come to escort him out into the makeshift boxing ring. Nandi tried to swallow as he walked nervously towards a raised square platform, four wooden fence posts with two lengths of ropes attached to them to form the boxing ring. He wasn't paying much attention to the clapping and cheering audience who were eagerly awaiting two young lads having a scrap. His opponent was already in his corner when Nandi climbed into the ring and they eyeballed each other throughout the principal's introduction who was explaining the rules and asked everyone to be sensible and to enjoy the clash.

The referee gave them their instructions and signalled for the bell to be rang to begin round one.

Nandi charged to the centre where he met his older foe. Nandi swung a sharp right and a left in succession that was dealt with by two solid forearm blocks. Then with a shrewd change of foot direction enabling Nandi to weave his body in to a closer position, he was able to notice a welcoming opening through his defence. Nandi took advantage of it and thumped his opponent three times around the chest area and lower stomach.

In the first few seconds he felt he had started with confidence until; there was a few second time lapse and Nandi found himself on his hands and knees trying to open his right eye. He was confused and for a while was wondering how he had come to end up in this position. The referee was counting seven then eight and Nandi staggered a little when he rose to his feet.

"Can you carry on son?" The referee questioned.

"Yeah, I'm okay. Let's go."

Before the fight continued it had dawned on Nandi that something very hard had struck his eyeball and he knew it had been a very quick fist. As much as Nandi tried, he couldn't open his eyes and when he made them open his vision remained blurred owing to the overflow of tears and blood dripping from the right eye. The referee had allowed them to battle on, but Nandi only ducked and ran under the fists of his attacking opponent holding closed his right eye with his glove allowing the left eye to guide him. Now the referee had seen enough and waved the fight to be over ordering some medical assistance from the side of the ring.

After a cold water bathing at the side of the ring, it was established that there wasn't any serious damage, but it was joked that Nandi had received a shiner for his birthday present.

The stinging sensation eased after Nandi took a bath in the river and soaked his face under the cold water for as long as possible in order to reduce any swelling. He wrapped the mustard robe around himself and sat on a large riverside rock allowing him to dry naturally under the warm summer sun. His hair was drenched and cold water dripped from it and ran down his face. He checked all around before lighting a cigarette and took advantage to relax alone whilst he wound down from his hyped up day and his sore face.

"Go for the solar plexus? What a dick head Horvath is." He said to himself.

Nandi had finished his smoke and had watched the cigarette butt float downstream and get lost in a mass of marsh grass with jointed hollow stalks.

"I bet if we pulled those reeds up we'd find dozens maybe even hundreds of cigarette butts under there." Nandi thought.

Just then, he heard footsteps, he turned to see who was the intruder and could see it was Jancsi.

"Let me see that eye." Jancsi insisted.

"Oh, it doesn't feel as sore as it did do an hour ago, good God I thought I was going blind.

"It'll certainly be bruised black by tomorrow." Jancsi assessed

"I can't even remember him hitting me. It all seemed to happen so quickly."

"I had a good view. You went for him good and hard, but then all of a sudden, you dropped your guard for a second, he saw it and bang, he socked you in the eye."

Nandi squirmed a little when he imagined the impact as he knew he hadn't even had chance to shut his eyes and the full glove had struck him right in the eyeball.

"Well there's one thing I've learnt from it."

"What's that then? Duck."

"Yeah duck. And if you are going to hit someone; hit them in the bloody eye. Christ there wasn't anything I could do. I couldn't see, I couldn't breath. If that had been a street fight or a war with an enemy soldier, he would have killed me. I wasn't able to defend myself. If a man can't see, a man can't fight."

Jancsi sat down beside Nandi, took out a cigarette of his own, picked up the box of matches Nandi had left on the ground and lit it.

"I've just seen the teams for the twenty four hour survival course."

"Oh yeah. I hope you are not going to tell me I am in the same team as the bloke who's just blacked my eye." Nandi joked.

"No, no. Although you could have suffocated him when he was asleep. They've split all our gang up and you are with Istvan Feher, Peter Sipos, Gabriel Zold and Tomi Megyesi. Professor Horvath is your assessor."

"I hope he's a better boy scout than he is boxing coach"

Less than a week later Professor Horvath stood outside with his survival team explaining the rules. He pointed out the time to them as was the other lecturers to the other three teams.

"It is now 12 o'clock midday. Your mission is to trek through the forest and get to the top of that mountain. When you reach the peak, you will find your team's coloured ribbon. There are of course four ribbons tied to a tree, red which is ours, white, green and blue. You will obtain your teams colour and then head back to this exact spot here where principal Varadi will be awaiting the winning team. You will all be assessed on your survival and team working abilities. Each team has a tutor with them who will be scoring each of you as we go along. The points will be handed in to Principal Varadi who will then calculate them and announce the winner forthwith. This means that the first team back does not necessarily mean they have won although, the first team back will score 50 points, the second scores 40 points, third 30 points and fourth 20 points. Total distance there and back is around forty kilometres and we estimate will take you around twenty-four hours. There is some rough terrain through that forest so before we set out I suggest you inspect your backpacks once again and ensure you have everything you think you'll need for a night out in the middle of a dense forest."

Each team were then given a map explaining their separate routes. The red team marched forward and were the first to cross the river over a low wooden bridge indicating the start of a creepy, thickset, wooded coppice. As the four teams trudged deeper into the forest, they slowly vanished from each others vicinity whilst they concentrated on the routes they had been given which was engineered to separate the four teams forcing them to fend alone as a unit. Whilst the teams went their own way, the trees grew taller and more spacious but their branches stretched out wider blocking out any glimmer of sunlight. Nandi checked his map when the obvious sounds of running water drew nearer. He could see that the river they all knew so well that ran alongside the college and into Szanto, did actually loop back in a sort of 'S' shape. Their first obstacle had now presented itself. They stood on the high riverbank looking down into a faster flowing part of the river which was deeper and wider than the tamer water they had so often scrubbed their hands and faces in by their college. The difference was they couldn't see a way across. Various solutions were quickly discussed and dismissed until Nandi broke away from the group, released his backpack and began fumbling inside. He had only pulled out a few things when at last he grabbed on to what he was searching for.

"Here!" He shouted to the others.

He held up a coiled up rope and threw it at Tomi.

"That rope is six metres long. If I give you a foot up that tree Tomi, do you think you could crawl out across that thick branch over the river and tie it around tight?"

Tomi checked the tree and immediately realised Nandi's plan. The tree had a large, thick, round base trunk and was growing at an angle leaning out above the river. Its branches were solid also and continued growing in the same direction, sprawling long and wide overhanging the water below. Tomi unbuckled his backpack and let it drop to the floor. He wrapped the rope over his shoulder and nodded to Nandi. Whilst Nandi lifted Tomi up the trunk, he began explaining to the others.

"Okay, when Tomi has tied it tight we will swing across one by one. As quick as we can, time is of the essence here, if we can get across quickly this is where we will make up some ground if the others are struggling to get over."

Tomi managed to ensure he had thread the end of the rope up, around and in between many smaller offshoots as well as the final knot pulled around the main limb of the tree. He let the rope dangle loosely to check the distance from the water and was given the thumbs up from the rest of them when they paid attention to its length and particularly the strength.

"Are you coming down?" Nandi called up to Tomi.

"No, I think it would be safer if I stayed here and monitor the knots. That way if they start to undo I can retie them."

The rope hung freely over the centre of the river and could not be reached from the riverbank. Tomi realised this and began to swing the rope towards the red team members. Gabriel was the first to reach it and tested its security by pulling and yanking at it as hard as he could.

"Well volunteered. Gabi is going first." Nandi announced.

Gabi laughed out loud and then responded by forcing the rope into Nandi's hand.

"It's your idea Nandi. Lead by example."

Nandi didn't answer. He looped the rope around a short branch, picked up his backpack and threw it over to the other side. It cleared the river and simply landed where Nandi had intended in a soft patch of grass well in land away from the river. He retrieved the rope, held it tight with two hands letting the end just drag on the ground. Nandi then pulled the rope and walked backwards until the tension of the rope was taut and Tomi complained Nandi was bending his branch. He dug his heels firmly into the soil, bent his knees slightly whilst the rest of the team watched with a curious concern for Nandi's method. Bravely, Nandi didn't ponder over his quest for more than a few seconds before he leapt high and hard, held the rope firmly with both hands and then let the tension of the rope and the elasticity of the branch pull and swing him dangerously over the flowing water beneath. He timed his jump to perfection and landed with elegance well away from the muddy riverbank. He turned and didn't wait for any applause, just reached out for the swinging rope, grabbed it before its momentum declined and, modestly but sternly threw it back to the rest of the team.

Nandi clapped his hands twice and said encouragingly,

"C'mon who's next? I'll grab you."

Much more confident now, Gabi took hold of the rope and poised himself in a similar stance to Nandi.

He hadn't managed to launch himself as successfully as Nandi but nevertheless Gabi achieved the jump with a little help from Nandi and without getting wet. As each one swung across it became evident that Nandi's abilities had brushed off onto them all and created a buzzing atmosphere filling them with a strong exaltation; maybe they were going to win?

Finally, Mr. Horvath helped Tomi down from the tree and insisted that Tomi would go next followed by himself last. Tomi decided that he wouldn't throw his backpack across as the others had done because he had some breakables inside and didn't want to risk smashing them. He secured it onto his back and grasped the rope with some hesitation.

"You'll be okay." Mr. Horvath reassured him. "I'll give you a good push."

They decided to count to three and with a huge shove Tomi swung out with tremendous speed.

"Oh shit." Tomi heard Mr. Horvath say as he began his swoop to the opposite riverbank.

He was about half way across when he realised something had happened. His backpack had unbuckled somehow and was slipping off his left shoulder. Nandi had realised it too in an instant and positioned himself nearer to the edge and warned the others.

"Grab meeee". Tomi called out as he crashed into the awaiting lads.

Nandi ensured Tomi was safe on the ground and then sharply attempted to retrieve the falling backpack. By now it had twisted around off his back and the harness straps were slipping from around his shoulders. It plunged to the ground and hit the top of the riverbank face before Nandi dived to the ground and gripped it by the side. Nandi managed to drag it to safety but not without losing a large proportion of its contents, watching a mass of small oddments along with three large packages plunge into the river and disappear beneath the uneven current.

"What have we lost?" Nandi asked Tomi when he passed him his much lighter backpack.

"I don't know exactly until I've checked."

"You have a look then while we help Mr. Horvath across."

Their lecturer landed safely with the aid of the lads steadying his awkward touchdown. By then Tomi, realising the importance of their equipment, had evenly sprawled out the remnants all over a shortcut grassy patch. He knew immediately what was missing and began reeling them off,

"Bread, salami, some ham, cheese, a corkscrew, a sharpening stone, various cutlery and a box of matches."

"Is that it?" Mr. Horvath questioned.

"Yeah, I think so. If there's anything else I'm sure it'll come back to me."

"Okay gents. Anyone else carrying any of the missing items?" Nandi asked.

Peter and Istvan confirmed they had got some similar foods but were sure they were without any of the other lost accessories.

"Well, it's no good crying over spilt milk. Let's take advantage of our quick crossing, which I am sure is causing the others more problems than it's caused us. Pack everything together and let's get moving."

Whilst Tomi stuffed his gear back, Nandi pulled the rope tight and tied it to another nearby tree explaining it was better to leave it there, as it would speed up the crossing on their return.

They plodded deeper into the forest systematically checking the magnetic compass following a south-easterly direction. The hot afternoon sun forced its way through the trees above ensuring an airless, muggy temperature inside the leafy copse. Sweat streamed through their hair and off their backs and they found much comfort in their plastic bottles of water used to cool them down and quench their thirsts. A small clearing after a few kilometres of forest was welcomed allowing them to visually see the advancing mountain. They all took turns in guessing the distance from where they stood to the foot and after short deliberation, they compromised and decided it must be approximately fourteen kilometres away. They knew the mountain that they must ascend was around 700 metres high and so the rest was a sensible calculated guess. They marched on in single file formation with Nandi leading the way. Bees and wasps appeared to be attracted to their presence as the insects irritated the team hovering only a few centimetres from their ears. All except Nandi were attempting to swot the pests but Nandi's concentration remained captivated on a small farmhouse standing alone, slightly southwest in direction, but a kilometre or so before the mountain. The team didn't speak for another two kilometres until Nandi stopped in his tracks, broke the silence, turned and said,

"I have a plan."

"What kind of plan?" Peter questioned and as they all stood, mouths half open breathing heavy, awaited Nandi's explanation.

"We all jog to the foot of the mountain."

"And that's it, your plan?" Retorted Peter disappointingly.

"Run? Why? We'll bloody collapse with dehydration?" Tomi reinforced Peter's reaction.

At first Nandi didn't answer until Mr. Horvath questioned his ambition.

"Well Nandi, do you have good reason for us all to run ten kilometres?"

"Okay listen. I know it sounds ridiculous in this heat, but in a few hours it will start to go dark. We have already lost some supplies, if needs be we can refuel our water supplies at the well just outside that farmhouse. We are going to need to set up camp in a suitable area and we are going to have to light a campfire. And if none of you have realised it, we haven't any matches. I can light a fire but only in daylight, I cannot do it when the sun goes down."

"Some kind of a magician are you Nandi?" Istvan joked.

Nandi smiled with his eyes but then seriously continued,

"Please trust me. And, you want to win don't you?"

Nandi's convincing speech inspired the team to at least attempt the ten-kilometre jog. Once they began and established a favourable running speed they seemed not to mind it so much owing to the prospect of freezing well water at the end. Nandi took his mind of the strenuous workout by imagining he was in a life or death situation. He was in the middle of a war zone being bombed by enemy aircraft from above. He dodged the bullets raining all around him and hurdled the anthills imagined them to be hidden mines. Nandi condemned himself to death as he accidentally crushed an anthill with his right boot, but sprinted on anyway imagining the well water to be a cure for a blown off leg.

In succession, the six of them circled the well awaiting for Mr. Horvath to heave up a full bucket of fresh, cold, water. They each took turns to soak themselves and after they'd caught their breath and cooled down, they all released their backpacks and slumped wearily onto the ground.

"What now?" Tomi asked wiping his nose.

"Well it is tea time." Nandi said leaving the question not completely answered.

"Yeah, so what."

"So let's find a suitable area to camp, get a good fire going and then let's eat."

"Over there I reckon." Istvan pointed to a large flat area in front of the forest trees that covered the mountain.

Gabi agreed immediately. " Yes; then when we wake up in the morning we will be refreshed and ready to climb the mountain.

After a short while they proceeded over to the spot, checked the texture of the earth, stripped down to their wastes and set to work erecting their two man canvas tents. It didn't take them too long and Nandi volunteered to venture off into the forest to collect some firewood whilst the others ensured their chosen campsite was tidy and that some food was prepared.

Nandi was chopping up branches with his short-handled axe making large piles here and there. It wasn't long before Tomi joined him helping by carrying the cut up sticks back and forth to their built up fireplace outside the tents.

They had both walked a little into the forest when Nandi noticed and pointed out a familiar type of tree.

"Do you know what type of trees these are?"

"I don't recognise them, but those over there are Oak trees. Why what are they?"

Nandi stroked the bark before he answered.

"This is a Hickory tree recognisable by the light grey, smooth, slightly rigid bark. Look at the height of this one, must be 3o metres high. Their leaves turn bright yellow in the autumn. Look at the flowers on it now, the flowers that you see along the stems hanging in three branch catkins are the male flowers and the ones you can see at the twig ends in small, petal less clusters are the female flowers."

Tomi looked up at the tree, frowned and said,

"Nandi, who gives a shit?"

Nandi sniggered at first and then they both laughed out loud and then Nandi explained,

"You will see. I am going to cut down a dozen of its branches. I need those very, very long ones there, but they are not for burning."

"So what do you need them for?"

"I'll show you later."

After Nandi had cut down about 15 long, straight Hickory branches of about half an inch thick, and Tomi had tied them together at each end; they both heard a rustling sound beyond some shorter bushes at about 40 metres away from them. Together they looked at each other, put one finger over their lips and crouched down very slowly. The rustling drew nearer and they both wondered what animal it could be. By now they could hear it chomping and chewing on something and they both stared hard patiently waiting for it to show itself. Nandi beckoned to Tomi so as they could both slowly creep behind the Hickory tree. When they were sure their movement hadn't disturbed it, they peeped out to see. It stepped out from behind a pile of sawn off tree trunks and hadn't noticed the lads behind it.

Nandi and Tomi moved their heads back out of sight.

"What are you doing?" Tomi whispered when Nandi picked up his axe off the floor.

"Looks like we are having venison for tea." Nandi whispered back.

Tomi stared at Nandi in disbelief as he slowly stood up brushing his back against the trunk of the Hickory tree. Nandi gripped the axe tight in his right hand and then peeped at the deer again, who still showed its bottom towards the lads completely engrossed with whatever it was eating off the ground. Nandi's heart beat faster; he stared back at the axe and then at the deer. Tomi grew scared but before he could dissuade him, Nandi turned and leapt out from behind the tree and raised the axe high behind his head. The deer lifted its nose up slightly to the left, but before it could run for safety Nandi had took aim and flung the axe. It whistled as it left his hand, spun around three times and landed with a deep thud and a crack into the skull of the deer. It seemed to walk forward a few inches but then its legs buckled and it wasn't long before it collapsed to the floor. Tomi came from behind the tree and stood beside Nandi, they both awaited for the animal to finish twitching and when they were sure it was dead, they walked over to it.

Tomi couldn't say anything, only stared at it. A few seconds passed and then Nandi pulled his axe from the head of the deer. It squelched and made a snapping noise as he did it and he wiped it clean it a bunch of rhubarb leaves.

"Don't just stand there, help me lift it over my back."

Tomi responded with Nandi and together they put it over the back of Nandi so as he was holding its hooves, two in each hand.

"Let's go and show the rest of them what we've caught." Nandi said proudly. "And Tomi, please don't forget my Hickory branches."

Tomi was in somewhat of a daze but soon snapped out of it when he began explaining to the rest of the team when they got back.

"I've never seen nothing like it. I don't know whether it was luck or what, but from a distance of I don't know, 15 metres or more, Nandi hit it straight in the head with his axe."

Astonished at first the lads with Mr. Horvath, congratulated Nandi and a kind of party atmosphere began.

"So how do you cook a deer then?" Mr. Horvath asked.

"I'll show you as soon as I get this fire going."

Nandi took Mr. Horvath's binoculars from around his neck and began stuffing some paper into the crevices of the unlit fire that had been piled up by the others. He then held the binoculars over the paper and manoeuvred them until he caught the sunlight and made a small, bright circular dot onto the tip of the paper. The paper quickly began to char and smoulder until it burst into flame. They all gathered around and helped to ensure the wood caught fire.

"So that's how you planned to start a fire without matches. And that's why you needed us to get here before the sun went down. You clever bastard. But I'm glad you are on my team." Istvan said with a chuffed tone and finished by patting Nandi on the back.

"Well, if Tomi hadn't lost half our food and our matches, I wouldn't have had to go hunting and we wouldn't have had to jog 10 kilometres in the blistering heat. So, in my opinion, it's all his fault."

The rest of them jokingly agreed, laughed and wrestled Tomi to the floor playfully. Tomi called out beneath a giggling bunch of friends,

"I'll get you Pekar."

When the fire was roaring it then became time for Nandi to give lessons in cleaning and cooking a deer. He led the way whilst explaining his actions as he went. They hung the body from a tree by its split open head. Using a stick, he held open the body and its hind legs so the air could freely circulate. Nandi then passed a sharp knife to Istvan and told him to cut the skin around the neck followed by a lengthwise incision under the neck to the abdominal cavity. Nandi carved up the inside of the legs in such a way so that the two sides met together. He then began to peel off the skin in big chunk sizes by pressing his fist between the flesh and the skin. He noticed his audience squirming as he did it and explained to them,

"You know it's easier to skin an animal when the flesh is still warm. But if you're squirming now wait until I remove its testicles."

The experience was exciting for the lads and Mr. Horvath and after a while they all grabbed a knife and joined in removing the skin, the hide, the legs, the scent glands, taking good care not to cut into the stomach or digestive organs. At last, it had been sectioned, washed, and sliced into cubes. Mr. Horvath took charge of the cooking and began by frying the venison in a pan over the open fire. It wasn't long before the air was filled with a hot, tasty, aroma and Nandi added to his impressive talents by picking some nearby mushrooms and passed them to Mr. Horvath.

"Are you sure these aren't poisonous?" Mr. Horvath looked at Nandi and then realised his mistake. "Stupid question. You don't need to answer that Nandi."

A relaxing, refreshing open-air bath revitalised the boys that simply required stripping naked, a bucket of cold water each, a bar of soap and a towel.

The lads devoured their meal and felt a moment of self disciplined joy, realising they had succeeded and were able to survive like an ancient caveman. The meal didn't come too late as they were all famished but now felt reenergized.

"So, what are you going to do with these Hickory branches?" Tomi asked.

Nandi burped out loud and then remembered his plan,

"Ah, almost forgot about them. Quick pass them here and everyone watch because you can help me."

They all watched with a speculative interest as Nandi cut away the string with a long bladed carving knife.

"This bloody knife has gone blunt." Nandi said and without thinking, realising they had lost the sharpening stone in the river, Nandi picked up another knife and began sharpening it by somehow slicing the sharp ends of the blades together metal against metal. Within minutes, he tested the carving knife by gently slivering it against a long blade of grass. When the grass blade fell into two without any effort the rest of the team sighed and Peter said,

"Doesn't he piss you off?"

"If you think that's clever watch this. Okay everybody grab a branch and start trimming off all the lateral twigs. Like this."

Nandi began sheering and the rest of the lads picked up a branch, a knife and copied.

"Then hold the branch firmly with both hands, bend it like this from butt to tip in every direction, gently now, must avoid any kinks. Keep on doing that until the entire branch is supple."

They all worked their branches until all were complete and Nandi continued with his demonstration. He then tied it into an overhand knot, large at first, then reduced the size of the bight by sliding along the end and standing (tip to butt). They simulated every piece of work as he continued to wrap the ends around the original loop until they were used up.

Nandi finished his branch first and said,

"Now look at that. A good wythe when completed should have three strands in every part, be free from kinks and nearly circular. Just like mine."

Peter who was working hard to replicate Nandi's said,

"What the hell is it?"

Istvan answered before Nandi.

"Are you stupid? It's a rope of course." It was perfection hidden under a cloak of simplicity.

"Exactly. When you've all finished attach them together and we will have one massive length of rope. We'll need it tomorrow to get up that bloody mountain."

"Good God. We've got Tarzan with us." Istvan announced.

Nandi laughed and then ushered Tomi away from the others.

"Have you still got that wine?"

"Of course. That's why I didn't throw my backpack across the river."

"Great. Do you think Horvath will let us have a drink?"

"Go and ask him"

After little persuasion, the lads managed to convince their teacher that they had all deserved to have a tipple but he did point out that they hadn't got a corkscrew.

Nandi pulled out a bottle of the medium sweet red wine and said,

"And for my final trick of the day…."

He wrapped up a large tea towel and held it against the trunk of a nearby tree with his left hand and then, holding the bottle by its neck with his right, began banging the base of the bottle against the tea towel and the tree. Slowly but surely, with every strike, the cork began popping out bit by bit until it showed large enough to be pulled out with his fingers. Everyone cheered and Nandi threw the cork into the fire and began filling six mugs. Peter stood up grinning slightly.

"I would like to propose a toast." They all lifted their mugs. "To Nandi, Tarzan of our Hungarian jungle."

July 18th 1953

Nandi helped his mother down off the cart and she showed appreciation for his gentlemanly conduct by hugging him and kissing him on both cheeks. He greeted his father in a smarter approach, shook his right hand firmly, embraced with their left arm, and a welcoming kiss one on each cheek. Margit couldn't resist another hug and pulled her tall son towards her and pressed her head against his hard chest. Finally, she released, but began raking through his thick black hair with her fingers and then followed up by straightening his thin, dark blue tie.

"Oh my son you look so smart. I'm so proud of you. Have they given you your results yet? Oh, it doesn't matter if you haven't done well, there's always next year. I love you whatever happens. And we are going to have a fantastic summer; your father has worked so hard on the land preparing for your homecoming. The pears, cherries, walnuts and all the fruit trees are ripe already. Where is everybody? Where's Laszi and Jancsi?"

"Give the boy a chance to answer" Janos interrupted

Margit touched Nandi's cheeks with both hands, smiles lit up her face and eyes. "So, sorry son, so excited and nervous, don't know what I'm saying."

"That's okay mother. I've missed you too. They haven't given out any results yet; and all my friends along with about 400 lads, teachers and parents are congregating in the main hall. Come on let's go inside, you can have a look at some of my work."

They had only been in the hall for a few minutes when Mr. Horvath spotted them and made an immediate beeline for them.

"Good afternoon Mr and Mrs. Pekar and what a pleasure it is to meet you both. I suppose Nandi has been telling you about our twenty-four hour expedition."

Janos answered, "No he hasn't, but we haven't had much time to discuss anything yet, we've only just arrived."

"Let me tell you. We had four separate teams with a task to get to the top of that mountain over yonder, and get back here in 24 hours, each team to be scored on their abilities to improvise, adapt, overcome. What an inspiring pioneer your son turned out to be. We saw acts of bravery, imagination, an ability to survive under extreme conditions, teamwork, strength, determination, your son possesses them all. It was all finished off with a climatic finish when Nandi's red team had to sprint for the finish line against a closely followed green team. But the red team finished first to claim maximum points. And the next day after all the points had been calculated they won by a landslide margin and I was proud to present them with their medals. But to be honest, they wouldn't have won it without Nandi."

Margit and Janos couldn't help feeling superciliously disdainful as Mr. Horvath's words of praise tumbled over each other.

"Yes my son has had a good teacher." Janos boasted.

"Oh yes, he has told me of his intelligent source."

"What about his science? Has he done well?" Margit remembered which subject Mr. Horvath was teaching.

"With flying colours Mrs. Pekar; with flying colours."

After half an hour of mingling and filtering from classroom to classroom, Principal Varadi announced to the parents that school reports were now ready for collection at the front of the stage. He advised one parent at a time to queue to avoid a stampede. The wait was worth waiting for. The report of their only son read as follows:-

ABAUJSZANTO COLLEGE ANNUAL REPORT OF ACHIEVEMENT

NAME.. *Nandor Pekar*

D.O.B. *5/07/38*

ACADEMIC YEAR. *1952/53*

REPORT DATE. *July 1953*

HOME TOWN/VILLAGE. *Mogyoroska*

HUNGARIAN

Nandi is a hardworking student who completes every task that he is given with enthusiasm and imagination. He should be congratulated on his recent examination result of grade 1, as this achievement is beyond his target level.

MATHEMATICS

Nandi sometimes lacks confidence, however his excellent grade 1 performance should give him the boost he requires. His year's work has been full of effort and he is now reaping the benefits of that. Well done.

HISTORY

Nandor has a good knowledge and understanding of not only Hungarian history but world history too. His appreciation of that 'yesterday' reflects on your way of living today, has contributed to the lessons and his very satisfactory exam result speaks for itself.

GEOGRAPHY

A solid exam performance mirror imaging his terms work. He is capable of achieving a grade 1 next year and I am more than confident he will do exactly that.

SCIENCE

I am very pleased with Nandi's continual progress this year. He has shown abilities that could see him in a scientific occupation; demonstrating a good understanding of both practical and theoretical science. He was only two marks away from a grade 1. Excellent.

RUSSIAN

Average exam result but a satisfactory terms work. Well done.

AGRICULTURE

Nandi has performed without a blemish all year. He has natural abilities for the rearing of crops and livestock. A very practical, self-disciplined lad, backed up by neat and organised theory. Been a pleasure to teach and I will be looking forward to teaching him again next year.

PHYSICAL EDUCATION

Nandi is a very keen and enthusiastic member of his class. His effort and attitude have been a credit to him and he can always be relied upon to give his best at all times. Progress has been outstanding in all activities, especially football and shot-put. He also showed an intense determination to train at an incredible endurance, pushing his body well beyond the pain barrier during his efforts to learn boxing. But, above all, the end of the school year was blessed with a performance from Nandor Pekar that defied logic when he displayed an array of personal attributes that shone like a blinding light. The organised survival course brought out his personal qualities showing both brain and brawn earning his team a massive win. Well Done!!

PRINCIPAL COMMENTS.

I am very proud to have Nandor at our boarding college. He is without a doubt an inspirational character and in addition he has a well-distinguished mannerism using his manners at all times. I have no fear in my mind that Nandor will succeed in getting his intended qualifications and moving into the career of his choice if he continues in this vein. There is nothing stopping him.

Best Regards

Mr. Varadi

CHAPTER 9

November 25th 1953

SZANTO BOARDING COLLEGE

Thirty or more students crammed themselves into the library whilst Professor Horvath tuned the college wireless into Radio Budapest. It crackled and whistled but eventually the Hungarian commentator could be heard through a roaring crowd. Today was the climax of an intense couple of weeks, not just for the college students but also for the lecturers, and for the whole country. The Hungarian national football team were making their mark on world football putting Hungary back on the map. They had displayed some marvellous, entertaining skill, and had produced results to go with it. Children all over the world were imitating the Hungarian stars and a national pride enveloped the country. A small Hungarian force had managed to break through the communist prison gates that surrounded Hungary, traipse through Europe and other footballing continents, show their talents creating havoc annihilating their opponents and returning home to Hungary to a hero's welcome. At last, the people of Hungary were feeling that maybe someone would begin to realize that Hungary still exists.

Today Hungary were playing England at Wembley Stadium in London. Nandi and his friends listened attentively as the commentator began reading out the Hungarian team. Gyula Grosics Goalkeeper, Jeno Buzansky Right Back, Mihaly Lantos Left Back, Jozsef Bozsik Right Half, Gyula Lorant Centre Half, Jozsef Zakarias Left Half, Lazslo Budai Right Wing, Sandor Kocsis Inside Right, Ferenc Puskas Inside Left, Zoltan Czibor Left Wing and Nandor Hidegkuti Centre Forward.

Nandi smiled to himself as a surge of accomplishment gushed through his body. The English team was then read out and Nandi tried hard to pronounce their names.

"Walter Winterbottom, England's Manager, Alf Ramsey Right Back, Billy Wright Right Half."

And then the commentator read out a familiar name.

"Ah, I've heard of him, Stanley Mathews! Plays for Blackpool." Nandi recalled.

After the two teams had been announced Nandi bit his nails and said,

"My prediction is the bloody English are about to get a lesson they deserve. In politics and war, they have abandoned us leaving us to the lions. So now they are about to get the three lions on their English badge kicked to shit. Gil Merrick their goalkeeper is about to have the hardest match of his career and if Lantos has a crack at goal and he tries to save it, it will probably break his hand. Ninety years without losing at Wembley Stadium is about to be a forgotten dream." Nandi's bitterness for Western Europe showed, but today Hungary had the chance to get its own back.

The whistle blew at Wembley Stadium and what followed could only be described as football elegance from an invincible Hungarian team and total humiliation from a home side that clearly looked stunned by a style of football it couldn't handle. Within sixty seconds, they took the lead when Hidegkuti successfully sold the dummy to Johnston before sending in a devastating shot. England drew level after Mortensen made a well timed pass for Sewell to find the net, but were crushed by some tactical interchanging positioning from Hidegkuti, a mingling of short, long and triangle passes coupled with geometrical accuracy and ball control. The pressure from

Hungary caused the English team to be running around like headless chickens and the Hungarian broadcaster on the wireless made it sound as such. The students were excited; even at one a piece. But they didn't stay level for long when Hidegkuti scored again from a poor England clearance. They all stood on their feet as the panic stricken commentator broadcast the next Hungarian sequence.

"Puskas receives a long, low, sizzling pass from Kocsis. Puskas turns towards goal. But here comes Billy Wright flying in with a challenge. **My word what a GOAL**. Billy Wright left for dead, flat on his backside. Puskas made it look as if he wasn't even there. Puskas simply drew the ball back with the sole of his boot and Wright went past him like a fire engine going to the wrong fire. It's a goal and Hungary lead three goals to one and England are in trouble." The library at Szanto college was in glorious uproar. Books and papers were thrown into the air, celebratory songs echoed throughout the building and they hardly drew breath when a fourth goal from Hungary went in again from Puskas who had diverted a free kick from Bozsik.

England pulled another goal back before half time but Nandi and his friends were in good voice as they sang their national anthem awaiting another forty-five minutes of delight.

Ten minutes after the interval Bozsik scored again and Hidegkuti quickly succeeded him who completed Hungary's triumph with a hat-trick. Though Ramsey converted a penalty to make the final score 6-3, the issue by then was no longer really at stake and a new page in the history of football had been turned.

For Nandi it was more than a 6-3 victory. It was a statement from a forgotten land. "We are still here; persecuted but still kicking! Still strong! Subject to evil, but still have fighting spirit! We are proud Hungarians!"

November 25th1953

The wireless was turned down as the commentator pointed out that as well has smacking the backsides of the creator of football; Hungary had overcome the traditional continental weakness at finishing and shot four of their goals from outside the penalty area.

Mr. Horvath raised his arms and encouraged the students to be silent. "It is a great victory, but please be quiet and go back to your rooms sensibly."

The students were in no mood to take their win over England lightly, they wanted to celebrate, they'd just beaten a country that had managed to survive the Second World War without being occupied by Germany. One of few who had actually achieved that. Hungary had pulled to pieces a pompous nation and the students felt fulfilment.

Squeezing out of the library, most of the lads talked of their hidden away stashes of beer, but Nandi whispered to Jancsi his intentions,

"I'm going into town to see Irinka. Coming?"

"No, I'm going to have some fun here."

"Okay I'll go alone. But will you keep look out for me?"

"Sure, let's slip out around the back and then I'll put the ladder in place ready for your return."

Jancsi helped Nandi bounce over the fence and Nandi strolled off towards town in a flamboyant tempo whistling as he went.

There was something amiss in Szanto Town. There was a chilling atmosphere. Nandi grew concerned and sensed a feeling of silent fear amongst the few people he passed as he entered the outskirts of the centre. There was something that had been unknowingly instilled into the idiosyncrasies of all Hungarian people. Years of oppression and tyranny had impelled them, steered them to survive and fend for themselves in any way they could. In the midst of numerous survival methods a secret language had been developed. A language that was so surreptitious not even the speakers knew when they were saying it, the listeners didn't know who was saying it and only at certain times was it spoken and could be deciphered by particular listeners. This silent code was at this moment being transmitted around Szanto. Nandi was reading it and smelling danger. Small groups of people, pale faced, vacant, trembling, glancing at Nandi as he strolled passed. Shops showed closed signs in their windows. Curtains drawn, doors locked. In

the distance beyond the church, he could see some activity, and then, like a bolt of lightening, forcing Nandi to jump, a dark blue Skoda sped from behind the church heading towards Nandi leaving a trail of burnt rubber. As the car approached, he could see two men in the front but the backseat had at least four people crammed in. Their heads bobbed around as if some kind of a struggle was happening. Nandi caught sight of the driver and had a familiar feeling when his face became clear with his short, black straight hair flattened to his head, a thin, long moustache that crept long over his bulging chin and his small, dark eyes. Nandi's moment of déjà vu was soon over when he saw who was riding in the backseat. One man was choking Irinka and another held a pistol to her head. A hand covered her mouth and her face clearly smeared in bright red blood. The car sped passed and Nandi replayed the split second image in his mind. He squeezed his eyes closed firmly for a second and screamed out loud before he decided to sprint after the car. He hadn't ran very far when he disappeared in a cloud of dust caused by the spinning wheels of the Skoda. Lost and in a dizzy daze, he halted, spitting gobs of dust from his mouth. Another speeding car sounding his horn as it swerved around Nandi and came hurtling passed. When the dust settled it became apparent that there was a convoy of AVO unmarked cars seemingly running rampage in Szanto. Nandi wanted to find out what was going on but when he checked around him for assistance the road was deserted. His rage rumbled inside his stomach, for a moment he paced towards the disappearing cars and then he turned back and paced towards the town centre. The burning sensation erupted into his legs forcing him to run at top speed towards the church. He bombed around the temple building only to find four more AVO policemen waving their guns in the air and herding two gypsy men into another car. Nandi stopped dead in his tracks and observed. It seemed one AVO man had had enough of his prisoner; he slung him against the iron fence that wound around the communist red star. He didn't think about it, he didn't consider what he was doing nor did he care, in cold blood he shot the gypsy straight through the head. A trickle of blood rolled out of the circular bullet wound and the gypsy fell forward and slumped onto the shoulder of the AVO policeman. He ordered one of the others to open the boot of the car, then with no remorse he dumped the body of the man into the boot and slammed it shut. Shocked and disorientated Nandi stood and stared when the final AVO car left Szanto.

The wind blew his hair, the town stood at the moment like a ghost town. It was deserted. A tin can rattled as it blew across the street. It was many minutes before a choking sob rose in his throat. Nandi sat on a wide sawn off tree trunk with his elbows resting on his knees and his fists pressed against his forehead. Streams of tears flowed down his lean cheeks but no sound was heard. After a while he stood up wiping his face dry and walked over to the red star. Blood and pieces of flesh decorated the floor and Nandi noticed something swirling gently about him on the floor. He stopped its light movement with his shoe and then slowly knelt down to pick it up. A large white rose with only about seven petals remaining. He was sure it belonged to Irinka and when he smelled it he was certain that it had fallen from her hair during her arrest. Unobtrusively, he stood up straight and carefully placed the rose into his right jacket pocket. He plucked a petal from it when he pulled his hand away and held it in his palm. Gripping the petal tight in his fist he kissed his white knuckles allowing his tears to fall once again dripping onto the back of his hand. He prayed hard and repeated the same words over and over. "God help us, when will we be free? Where have they taken her? I swear by the almighty I will avenge Hungary's condemners."

Nandi was now experiencing a national prisoner's brutality. Rough justice from an occupying nation. For what, he had no idea. Why should Irinka and her family be treated in this way? At least one had been murdered in front of his very eyes. Who could he tell? Who could he complain to? To protest would be suicide. He was alone, frustrated, angry and he realised there wasn't anything he could do. He wanted to find out what had happened to her and why. To ask too many questions could result in his own arrest he knew that. Ironically, it was a familiar feeling that all of Hungary had grown to accept as a relating fundamental, natural part of their lives. It supposed to have improved after Jozsef Stalin's death, but Khrushchev hadn't shown any signs of pulling down the Iron Curtain and the rest of the world were growing to accept it. Like everyone who lived in Hungary, Nandi was trapped. The leaders were corrupt and their henchman who were policing the country were full of dead mans bones and had created a home for the lizard and the spider. No way out. Nandi felt devastated.

Eventually, he made his way back to his college room and told nobody of what he'd witnessed. He bore the worst kind of hatred, the silent kind. The sadness, the numbness became his persistent mood. The ceiling above his bed was the area of room where his innermost thoughts were played out, gazing up, hands behind head, staring behind tear filled eyes, almost burning holes in the outer fabric of the bedroom ceiling above him. At one stage, he thought his sombre depression was sending him out of his mind.

He spent days in a speechless cyclone, each night roving through Szanto town searching for a clue. Hoping, praying for some news, some evidence she was still alive. It was sure now to Nandi the AVO had wiped out the whole family. Not any one person from Irinka's family was present in Szanto. Their house was deserted and had been ransacked. Nandi didn't dare to ask residents of their whereabouts in case of reprisals. After one week since her disappearance Nandi had to accept the communists had probably killed her. He had no answers or reasons why **they** should do such a thing. But then, did **they** need a reason? Anger, sadness and frustration are deadly cocktails to bottle up inside a human. Together these emotions could equate to two outcomes, self-destruction or violent retaliation. Nandi felt alone with these feelings. Little did he realise, **he wasn't.**

CHAPTER 10

1956

It had been seven years since the execution of the Hungarian Communist leader Laszlo Rajk. His trial had been a traumatic event and had been a much talked about controversy throughout Hungary and the world. After Laszlo had fought in the Spanish civil war from 1936-1939 he returned to Hungary in 1941 and became First Secretary of the Communist Party. He participated in the Hungarian underground movement against the Nazi's and for a while was captured and imprisoned by the Gestapo. After the Second World War he worked his way up in the Communist Party to become Foreign Minister by 1948.

The Laszlo Rajk trial of 1949 had since circulated many widespread rumours and was the most notorious of Stalin's fabricated exhibitions. Rajk confessed to conspiring to overthrow the Hungarian government, he and eighteen others were convicted, executed and buried in unmarked graves. Cardinal Mindszenty was among the accused that had been imprisoned one year earlier to the Rajk trial. The truth was Laszlo Rajk had been set up on trumped up charges and been the victim to the message Stalin was to broadcast in a theatrical demonstration known as the Rajk trial. His message was simple and was intended to instil a political fear throughout Hungary. "To betray Communism, to desert Communism, to conspire against Communism, to simply talk against Communism will result in your own execution." Laszlo Rajk had been a political pawn in a dangerous game and paid with his life. A confession had been beaten from him.

At the 20th Party Congress at Moscow in February 1956 Russian leader Nikita Khrushchev, in a closed-door speech, denounced Jozsef Stalin. Word of this filtered out and was fed to the attentive listeners in Hungary. Hearing of these words influential elements within the communist Party began to criticize Matyas Rakosi. One month later in March, owing to pressure from Laszlo Rajk's wife, who had been imprisoned by Stalin in 1949 for supporting her husband's subversive policy, the Matyas Rakosi Hungarian government declared his trial to of been an error. In view of that, it was decided that Laszlo Rajk would receive a ceremonial reburial in Budapest later in the year.

In the Polish city of Poznan, a workers revolt erupted in June 1956. Demonstrations and protests were made which led to discussions with regard to changes in the leadership of the Polish Communist Party. Hungary's mood was changing. Hearing this, a silent, slight hope circulated across the land mixed with a national unrest. The Kremlin sensed a mood swing in its web and made a political shift moving Matyas Rakosi from leader replacing him with Erno Gero.

Nikita Khrushchev's gestures were intended to keep Hungary's unrest under control. He and the Kremlin were about to find out if their gesticulations were as influential as they had expected.

October 6th 1956 Budapest

No one in Hungary was expecting a 200,000 strong crowd to turn out for the reburial of Laszlo Rajk. The surrounding streets, avenues and squares were bulging and swelling with the masses of people. The cemetery was jam packed, people climbed on high walls, buildings, cars, tractors, anything just to take a peak at this famous moment that was certain to go down in Hungarian History. 200,000 people of all ages and classes grouped and studied each moment and stared with respect at his wife and son as they tearfully watched him being lowered into a new and honourable grave.

A twenty strong group of young university students huddled together, began to discuss the moment with interest.

"I wonder if she will be able to go back to using Mrs. Rajk. You know when she was released from prison Stalin forced her to change her name with an intent to doom his name into oblivion."

"Who cares anyway?" A person standing nearby commented.

"That's a callous statement isn't it friend?" Someone else asked him.

"It may sound callous but if you were all to admit why you are here, it isn't particularly to pay tribute to Laszlo Rajk, we are considering this burial a final burial of Jozsef bloody Stalin. Stalinism!"

"Yeah, he's absolutely correct. This funeral is a symbol of Communist perfidy. An example of the treacherous Stalin Communist regime. Look at that!" All nearby onlookers who were listening turned their heads towards the ceremony.

"The widow and her son, the reburial of Laszlo Rajk, his coffin, symbols of Stalin victims."

About thirty people in the crowd shouted out at the same time,

"Here, here." The crowd of voices agreeing and repeated the same words in one breath, together sounded like one voice and before long the identical topic of conversation was being discussed throughout and spreading like wildfire.

"Nikita Khrushchev thinks he's doing something good for us. He insults our intelligence that's what he does. Digging up an example of Stalin's butchery and deceit and then reburying him in Budapest. Moving aside Matyas Rakosi and putting another Communist bully in his place. If he wants to do something for us, he could fuck off back to Russia and leave us to be free."

It seemed like 200, 000 people had heard his comments as it was followed by a nervous resonance that sounded like the bottom of a rattlesnake's pit.

"**Shush**, you'll get us all **sh**ot. **Shush**."

These kinds of words were taken advantage of by the university students who were using this uncommon gathering of oppressed Hungarians to distribute their beliefs and intentions. Elected university speakers from universities all around Budapest were intermingling with the masses and going ahead with their planned speeches. They talked openly to large groups of people and asked for them to unite and support their mission to persuade the Communists to let Hungary be free. The interest and opinionated people spoke out for the first time and led to hours of street debate. Other students were distributing their leaflets and pamphlets explaining a brief plan and a request for the people of Hungary to rise up and stand together and request freedom.

A young student was handing out his piles of typed out documents when a friend of his called out,

"Eh, eh, which leaflets are you handing out?"

The student held one up so as he could see it.

"This one, why?"

He read the first few lines quickly and then breathed a sigh of relief.

"For a moment then I thought you were distributing the other ones, you know the secret ones. Where have you put them?"

"Don't worry; most of them have been posted or hand delivered to colleges and universities around the country. What we've got left over are hidden back at the university."

"Good God. Just for a second I had a horrible vision we had been giving out the wrong ones, Christ we'd of all been shot on the spot."

"Perish the thought, perish the thought."

A few hours after the funeral had finished a few dozen students began feeling a little brave and began discussing, almost daring each other to march on towards the centre under a banner of protest.

"C'mon lads lets march together arm in arm, make our views known, sing our national anthem or something get to the city centre and see what happens."

"It against the law. We could get arrested."

"Nobody was arrested in Poznan Poland. Eh, same thing."

"Yeah c'mon, I'll do it."

"What do you lot think?"

Nods of agreement and words of promising acceptance harmonized the crowd and rippled through the masses like a Mexican wave. Before long the talking progressed into action when a large Hungarian flag was pulled out by a student and stretched over a group of about two-dozen people. This was it, their moment of honour.

"**Let's go!**" Someone cried out, and then the march began. Twenty abreast, the streets swelled with a brave bunch of folk requesting a right to speak freely. It was almost incredible to see and realise that the long line of protesters was bulging and seemed it wouldn't stop. When the front liners looked back, a sea of people was a welcoming sight, knowing what support the idea to march to the city centre had had; now encouraged the peaceful mob to sing revolutionary songs. The singing grew louder until eventually all 300 demonstrators sang in unison, a few passing cars showed their salute by attempting to play the national anthem on their car horns.

"Only two more kilometres to the city centre. No interference from the police yet, c'mon let's really test the water. Turn up the heat with this song. `We will not stop halfway, Stalinism must be destroyed, we will not stop halfway, Stalinism must be destroyed, we will not stop halfway, Stalinism must be destroyed,`"

It wasn't long before the tune had turned into a chant and the length of a 300 healthy multitude of people intonating in unity echoed around the walls of the approaching city centre.

The evening of October 6th 1956 fell into a satisfactory shadow for the organisers of the rally. Universities and industries alike relaxed in their homes with an unfamiliar feeling of dignity. They had pulled it off. Not too big though, but nevertheless the day had closed peacefully and more importantly their voices had been raised. A small tad of their heavy burden carried with them for countless years, had been lifted and they liked the taste of it.

SZANTO BOARDING COLLEGE. October 17th 1956

Twenty students packed out the library sitting on wooden stools or leaning against the high bookshelves.
Peter began opening a wide, padded, brown, envelope marked Top Secret whilst Nandi locked the library doors to ensure their meeting could not be disturbed.
"What news from Budapest?" Jancsi asked Peter.
"This package is from the University of Buda. Now let's see, aha, a pile of propaganda information. Okay while Attila hands them around I'll read them out loud."

"Dear Student colleagues,

October 17th 1956

Please distribute the attached information to any trusted
Hungarian companion.
It is now time for action. Far too long the Iron Fist of the Kremlin
has trampled on our nation. We are in the process of setting up an
independent student organisation where we will discuss our
concerns and set about changing the policies of the Communist
system in the good of the future of our country. We ask your
support and request for you to attend our next meeting held at the
University of Szeged at Szeged city on October 16th.

We should all bear in mind at this moment of the way our Russian
rulers are treating our people. We know of innocent people being
imprisoned for crimes against the state some have being held
since the War, they have not been charged and have no prospect
of release. These people remain illegally in prison, many assumed
by their relatives to be dead. We know the prison camps are full of
innocent common people, workers, poor peasants, small
stallholders etc. The prisons are packed full of
dejected demoralised prisoners, who have never been tried,
imprisoned for petty crimes such as chicken stealing."

"October 16th was yesterday." Attila interrupted.
"So it was. Well if their mail is one day late how can we make it?"
Peter complained
A disappointing brief pause loomed over the small congregation
for about half a minute before Peter continued reading the final
part of the one page leaflet.
" And finally we find it necessary to remind all of our patriotic
brothers of Hungary, of October 1849 exactly 109 years ago
almost to the very day, when the Governor of Hungary Lajos
Kossuth, joined with Polish General Jozsef Bem and fought for
Hungarian Independence winning many victories at the beginning
only to have our hopes and dreams dashed when Russia
intervened on the side of the Austrians and deprived Hungary of
the freedom we humanly deserve. Once again we find ourselves

dominated by the same invading aggressor, or have we ever been free from them? Early this year Polish workers demonstrated against <u>that</u> aggressor and as a result, it was revealed yesterday they have won for themselves substantial concessions. And don't forget all Russian troops pulled out of Austria last year.
Can you see the significance of why we must unite and act now?
See you soon our fellow patriots.**"**

No one passed comment at first until Peter requested that someone should say something.
Nandi took a deep breath through his nose before responding,

"Did you all know there is a stone tablet in Hero's Square Budapest with commemorative words carved into it paying tribute to those who died for national freedom and independence in 1849? And did any of you know that the Chain Bridge in Budapest was built in November 1849 and then rebuilt exactly 100 years later to the day in 1949?"

Each student shrugged to each other in a puzzled mannerism until one of them asked,
"And your point is..?"

"My point is simply this.. How history evolves!"

"But what about the request from the Budapest students to rise up and gel together in a hope to challenge the Soviet system to give us our freedom?"

Jancsi decided to answer Attila's question.

"I think we must first find out what happened in yesterday's meeting at Szeged, then find out what they plan to do next. But I can't help feeling that this is going to get bloody. As Nandi says and I'm sure he means when he says, how history evolves, that

this could be a repeat of the uprising of 1849. I cannot see Russia
bending easily; they are still smarting from World War 2. So if we
join up, then we must be prepared to die for our country. What say
the rest of you?"

The library was in full agreement with the room full of feeling
that after years of suffocation they could be finally in a position
when they could do something about it. But Nandi spoke out
again.

"I feel we cannot win a battle with Russia without any backing
from the west for what we do. We have been ignored and deserted
by the likes of England, France and America before. The cold war
divides Europe; I really don't know how the west would respond
to us standing up to Russia. I would hope they would back us but I
just don't know."

"Surely they wouldn't leave us to the slaughter?" A younger
student Tibor piped up and asked.
Nandi continued.

"Well, I am eighteen years of age, I have many certificates of
education already and next year is my final graduation year before
I move on to University. I think to negotiate with the west is our
only chance forward. If that fails, education is the key to freedom,
not violence."
Imre then decided to challenge Nandi's comments.

"Nandi, maybe there will not be any violence. Maybe violence
isn't necessary. But I can tell you Nandi if violence comes our
way then I for one am prepared to stand up to these Russian
bastards. Do you know they have tortured my entire family? My
father committed suicide two years ago because of the Russian
bullies. Do you know why they bullied him? Because he couldn't
remember some history about Matyas Rakosi's life, they asked

him to repeat a certain page from the Communist book at a
seminar and he couldn't remember it. Are you a coward Nandi?"

Nandi stood up slowly and brushed the creases from his trousers.
The room stared at Nandi and Imre with an uncomfortable glare.
Step by step, slowly he moved a little closer to Imre ensuring his
frown scorched Imre's face.

"In answer to your first questions about your father. No I didn't
know what they had done to him. And the answer to your last
question. Is **no** also. I am not a coward; I like to think I would use
my brain first before my brawn. I would die for my country, but
these are only words, when the words are carved into your heart
that is what will make you a true Hungarian. Faithful towards
your country's honour, to the bitter end. Can you really tell me
that these words are truly carved into your heart or are your words
just rage? Because I can tell you that what is in my heart goes
beyond rage. Now I have a question for you Imre, could you make
your words count? Like on a battlefield?"
Nandi gave Imre a chance to answer but he said nothing only
bowed his head towards the floor.
"So you don't know the answer. Well I will tell you and I will tell
you all, I will continue to monitor this situation with much
attention. But that is my position today and I will leave you all to
continue the meeting without me."
Nandi walked over to the library door, unlocked it, threw the key
to Jancsi and left closing the door behind him.

A younger student called out from the back.
"Is he a coward? Because he his bigger than anyone in this room,
I would imagine he could stand up for himself."
Jancsi came to Nandi's defence.
"Let me put it this way, if I were to face a gang or an army, I
would want Nandi to be on my side."
Peter then diffused the concern for Nandi.

"Okay, let's forget him for the moment. I know Nandi! He will be with us when the time is right when it is crucial. I put forward that our position is to back up their move towards challenging the Communist system, but find out what happened yesterday in Szeged and find out what they plan to do next. All those who agree raise their hands."

All agreed.

SZANTO BOARDING COLLEGE. October 23rd 1956. 4:a.m.

Nandi was sharply awakened by Laszi excitedly shaking him by his right shoulder and whispering as loud as he dared.
"Nandi, Nandi, wake up, quickly."

"What the hell is going on? What time is it?"

"It's four o'clock in the morning. C'mon get dressed, big news just in from Budapest."

Nandi threw back his quilt and lifted his feet out of the bed onto the floor. Laszi lit two large candles in order to keep the early meeting as concealed and conspicuous as possible but at the same time allowing enough light to help Nandi find his clothes. Nandi checked the other beds.

"Where are the others?"

"They went down to the library half an hour ago, everybody is gathering in there but we all insisted you should be there to hear it."

"Okay Laszi, you go to them. Tell them I will be five minutes."

Nandi entered the dim lit library illuminated only by a lantern that Peter was holding and seven or eight cigarette ends.

October 23rd 1956

As Jancsi locked the door behind Nandi, Peter began,

"Okay now everyone is here I can tell you that a huge meeting has been taking place all night in Budapest between their newly formed student organisation. According to sources, there has been much talked about and plenty decided. In order to get the message throughout the country, representatives on motorcycles have delivered the information from one college to another."

"You mean someone from Budapest has travelled all the way to here on a motorcycle?" Tibor questioned.

"No not like that. What they have organised is, they have drove to a few universities on the outskirts of Budapest, passed out the information, then delegates from there have delivered to further colleges and so on. For example this information we have here has come from Szikszo, they got it from Miskolc, they from Mezokovesd, they received theirs from Gyongyos and of course Gyongyos received their information from Budapest. The plan has spread like a forest fire."

"So what is happening? What do they plan to do?" Bela called out to Peter.

"If everyone grabs a sheet off this pile you will see what they are proposing in writing. What we have here is a copy of sixteen points the people of Hungary are demanding, compiled by the students of Budapest."
Everyone took a copy but found it difficult to read owing to the dullness in the library. Peter took held the lantern over the paper and began reading it.

" The Students Sixteen Points

Copy this and spread it among the Hungarian Population

The Sixteen Political, Economical and Ideological Points of the Resolution

Adopted at The Plenary Meeting of the Building Industry Technological University

Students of Budapest!

The following resolution was born on 22 October 1956, at the dawn of a new period in Hungarian history, in the Hall of the Building Industry Technological University as a result of the spontaneous movement of several thousand of the Hungarian youth who love their Fatherland:

(1) We demand the immediate withdrawal of all Soviet troops in accordance with the provisions of the Peace Treaty.

(2) We demand the election of new leaders in the Hungarian Workers' Party on the low, medium and high levels by secret ballot from the ranks upwards. These leaders should convene the Party Congress within the shortest possible time and should elect a new central body of leaders.

(3) The Government should be reconstituted under the leadership of Comrade Imre Nagy; all criminal leaders of the Stalinist-Rakosi era should be relieved of their posts at once.

(4) We demand a public trial in the criminal case of Milidly Farkas and his accomplices. Matyas Rakosi, who is primarily responsible for all the crimes of the recent past and for the ruin of this country, should be brought home and brought before a People's Court of judgment.

(5) We demand general elections in this country, with universal suffrage, secret ballot and the participation of several Parties for the purpose of electing a new National Assembly. We demand that the workers should have the right to strike.

(6) We demand a re-examination and re-adjustment of Hungarian-Soviet and Hungarian-Yugoslav political, economic and intellectual relations on the basis of complete political and economic equality and of non-intervention in each other's internal affairs.

(7) We demand the re-organization of the entire economic life of Hungary, with the assistance of specialists. Our whole economic system based on planned economy should be re-examined with an eve to Hungarian conditions and to the vital interests of the Hungarian people.

(8) Our foreign trade agreements and the real figures in respect of reparations that can never be paid should be made public. We demand frank and sincere information concerning the country's uranium deposits, their exploitation and the Russian concession. We demand that Hungary should have the right to sell the uranium ore freely

at world market prices in exchange for hard currency.

(9) We demand the complete revision of norms in industry and an urgent and radical adjustment of wages to meet the demands of workers and intellectuals. We demand that minimum living wages for workers should be fixed.

(10) We demand that the delivery system should be placed on new basis and that produce should be used rationally. We demand equal treatment of peasants farming individually.

(11) We demand the re-examination of all political and economic trials by independent courts and the release and rehabilitation of innocent persons. We demand the immediate repatriation of prisoners-of-war and of civilians deported to the Soviet Union, including prisoners who have been condemned beyond the frontiers of Hungary.

(12) We demand complete freedom of opinion and expression, freedom of the Press and a free Radio, as well as a new daily newspaper of large circulation for the MEFESZ League of Hungarian University and College Student Associations organization. We demand that the existing 'screening material' should be made public and destroyed.

(13) We demand that the Stalin statue-the symbol of Stalinist tyranny and political oppression-should be removed as quickly as possible and that a

memorial worthy of the freedom fighters and martyrs of 1848-49 should be erected on its site.

(14) In place of the existing coat of arms, which is foreign to the Hungarian people, we wish the re-introduction of the old Hungarian Kossuth arms. We demand for the

Hungarian Army new uniforms worthy of our national traditions. We demand that 15th March should be a national holiday and a nonworking day and that 6 October should be a day of national mourning and a school holiday.

(15) The youth of the Technological University of Budapest unanimously express their complete solidarity with the Polish and Warsaw workers and youth in connection with the Polish national independence movement.

(16) The students of the Building Industry Technological University will organize local units of MEFESZ as quickly as possible, and have resolved to convene a Youth Parliament in Budapest for the 27th of this month (Saturday) at which the entire youth of this country will be represented by their delegates.

The students of the Technological University and of the various other Universities will gather in the Gorkij Fasor before the Writers' Union Headquarters tomorrow, the 23rd. of this month, at 2.30 P.M, whence they will proceed to the Bem Square to the Bem statue, on which they will lay wreaths in sign of their sympathy with the Polish

freedom movement. The workers of the factories
are invited to join in this procession."

"Wow." Attila said standing back in amazement. "I don't know
about any of you lot but all this is giving me an incredible rush."

"Do you think it will happen? Do y' think the Russians will buy it
and bugger off?"

"Why shouldn't they? They aren't needed or wanted here."

"It would be a miracle if they only accepted about ten out of the
sixteen points."

"We shouldn't accept nothing less than the sixteen. There would
have been a seventeen if I had been there. I would have demanded
they apologised to each and every Hungarian before they left on
their way out for all the years of kidnapping, rape, murder and to
say sorry for the inhuman experiment they have been carrying out
on our people since 1945."

Peter held the lantern over towards someone at the back of the
room after he had heard something. "Are you alright there at the
back Matyas?" Peter checked.
Matyas was a younger student and was experiencing his first year
at the boarding college. He faced the lantern light and it was
evident that tears were reflecting off his eyes and cheeks.
" I don't why I am crying, I'm not ashamed of my tears, and this
feels like a very special moment, I'm just so glad I am a part of it.
I think we should all support them brave patriots in Budapest, my
prayers are with them and will be with them all day. For me
whatever happens today I am behind the protest march."

"It doesn't say there will be a protest march."

"So what are they meeting at the Jozsef Bem statue for?"

"Yeah it will be a demonstration all right. And I can bet these sixteen points will be pushed under the nose of Erno Gero at the Parliament Buildings. God I'd love to be there to see that. Can you imagine Gero and Rakosi's face when they read it? I hope they choke on their own guilt. Bastards."

"What do you think Nandi?" Peter's right eyebrow cocked up as he asked.

"Well, let's do as Matyas suggests. Let's pray. But at the same time pray for assistance from the west.
I think all our lessons are over by 2:30p.m this afternoon, so let's get back here for then, tune in to Radio Budapest and, take it from there."

Four younger students Matyas, Dinyi, Adam and Edvard stood up and Edvard spoke out for them volunteering more aid to the cause explaining that each only had one early morning lesson that finished before 10a.m.
After a little discussion Nandi asked them,

"See if you can hitch a ride to Miskolc city. When you get there go to the University in the centre, speak to the students there, listen to their radio, see what you can find out. If you manage to get back here for say late afternoon or early evening we can compare and entwine our information. What do you think Peter?"

Peter nodded and so did the rest.
"Yeah it's a good idea, if you four are up to it of course."

"Sure no problem." They all answered together.

Peter decided to adjourn the meeting from that point.
"Okay if there's nothing else I think we should get back to our
rooms before we stir up any suspicion. Our destiny is now in the
hands of the days events in Budapest, may we all prosper."

6p.m That Evening

"Perhaps you should give it up as a bad job Nandi. You've been
trying for two hours to tune the blasted thing in. The bloody things
knackered." Peter said irritably.

"Have you tried kicking it?" Attila remarked

"I've tried bloody everything. What a day for the radio to be
playing funny buggers. All I keep getting is some stupid women
singing and dancing the Csardas. Probably some bloody radio
station in Transylvania or somewhere."

Just then Professor Horvath entered the library.
"Problems there Nandi?"

"Yeah can't find Radio Budapest."

"How long have you been trying?"

"For two hours now. It was doing okay up until about 4o'clock
this afternoon and then kaput, haven't been able to tune sod all in
since. Except some opera singer singing about her true love has
buggered off with her sister or something."

Professor Horvath chuckled at Nandi's frustrations and asked,

"Well what news did you have up to then?"
Nandi decided to stand up and take a break picking up his
notebook as he rose to his feet.

Turning over a page of it Nandi began reading the notes he'd made from the broadcasts off the radio.

"The demonstrations began peacefully. It seemed only the law students had turned up with placards and were handing out their duplicated lists of demands. That would be the sixteen points. The placards read various slogans such as 'we want human rights', 'we don't want any form of oppression', even one had been reported to say 'Russians go home', I think he'd probably been drinking Palinka all day or something. More and more people joined the students, some probably out of curiosity, others fully agreeing with the demands and aims. The radio reporter said there were

people applauding the marchers from balconies; strangers from all over were running up kissing and hugging the demonstrators. There were red, white and green flags waving everywhere. People were wearing the same colour ribbons on their arms. The reporter explained how they congregated around the statue of Jozsef Bem and the Polish Embassy and by now after the morning factories had finished their shift, the industrial workers were joining in adding to the social weight of the crowd and the broadcaster on the radio estimated there was over half a million people in Budapest who had joined the protest. Finally, the last thing we heard was that there was some Russian tanks manoeuvring but weren't showing any signs of engaging and the crowds were now splitting into several other still large crowds. And that was the last we heard before we lost radio contact."

"Shall I see what I can do with the radio gents?" Mr. Horvath offered

"Please do." Nandi answered. "I'm going outside for a cigarette anyway; I need to get out of this stuffy library."

They all followed leaving Mr. Horvath to tamper around with the radio.

The lads stood outside the college grounds in small groups opposite the train station smoking cigarettes and exchanging conversations concerning the day's events in Budapest. Nandi stood quiet for a while just listening to the views. After he'd listening to the same conversation repeating in different forms he turned his back on them not in a rude manner and crossed over the road to the train station. He bit his cigarette tight between his teeth while he climbed over the low white gate and onto the train station platform. Curious, Jancsi followed him and also climbed onto the platform moments after only to notice Nandi scrutinising the train departure times.

"What you looking for Nandi?"

Nandi carried on reading and answered,

"Oh, just wondering what time the trains leave to Budapest each day."

"Why you're not thinking of joining the protest are you?"

"No, no. But I have just been thinking that this time next year I hope to be attending a university in Budapest. If this was then, I would be a part of this march most probably. Missed out by about ten months."

"Never mind that. This time next year we could be a free country. Able to start a family in a free Hungary, without any of the asphyxiation we've had to experience."

"Wouldn't that be fantastic? You know I'm going to marry a beautiful woman and I'm going to have two or three children."

"Yeah and me. What do you want Nandi, girls or boys?"

"Don't mind as long as they are free. Although my father has instructed me that I have got to have at least one son to carry on our family name Pekar." Nandi mimicked his father. "The more bloody Pekar's in the world the better.!"

"There are two too many in the world today in my opinion. Don't bloody want anymore." Jancsi joked
Nandi sniggered with Jancsi and then they both decided to scarper when they heard a train approaching the station.

Mr. Horvath met the students in the college hall and quickly explained that he too was unable to tune into any radio station that had made any sense. The lads decided to switch the main power off the radio and retire to their rooms reminding each other that Matyas, Dinyi, Adam and Edvard were due back at any time and would probably have more information.
As Attila, Laszi, Jancsi and Nandi began climbing the steps to their second floor dormitories they reassured the others heading to their rooms,
"Well you could say no news is good news."

It wasn't long before the four of them had fallen into an early evening sleep; a consequence of holding early morning meetings before a long day of rigorous subjects. Their nap was dreamless but restless and was interrupted by the last 10:19p.m train to Budapest, screeching, hooting and chugging as it departed.
"Shit! What time is it lads?" Jancsi called out fumbling for his pocket watch.

They all stretched their arms and legs without answering until Jancsi found his watch and held it to the moonlight.
"Bloody hell it's almost half past ten."

"We'd better go down to see if they've got back from Miskolc yet."

They trotted down the steps zipping up their cardigans as they went. Outside were groups of students and teachers in various group formations some on the grounds, others standing in the road outside. Conversations were calm but concerned. Nandi, first outside, checked all around systematically looking for Matyas, Adam or any of them. They weren't to be seen anywhere and then as they all shuffled closer to the road outside, Peter spotted them.

"Suppose you lot fell asleep did you? They haven't returned yet; don't know where the fuck they've got to but we are all getting a bit worried. The lecturers are shitting themselves and we are all in trouble if something has happened to them."

"Sod the bloody lecturers. C'mon we should form a few search parties and go and look for them." Laszi suggested.

"Not so hasty Laszi, perhaps we should give them a little longer." Said Attila.

Peter thought for a second and then told the four of them.

 "You know we've just been told by a passer-by dragging a cart load of hay that there has been shots fired in Budapest."
Nandi's eyes opened wide as he felt a sudden shriek of panic fill his thoughts.

"Oh my lord. How many shots? Anyone killed? Who fired the shots?"
Peter interrupted Nandi so as he could calm his reaction.

"That's all he said, that he'd been told by the landlord in Encs that there had been shots fired in Budapest."

October 23rd 1956

No one spoke for a time until Nandi lit his last cigarette. As he exhaled the smoke from the first drag he ranted out loud, "Has anybody had any luck with that fuckin' radio yet?"

Peter answered Nandi's question.
"We've just tried it, it's still buggered. Listen, we should all have a quick cup of coffee then we can think about walking in groups towards the number 3 road. I would have thought that they would come back that way, it is the shortest route back from Miskolc."

Nandi and the others agreed but suggested they should all sit on the benches in the train station, that way they would have a view across the fields towards Encs and the number 3 road.

It was almost an hour later when the relieving silhouetted sight of four lads could be seen approaching, traipsing over the fields. The pitch black field was camouflaging their lower bodies but the lighter darkness in the sky brightened by a half moon and a million tiny stars stood behind them outlining their heads and shoulders. Everyone stood to attention pointing and calling out their names. A few of them ran back to their rooms to acquire some blankets and a hot drink for each of them. Nandi and a few others ran over the railway tracks, leaped over the bare privets into the field, then strode stealthily over the frozen mud. As they met it was obvious the boys were weary and slightly disorientated, they leaned clumsily into Nandi and the others for a welcomed walking aid to the train station platform where the waiting students wrapped them in blankets and passed them mugs of steaming black coffee. There was an awful lot of concern for these lads and a thirsty intrigue for information. The four of them sat side by side on the wooden bench cradling their coffee's with dirty hands, smudging fingerprints against the enamel. Twenty or more students circled them talking to each other, firing unanswered questions to them one after another. Neither Matyas, Adam, Dinyi or Edvard said a word; overwhelmed with the attention they just slurped their hot coffees and let the steam rise

onto their faces and into their sinuses. Slowly, everybody
quietened down until finally nobody was saying a word. There
was complete silence only the sound of the lads lips sucking in the
edges of their coffee from inside the rim until Matyas spoke first,

"Have you heard?"

"Heard what?"

"What is happening in Budapest?"

"We haven't heard a thing, hardly. The stupid radio packed up on
us this afternoon. Nandi will tell you as much as we know."

Nandi continued.

"All as we know is the demonstrations began peacefully. The law
students had turned up with placards with various slogans such as
'we want human rights', 'we don't want any form of oppression',
'Russians go home'. More and more people joined the students.
The radio reporter said there were people applauding the marchers
from balconies; strangers from all over were running up kissing
and hugging the demonstrators. There were red, white and green
flags waving everywhere. The reporter explained how they
congregated around the statue of Jozsef Bem and the Polish
Embassy. When the morning factories had finished their shift, the
industrial workers joined in also. Finally, the last thing we heard
was that there was some Russian tanks manoeuvring but weren't
showing any signs of engaging and the crowds were splitting into
several other still large crowds."

Peter then added to Nandi's news.
"But we have heard a rumour only about an hour ago that there
has been some shooting in Budapest. So what do you know?"

Dinyi decided to begin explaining,

October 23rd 1956

"Everyone expected the students of Budapest to demonstrate against the Russian occupation. Instead, the entire population of Budapest have united. Students, workers, common people, women, children, professors, people of all classes came out onto the streets to raise a banner for freedom and have discovered they are not alone.

Everything was going according to plan until Erno Gero made his speech on the radio, which totally inflamed the situation and quickly changed the mood of the people. He denounced the demonstrators as enemies of the people and refused to even consider any of their sixteen points, threatening them with arrest, unless they dispersed immediately. But by this time the demonstration had split up into several different ones. One of them approached the Parliament building, asking for Imre Nagy to come and address them, while another group moved to the Budapest Radio building, requesting air time to broadcast the sixteen points themselves, another crowd headed towards Stalin square."

Dinyi broke off for a second and sipped his coffee.

They remained wide-eyed but silent as they waited patiently for Dinyi to continue but he didn't, Adam decided to take up from there.

"There were songs being sung all over Budapest, old men on street corners blowing the clarinet playing revolutionary songs 'Long Live Hungarian Freedom! Long Live our Native Land!' Other groups chanting 'We swear, we swear, we will no longer remain slaves.' And when 60,000 of them marched over the Chain Bridge to Buda and to the Bem statue hundreds of them were cutting and tearing the hammer and sickle Russian insignia from out of the middle of our flags, shouting and balling

'get this Russian emblem out of our sacred flag.' Everyone took up the patriotic singing and shouting and it roared across Budapest and bounced off the walls of the city. The hundreds of thousands of people taking part in this massive event wept unashamedly and apparently as well as the songs that could be heard for miles, so could the tears of joy."

Edvard then decided to chirp in to remind his friends of the feeling,
"So I know every patriotic Hungarian is feeling it now but can you imagine how the organisers of this rally were feeling when Gero shunned them. When he dismissed the points we all felt wounded of our national pride. We are hungry for freedom and independence and he shatters our hopes and dreams in one radio announcement. Then Imre Nagy, the one we pin our hopes upon, comes out at the Parliament buildings and makes a complete cock up. When he appeared, what happened? The Red Star on top of the Parliament Building lights up. Inevitably the crowd roars 'Put out the Red Star.' The light goes off. He starts talking to the crowd and begins, 'Dear Comrades.' Again everybody roars and hurls abuse at him 'Dear Comrades is a Russian salutation.' His speech eventually continued but was not a success he warned the people to stay calm and said the situation was delicate and everyone should go home and wait for developments. This simply enraged the crowd more and we all know why. He has totally missed the point; he's lost the fuckin plot. He just doesn't know what we want. It's now time for action; we will no longer be satisfied with the uncertain promise of gradual changes within the party and he thinks he can promise that kind of shit to us and we will roll over like some animal. Who is he trying to kid? Anyway, what happened at Stalin Square was the consequence of Gero and Nagy."

Jancsi, eager to know urged them to carry on. This time Matyas thought it his turn to tell the tale.
"Workers turned up there with acetylene torches." Matyas grinned inanely
"Acetylene torches, what for?" Attila asked him, puzzled.

October 23rd 1956

"They have cut down the statue of Stalin. It's true they burnt through his boots. Attached cables to it fastening them to tractors, pulling, cutting hammering until finally it came crashing down. The crowd cheered and cheered as it broke, crashed and cracked on the ground."

Nandi and all the other students cocked their eyebrows up in a stunned disbelief, silent for a minute until Peter began to applaud frantically and the rest followed. But they couldn't help noticing the four lads from Miskolc were not sharing the same enthusiasm. "There must be more. What happened next? Were there shots fired?" Nandi questioned.

Adam threw the dregs of his coffee onto the floor and took a deep breath to speak whilst the others bowed their heads in silence.

"At the Radio Budapest the crowd were growing anxious for some news because the authorities had allowed a small delegation in there to allow them to broadcast the sixteen points to the nation. The AVO sprung up and began throwing tear-gas grenades at them. Reports say it wanted to create confusion because then they began to make arrests in the crowd. Some people surged forward and tried to rescue the arrested and then…"
Adam swallowed before he continued as the words stuck in his throat.
"And then they, the AVO, opened fire with machine guns on the crowd. On an unarmed crowd they fired rounds and rounds of bullets into civilians. Women, children, old people, young people, mowed down, killed, murdered. The streets were flowing with blood and dead bodies."

Adam paused to give everybody a moment to reflect on the atrocity, the cold-blooded murders in full view of the entire world. Eyes were full; each student choked holding back their sobs. Nandi clenched his teeth tight and said,

"So is that it then? The AVO open fire on innocent unarmed people, killing children, just because we are asking to be able to live in our own country as free people. So because they are evil murderers it's all over. We are just to forget about our needs to be treated like human beings."

"That's just it Nandi. It's not over. The crowds have retaliated. They fought back. A people's wrath is a frightening weapon. They have taken cover, ran to some barracks somewhere, ransacked it, seized some weapons and are at this moment fighting in Budapest."

Nandi took a very deep breath through his nose and placed his fists on his sides below his ribcage. This news began an immediate surge of serious debate with them all, but Nandi turned and walked away from the group and stared coldly into the darkness. He frowned and began telling himself,

"The moment of impact has come. It has been growing like a large boil and now we are going to attempt to lance it. This is not just a movement of self-defence, but this is going to develop into an armed uprising to establish a new society…God be with us."

Nandi tilted his head upwards towards the horizon into the direction of Budapest, thoughts flashing through his mind. 'People of all classes onto the streets to raise a banner for freedom and have discovered they are not alone, Parliament building, Budapest Radio building, Stalin Square, the Stalin statue collapsed, Long Live Hungarian Freedom! Long Live our Native Land! Other groups chanting 'We swear, we swear, we will no longer remain slaves, cutting and tearing the hammer and sickle Russian insignia from out of the middle of our flags, it roared across Budapest and bounced off the walls of the city, hungry for freedom and independence, tear-gas grenades, opened fire with machine guns on the crowd, mowed down, killed, murdered, the streets flowing with blood, dead bodies, The crowds have retaliated, they fought back. We <u>are</u> at war with Russia.' "Dear Lord watch over our brothers in Budapest."

Nandi turned back towards the others and joined them. Adam stood to announce he had more to tell them.

"As we were leaving Miskolc there were crowds gathered there too. We have decided not stick around any longer because it was getting late and the students from the university have pooled funds for us to catch a bus back and the last one was nearing. We have turned a corner and in the courtyard of someone's flats we heard and could see gunshots flashing in the dark. We decided to take a peak and we noticed our flags hanging up around the courtyard with the Russian insignia cut out. When we moved in a little closer we saw them, the AVO policeman, stepping over about ten dead bodies on the floor. They were checking them to see if they were breathing and if any of them were, bang! They shot them again in the head. We panicked, luckily they didn't see us and when they were sure all were dead, they left at the back entrance. Within seconds dozens of family members of the dead ran to them screaming, crying, hugging them pleading with them to wake up. We began crying too and we fell to our knees when we saw that the people killed were girls and boys. Oldest was about thirteen and the youngest only three years old. Apparently they had hung up the flags all around and were singing freedom songs when a detachment of the AVO overheard from outside. A few minutes after, we arrived to witness the massacre."

Nandi felt dizzy with emotion. The feeling that was taking over his body was spreading through his soul like a cancerous growth. He was imagining visions from his childhood and the one that stood out at the moment was his own experiences in Budapest with his father years ago. He was remembering the lines of Hungarian flags perched out of every top floor window, leading towards the bridges of Budapest and his father scowling at the hammer and sickle. The clear waters of the Danube that stretched away into the distance under the sun. The edges of the river frozen but thawing slowly. The cliffs of Buda rising high above the flat plane of Pest. A thousand proud Hungarians encircling the re-opening of The Chain Bridge. A visit to the Parliament Buildings with the huge red star on its roof. The Arpad Bridge being renamed The Stalin Bridge. Nandi staring at the Stalin Statue's boots and trying to reach it with a mouthful spit. Heroes Square housing the statues of the most famous Hungarian rulers in Hungarian history. The words that paid tribute to those who died for national freedom and independence.

Nandi couldn't listen any longer and so he stormed off towards the college. "Where the hell are you going Nandi?"
"I'm going to get some sleep."
"How in God's name can you sleep on a night like this?"
Nandi didn't answer only continued on across the road to his room. As he disappeared into the darkness Matyas remarked, "So, he is a coward."

✳✳✳

The next morning all of the students had arranged to meet in the library for a meeting to discuss events. As the first bunch entered the room Nandi was already there fiddling with the radio.
"Nandi. Any luck with it?"
"Yeah, I did manage to get something. I was listening to it for about an hour when I lost it again."
Peter asked Nandi to wait until everybody was present before saying what he'd heard. Nandi revealed that fighting had progressed all through the night, resistance groups were forming all over Budapest and rumours of fighting in Debrecen and Szeged were filtering through.
"Oh and they have made Imre Nagy prime minister over night and he has called once again for order, calm and discipline."
"He is a dick head isn't he?" Peter stated and then Nandi excused himself from the meeting.

"Sorry but if you'll all excuse me, I have a 9:30 lesson and I want to have a cigarette before it starts. I'll be back later to see what I can do with the radio. In the meantime any of you feel free to have a go. See you later."

Nandi sat on the outside wall alone and then lit his cigarette. He was deep in thought when a rumbling sound interrupted his trance. He hopped off the wall and stood in the middle of the road where he had a better view of everything from all directions. He then saw what he thought was making the unfamiliar rumbling sound. Two 36ton tanks, about 9metres in length, 3 ½ metres wide and a huge 100mm gun spouting from them pointing towards Nandi and travelling from Szanto along the road towards the college. Nandi moved off the road and leaned against the wall and waited patiently for them.
"These have got to be the Russian T54 tanks." He said to himself

The ground shook and felt like a small earth tremor vibrating beneath his feet vigorously as the heavy armoured tanks rolled up and gallantly droned passed leaving a trail of smoke behind. Nandi made a mental note of the position of the grill, which he noticed it was beneath the turret.

Jancsi had heard the rumblings and came outside to investigate, leapt over the wall and joined Nandi.

"How many of them are there Nandi?"

"Two of them, travelling in single-file formation. Probably going to meet up with a few more on the number 3 road travelling from Kassa. They're going to Budapest. We are going to see a lot more of that in the next few days. Something I forgot to mention in the library. Erno Gero has requested for military assistance from Russia."

"Oh my God. We really are at war now aren't we?"

"Well let's see how long we can hold out for."

"Do you think we can win Nandi?"

"Yes. One man defending his home is more of a warrior than ten hired soldiers. We can win, but we need heart, passion, guts and if we can do that and win initially; we will then need military assistance from the west and then and only then we will be free. It's a pity we haven't got a bloody army though. You would never believe that in this day and age civilians would have to fight against a military trained army. You know the Russians will be no push over. The Nazi's killed 20 million of them but they still kept going and then pushed them all the way back to Berlin. We are not military trained our only weapon is our hearts."

"Who are these pair coming on bikes here?" Jancsi noticed them pedalling wildly towards them. As they got nearer they dismounted the bikes and pushed them alongside Nandi and Jancsi. They were two strapping size men aged about thirty and had a bag each hanging off their front handle bars with something heavy inside shaped like a bottle. A little breathless one of them asked,
"Eh have you seen two Russian tanks go passed here."

"Yeah. They've just gone passed. In fact, if you carry straight on just around the first bend you'll see them. It was only a few minutes ago. Why?"

The two men looked at each other but didn't answer Nandi; they just nodded, jumped onto their bikes and began peddling away quickly. As they got to about 20 metres away one of them turned around and shouted,

"Haven't you heard? We are at war with the Russians."

October 24th 1956

Startled by his remark Jancsi and Nandi began jogging along the
road towards the bikes. They hadn't reached the bend when two
huge explosions shook the air around them. They both dived down
into the ditch beside the road and covered their heads. What
followed was a shocking, repetitive hurricane of explosions like a
succession of firecrackers being let off one after another. Nandi
and Jancsi pushed their noses deeper into the grassy soil as earth
and stones burst into the air and clattered the road in front of
them. They were certain the explosions had finished but didn't
care anyway, and so driven by a concern for the men on bikes and
a sudden impulse to fight, they clawed their way out of the ditch,
back onto the road. Immediately they could see fierce flames
showing through the gaps between the tall trees that spanned the
roadside. Before they launched into a rapid sprint they both
glanced to the sky, forced to do so by a thick cluster of black
smoke that was swirling and spiralling upwards at great speed.
Nandi called out to Jancsi "Quickly, Jancsi move, move."
As Nandi turned the bend and approached the burning wreckages,
the intense heat from the glowing steel almost scorched his face.
He held his hand in front of his eyes to protect them and bowed
his head like a bull attacking his foe. He was only a few meters
away when the two bikes fell out of the flames onto their sides.
Nandi stopped in his tracks looking for any signs of life. By now
Jancsi had caught up with Nandi and stood at his side, both of
them now looking for any movement.
"Oh my God! There!" Jancsi pointed a finger

Nandi could see too, on the back of the first tank was one man
lying sprawled face down and on top of the second tank the other
man lay facing up.
"Christ they are roasting to death." As Nandi said it, a vile stench
reached them stinking of burning flesh. Nandi dashed like a
whippet and hurdled the fence of an opposite deserted farmhouse.
He quickly peered down the open counter-weighted well and was
glad to see it half full of water. With sharp speed, he unhooked the
metal bucket and spun the wheel with full force allowing the

bucket to plummet into the water. When it filled the tension from the chain tightened with a thud. Jancsi, realising Nandi's intentions, arrived and together they began rotating the well wheel as quickly as they could hauling the full bucket to the top.
"Okay it's here Jancsi fetch me that other bucket from over there." Jancsi darted over to it and brought it over, without hesitation it was filled and Nandi ran over to the tanks and attempted to quench the two bike riders. The water hissed as it was thrown onto the men but made no difference to the smouldering human bodies now almost melted completely into the tanks. Nandi stared in shock at their black charred skin. Jancsi called out to Nandi. "Nandi there was nothing we could do; they were dead before we got here."

Nandi stared for a few more seconds and then threw the empty bucket at the tanks in a rage.
"Bastard! BASTARD!" He shouted

Jancsi pulled at Nandi's arm and led him away from the burning wreckages into a safer spot.
They both turned and watched the bikes almost disintegrating to nothing and the remains of two broken bottles showed from time to time inside the orange and blue flames. Nandi wiped his streaming nose with the back of his hand,
"You know what they did don't you?"
"What?" Jancsi asked.

"Look, you can see. They have ridden up beside the tanks, one tank each. And then they've bombed it with a petrol bomb. They've aimed at the grill in the back, it sucked in the burning fuel and before they could get away it's ignited the fuel tank and boom. Killed the Russians yeah, but they've paid with their lives."

"How do you know they've used a petrol bomb?"

"I saw bottles in their bags. I can smell the fuel burning, blue flames, there are the broken bottles."

"Nandi. They are dead. They have just cooked before my very eyes."

Jancsi fell to his knees and began shedding a stream of tears. He was in shock and Nandi lifted him back to his feet.

"Jancsi. I too have never seen the likes of it before in my life. But we must be strong just think about our freedom fighters in Budapest. Right in the middle of the action, death all around them probably. They need us as much as we need them. As he said on the bike. 'We are at war with Russia.' It's time for rational thinking; so I'm sure someone will be here soon, emergency services, the AVO for certain. I don't want to be around when they get here. As far as we are concerned, we've seen nothing. So let's get back to the college, clean ourselves up and act like nothing's happened. C'mon we'll circle around the back and sneak in that way."

Jancsi wiped his tears and agreed, and then they both made the sign of the cross towards the men on bikes and made their way back to the college.

Luckily, the entrance behind the college was deserted and as they tiptoed along the corridors, through the hallways and main hall it became apparent that there wasn't a soul inside the college building. They both agreed that everyone must be aware by now of the tanks outside and as they realised that, they could see and hear a crowd gathering in the road through a classroom window. The assembly of students and teachers outside made it easier for Jancsi and Nandi to slip away to their dormitories without being seen allowing them to successfully conceal their involvement. By the time they had changed their smoke scented clothes, washed clean any dirt from their hands and faces and then joined the rest of the intrigued crowd, the area of road had been quarantined off by the authorities and the blazing inferno was now just a smoulder of small flickering flames. A few ordinary Hungarian policemen closely followed by members of the AVO approached the crowd; spoke to a few individually and then addressed everybody asking anyone to come forward if they'd seen anything. Mr. Horvath leaned forward slightly and explained to the policeman that he was certain that all of the students had been inside the building at the time of the incident. After a while they seemed happy enough with that explanation; Nandi and Jancsi were relieved but knew they could probably tell at first glance that two civilians on bikes had attacked the unsuspecting tanks and couldn't get away quick enough, consequently blowing themselves up. That was probably enough for them to know the assailants had failed to escape the blast.

News of events in Budapest crept in throughout the day and into the evening. The radio provided information at times when it was functional, passers-by obtaining rumours passed on what they'd heard. Fighting in Budapest and many major cities was now in full force. Rebels had seized factories, barricades were built. Ordinary people, who two days before had been factory workers, students, pig farmers, office workers, or anybody, were now seizing guns, ammunition, building a growing army and fighting the Russian army. Strongholds everywhere were spontaneously sprouting from within and standing up to an almighty superpower of the world. Their task was to defeat what appeared to be an invincible opponent with a ramshackle army of civilians, and to destroy anything in their country that was associated with the occupying forces. Reports were coming in that all communist symbols were being publicly annihilated. The fighting was ongoing but a winner had not yet been established. Nandi and the rest of the students sat peering from their dormitory windows occasionally watching a convoy of Russian military vehicles far in the distance assumingly heading for Miskolc, Debrecen or Budapest. That evening ended with an anxious, depressing emotion, as Szanto college silenced under a unified prayer for the brave, the dead and for the future of Hungary.

Thursday Morning October 25th 1956.

All lessons had been cancelled until Monday at the earliest the students at Szanto College were informed. Their instructions were to revise all the terms work from all subjects until then. A few had requested and were allowed to go home until Monday although Nandi and most of his close acquaintances had opted to stay. The water pipes to the college had frozen solid that morning and so after they'd all eaten breakfast they were forced to trek down to the river, break the thin ice and scrub their hands and face on the riverbank. After they'd dried themselves off Peter and Jancsi suggested parading into the centre of Szanto to attempt to hear the latest on the uprising. Matyas, Edvard, Dinyi, Adam, Attila, Laszi, along with seven others immediately agreed and jumped at the idea eager to get outside and weigh up the recent and local situation. Each of them hurried back to their rooms for certain supplies; cigarettes, hats and coats were the main things and as they scurried off Nandi announced to Peter and Jancsi he wouldn't be joining them.

"Why Nandi, why don't you come with us?"

"Well I've borrowed a screwdriver from Miklos I'm going to have another go at repairing the radio. It's our only communication with what's going on so it makes good sense to have it in working order."

Jancsi frowned at first but after, he nodded and said,

"Okay Nandi. But if you mange to hear something of importance on it catch us up and let us know."

"Of course, you can count on it."

The small gang of fifteen Szanto college students had been gone for almost an hour when Nandi had completely stripped down almost the entire component contents of the radio. All about him on the library floor were wires, electric circuits, large screws, and tiny screws until Nandi picked up the radio's transducer.

"What's that?" Miklos asked.

"I think this maybe buggered. It's the transducer."

"What does it do?"

"Well." Said Nandi. "It is a device that transfers energy from one system to another; it converts non electrical energy into electrical energy."

Miklos the janitor wore a blank expression until Nandi said,

"It enables the sound from the radio to be heard."

"Oh why didn't you say that, I've got one of them in my shed."

"Well Christ go and get it then."

"No, I can't, I've got to wash down the walls in the corridor, but here is the key to the shed go and get it yourself. You'll find it on the right hand side of the top shelf as you go in."

Miklos lobbed the key to Nandi and he ran outside to the shed with excitement and unlocked the shed door. The top shelf was high so Nandi had to stretch his arm up and feel along the top for it. At first he couldn't find it owing to a short handled axe obstructing his way as it lay across the transducer. He lifted the axe down and buried the sharp head into the bench top leaving the handle at a 45-degree angle. He reached up again and to his delight the transducer looked almost identical to the broken one from the radio.

Nandi didn't waste any time piecing the radio back together and he held his breath when he switched on the power. He turned the tuning knob with anticipation and found in an instant he had a clear radio station from somewhere. He listened hard to the broadcast for a few minutes until he heard Miklos enter the library behind him. Nandi didn't turn to look but said,

"I've fixed it at last Miklos. Your transducer has worked. Haven't heard anything yet though, just some news presenter talking about some trouble with the Suez Canal in north-eastern Egypt and England and France were getting into some argument. We could be about to have our country atom bombed by Russia and he was talking about some trivial issue in bloody Egypt."

"STAND UP NOW!" A loud deep voice demanded.

Startled, Nandi jumped with a hard jolt and turned his head sharpish. To his amazement, Miklos wasn't standing there but five members of the AVO had sneaked into the library behind him. Nandi's face clouded suddenly as he stared into the eyes of the AVO captain with his short, black straight hair flattened to his head, and a thin, long moustache that crept long over his bulging chin. His small, dark eyes looked back at Nandi at the wrong time. In a sharp flash of recollection, in a single second, the memory that had become a baffling cup shaped curve, making the most recent times clear, early in his life clear, but the part in the middle dip down into darkness, had now, in a split second, come flooding back.

"Captain Nistor." Nandi said out loud as his eyes almost burned a hole through him.

"I SAID STAND UP NOW!" Captain Nistor repeated but this time pointed his sub-machine gun at Nandi. Without redirecting his stare, Nandi slowly rose to his feet and raised his hands. Captain Nistor moved the barrel of his weapon slightly to the right of Nandi, paused, pulled the trigger firing a round of bullets into the radio, shattering and splintering it until it split open and spewed out thousands of tiny fragments onto the floor. Nandi didn't flinch, nor was he deterred from holding his stare at the captain. He continued to glare hard as parts of his forgotten past poured back. Flashbacks... Nandi was ten years old, he was in Mogyoroska, everywhere was covered in thick snow, Captain Nistor was striding towards Nandi, he began to unbutton his long leather coat and then removed his black leather glove from his right hand and stuffed it into his left coat pocket he stopped within inches from him. As sharp as lightening Nandi's head jolted to one side as the captain swung and slapped Nandi's left cheek with the flat of his right hand. Then it was three years ago... As the car approached he could see two men in the front but the backseat had at least four people crammed in. Their heads bobbed around as if some kind of a struggle was happening. Nandi caught sight of the driver and had a familiar feeling when his face became clear with his short, black straight hair flattened to his head, a thin, long moustache that crept long over his bulging chin and his small, dark eyes. A man was choking Irinka on the backseat and another held a pistol to her head. A hand covered her mouth and her face clearly smeared in bright red blood.

For three years that scene had tormented Nandi until he almost went out of his mind. And now, it had come together. The hours, weeks and months of persistent agonizing mental torture, trying to put together the missing jigsaw piece had now emerged. It was Captain Nistor who had probably ordered the arrest and murder of Irinka, the same Captain Nistor who had arrested Peter Csonka, the same Captain Nistor who had slapped his face as a child and the same Captain Nistor who stood before him now with a submachine gun in his hand.

"How do you know my name?" Nandi then knew he hadn't recognised him and he didn't answer.

Captain Nistor walked to Nandi, grabbed him by his collar and brutally pushed him against the wall.

"I said.." Before he continued he pushed the barrel of the submachine gun under Nandi's chin.
"How do you know my name? And where are the rest of the students?"

Nandi stared down at Captain Nistor and replied,

"I know your name because I have a good memory for names and the rest of the students have gone for a walk into the town."

The captain responded with a grin, released Nandi and pulled the barrel away from his jaw.

"Thank you." He turned to the other four AVO policemen and gave his orders.

"Okay. You heard him they're in town. Let's go and make sure they aren't up to any mischief."
They all rushed out of the library leaving Nandi standing alone with the shot up radio. He turned to face the wall with gritted teeth. He panted through his nose heavily until. Then, the volcano erupted. He ran with leopard like stealth out of the library along the corridor, through the main hall outside to the shed. Before he reached the shed door, one of the AVO policeman stepped out from the blindside of the shed.

"What's the hurry?" He said with his arms folded and his legs astride blocking Nandi's way.

Nandi halted his sprint only two metres away from him. He stared coldly at him without saying a word. He felt the sweat gathered on his back and begin trickling down his spine, and then, Nandi booted the policeman with full force into his groin. He felt the pain immediately shoot up through his abdomen and into his mouth and he thought he was going to be sick. He yelped out loud but before he could vomit, Nandi punched him once, twice and then three times in both eyes until he collapsed into a heap on the ground. As he did, Nandi toe bunted him in the back of the neck ensuring he went limp before retrieving him of his revolver from his inside pocket. Without any hesitation, his bottled up exasperation that had now been released, causing him to cock back the hammer of the revolver, hold it to the AVO policeman's head and without any remorse he stared into his bloodshot eyes and said,

"The murderer will now receive his final payment." He pulled the trigger and then watched him die.

Nandi didn't ponder for long; he dragged him behind the shed and began searching his pockets. He pulled out thousands and thousands of Forints in crisp new notes, he was about to stuff the money into his own pocket when he imagined the AVO being paid by the leaders of the Kremlin for killing innocent Hungarian children, like the one's Matyas and his friends had witnessed in Miskolc. Instead, Nandi began shoving the notes one by one into the mouth of the AVO policeman,

"Choke on it you bastard."

Finally, Nandi removed his expensive leather boots and put them on before covering him with a Hessian sack from out of the shed. Before closing the shed door he pulled the axe from the workbench and ran with it back to his room, put on his long overcoat with the deep inside pockets, hid the axe in it, buttoned it half way up and shot back down the stairs. He held the axe firm against his chest through the coat when he leapt over the wall in an attempt to prevent it from falling out. Driven by panic and an overload of wrath, Nandi sprinted towards the town centre with one thought in his mind. He stopped when he was a short distance from the church and decided to check how many bullets remained in the revolver.

"Christ, there's only two left." He closed the cylinder and turned it positioned at the first bullet.

Listening to the shouting from beyond the church, he wasn't able to see anything yet but that enabled him to be unseen himself. He cautiously made his way to the church building and pressed his back against the church wall. His heart was pounding and he sensed some violent activity behind him. He clutched the handle of the revolver in his pocket, let go and then rubbed his hand against the handle of the axe. He wanted to look around him to see what was going on but before he did he looked down at both of his boots taken from the dead body of the AVO policeman. He was now ready to peep around the corner. As he did the shouting became clearer.

"On your knees! Both of you now!"

Only his right eye peered around, he stared at the situation like a primeval predator surveying his prey. Captain Nistor and another were standing together pointing their weapons at thirteen of Nandi's friends who were grouped in front of the red star with their hands behind their heads. Captain Nistor fired his sub-machine gun over their heads and demanded they stand still. Over to the right of the group, almost directly in front of where Nandi was hiding, about twenty metres away, to Nandi's horror the other two AVO policemen had forced Matyas and Imre to kneel down with hands behind their heads, fingers clasped together and were pressing the barrels of their pistols firm against the backs of their heads.

October 25th 1956

"What were you about to do to the red star?" Matyas and Imre couldn't answer; one of them was crying uncontrollably, Nandi couldn't tell which. Suddenly, one of the AVO holding the pistol began to laugh.

"Just look, they get caught in the act of treason then they lose control of their bodily functions. Look, this one's pissed himself."

"Get it over and done with!" Captain Nistor shouted over to them.

Nandi was sure they were going to kill Matyas and Imre. He turned and leapt out from behind the church and raised the axe high behind his head. As he took aim, his memory, that was playing curious tricks on him, showed flashes of his past again; in front of his eyes, he could see Irinka, they had both stood on the very spot where Matyas and Imre now kneeled. He could see Irinka gently waving to him and begin to walk nearer. Her image was ghostly but compelling. Petite, ten inches shorter than Nandi. The face of an angel. Fragile. Mystical. Her long dark hair flowing like a river and kinked at the ends just below her shoulders. The tight, yellow bodice clung to her shapely bosom leaving her neck and tops of her shoulders exposed. Her long dirndl skirt was a matching, paler yellow. A large white rose attached to her parted hair complimented her thick, dark red, sensuous lips that beamed across her dark tanned skin unveiling her bright white teeth. He could see Irinka and himself standing toe to toe beside the red star gazing at each other, smiles of joy breaking out across their faces. Slowly, he cupped her delicate cheek with his hand catching a finger in her large circular gold coloured earring. He gave her a soft but long lingering kiss on her mouth, she was pulling him closer. Then he flashed back to his heart stabbing tormenting moment imagining the occasion, also at the same spot, when he was staring down at the floor beside the red star at blood and pieces of flesh. Then, he noticed something swirling gently about him. He stopped its light movement with his shoe and then slowly knelt down to pick it up. It was Irinka's large white rose with only about seven petals remaining. He smelled it, he was certain that it had fallen from her hair during her arrest. He carefully placed the rose into his right jacket pocket.

The memory surge that stretched around him in a second hadn't affected his aim; he flung the axe towards one of the AVO policemen who was about to pull his trigger. It whistled as it left his hand, spun around three times and landed with a deep thud and a crack into the skull of the AVO man. He didn't move at first until he dropped his gun, and then, the other secret policeman noticed the axe jammed at the back of his head. Baffled and shocked, he looked towards Nandi only to be greeted by a gun blast fired from Nandi's revolver that pierced his chest instantly killing him before he hit the floor. The axed Avu fell forward onto Matyas by now spraying jets of blood by the litre load. Streams and streams of the red liquid gushed onto the pavement from his head, which was almost in two halves. By now, it had dawned on Captain Nistor and his partner that they were under attack. Nistor fired his machine gun towards the corner of the church where Nandi had stood, but he had moved back out of sight. Matyas and Imre pushed the two bodies aside, looked around and scampered for cover out of sight behind the red star. Jancsi and Peter who were standing at the front of the crowd managed to grab Nistor's partner, disarm him, and drag him into the middle of the seething students that now were attempting to kick him to death. Complete mayhem had erupted, everyone was an animal. Nistor had darted out of sight and hid with his machine gun in his right hand behind an opposite church wall. Nandi checked the area again and could account for three AVO policemen. But where was Nistor?

With only one bullet left, it had to count.

"Jancsi. Where's the other one?" Nandi called out, now squatting behind the church.

"I didn't see which way he went." Jancsi answered

"I'm right behind you." Nistor had crept around and Nandi now felt the barrel of his sub-machine pressing against his spine.

"Drop your weapon now!"

Nandi let it fall to the floor.

"Good. Now this is what we are going to do. You are going to walk out into the open where your fellow students can see you, with your arms raised and you are going to tell them to stop kicking the policeman. If they don't I'm going to fill your spine full of bullets, thus splitting you in two. Now move!"

Nandi stepped forward with his arms raised and shouted across to the others.

"Oy!"

They didn't hear him but just as Nandi was about to call out again, he turned around quickly and knocked the barrel of the sub-machine gun away from his body and then grabbed it with both hands. Nistor fired it but the bullets ricocheted across the floor. Like a tug-o-war fight, they both pulled and pushed at the machine gun. Nandi wrenched hard and swung the captain around, but he wouldn't let go. Jancsi and Peter shouted to the others to take cover in case the machine gun fired again.

"C'mon Nandi kill that bastard." Peter shouted over to him.

Nandi kept a firm grip with his left hand but released with his right and tried to punch Nistor in the eyes. He jabbed and jabbed hitting him around the cheeks and head, Nistor managing to avoid any direct blows. Suddenly, the machine gun went off again causing Nandi to clasp it with both hands. This time Nandi used every muscle in his body to shunt Nistor from this way and that, until he smashed him against the church wall. As he did, the machine gun slipped from both of their grasps and slid away from their reach across the floor. Nistor head butted Nandi in the mouth and punched him in the chest only to then be yanked to the floor. But, he found himself on top of Nandi clutching hold of his windpipe. Choking and breathless, he reached down with his right hand and drew a parachute knife from his boot-top. He directed the tip of the blade into his stomach and before he shoved it in, he caught the eye of Nistor and spoke to him in Russian. "The Russian language will die with you. This is for Irinka."

The blade got stuck on his lower rib so he had to thrust a little harder to ensure it sank all the way into his body. Within a second or two, blood curdled at the back of his throat and he fought for gasps of air. Nandi pushed him away with ease, then, stood up to watch a gallon of blood clog every air vent, choking the life from him.

Everything went silent and still…

"Fuckin good boots these."

Jancsi walked up and stood by Nandi putting his hand on his shoulder.

"Where did you get them from?"

"It's a long story. Well, we are well and truly at war now aren't we?"

Nandi strolled over to the revolver that had one bullet left, picked it up and put it in his pocket. Peter and Jancsi were following Nandi. He picked up the machine-gun and turned it towards the AVO policeman that now lay sprawled over the iron fence that wound around the red star. He opened fire on him but the magazine was empty.

"Fuckin typical. Here I am fighting for my life against a man who hasn't any bullets left in his gun."

"Wipe your mouth Nandi you've got blood around your lips." Attila told him.

The rest of the students had now hurried over to Nandi and stood around him.

"So what do we do now?" Tibor asked.

Nandi opened his mouth to speak but stopped when Imre and Matyas stepped right up to his face.

"You saved our lives. You saved our lives. We don't know how to thank you."

Imre put his head on Nandi's left shoulder and Matyas the other sobbing into his coat. Nandi was choked, emotionally; he patted them both across their backs.

The two lads moved their heads off Nandi's shoulders and then began shaking his hands and smiling.

By now they had all clustered closer to Nandi and one of them called out,

"He saved all of our lives." Then followed it up by giving Nandi a big round of applause. The claps were vigorous and Imre and Matyas apologised to Nandi,

"And to think we called you a coward. We are sorry."

When the celebrations stopped Nandi got back to reality wiped the blood from his parachute knife on his sleeve, slipped it back into his boot-top and said to Imre and Matyas.

"Okay time for you two to be heroic. Can any of you drive?"

"I can." Matyas revealed

"Right. We must throw the bodies of the AVO men into their car, but not before we have relieved them of their weapons especially my axe. Then drive them away as far as the village of Tokaj, dump the car with them inside in the forest somewhere. That way when they are found they won't relate them to us."

"Okay. But how do I get back?"

"Improvise, adapt, overcome."

"Shall we take their money? They have thousands of Forints in their wallets." Tomi told them all.

"What does your heart tell you to do?" Nandi asked

Tomi thought hard and everyone listened for his answer.

"I don't want their money, it's blood money."

"Precisely. Does everyone else share the same view?" Nandi called out to them all and got the response he expected. "Stuff their money up their arses."

"While they dispose of the bodies in Tokaj what are we going to do Nandi?" Peter asked.

"Us. We are going to continue the war, starting right there." Nandi pulled the revolver from his pocket, aimed it at the red star and shot a hole dead centre with the last bullet.

Nandi shouted to Imre.

"And Imre, this is your chance to get revenge for your father. Any nationalised communist, Marxist bookstores must be destroyed. There is one in Encs."

That day the students from Szanto went on the rampage simulating events in Budapest. Anything associated with communism was publicly and gleefully destroyed. The red star in Szanto centre was smashed up into tiny pieces, a replica of the Russian World War 2 plane was torn down off the post office and smashed up, red star flags were burnt. Then they did march on into Encs and continued their communist ridding campaign and ransacked the communist bookstore throwing all the books about Stalin's life, Rakosi's life out into the street. When the bookshop was empty Nandi passed Imre a box of matches and gave him the satisfaction of setting fire to them. Imre was pleased to strike one match after another and throw them onto the books and communist papers. When the flames soared Imre said to Nandi,

"My father is smiling down on me now."

"I'm sure he is. Have you noticed even when all this stuff is in flames, it still smells of shit?" Nandi joked making light of a serious moment.

Their mood was full of optimism, but although they felt like a gallant force and had contributed an amount to their country's task, they decided in good time to make their way back to the college before they went too far. They discussed their intentions, first reactions was of single minded tenacity and to hack their way through the Russian troops all the way to Budapest. But after sensible plans were decided, the main being to cut back across to Szanto through fields hoping to be able to conceal themselves behind mounds of earth, haystacks, tractors anything that might have been left lying around by farmers.

The weather was cold and gusty, and there was a light fog that softened the contours of the village houses in the distance. Infected by a kind of gaiety they walked in a military type fashion across the fields with the weapons they had retrieved in a zigzagged shape line, keeping equal distances apart. It had happened, the war that began in Budapest had spread throughout Hungary; they believed in what they were doing. There were no Communists any longer, they were Hungarians and they were ready to die.

Back at the college they all spontaneously knew exactly what to do, weapons were hidden, plans put into place. Nandi ran over to the shed knowing he must dispose of the body he'd hidden there. He was met by Miklos, who blocked his way and asked him,

"Looking for something Nandi?"

"Err, okay Miklos, where is it?"

Miklos picked up a shovel that was leaning against the wall and reassured Nandi,

"It is six foot under beneath the shed. I've had to drag the shed around a bit but it was necessary to conceal the freshly dug up earth. But don't worry it's gone, for good."

"Great! And, thank you Miklos."

Just then Matyas walked onto the college grounds returned from Tokaj. Smiling widely, he winked at Nandi and told him.

"Mission successful!"

Nandi was pleased about that and could forget about it now for a while, so he decided he had to organise something else.

"Jancsi, Attila, come here for a moment… Listen can you do me a favour and get me some copper wire, some Iron Pyrite, headphones, a cardboard toilet paper tube, some fine sandpaper and a small piece of metal for a connector."

Jancsi and Attila smiled at each other and they both said at the same time,
"He's going to build a radio."

302

"How did you guess? Because you'll find ours in the library in a thousand bits, machined gunned by that tosser I knifed in the guts. Serves him right, I'd just fixed it too."

Jancsi and Attila smirked and set off to get the required bits for Nandi's homemade radio but then Attila stopped before he went into the college, turned and reminded Nandi,

"Don't forget to earth it!"
"Ha! That's what you are here for my friend, to help me with the technicalities."

That evening the students retreated to Nandi's dormitory that was now looking something like a code breaking laboratory. Screw drivers, clips, transducers, coils of wire were the remnants of their makeshift radio scattered across his bed, on the floor and peppered here and there on his circular bedside table. Nandi had managed to rig up the bare boned radio to two speakers taken from the shot up radio out of the library. Two large candles allowing enough illumination to see the radio, lit up the table. Nandi sat in front of his contraption tweaking at the wires and its components, the others kneeled or crouched in a semi-circle, and acted as foundations for the taller lads who were leaning against their backs either sides of Nandi. The uncomfortable compression was somehow ignored or overlooked, the heart stopping suspense pumping their adrenalin reaching fever pitch took care of their needs to complain about someone who were digging their elbows in someone's back or standing on somebody's toe. No, the air outside was below freezing but body heat in the dormitory had soared the temperature to boiling point. The silence was broken when radio interference crackled through the speakers. Everyone turned their right or left ear towards the sound and then like a miracle a deep familiar voice began talking to the students from

October 25th 1956

somewhere in Budapest. " *So Janos Kadar replaces Erno Gero as first Secretary as a gesture, fighting still goes on in Budapest and throughout the country. Casualties are high on both sides; the streets of Budapest are red. The ordinary people of Hungary are now combat soldiers defending their land.*

Imre Nagy and Janos Kadar have announced that following restoration of order, negotiations for the withdrawal of Soviet Troops will go ahead and a reorganization of the government will be considered.

Avo policemen have been arrested, humiliated and hung from trees by the freedom fighters. . . . "

Just then the broadcast was lost, but it didn't matter. Nandi stood up and moved over to the window and his friends eased aside to let him through and then followed grouping together in front of the sill. Nandi folded his arms and stared out into the distance listening to the comments from the others. Janos interposed pointing out six warplanes overhead travelling from East to West. "Yes and look over there; a continuous convoy of Russian tanks invading, reinforcing their positions. 'Following restoration of order negotiations for the withdrawal of the Russians will go ahead' who are they trying to kid? Bloody Nagy and Kadar are nuts, for fuck sake we don't want a negotiation to rid our country of someone who shouldn't be here in the first place. We don't need talks, we are going to get rid of them our selves, and we, the people are going to reorganize the government." Nandi was angry and his words inspired his mates and encouraged Jancsi to continue,

"And that bit at the end about the Avo. At last the men who have spent years inflicting pain and suffering on others now have to fear being arrested themselves. It's great we shouldn't leave a single one of them alive."
Attila thought and then jumped in,

"But if there are heavy casualties on both sides, how the hell are we fighting against tanks and heavy artillery?"

Nandi answered,
"If there is one thing a Hungarian can do, he can fight for what he
believes in. We are fighting with our passion and patriotism and
that is stronger than any bullet. Free men we deserve and free men
we shall be. And I have a plan."

Before Nandi could explain what he had in mind the radio
broadcast recommenced causing them all to walk back to the
speakers.

" *Fierce fighting goes ahead as J speak, death in every corner, tanks
taken out, smouldering. There are reports more and more tanks have
been called in to deal with the situation. Jn front of the Parliament
Buildings today Russian machine guns situated on roof-tops
massacred 200 hundred unarmed civilians. We will continue the
struggle, long live freedom.*"
The radio cut off again for a second time and Matyas whispered,

"That wasn't the same broadcaster."

"No it wasn't. Probably wasn't the same radio station."

"That was a freedom fighter I'll bet. He's managed to get on the
air from somewhere trying to inform whoever maybe listening."

"That's right." Nandi said, wanting to be heard. "They need more
of our help. What we have achieved today is only the beginning.
We have now realised how it feels to kill and it's not a good
feeling. In fact it sickens me to the stomach and when this is over
I don't know how I am going to live with myself. But I have also
realised how much I love my country and fellow countrymen for I
would not attack anyone who hadn't attacked me or my country
first. And now the Russians aim is to succeed in one thing,
eliminating its enemy. It will crush and exterminate anything in its
path, so we must defend our country from being attacked in the

same manner as we have succeeded today. There is no way Russia will allow us to inflict humiliation on them in front of the western world, so now we must continue our crusade. We must prevent these tanks ever reaching Budapest. For every tank we take out, we save fifty lives of the freedom fighters in Budapest. This is my plan."

"How will we pull this off? We must have some kind of strategy." Adam quizzed.

For the rest of the evening they all sat around troubleshooting the plan. Nandi used oddments such as wooden rulers, pencils, paperclips, matchboxes and others to build and illustrate his military delineate. The quilt on his bed had become a bird's eye view of their strategic positioning and targets.
" This is the art of capture gentlemen; ambush!" Nandi said with a satisfied tone to his voice. "Now if you all have your objectives memorized, we should all get some sleep and remember, tomorrow we go to war."

All the students experienced an emotional nights rest mixed with a catalogue of fervency haunting their sleep. Fear, eagerness, nervousness, belligerency intruded a much needed rest but the rigours of the day aided them to achieve some hours of dream filled sleep.

Nandi awoke first the next morning but didn't rush after he'd seen it had only just turned 6a.m, instead he lay on his side staring at the floor running his tongue against the inside of his wounded lower lip. When he heard Jancsi stir he used that as a signal to go and boil some water for an early morning hot coffee.

An hour later they all met at the front gate and quietly they all outlined their personal role towards their primary objective to knockout as many Russian tanks as possible.

October 26th 1956

ADAM: "I am going to the pub at the village of Halmaj and there I am going to get pissed. Unfortunately I am not, but I will obtain as many empty beer bottles as possible and somehow transport them to the sunflower fields alongside the number 3 road and hide them in the dirt.

When I arrive I am going to find a shovel and dig up some large mounds of earth."

JANCSI: "At 10 a.m I will make my way towards the sunflower fields with my rubber tube, 5 of the largest plastic containers I can find, preferably enough containers to hold at least thirty to forty litres of liquid and I will transport them with the go-cart I am going to build now out of the wooden planks and pram wheels from the shed. When I am approximately six kilometres from the number 3 road I will look for any parked cars or tractors and I will siphon the fuel from them and fill the containers and then continue with the filled containers to the sunflower field."

ATTILA: " I am going to dress up as a farmer with dungarees and knee length rubber boots. Get to the rendezvous point as early as possible and with my pitchfork, collect as much paper as possible from the roadside putting them into carrier bags, hiding them behind a tree or something. Throughout the day I will note the times and details of any military activity that I see along the Number 3 road."

LASZI: "I'm leaving now to the sunflower fields but taking a different route towards the number 3 road passing through Inancs and then will walk east along the 3 road until I get one kilometre passed the Halmaj crossroads which is approximately the area of our rendezvous point. I have in my rucksack ten penknives, a small pick axe, Nandi's axe, drinks of water, 20 cooked chicken wings taken from the kitchen, six boxes of matches, a ball of string and some canvas bed sheets. If I'm stopped and asked where I'm going, I'm to say I am going to visit my aunt Zsoka who lives in Szikszo. She hasn't a bedroom for me so I am going to sleep in a tent in the back garden."

MATYAS: "With the money we've pooled I will take the train to Miskolc, find some students and request for some bullets for the guns we have acquired. If I'm successful, with my roll of sticky tape I will stick the bullets to my back in order to conceal them in case I'm stopped and searched. I will then try to get to the sunflower field without using the remainder of the money by hitching a ride or something."

PETER: " The same as Attila I'm dressing as a farmer and my objective is to dig four holes in the sunflower field approx. two metres deep, cover them with wooden planks and camouflage the planks with branches and straw."

TIBOR: "I'm going in the other direction, first to Encs and then into the village of Foro, at the side of the number 3 road there, is the beginning of a dense forest. I'm going to find a well hidden area there but what has a good view of the road and will also find a way to dig four two metre deep holes and keep them well covered. When that is achieved I will make my way to the sunflower field."

Adam, Jancsi, Attila, Laszi, Matyas, Peter and Tibor expected to be all together in the sunflower field by 3 o'clock in the afternoon.

Imre, Bela, Dinyi, and Edvard were going to travel together to the number 3 road but were to sought sanctuary on the opposite side of the road in a field full of evergreen trees, where they were to simulate the plans in the sunflower field. Holes, mounds of earth etc. When the day began to grow dark then the plans were to continue. Peter explained,

"At this time we will all be together, except for Nandi, when we will begin filling the empty beer bottles with fuel and stuffing the neck of the bottles with paper. We will then hide a quantity of the bottles in the dug out holes on both sides of the road and we will also place at least ten filled bottles behind the mounds of earth closer to the side of the road. When this is all prepared we will lie low, stay quiet and wait for Nandi."

NANDI: "I will be the last to leave for the field. At about midday today I will begin to discretely transport the guns into Szanto and hide them at the back of the pub. When Mr. Csepel returns from his wood cutting in the forest he always goes for a belly full of beer and leaves his horse and cart in the side street full of his logs and tree trunks. I will be waiting somewhere near to, when he is out of sight I will hide the weapons amongst the wood, steal the horse and cart and head to meet you all. I should arrive there for about 6p.m.

Have you all informed the teachers that you are going home to your parents for the day and that you may not be back tonight?"

After they all confirmed that they had, Nandi dished out a round of bread for each of them and they all decided they would have to nibble at it throughout the day.

"Well, good luck to you all and...See you at 6.p.m." After they'd all tucked their bread into pockets or socks they shook hands but there was no more need for words, their anxious commitment quietly concealed the nervous sensations that they were experiencing and, as if they had done it all before, they set off accepting the moment like it was a basic fundamental inborn part of their lives.

Nandi and Jancsi turned away from their departing friends and set out together to assemble the go-cart.

October 26th 1956

Nandi stamped out his cigarette on the dusty roadside. It was almost midday and he had been standing alone outside the college for almost two hours lost in the silence, meditating, studying the unsteady airflow blowing through the bare trees at the side of the road. His face was stern and serious, oblivious to any danger he was overwhelmed with thoughts of the task ahead with one objective, sacrifice his own safety, for the freedom of the nation.

In his room, he stared at himself for over five minutes through a broken mirror in his drawer until he gave himself a military salute followed by the sign of the cross against his chest. He bit the skin off the inside of his wounded lip and then began to dress for the occasion. His long overcoat concealed his baggy brown trousers held up with elasticised braces, covered with a collarless black-cottoned shirt. But more importantly, the dark blue coat buttoned half way, would cloak the 8mm Huzagol 35 M. rifle. Nandi held it up in front of his face and gave it a visual inspection checking the integral charger and empty box magazine. He then checked the turning bolt action physically unlocking the rotating lugs on the detachable bolt head that went into the receiver. The sights looked okay as he aimed it at the wall and then pulled the trigger. Satisfied, Nandi tucked the short rifle into his long, deep inside pocket. He had to smuggle five weapons in total out of the college, three 9mm Femaru 37M Pistols, the Huzagol rifle and the German made Mpi-40 Machine-Gun with its empty 32 round detachable magazine box. After lacing up his boots and checking the short, fat steel bladed parachute knife was secure in his boot-top, Nandi told himself,

"I'll do this in two journeys. I can stuff the three pistols into my pockets now and then come back for Nistor's machine gun."

The jaunt to the Szanto pub was nerve racking and seemed to take forever but within one hour Nandi had made two journeys to and from the college and had safely hidden the weapons under a heap of broken beer bottles behind the horse trough.

"I hope Matyas manages to get us some ammunition or it really will be bows and arrows against the lightening." Nandi muttered to himself quietly.

He then discretely searched all around him with his eyes and was satisfied that he hadn't been seen but nevertheless, he wasn't going to go too far away so as he would have one eye on the back area of the pub whilst he waited for Mr. Csepel. Eventually Nandi sat on an opposite wooden bench, pulled a pencil and his penknife out of his pocket and began sharpening it for something to do. Just as the nib had become long and sharp to a fine point he held it up against the ashy coloured crumbling fabric walls of the pub. Vision of the pencil was clear with everything in the background a blur; even the identity of the approaching man and his dog was unclear until he called out,

"Nandi! What are you doing out here?"

Startled, Nandi jumped up to his feet and stuffed away the penknife and pencil into his pocket. He swallowed twice before he responded,

"Father. It's great to see you….But, what, what are you doing here?"

Blackie jumped up with his paws on Nandi's chest and began licking his face. Nandi ruffled and patted his dog vigorously on the head. "How are you Blackie, how are you boy, good boy, give me a kiss."

Blackie pulled his paws away and began chasing his tail with excitement allowing Nandi to stroke his thick fur. "Goodness you've put some weight on lad."
After he had finished greeting his excited pet he ripped a small piece of his bread off and threw it under the wooden bench and then ordered Blackie to lie under there.

"Come here son; give your father a hug."

Janos clasped Nandi's shoulders with his large hands, squeezed hard and pulled him closer and kissed both of his cheeks. Nandi smiled appreciatively and said,

"I hope there isn't anything wrong. How's mama?"

"She's fine, she's okay. I've only been to Encs for some tomatoes and just thought I would see if you were around. In fact I've been thinking about you a lot just lately and to be honest I'm a bit worried about this war with the Russians you know, and I don't want you to get involved. I've heard that deaths on both sides are already in the thousands. It must be incredible for the winners and losers, if it's true we could be actually beating the Russians."
Janos paused while Nandi looked up at the clouds above.
"Anyway, that's another reason why I've come to see you. Don't you be getting any ideas you know about joining the fight. Today is Friday October 26th I hope you are coming home for the weekend, your mother is missing you and she told me to make sure you come home for a few days."

Nandi frowned hard and took a long few seconds to thinks before he answered his father.

"Papa, sit down for a minute." They both sat side by side on the wooden bench. "By the end of the day today Insurgent heroes from all over Hungary will have taken over the entire area between Magyarovar and the Hungarian frontier station of

Hegyesalom. In Budapest they are fighting the red army to a standstill. In order for us to achieve the freedom of our nation we must unite, if new political parties are to be born we must unite; if negotiations with Russia for the withdrawal of their troops are to succeed we must unite, if we are to get a complete amnesty for all the freedom fighters we must unite."

"But Nandi, we can't win!"

Nandi's eyes opened wider with a look of dismay and disappointment.

"Oh no! Father, father; no maybe we can't win. But it feels wonderful to be a part of the Hungarian history that has attempted to win back its freedom. No maybe we can't win, but we should show the Russian aggressors that we are humans and we will not let our country and our people be persecuted any more. We must make a stand and tell them that Hungary's sons and daughters are theirs no more and to fight for that is honourable and I for one will fight for that and to do that I am willing to take everything that Russia has got, I will rip out its heart, for my Hungarian heart is stronger than theirs."

"No son it's suicide."

"Father listen! In the year 1526 the Sultan of Turkey, emperor of all the Ottoman lands, turned his attentions to our small and proud country. Lajos, the brave King of Hungary was an inspiring leader of men. He knew he had to re-establish Hungary's army. Hungary had no chance of defending itself against an army of half a million soldiers. The armies of Turkey's empire were feared throughout the world, they had reputations of ferocious bravery. King Lajos asked for help from the West, England and France, closer to home, Poland. He was shunned, nobody was interested to go into battle and help Hungary. 'Let Hungary look after itself.' Were the words from the West. But still Lajos took to the field with his small army; he was not the kind of man who would bow down to this Turkish bully without a fight. The Turkish army invaded Hungary on horseback and the Hungarian army confronted them on the battlefield in Mohacs, vowing to defend their land and fight to their death. Thousands upon thousands of Hungarians were killed that day; they went down fighting with honour for the freedom of Hungary against a foreign invader."

"I told you this story Nandi when you were a boy."

"Yes father I have remembered it. In fact it is happening all over again only this time we are going to win. I asked you back then when I was a boy; I asked you what would King Lajos do about the Russians? And you told me…"

Janos interrupted
"That's something you will have to figure out for yourself, but I can tell you, in the   clutches of the Soviet Union, you have to put Hungary first, before your family, before your friends; if you believe in freedom."

He stopped and then looked back at Nandi.

"I have now figured it out father, King Lajos would do exactly as I am doing and every other freedom fighter is doing today. For centuries we have been plagued by an invading army, today I intend to do my bit to put a stop to it. And I do believe we should be free and to get that, I must put Hungary first.
Papa you have been teaching me this all of my life. What would happen to this country if all parents of the freedom fighters came to them today as you are; and said 'it's too dangerous you must come home for the weekend.'"

Janos turned away and pulled a clean handkerchief from up his sleeve and began wiping the tears from his eyes.

"Son, son, after Bela died when you were very young I made you promise that you would never leave me; and you did promise. I am so very proud of you my boy. You are still my baby son, but I can see you have become a young man before I knew it. A fine strong young man with broad shoulders. When you talk like this it sends a chill through my body, you are a patriot, a patriot with brains. Yes I have been teaching you, preparing you for this all your life. It's as if I knew this day would come."

Nandi intervened for a second,

"This war began for me from a baby."

" I want you to remember your promise to me. You promised that you would never leave me and I need you to tell me you are going to keep that promise. I do not want to know what are your intentions, I just need you to tell me that you will never leave me and that you will be with us at home in Mogyoroska when it is over."

"I will endeavour to keep my promise Papa you know that; but I want to be free."

Janos stood up quickly and Nandi too. They stood face-to-face, Janos exploring Nandi's expressions. He was satisfied with his son and was now certain he would survive and return home. With tears once again inflating his lower eyelid, Janos embraced Nandi tightly holding him close to his chest. When he released he pulled something from his inside pocket and passed it to Nandi.

"What's this?" Nandi asked.

"It's from me to you son. Don't open it yet. Wait until you are alone."

Nandi noticed Mr. Csepel approaching in the distance, which seemed to change his mood. He put the small pocket size gift into his pocket and hugged his father once more.

"Don't worry Papa; I'm going to be fine. Give mother my love and tell her I'll be home in a few days time."

"Okay son and just you make sure that you **are** home in a few days time."

Janos walked away along the road with Blackie strolling beside him passing Mr. Csepel's horse and cart filled with half trees, logs and branches. Janos and Blackie turned and waved to Nandi before they disappeared out of sight.

By now Mr. Csepel had parked the horse and cart in the side street as Nandi had predicted and had gone into the bar. Nandi decided to light a cigarette before rushing across, if there had been any suspicions from the locals Nandi aimed to diffuse it. After smoking it half way down he was growing impatient and so he couldn't wait any longer. He turned up the collar on his coat and walked briskly over to the horse trough. With one eye on the broken beer bottles he caressed the neck of the mare who snorted aloud and was appreciative to Nandi when he offered the remainder of his bread in his cupped hand. There wasn't anyone in sight so Nandi removed a layer of beer bottles with his foot exposing the three 9mm Femaru 37M Pistols. He picked them up and quickly crammed them beneath a very twiggy branch deep and out of sight. The Huzagol rifle was next, he shielded it with his body rushed to the back and slid it between the gaps of the bottom bundles of thin tree trunks. His heart beat loud and hard, he turned from side to side all was still clear and so, the German made Mpi-40 Machine-Gun and the empty 32 round detachable magazine was the next and excitedly he managed to conceal it in the other corner of the cart but made sure it was completely out of sight by dragging extra branches over the top. As an extra precaution, Nandi threw some of the broken empty beer bottles roughly around the areas of the guns because he thought if it was searched at least these areas might be avoided owing to the sharp beer bottles. He didn't want to delay any longer; he pounced on the quiet opportunity, untied the horse and jumped aboard whipping the horse twice sharply. It obeyed jerking the heavy load causing the cart to drag itself forward. The cart made loud wood snapping noises as it picked up momentum. Nandi decided not to check behind just buried his face behind the collars of his coat. "If Mr. Csepel comes out there isn't much I can do about it, so just keep going."

He was five minutes into the journey before it seemed he could breathe normally, he relaxed a little and lit another cigarette.

"Piece of cake." He said to himself.

Before he reached the village Felsodobsza Mr. Csepel's horse was strong and seemed familiar with the route and it allowed Nandi to pull out the gift from his father. It was wrapped in brown paper and the shape of it could easily be recognized as a small book or a box of some kind. As he folded over the corner, the dark green hardback cover of Janos's Greek Orthodox bible in the Hungarian language was slowly unveiling. Nandi looked delighted and turned over the first two pages to find a handwritten message from his father that read,

King Herrod asked John the Baptist 'if I gave you your freedom, what would you do with it?' John answered 'I would follow the one who I have made the way for.'
Nandi, if you were in chains as was John the Baptist and you were asked the same question, what would be your answer?

To find your true answer you must search your soul.

*Son, to handle yourself use your head. To find the
courage to seek freedom and confront others, use your
heart.
Time and space will never divide
Or keep my son from my side
My memories paint in colours true
The happy times I spend with you
To Nandor Pekar 26-10-56
From your ever loving father.*

Nandi inhaled deeply and then thumbed over the next few pages
quickly only to find a single pressed stem and petals of a Lilly of
the Valley plant. He very carefully ran his index finger over the
brittle stalk and then slowly closed the bible taking care not to
damage the delicate flower. He squeezed it firmly shut and placed
it back into his pocket. The message from his father repeated a
few times in his head until he answered the question of freedom,

"If I was in chains and was asked what I would do with my
freedom… Well, I am in chains and have been all my life, and
with my freedom, I would share it with others. Because, what you
keep for yourself is never really your own, but what you share
with others, will always belong to you."

Nandi was pleased with his philosophy; that, combined with his
father's message somehow inspired him and lifted his spirits. He
whipped the horse a little faster eager to meet up with his small
army at the sunflower field.

Nandi reached the borders of the sunflower field in good time. It
was almost dark but now he had planned to abandon the horse and
cart. Over to the right of him, off the roadside, was a manmade
pathway leading towards the planned rendezvous point. He made
the horse heave the cart over a small mound of earth and into the
field. Over to his left was a large cluster of trees of all types.

Some were bare some were evergreen and they had been arranged in a circular fashion. Nandi was sure from the centre of the clump would be concealed from the outside especially as it grew dark. "Perfect, I'll hide the horse and cart inside there."

Nandi pulled the reigns hard to the left and when the horse had realised Nandi's intentions, he began striding the cart towards the hideout. Looking down at his feet he was relieved to see a gunnysack full of grain and a canvas feedbag next to it. The nucleus of the trees was a perfect place for the horse to rest. Nandi tied the horse tight to a tree and then uncoupled the heavy cart from it. The horse immediately lay itself down on the ground but kept its head high, alert, hungry. Nandi stroked it and then decided not to attach the feedbag to his ears.

"Here boy, take the lot." He threw the gunnysack half full of grain down by the side of him and the horse put its nose inside and began chomping at it.

"Sorry boy, I will try to bring you some water later. But duty calls and it's time to go to war; and you are my get away." Nandi said to the horse as he climbed on the back of the cart and fished for the guns amongst the dark shadows. Nandi put the pistols in his pockets, held the rifle and the machine gun in his right and left hand. He ran to the perimeter of the trees and peered across the field in the meeting place direction.
"They're hidden well I cannot see them at all." Nandi said to himself

Night was falling fast and he decided that it was dark enough not to be seen so he began strolling casually across the field towards the number 3 road.

"Somebody's coming." Peter whispered.
Matyas crawled through the dirt towards Peter

"I hope it's Nandi… It is Nandi."

They all sat up and leaned their backs against the high mounds of freshly dug earth.
"Nandi over here." Adam whispered out loud.

Nandi heard him and started to jog and then sat down amongst his friends against the soil barricade blocking out any sight of them from the road.
Nandi's first question asked if they'd all managed to complete their intended tasks and they had. Up to now everything had ran like clockwork and while Nandi passed the guns to Imre to hide in the two metre deep holes dug out by Peter, Laszi passed Nandi three chicken wings to chew on whilst he relaxed for a few minutes. Nandi bit and peeled the skin off with his teeth and simultaneously checked around him.

"Molotov cocktails ready? Yes I can see them, and smell them. Matyas what's happening in Miskolc?"

"Good God you wouldn't believe it Nandi. I had to get off the train before it reached the city but from there I could hear explosions. I asked some people for directions to the nearest college and they showed me to one on the outskirts of the city. When I got there I saw a group of lads standing on the corner with rifles. I approached them and explained who I was and then one of them took me inside into a room where they were hiding some ammunition. I managed to get some for our few weapons but they hadn't got any spare guns or anything for me. When I asked for an update on the fighting they led me around onto the college gardens and there, lying side by side covered over with Hungarian flags were at least eighty people. I was told they had been massacred by the Avo two days before. When I showed my grief and anger he told me they had killed the man responsible for ordering the massacre and had retaliated well, wiping out tanks and soldiers in response.

The revenge was slightly reassuring but still sickened me at heart. I left shortly after and promised to help them all I could."

"As I suspected the whole country has united and are fighting. Okay quickly Matyas there isn't any time to waste. Get your bullets and load up the guns… Attila! What about military activity?"

"Every hour and a half tanks or armoured vehicles in convoys of two's or three's have been heading west."

"How close are they to each other?"

"Oh, sometimes just a cars length between them and sometimes as much as a kilometre between them."

"When was the last convoy?"

"Over one hour ago Nandi."

"Then there is probably another due any time now."

Matyas called Nandi over after he'd finished loading the guns.

"Nandi come look. Which one is yours?" Matyas held the plank of wood high and held a match down the hole in order so Nandi could see the loaded weapons.

"Mine is the machine gun of course… Okay guys here's the plan."

The sky had darkened quickly and it was now dark enough for them to manoeuvre about more freely. Imre, Bela, Dinyi, and Edvard had slipped over to the other side of the road out of sight. Nandi sat behind a wide roadside tree with his machine gun gripped in his hands. The magazine with its 32 round detachable box had been loaded to the gun; Nandi stared the 248mm barrel up and down and couldn't decide if the gun was shaking because he was cold or nervous. Peter signalled over to Nandi from behind the mounds of earth and then made a loud fox like yelp. Dinyi returned the call from over the road and now they knew the moment they had prepared for had finally arrived. In the distance the deep, droning, rumbling sound of three Russian T34 tanks reverberated the air and sent a vibrating sensation to the pit of their stomach. Nandi observed their approach from behind the tree and after he'd checked out their headlights he moved his head back out of sight in case the lights reflected against him when they got closer. The engines grew louder and Nandi tightened his grip on the machine gun until his knuckles showed white. By now he was sweating with dirt all over his face, his pulse rate soared but then they all felt a moment of shock when the tanks screeched to a halt. Their engines remained loud and roared a few times when the operator revved. They froze in their positions not daring to move or even breathe. Nandi couldn't see what was happening but he knew Peter and Jancsi must have an excellent view; he caught sight of Jancsi and beckoned to him. After a minute Jancsi crawled stealthily through the dirt to the foot of the tree to Nandi. "Keep your head down." Nandi told Jancsi able to talk clearly owing to the engines from the T34's drowning out his voice.

"What's happening? Why have they stopped and how far are they from us?" He inquired

"There are three tanks and it looks like they've stopped for a break or something. The tank commander in the front tank has his head popped out of the steel hatch and looks as if he is reading something. Nobody has appeared from the middle tank, but a soldier has got out of the last tank and lit a cigarette."

"Thank God for that, I thought they'd stopped because they'd spotted us. How far are they?

"They are about five hundred metres from us."

Nandi brushed the bristles from his chin with the back of his left hand and then said,
"Plans stay as they were, three tanks, hit the front and back tank first, any more than three we abandon the ambush. So if any more vehicles join them, we abort. When the three of them decide to continue we proceed as planned."

It was almost a quarter of an hour later when the steel hatch from above the turret of the last tank slammed open and a soldier appeared and began shouting something to the commander at the front. There was a brief exchange of words and although they couldn't be heard it was obvious that they were about to continue. Nandi slowly lay face down in the dirt next to Jancsi and aimed his machine gun towards the approaching tanks. Visibility was limited at first owing to a sudden wind that had caused the dust and dirt around them to whip and the twigs from bare bushes between Nandi and the road to flap with ghostly abandon. But the heart stopping reality of the situation dawned quickly on Nandi when the headlights of the front two tanks grew larger but the last tank had remained putt.
Nandi leaned his head away from the sights of his gun and realised it was true.

"Shit! The last tank isn't moving. The bastard is staying where he is. Look, that guy has lit another cigarette and the soldier from the steel hatch is smoking also."

"Shall we abort?"

"No!"

"But if we petrol bomb the first two tanks the last one will see us and no doubt he will pick us off one by bloody one. He'll probably blow the whole sunflower field to a pulp."

"We will not abort." Nandi stretched the strap from the machine gun over his shoulder so as the gun lay on his back.

"Nandi, what are you going to do?"

"Tell everyone to proceed as planned; I'm going to take care of that tank."

Jancsi had seen this look in Nandi's face before and knew there was no point in trying to dissuade him. His eyes had blackened like a shark about to attack its prey; he picked up one bottle of petrol with paper stuffed into the neck, crouched down low with his back arched and began to run, first away from the roadside, deeper into the field and then east adjacent to the number 3 road towards the obstinate T34 Russian tank. When he was opposite the tank he was about 100 meters from it and from here he had a decent view. He had to be quick if this was to succeed. His friend's lives were now in Nandi's hands, if they attacked before Nandi could put the last tank out of action they would pay dearly and Nandi knew it. By now the first two tanks were travelling slowly but were less than two hundred metres from the area of bombardment. Nandi scrambled through the earth and clawed his way as quickly as he could towards the parked tank. He could see one Russian soldier still smoking with his head out of the hatch, the other was now standing on the other side shielded by the tank. The rough terrain had ripped the knees of Nandi's trousers and blood oozed out of his wounds but as he crawled, the dirt seemed to press into the severed flesh and block the bleeding. Nandi was oblivious to this and couldn't feel any pain, he'd made it to the roadside without being heard or seen. Then it happened, there were two flashes of light, the chinking of smashing glass followed by a swift roar from burning fuel. Nandi knew they had bombed the first two tanks and as he stared at the Russian soldier he knew that he'd realised it also. He reached for the hatch but Nandi was too quick, he had already aimed his machine gun at him and followed by squeezing the trigger firing ten rounds into his head and body. He slumped forward and then fell into the tank. The other soldier hadn't realised his comrade had been shot. Nandi hid behind a tree and waited for him to show himself but he stayed out of sight for now. Suddenly the turret began to rotate and the 100mm gun lifted slightly towards the burning tanks and the surrounding ambushers. Nandi knew that there must be another Russian soldier inside who was taking aim. The moment was interrupted when one of the tanks exploded sending a gust of smoke and fire hurtling into the air setting alight nearby bushes and trees but illuminating the field. Nandi could see his friends now still firing their pistols at the tanks. The tank next to him began taking up aim again.

"Think, think, defeat the enemy, defeat Communism." Nandi looked up the tree and could see a small gap between two entwined branches. He jammed the bottle of petrol in it, which began to seep slightly through the paper. Then, with the machine gun on his back he quickly began scaling the trunk jamming his toes and fingers inside crevices in the bark. Eventually he reached an overhanging branch, which stretched out far and long arching over the tank. He cocked his left leg over parking his bottom between the tree trunk and the branch. Sitting secure, Nandi then leaned down to the side, stretched out an arm and recovered the petrol bomb. As he crawled across the branch he could see the other soldier below him, kneeling behind the far side of the tank, he was firing his rifle crazily one shot after another towards Nandi's friends, screaming. Nandi wondered why he couldn't hear a thing, the shots from the guns were muffled, there wasn't any sound coming from the Russian's mouth although he could see him screaming very loud. He looked over to the two tanks, the flames had stopped flickering and his friends were running, diving, throwing more petrol bombs, but it was as if the whole world around him had been put on slow motion. Suddenly the scene became familiar to him, for a second he couldn't see the tank or the soldier below him but could hear his dog barking, the grunts from a wild boar. It only lasted for a second; he shook his head vigorously when the tank fired a shell direct into the open field. The force beneath him almost caused him to fall from the branch; he had slipped but clung on tight pressing his right cheek against the splintered bark. His ears rang out and he spluttered and spat when the smoke from the cannon attacked his throat and eyes. He couldn't see if there had been any casualties, he was covered in a whirlwind of dust, smoke, fire and a smell of charred rubber. He hoped the soldier below hadn't seen him but he had to reach for the matchbox in his pocket and strike a match. As he fumbled he touched his father's bible and squeezed the cover. An instant later he was striking a match against his leather boot and holding the drenched bottle of petrol in his other hand; he was motivated and aware that he must move like lightening. Before the tank was able to fire off another shell, Nandi dropped the lighted bomb through the open hatch of the tank; a split second later he turned the machine gun on the unsuspecting soldier and shot him through the centre from his groin up to his forehead. Before Nandi could do much more he was engulfed in a hot flurry of flames erupting from the tank. He reacted, throwing himself onto the road behind the tank and then rolling away from the intense heat.

"Oh shit!" Nandi called out when he noticed his sleeve was on fire. He rubbed it hard into the soil at the side of the road but it burnt into his wrist. It was more than relieving when Jancsi poured a beer bottle full of water over it, but when Nandi saw it was a beer bottle he jumped and shouted at Jancsi,

"Christ it isn't petrol is it?"

"Don't be stupid man; it's bloody water. Here pour it all over and then let's go join the others."

"Oh my God the shell. The tank, it fired a shell; I, I tried to stop it Jancsi but I couldn't get to it quick enough…What happened?"

"Everyone's okay. A few cuts and bruises but that bloody Russian tank driver must've been blind or something he missed by a mile. He managed to cover us with soil but that was about all."

"Yahoo!" Nandi shouted. "C'mon Jancsi we haven't a moment to lose." Nandi patted his friend across the back and then ran down the middle of the road alongside the first burning wreckage and then towards the others. They all emerged from behind the hazy orange flames in their large group, Nandi and Jancsi greeted them with pats of encouragement but Nandi insisted they continue as planned quickly before any rescuers turned up.

They grabbed as much equipment as possible including leftover petrol bombs, made their way deep into the darkness of the land on the opposite side where Imre, Bela, Dinyi, and Edvard had sought sanctuary amongst the evergreen forest; and with Tibor leading the way they began to jog in a single file line towards the village of Forro which was to be their hideout and next part of their ambush plans.

Tibor and Nandi were the first to reach the hideout. Tibor had done well to find a suitable position just before Forro on a high natural hilly elevation amongst dense woodland overlooking the number 3 road in and out of Forro. Quickly, Tibor raised the branches that camouflaged the holes he'd dug and they both began to offload their equipment into them. They had just jogged fifteen kilometres across sludgy, uneven ground and were desperately in need of a rest as they slumped to the ground and panted heavily. The rest of them arrived within minutes of each other and did exactly the same dropping their equipment into the holes. Laszi was the last to arrive and after he'd placed two petrol bombs into the holes he unbuckled his rucksack and began emptying it until he pulled out three canvas bed sheets and laid them across the ground. He then instructed anyone who was injured to lie on them, while he would use the water to rinse them clean. Fortunately, there weren't too many severe cuts or gashes but Nandi took the opportunity to soak his wrist and allow Laszi to bathe his knees and tie some torn, clean material around them to prevent the bleeding. Attila complained of a blow to his head and when examined by Laszi he could see it had begun to swell. Nandi took a large knife and ensured the steel blade was cold; he passed it to Attila and told him to press it against the swelling for a few minutes promising it would reduce the bruised lump.

It was a long time after before they'd all got their breath back and began to relax. They had been through a traumatic event and were trying to come to terms with it. They huddled together sharing the remnants of the chicken wings and water and were awaiting their next victim. Their faces were streaked with blood, sweat and dirt but they all decided it was a good subterfuge and would aid them if the enemy decided to shine a search light towards them.

It was almost midnight when Bela returned from a lookout stroll and told them he had seen on the horizon in the direction of Kassa some kind of a vehicle approaching. From there it would be another ten minutes before it reached Forro if it was to pass them. Nandi jumped to his feet and insisted they take up their positions, check and re-load their weapons. As they examined the road below them Nandi quickly noticed a possible flaw in their plan and so he called everyone over quickly.

"Listen, if it's a tank we aim at the grill beneath the turret. If it's a military car we shoot the side window and then lob petrol bombs into the car… I can see a problem, we are too high up here we will never be able to hit the grill with our first shot. If we miss it could prove fatal for us."

"So what shall we do?"

Nandi walked a few steps away knocking the but of the machine gun against the palm of his hand. He stopped and then turned back.

"Look down there at the side of the road, there is a shallow pool of muddy water with a few rocks and bamboo stems sticking out above the water. If I was to hide in that with a petrol bomb at my side, as the vehicle passed I could easily get the petrol bomb into the radiator."

"What happens if they see you first?"

"Then I'll be dead, unless you can shoot them first of course."

Nandi was convinced his idea would work so he didn't waste any more time, he emptied his pockets passing his bible to Jancsi. He left his machine gun with Matyas but swapped it for his pistol. A box of matches and the petrol bomb was all as he needed to ensure he succeeded. Nandi ran and slid down the bank onto the road and ran across to the shallow muddy pool. Up to yet he couldn't here anything apart from the occasional hoot from a nearby owl. He stared down at the water and noticed a thin layer of crusty ice forming across the surface. Pulling the stem of a bamboo shoot out of the pool he realised the depth was probably just right to conceal his body and so with no more ado, he blew through the bamboo shoot ensuring the airway was clear and then undressed down to his underpants and boots folding his trousers, coat and shirt and hiding them behind a nearby rock.

"What the hell is he stripping off for? Is he mad? He must be freezing." Dinyi said to the others.

"Quick here it comes. Christ it's a tank. All alone too. Nandi get down!" Matyas called out from the trees.

Nandi didn't need any more warning and without thinking he lay himself down on his back in the freezing muddy water. His body stiffened as a thousand needles seemed to pierce his skin. He bit hard on the bamboo shoot and when he'd got used to the rapid temperature change in his body he quickly began breathing through the shoot. He was sure the black muddy water had concealed his body and he was almost grateful when he could feel the vibrations from the tank around him and could hear the droning engine from under the water. As the tank passed him, a dark shadow fell across the water and he was forced to sway due to the vibrating undercurrent caused by the heavy wheels and tracks of the tank trembling the ground beneath it. The shadow moved away and it signalled the moment for Nandi to pounce. Dripping wet, he leapt from the pool, snatched the petrol bomb and struck a match. It sparked but the water from his hands quenched it,

"Bollocks!" He ranted, but spontaneously flung the unlit petrol bomb directly at the radiator. The bottle shattered and flooded the grill and crevices with fuel and then the tank slammed on its brakes and ground to an instant halt. The large, pulsating, chunk of lumbering metal slid across the road slightly before it had completely come to rest. There was a second of silence, then a large clunking sound as if steel was scraping against steel and then the tank began to reverse itself, simultaneously the large barrel of the gun started its rotation towards Nandi. He didn't move at first as if enticing, almost daring the tank to attack him and then, he fired a single shot from his pistol towards the grill. When Nandi saw the bullet strike the steel body of the tank, he knew the spark would have been enough to ignite the fuel and flood the grill with flames. It was fierce, but when Nandi heard the screams from within the tank as the grill sucked the burning fuel into its body, he threw himself back into the freezing water to protect himself from the explosion. He stayed beneath the water until forced up to breathe and then flung his head back out of the water throwing curved shape droplets of spray behind him. He kneeled in the mud and turned his head towards his friends who had now encircled the burning wreckage. One of them fired two shots into the tank and then cheered.

"C'mon Nandi get out of that shit." Jancsi shouted to him

Nandi smiled and shook his head but did as he said. Even though there was a chilling fear inside the lads and a nagging trepidation that a consequence for their acts could at any moment present itself, they could not help but to almost fall about and roar with laughter as Nandi stood drenched to the bone, hair streaked with mud glistening like wet leather, wearing nothing but dirt stained white underpants and black lace up boots. He looked down and sniggered at himself but stepped closer to the burning tank and began turning like a pig on a spit which encouraged more laughter when the heat began scorching his naked body causing steam to rise from his skin.

"That's why he stripped; he didn't want to wet his clothes." Dinyi realised when Nandi pulled up his trousers.

"Of course… But I wish I'd had time to take off my boots too."

When Nandi had finished buttoning up his coat Jancsi brushed passed him and slipped the bible back into his pocket. Nandi squeezed it through his coat, nodded and winked to his friend.

Without anything but their reloaded weapons, abandoning their posts was deliberate at this stage to avoid capture. They were splitting up, keeping equal distances of about thirty metres between them taking a diagonal trek across field deep into the darkness intending to reach the awaiting horse and cart. Any sort of lighting aid such as a torch, cigarette or match was agreeably forbidden and signs of danger would result in everyone laying face down in the dirt until it passed. If an enemy were to be engaged upon, the lad with the machine gun would shoot first. The deeper they trudged into the marrow of the countryside, the darker it became and the louder their marching strides sounded crunching into the heavy ground. The burning tank was now a small flickering dot in the distance behind them and over to their diagonal right, dark smoke could be seen rising into the black sky beyond the crest of a high hump in the number 3 road. From a view from heaven, if the blown up tanks, Nandi and the others were joined up with a pencil, a scalene triangle could be drawn with the students at the tip and the first 3 tanks and the single tank at Forro in the bottom two corners. Now Nandi slowed his jog into a fast walk and the others simulated keeping their straight-line advances intact, but side stepped closer to each other narrowing the thirty-metre gap between them. Nandi turned, but continued by walking backwards and pointed out the triangular shape,

"Hey lads look! We have destroyed tanks on the road about seven kilometres obliquely to our right at Forro and then probably about the same, seven kilometres obliquely to our left."

"So what?" Peter managed to force out between pants.

"Well, we are here, seven kilometres from both recipients in the middle of baron land. We are the tip of a triangle."
They all thought about it for a while until Jancsi spoke out jokingly,

"Nandi, are your shell shocked or something from the tank? Shut the fuck up."
They all tried to laugh including Nandi through their breathless mouths,

"No listen, it just reminds me of our brilliant Hungarian football team, you know how they pass the ball around with tactical interchanging positioning from Hidegkuti and a mingling of short, long and triangle passes. Maybe triangles are Hungary's calling card in sport and in battle."

"Don't say that Nandi; don't forget we lost the World Cup final two years ago 3-2 to West Germany after being two goals in front." Attila reminded them all.

"Yeah, that's true. But if we are epitomising the Hungarian football team, you know winning battle after battle, triangles and everything, the only reason we lost our lead was because our star player Ferenc Puskas was injured. So, provided our star player in this war doesn't get injured, then we will go on to win it." Matyas added to the philosophy.

"And who is our hero, our star player?" Bela called over.

Nandi intervened
"The difference between the hero and the coward is, the hero is prepared to die. I think we are all star players and if we look out for each other then we will all be hero's and live to tell the tail."

Closer to the hidden horse Peter and Jancsi had spotted a farmhouse and went off to steal a bucket of water for it while the others took the opportunity to stop, sit down on the ground and catch their breath. There was an added feeling of accomplishment apparent in their term of phrase followed by apprehension knowing the mission was not yet complete. Returning back to the college, safe without detection, without serious injury or a fatality was approaching and it felt satisfying. They had intercepted four war machines, put them out of action, and killed maybe a dozen Russian soldiers consequently saving hundreds of Hungarian lives. Their part in the conquest to free Hungary was happening and was executed with courage and determination; they had added to the might of the Hungarian mutineer and for the moment, it felt gratifying.

By 4:00 a.m they had uncoupled the horse from the cart two kilometres from the college and left the horse to find its own

way home. Most of the lads had hid amongst the logs and tree branches in the cart, and when they respectfully dragged the cart to the side of the lane, they all donated a few Forints each, tied the coins up in a handkerchief and left it in the hope that Mr. Csepel would retrieve back his loss and receive the money as a thank you, as it was intended.

It was a relief and they felt impregnable when they each scrambled into their rooms and sank into their mattress. A short time after they had wrapped a blanket around their weary body, their sore eyelids fell tightly shut and a long sleep had barely began.

Midday was approaching when the last of the lads awoke. Very little discussion took place and for a while the day unfolded just like any other. Emotions were running high; no-one could make much sense of their thoughts and sentiments that could have been guilt or joy. So, instead of trying to fathom it out, it felt better to remain silent and just to continue with the normal chores of the day without disruption. After Nandi had bathed and eaten, he felt much comfort lying alone on the riverbank holding his burnt wrist beneath the icy cold riverbed and smoking a cigarette with his free hand. As the afternoon grew so did reality, Nandi lobbed a stone upstream into the river before heading towards the dinner room where the rest were congregating. They had already pushed four wooden, rectangle tables together to make a large square in the centre of the dinner room when Nandi entered. Nandi slid two chairs towards the tables and sat on one of them while everyone else did more or less the same to ensure there were enough seats for the meeting. Only a couple of lecturers hovered around the college grounds and under the circumstances lighting cigarettes in the dinner room seemed trivial.

"Fighting in Budapest and all over is escalating but there isn't any indication of a winner. The new government has been announced headed by Imre Nagy and Non-communists have been drafted in, like Zoltan Tildy and Bela Kovacs whoever they are."

"Tildy led the small Landholders Party, he's a good choice. Politically a good move. But what about Bela Kovacs?"

"Well, the Russians hate him; he was imprisoned by them years ago for his anti-communism and was only released last year. So, Imre Nagy's coalition is definitely the people's choice."

"Also they are negotiating around the clock with Soviet Troop commanders requesting their withdrawal. But the more casualties we can inflict on the Russian soldier the better this makes it for Imre Nagy in terms of getting the Russians out."

"It sounds like Nagy is at last coming to the party. Hesitant at first but now sounds like he's in full swing."

"What's next for us?"

"We must be cautious because I should imagine the tanks have been discovered by now which will mean a possible search of the area by the Number 3 road and certainly the next convoys will be more aware of an ambush."

"So, what do we do? When do we attack?"

"Tonight." Nandi spoke for the first time.

"Tonight could be dangerous." The response from Adam was cautious.

"War is dangerous."

"Perhaps a couple of us should make our way to Halmaj and check out the tanks and the area and then report back before we decide to charge in?"

The idea was immediately assented by all. Laszi and Peter volunteered to go.

"How much ammunition have we got with us?"

"There is a few rounds left in the machine gun and we have one full magazine and probably the same for the handguns and the Huzagol 35 M. rifle. But then there's some more hidden in the sunflower field with loads of petrol bombs hidden down the hole."

"If we can, we'll check they are still there." Laszi assured.

"We definitely need more weapons."

"This time we should probably forget tanks and wait for a couple of armoured cars or an unmarked Avo car or something, hold back with the petrol bombs, seize the vehicle and take their guns. If we blow them up, we blow their weapons up also."

Nandi then realised the best course of action and said,

"Okay then, this is what we should do. If Laszi and Peter go now the rest of us can set out an hour and a half later. Half of us can go along the lane towards Pere and Inancs and the other half head along the other route towards Hernadkercs and Halmaj, but we do not meet in the sunflower field. We cut across field and meet in the fields close to the Number 3 road at Csobad between Forro and Halmaj. Here we can rally all together, Laszi and Peter can give us the news and then we can decide what to do next. I think it would be better if you two grab what ammo you can carry to Csobad then we can be fully armed and prepared."

"So, it's decided then. Our mission for today is to seize more weapons. The time now is approaching 3 o'clock, we will go and get one handgun between us and a knife each and then we'll be off." Peter said and began to make a move.

"Yes and we'll set off at about half past four. See you in the fields of Csobad."

Three groups, two fives and a two, met as planned early evening in the centre of a very uneven field about one kilometre from the roadside. The chosen spot was heavy and hilly, deep in freshly ploughed soil. The twelve of them with their bare hands pushed the earth making a circular wall of dirt surrounding them. They crouched down keeping their heads below the barricade and counted the ammunition ensuring each weapon was fully loaded. Laszi and Peter couldn't wait much longer to tell everyone the news so before anyone decided what to do next, Peter began explaining;

"The three tanks haven't been removed they are still there but seem as if they have been shunted to the side. There aren't any bodies, they have been taken. They didn't find the petrol bombs or any of our ammunition, pick axe, axe or anything; but fifteen Avo policemen have taken over the village of Halmaj. They have ransacked the village made arrests throwing them into their own makeshift prisons. They are patrolling the village in armoured vehicles, they have rifles, machine guns, grenades and someone said they have killed two men. It is probably in response to our attacks and they are searching for clues."

Jancsi slumped back against the earth and angrily stamped his heel into the ground several times cursing as he pounded,

"Shit, shit, shit, what now? Shit, the bastards!"

Matyas added to the frustration and punched a hole into the soil and then snapped,

"We have too few weapons to do anything."

But then Bela suggested,

October 27th 1956

"We should go to Szikszo and find help, maybe more will join up with us and we can attack them in Halmaj."

"That's a good idea Bela. Hey and there is an Avo police station in Szikszo too we could burn it down." Attila pitilessly suggested.

Nandi then spoke out and summed the situation and plan,

"We need people, we need more guns and we can try and get them from Szikszo and then the plan is…Get back to Halmaj and shoot the fuckers."

Tibor laughed and then said,

"That's a great plan Nandi."

"Of course it is, simple. Shoot them all and so; what did one shepherd say to the other shepherd?" All faces sported half a grin and a blank expression waiting for the punch line. "Let's get the flock out of here."

They split into two groups of six and set out towards Szikszo in the darkness either side of the Number 3 road. When they passed last night's area of bombardment Nandi had a plan and decided to execute the plan alone explaining to the other five to carry on without him and he would catch them up. He proceeded over to the tree that he'd used to ambush and bomb the tank from. The tank had obviously been pushed forward away from its area of attack as it was a considerable distance from the tree and deep grooves were apparent scraped into the surface of the road where something had shoved it hard. Nandi dropped the pickaxe and his axe to the floor and then pulled his sharp parachute knife from his boot-top. Standing behind the tree, he began to mark out a doorway shape in the bark of the wide tree trunk of about half Nandi's height. The rectangular doorway was as wide as Nandi and went from the foot of the tree to Nandi's chest. He slipped the knife back into his boot, picked up the axe and began chopping into the knife grooves. The tree was old and felt hollow making it easy to dig out the doorway shape into the bark. When Nandi thought he was deep enough he used his knife again to try and wedge it in and peel off the thick layer of bark. After a while, working his way around, he managed it, and he pulled away a door shape from the trunk. He laid the rectangular bark on the ground, looked at the inner wooded tree trunk, tapped on it with his knuckles and then began to hack away at it with his pickaxe. A quarter of an hour later as he intended, the inside of the tree was now a small cut out room. He put the axe and pickaxe inside and filled the hole with the cut out bark. After he had cleared away a small pile of chopped splinters and threw them into the road, Nandi stepped back and checked out his work.

"Perfect; you couldn't tell if you stood right next to it."

A ten minute sprint and a five minute jog later Nandi caught up with the other five. By now Szikszo was only another ten minutes away.

Entering the outskirts of Szikszo was disturbing, there were gunshots in the distance and towards the south of the town, flashes of light stabbed the darkness. The two groups were now one, and now knew there was some fighting nearby. When they reached the centre, the shouting and screaming was somehow required to enhance the horrific scenes. There were bodies everywhere. Nothing was standing. Buildings were in ruins. There were cars wrecked and abandoned, some of them still burning. The worst sights were the dead, sprawled on every street corner, heaped in piles; some of them had rifles beside them. One of the frantic women ran to them when she saw there were a few guns amongst them. There had been an attack on the town only half an hour before and now the Avo had been chased back into the police station. Some students surrounded it and the woman begged for them to assist. The one's without guns ran immediately to the dead, armed themselves and then they all made for the police station. Moments away they saw grenades being thrown from the windows of the police station into the surrounding streets. The explosions shook the floor and then the lads split up and took up positions around the police station. Nandi joined two other lads hiding around an opposite street corner armed with rifles. The lads immediately noticed Nandi was armed with a sub-machine gun and began explaining what the Avo men had done and how many there were.

Suddenly a shot was fired from the police station and a loud scream followed. They looked across, visibility obscured owing to the dust from the exploding grenades, but through flying debris a man had been hit in the chest. Three men had rushed to him and were trying to stop the bleeding. Nandi stared at them panicking trying to drag him out of the line of fire behind an upturned car. When the victim coughed up a spray of blood that covered his face, Nandi bowed his head and when he looked up again he had had to have been left alone on the street as his helpers needed to take cover. Nandi retaliated along with the others and fired a string of shots towards the police station. Windows smashed, doors splintered, but the Avo had taken cover. Manoeuvrings around the station continued for another hour, they were hoping for the Avo to run out of ammunition then they would storm the building. But Nandi had grown impatient and insisted that he was given a grenade. Another group heard what Nandi wanted from nearby and even though they explained that it was their last, Nandi persuaded them to pass it to him. He took the grenade and put into his pocket. Before he set off, he attached a full magazine to his sub-machine gun and put the half used one into his pocket, firmly held in place next to the bible. With machine-gun over his shoulder he sprinted along a dark street and entered an empty house on the opposite corner. He ran up the outside steps to the top and climbed onto the roof and worked his way across the rooftops,

up ladders and down ladders until he came to the building
opposite the police station. From here he had an excellent view
of his target and the activity below. Now he could see exactly
which window and which room the Avo were occupying. He
pulled the pin from the grenade with his front teeth waited a few
seconds and then flung it onto the police station roof directly
above the Avo. Seconds after, there was a terrible explosion and
the front part of the roof collapsed. Nandi ducked and covered
his head to shield himself from the flying debris and grit that
rained all over him. It seemed ages before the earthshaking roar
ceased and Nandi could have a look. As he did, he saw the
damage the grenade had made. Smelling the smoke and tasting
the dust he peered over to see almost the entire roof, cratered,
and still shedding its structure. Still shots poured out towards the
surrounding army on the ground, but now they began throwing
petrol bombs towards the police station. Enormous flames
hurled from the ground making the nearby streets look like day.
Nandi fired his machine gun like a madman onto the surviving
Avo in the police station and after a while decided to go, and ran
to the chimney at the back of the roof to clamber down the
ladder.

Leaping from the last flight of stone steps, something prevented
him from continuing out into the street. A large dark figure of a
man appeared, still, but sturdy looking. His face was scarcely
visible behind the shadows, but he was clearly obstructing the
doorway. Nervously, he clutched the gun over his shoulder then
asked him.

"Who are you?" The man didn't answer he just stood still,
motionless. "Get out of my way, or I will have to shoot you."

Nandi stepped forward but so did the man. They both stopped
suddenly, suspecting danger, Nandi began to point the gun
towards him. Before he had a chance to fire a shot the man
struck Nandi in the face with his fist. The force threw him back

against the ground floor windowsill and the machine-gun continued on, smashing through the window and away into the dark shadows of the courtyard. Slumped in the windowsill, the foe drew a long knife from his inside pocket. The glare of the weapon reflected into Nandi's eye. He thought this was death but felt pretty calm.

"I am a member of the secret police, you are under arrest and you are guilty of treason. Your sentence is, death."

The man charged at Nandi with the knife raised high. Screaming he stuck out his boot burying it into his belly and held him far enough away so as he couldn't stab him. Instead, after swinging the knife and missing his target he sliced at Nandi's shinbone. Wincing from the pain, he shoved the man hard with his leg forcing him back towards the stone steps giving Nandi enough time to leap through the window onto the courtyard. Before he could retrieve his gun, the attacker had followed after him and managed to kick Nandi in his mouth. The kick forced him to the floor face up and the man had gone wild leaping on top of him. Nandi managed to grab his wrist and hold it tight preventing the knife from entering his body. They rolled and writhed, the fear increasing, knowing if he released the grip on his arm, he was dead. Suddenly, the steel blade of the knife plunged into his sinew shoulder. There wasn't much Nandi could do now, the blade was sinking deeper, blood was oozing and he could feel the knife scraping against the clavicle bone. He felt his arm screaming in pain and it was becoming weaker. In a desperate attempt to survive, he punched his face with his left fist and then clasped a handful of cheek. They both yelled when Nandi pushed a finger into his eyeball. Nandi poked hard and could hardly breathe and then the man jumped up pulling the knife from his shoulder at the same time. Stalling, wiping the blood from his eye, was fatal; Nandi pulled his knife from his boot and stiffly plunged it into his stomach. Watching him in the darkness, he fell backwards but stayed on his feet. The handle of the knife was butted right up to his skin. The length of the blade buried deep into the pit of his belly. He yelped out three times, didn't fall, just staggered out of the courtyard and into the street with a trail of dark red blood behind him.

Nandi shook himself, he had froze for a while, he couldn't get up so he reached for his gun and dragged it to his side. Then he didn't want to get up; instead he drew his knees into his chest and rested his forehead onto them. He started to cry uncontrollably. Eventually he tried wiping away the tears with his dirty blood soaked hands but it was useless, he couldn't prevent himself from sobbing. After, he gave up and just lay back on the cold cobblestone courtyard ground and wept aloud. His bawling was strident and echoed around him but shouting and explosions in the streets drowned out his own voice until he couldn't even hear it himself. Finally his emotional and physical pain choked his energy until he lost consciousness and lay as if in a coma, bleeding and hardly breathing on the floor.

Nandi groaned. His mouth tasted of blood, his eyes ached, every muscle in his body shrieked with pain. He made his eyes open wider whether the light hurt them or not.

There had been gunshots. He had better get up off the ground, he told himself, or there might be more. He tried to rise but it wasn't easy. He held on to a young tree growing in the courtyard for a while until the unsteadiness passed.

He wondered if he dared to take off his coat, the bleeding seemed to of stopped, but if he started wrenching off his coat he might disturb the wound. He did it anyway, by slow degrees, taking the sleeve off the left arm first, then letting the coat slide down, slip away off his right shoulder and right arm. He looked at the wound. It was a gaping, deep stab, into the front of his shoulder. Dried blood had clogged the bleeding and a large patch stained his black shirt. Fresh blood had begun trickling through recently probably as he'd woken, stood up and removed his coat. It was daylight, 'I have been here all night' he thought but where is everyone. He hadn't an idea of the time or what was happening outside. Eventually, he threw his coat over his left arm and with rubbery steps he limped to the outside. A strong breeze blew his hair as he popped his head out.

The street was desolate and untidy. Deserted barricades had been abandoned; trucks and carts had been tipped onto their sides. Newspapers and hay blew down the centre of the street and here and there Nandi could see bodies of the dead laying in the gutters. Sickened and panic-stricken, Nandi knew where the hospital was and decided he must leave this place and get to it.

As he entered the windowless corridor of the hospital he grew faint and a strange feeling of 'déjà vu' overwhelmed him. He was dizzy and thought he might pass-out so he held on to a wooden bench. And then, he was thrown into a frightening dream, a dream from the past. There was panic; it reminded him of illness and death. He could hear voices from the past all around him; he started to sweat profusely when the voices echoed. He tried to call out but couldn't, he'd been here before he sensed and now he had no choice but to examine the pictures from the past that were haunting him…

His mother carried Bela wrapped in a small white blanket into the hospital with Janos carrying Nandi at the right side of her and Doctor Molnar the other. The corridor leading to the hospitals reception area was long narrow and unclean. The floor was cobble stoned, the walls were bare brick and there was an aroma of vermin in the air. Equally spaced on either sides of the corridor were old wooden benches, littered every so often with gypsy type people who had found refuge, some were lying, sleeping. Doctor

October 27th 1956

Molnar opened the reception area door to allow them to enter. After they'd entered, they stood just inside the reception area. The doctor made his way towards a lady that sat behind a table. The room was dark, heavy damask curtains were drawn. There was a fire in the opposite right hand corner of the room burning a dull glow. The table had an inkpot in one corner and the gas in a single globe turned very low in the other.

Bela began to lash out a coughing fit; the nurses responded to Bela immediately holding him over a bucket at the side of the bed. Tenacious sputum loosened from his throat as he wrenched and with a fierce spurt, a rust coloured gob of saliva fell from Bela's mouth and covered the base of the bucket.

Nandi's vision was tormenting then as if in an outer body experience he was looking down onto his brother's hospital bed and could see and hear himself talking to his brother,

"I'm going home now Bela, but when I'm there, I'll make you a big prize, cuz I love you, when you come home you can have it; so, bye bye Bela, love you, see you later." Bela watched Nandi walking away from his bed and out of the ward. Nandi turned around and waved to Bela.. Before he disappeared, Bela managed to lift up his weak arm and struggled a wave back. "I love you too Nandi." Bela whispered.

✳✳✳

Someone squeezing cool water onto his face from a cloth disturbed him. He stared up at the nurse at first and then spoke to her,

"Where am I?"

"You are in Szikszo hospital. You've had ten stitches in your shoulder, I have put fresh dressings on your knees and your shin, also put an antiseptic solution in your mouth and all your cuts, grazes and burns have been tended to."

October 28th 1956

"How long have I been here?"

"You have been here since this morning. You were passed out, delirious in the corridor."

Nandi sat up startled,

"What time is it?"

"Please lie back." She eased him back onto the pillow. "You need to relax. I suspect you were involved in the Avo police station raid. Do not worry all the Avo men have been dealt with. Where are you from?"

"It's best you don't know Miss."

"Well wherever you are from it's good you came to help. The Russians were here before the attack on the police station but they left towards Budapest. The Avo and the Russians were animals together; they got drunk and went into the maternity ward here and repeatedly raped pregnant women. Their screaming went on for hours and hours; but they have been dealt with now, thanks to you freedom fighters."

"What time is it?"

"It's almost seven o'clock… Who is Bela?"

"Why do you ask?"

"Because you were saying his name in your sleep. You were repeating over and over, come back Bela don't leave me, I miss you, I love you."

Nandi pondered for a minute and sipped on the cup of water the nurse had passed to him. It couldn't be his classmate Bela…And then he remembered the dream,

"It was my older brother, I must have been dreaming about him."

"Oh older brother eh? If he's about my age and as handsome as you, send him to see me."

Nandi stared the woman up and down and guessed she must be about thirty something. He grinned a cheeky grin and replied,

"I'm sure he would have been, but you'll just have to settle for me because he died of pneumonia when I was a toddler. The last time I saw him alive was in this hospital, I think or certainly one like it."

The nurse caressed Nandi's forehead to check his temperature.

"You are much better now than you were this morning. Drink all that water, there's more if you need it, then have a good rest; tomorrow you can go home to your parents."

"But why? We must beat the Russians."

"Yes that's true, but your body has had enough pain. Your parents have had even more pain by the sounds of that, I'm sure they don't want to lose another son. Anyway a good looking lad like you should take care of his looks; maybe you should forget the war and think about settling down and having children."

"Is that a proposal?" The nurse chuckled and then Nandi continued. " You're probably right; my father wants me to have a son to continue our family surname for generations to come. But I know one thing for sure, my children will be free."

"Your father is a good man."

"How do you know that?"

The nurse looked over towards the wooden coat-peg in the corner where his dark blue, torn, bloodstained coat hung.

"The words in your bible, comforting; he's give it to you as a guardian angel to protect you. And so far it has worked."

Nandi sighed deeply, smiling at the same time.

"Did I bring a weapon in here with me?"

"No, nothing, apart from your father's bible of course."

"Shit." Nandi mumbled when he remembered. "I must have left it in the courtyard this morning."

Nandi licked his lips after finishing the remnants of water from the glass and said,

"I feel a little hungry."

He checked his attire beneath the covers and noticed his boots down beside him on the floor, his clothes on a nearby stool and wondered who had dressed him in a ridiculous white cotton gown smeared in spatters of red blood droplets.

"We have some slices of green pepper and salt. Shall I fetch you a few?"

Nandi blinked and nodded eagerly and then examined his shoulder dressing. The wound felt sore but was tightly wrapped in a single length of bandage that wound around his shoulder under his armpit and hugged the top of his arm around the bicep. He flexed

348

the muscle in his arm testing the stitching bending his arm two or three times at the elbow. He felt the repairs tug at his skin but the bandage had been wrapped enough times to form a thick padding and protection.

He chomped hungrily at eight thin slices of salty green pepper and swilled it down with another glass of water. His ward had only seven beds widely spaced with two other old men at the other end of the room. The other beds were untidy but the occupants were not present at the moment. His faculties were clearing by the minute, he had regained consciousness an hour ago and all events and dangers from the previous nights came flooding back. He became restless, fidgeting, tapping his foot, and twirling his thumbs until finally he threw back the bed sheet.

Before he moved his legs he thought hard of the whereabouts of his friends, Nandi knew he must find them. Were they dead? Had they been looking for him? Had they continued with their plans to liberate the village of Halmaj?

Nandi decided to stroll down the ward towards the two old men just to test and exercise his legs and joints.
The tingling sensations in his toes eased along with his stiff leg joints as he walked beside the bed of one of the old men. He had the face of a worker and Nandi felt at ease with the man's sympathetic expression.

"What should I do old man, fight or go home?"

The man reached out a hand and gripped Nandi's right wrist.

"The future of Hungary is in your hands son. It is better to live fighting for what you believe in than to die regretting what you could have done. But, remember this too, the loneliness of Hungary is a source of strength, an oasis in the European desert. Our fate is in our hands, we are a people that have been, and are being tragically left on our own between east and west. You have decided to set about the impossible in the middle of our loneliness. God be with you."

Nandi checked his wounds once more smiled at the man and rushed back to his bed. In a confident and certain manner, he was once again dressed for action somehow proud of his torn, black, blooded shirt and coat. They bore the scars of a battle for freedom and their tattered appearance warmed his heart.

Concerned he hadn't any kind weapon but not deterred, he left the hospital and searched the streets for something and found a half loaded handgun in the gutter a few feet away from a blown out Russian military car. That would do for now and soon after; his injuries were forgotten as he set for Halmaj on foot.

The walk was long but Nandi felt fit considering his wounds. The people he passed on the way weren't exchanging conversation but the few, to Nandi's surprise, seemed to be acting like this day was the same as any other. Feeding their chickens, sweeping the dust from their front porch were things to be done after freedom has been achieved, not something that is done when a world superpower is threatening your very existence he thought to himself and wasn't sure how to feel, but decided not to fathom it out.

"War does strange things to people." He whispered.

He found himself staring along the straight but now familiar number 3 road. As he marched along keeping tucked in off the road, he knew this area would now always have a battleground memory. The road scared him slightly like a dog sensing evil. He felt hairs on the back of his neck becoming erect; instantaneously he clutched the but of the gun that he had slipped into his trouser waste. Keeping hold of the weapon through his coat, he began to quicken his pace, striding, hurdling over mounds of mud. The turn off to Halmaj was in his sights and so he decided to cut across

October 28th 1956

field now and circle the village. When he was close enough to assess any risk to enter Halmaj, even though it was all quite calm, he cautiously took a route that would allow him to observe the village from the outskirts.

The night skies were pitch black and the stars weren't visible owing to thick smog that appeared to be hugging the heavens. Nandi ringed the village finding little signs of hostile behaviour. He now stood in a large garden on the eastside of Halmaj that showed signs of his own home. In the shadows, he could make out a pigsty, three haystacks a large henhouse and a barn over to his right. He could see a smoking chimney beyond, about two streets away. Nandi was certain that this building, illuminated by a single glowing street lantern, was Halmaj Police Station. He would know for sure in the morning but for now, he let himself into the barn, buried himself beneath a pile of straw and tried to sleep until at least sunrise.

October 29th 1956

He first stirred at around 4:30a.m disturbed by a restless cow that sat in a small compound in the opposite corner of the barn. He blew fragments of dusty straw off his face, rolled on his back, stiffened the muscles in his legs and clasped the fingers of both his hands together at the back of his head. He licked his dry lips as he made his eyes search the barn and focus on the shadows around trying to make out what was about him. He could see the outline of a pitchfork, a high shelf with different shapes neatly placed in a row and another row of garden implements leaning against the wall. When he rose to his feet the straw rustled and fell to the floor off him. Sensing an unfamiliar presence, the cow mooed once forcing Nandi to make his way over to it quickly. He patted it reassuringly knowing he needed the cow to remain silent. Holes in the wooden planks were convenient to check for intruders, when certain it was safe, he ventured out of the barn towards the henhouses returning to the barn with four eggs. He gestured and pulled the cow to its feet, dragged a small wooden milking stool over, placed an old chipped ceramic bowl under the cow's udder and began pouring his breakfast through her teats. He managed about half a litre of milk, cracked the four eggs into it and stirred it vigorously with the barrel of his gun. He lifted the bowl to his mouth and gulped it down hungrily letting the overspill soak his chin. After he'd slurped the last drops, appreciatively, loose coins from a torn pocket were emptied into the bowl and left on the dusty barn floor beside the broken eggshells. His gratitude was then shown with a deep belch from the pit of his stomach and the cow grunted her response as if to offer her manners. Instead of smearing the egg and milk across his chin with his coat sleeve, Nandi ignored the mess and let it dry naturally. He checked outside once more hoping for signs of first light. Halmaj, for the moment lay enveloped in darkness but for the dim light of the moon that shone through fleecy clouds, casting a pale light that of approaching dawn. Suddenly, rifles broke the silence somewhere in the village. Nandi counted the shots that fired spasmodically like dogs barking on lone farms. After seven far away gunshots it ceased and no other sounds could be heard. Nandi listened hard but he thought it was over. An hour later and the first signs of daylight made the view from the barn look grey. Nandi confirmed to himself he had four bullets in the handgun and decided to brave the streets. He leapfrogged the garden gate and set off to spy the police station.

Affirmation concluded when a Russian sniper on the rooftop lay watching and lit a cigarette. It was his give away; the flash from his match drew Nandi's attention to him. Maybe he thought it was safe to light up now daylight was looming. He hadn't seen Nandi, he was facing the opposite direction, but Nandi was close enough to observe he was eating a sandwich and his rifle lay beside him. Moving out of sight on the street corner, he planned his next move, looked up and noticed four youths in a nearby car. When he was certain they were Hungarian, he decided to walk by the car to assess their intentions. He made sure the collar of his coat was up covering part of his face and strolled passed the car innocently. Nandi recognised them immediately. Chuffed and excited he flung open the back car door and dived onto the knees of Adam and Jancsi. They must have all been dozing because they hadn't seen Nandi at all and responding by screaming aloud. Nandi laughed audibly and couldn't find the energy to stop himself. Matyas and Peter were in the front and demanded silence while Jancsi slammed the car door shut.

"Fuck me! You've scared the living daylights out of us. We thought you'd been killed. Where have you been Nandi?" Matyas asked while his hands gripped the steering wheel tight.

Nandi sat up and squeezed himself between Adam and Jancsi.

"Last night I slept with a cow, yesterday I slept with a nurse and the night before I slept in my own blood on a courtyard in Szikszo."

"What do you mean? What nurse?"

"I've been in hospital, had few stitches; it's a long story I'll explain later. Quickly tell me what's happening here."

"Most of the Avo have gone to Budapest but, we have been told there are a few left in the police station."

"How many is a few?"

"Three or four."

"So what's your plan?"

"We are going to lure them out, let them give chase out of Halmaj where the rest of us are waiting in the sunflower field armed with guns, petrol bombs, grenades…."

"You can't do that yet?"

"Why not Nandi?"

"Because we will have to take out the Russian sniper who is hiding on top of the Police Station."

"You've seen him."

"Yeah. Eh my parents don't think I'm dead do they?"

"No. Neither of us have been back to the college yet. After we'd garrotted the surviving Avo from lampposts we found refuge in local houses. The owners couldn't thank us enough. Then we heard that these bastards had vacated here and just left a few patrol units."

"We searched for you everywhere." Jancsi reassured and then embraced Nandi's head and kissed his left cheek. "Thank God you're still alive."

"Yeah thank God. But I am even more prepared now to die for my country. Anybody know what's happening in Budapest?"

"Last we heard the freedom fighters were winning but Russia are sending in more troops."

"Great! C'mon England get your fucking army into Budapest. The Russians would shit themselves and sod off for good."

"We've got to sort out this sniper, what do you suggest Nandi?"

"Me and Jancsi can climb onto an adjacent roof and take him out.
Got any rifles?"
"Yes. Two fully loaded in the boot. We've all got handguns and
four petrol bombs."

"Okay leave the rifles where they are, Jancsi and I can take out
the sniper. You lot keep us covered when he's dead wait for us to
get back into the car then we'll bomb the Police Station and speed
off to the others. No wait, on second thoughts we'll take one rifle;
and your cap." Nandi snatched Peter's dark brown cap from his
head, put it on himself, smiled at Peter when he looked at Nandi
with a puzzled expression and pulled the door handle to release
the catch.

"C'mon Jancsi; let's go and kill a Russian."

Jancsi and Nandi rolled over the roof to a chimneystack at the rear
positioning themselves directly opposite the Police Station. They
slowly drew themselves behind the chimneystack, until their eyes
were level with the top of the parapet. There was nothing to be
seen just the dim outline of the Police Station against the
brightening sky. The enemy was under cover.

"I can't see anybody. Are you sure he's there?" Jancsi whispered

Nandi didn't answer, he just concentrated hard.

After a while they were both sure the sniper could hear their get
away car advancing slowly. Matyas stopped a considerable
distance away but the dull panting of the engine must be alerting
the sniper. Then, round the corner of a side street came an old
woman, her head covered by a tattered shawl. She began to talk to
Matyas through his car window. Nandi and Jancsi stared at the
woman with a cold gleam and as she pointed towards the Police
Station rooftop, the sniper raised his rifle and fired. The woman

whirled around and fell with a shriek into the gutter. The sniper could be seen now and as he took up aim again, probably at the car, Jancsi fired two frantic shots at him.

"Did I hit him?"

" No. You missed. Now keep your head down he now knows we're here."

"What about the others in the Police Station."

"They'll be out soon. We must kill that bastard and get out of here. Quick, pass me the rifle."

Taking off the cap, Nandi placed it over the muzzle of the rifle. Then he pushed the rifle slowly over the parapet, until the cap was visible from the Police Station. Almost immediately, there was a single shot fired from the Russian that pierced the centre of the cap. Nandi slanted the rifle forward. The cap slipped down into the street. Nandi then grabbed the rifle at the middle with his left hand and let his arm and the rifle hang over the side lifelessly. After a few moments, he let the rifle drop to the street. Then he sank into the roof out of sight dragging his hand with him. They kept their heads down and crawled quickly over to the other side; they peered across to the Police Station. The ruse had succeeded. The Russian sniper, seeing the cap and rifle fall, thought he had killed his man. He was now standing before the smoking chimney pot, looking across, with his head clearly silhouetted against the western sky. Nandi and Jancsi smiled and lifted their revolvers above the edge of the parapet.

The distance was about sixty metres, a hard shot in the dim light. Nandi's wound was paining him but he took a steady aim. His hand trembled with eagerness. They both gritted their lips together, took a deep breath through their nostrils and fired at the same time. Nandi yelped slightly as his arm shook with the recoil. It seemed to irritate his stab wound. Then, when the smoke cleared, they peered across and uttered a cry of joy. He'd been hit. He was reeling over the parapet in his death agony. He struggled to keep his feet, but he was slowly falling forward as if in a dream. The rifle fell from his grasp, hit the parapet, fell over, bounded off the pole of a soup kitchen and then clattered on the pavement. Then the dying man crumpled up and fell forward. The body turned over and over in space and hit the ground with a dull thud. Then it lay still.

For a moment Nandi was stunned, the lust for battle had died in him. He became bitten by remorse. Sweat stood out in beads on his forehead. Weakened by his wound, he revolted from the sight of the shattered mass of the dead Russian. His teeth chattered, he began to gibber to himself cursing himself. He looked at the smoking revolver in his hand and wanted to end the fight; he wanted to go home.

"C'mon Nandi the Avo will be coming after us. Matyas is pulling the car around the back quickly let's go."

Suddenly a shot was fired from the doorway of the Police Station they had realised they were under attack. The bullet whizzed passed Nandi's head. He was frightened back to his senses by the shock. His nerves steadied. The cloud of fear and remorse scattered from his mind and he ran with Jancsi and climbed down quickly off the roof. Jancsi was the first to get into the car but Nandi couldn't cross the pavement because two Avo policemen had begun firing shots towards the car. Unsure what to do next, Nandi had to wait in a doorway out of the line of fire.

"Drive away, drive away!" Nandi shouted. But then noticed they had ignited the petrol bombs. When they exploded, it created a wall of fire and black smoke in the street allowing Nandi to run to the car. Panic fire from beyond the burning partition tore up the ground around him with a hail of bullets. He escaped being hit and Matyas wheel spun away and screeched around the corner.

"Faster Matyas, faster, they'll be following, be sure of that."

Matyas turned corners without breaking leaving a stench of burning rubber behind. The three in the back turned around, kneeled on the back seat and smashed out the back window with the rifles and revolvers. When the window was free from glass, they took up aim and rested their arms against the back window ledge awaiting their trackers. If they were coming, they hadn't caught up with them yet and now they were heading out of the village.

"Hold on!" Matyas cried as he ruthlessly yanked the steering wheel taking them off the road and into the fields. The car mercilessly revved, the clutch and gearbox clanked throwing them all about as it cut through turf and frozen soil.

"They're here.! They've seen us!" Jancsi shouted.

A green military jeep followed after them across the field.

"For fuck sake shoot the bastards."

They couldn't aim properly but the shots rang out from their car towards the approaching jeep.

"They're too far away, stop firing." Nandi shouted.

"Just a little further. Look over to our right it's Attila, Laszi, and the others."

They could see them behind their mound of earth.

"Go on Matyas, draw them in. Ambush, ambush."

Suddenly the car hit something in the ground and threw them forward. Peter hit his head on the windscreen but bounced back in his seat.

"What the fuck was that."

Matyas furiously accelerated but the car dug its wheels deeper into the ground.

"I can't move it we're stuck."

Spontaneously they all ducked their heads to the floor as a rain of bullets and grenades exploded all around them. The glass shattered, and covered them. They could hear bullets ricocheting hitting the metal body of the car. Explosions around increased in volume and Nandi was sure they were on fire. They could feel flames scorching and then they all began to choke as smoke filled the car.

"Get out, get out, all of you get of the car." Bela shouted to them from outside. Nandi obeyed the instruction immediately and kicked open the car door. Matyas followed. Dizzy and disorientated they fell onto their saviours.

"What happened? Where are the Avo?"

"They're there look. They're fleeing, driving towards the number 3 road. We ambushed them. As they got within shooting distance we plugged them all."

"So, who's driving?"

"We hit them all I'm sure of it and as we did, the driver didn't know what the hell had hit them so he sped off. But I'm sure I shot the driver, maybe I didn't kill him."

"Nandi, Nandi, what happened to you?"

"Never mind that now; if he's still alive he's going to radio for help we'd better get ready. I'm going to make my way to the roadside; everybody else get in your trenches closer to the roadside and get ready for an attack."

Nandi made it to the road. He looked left and then right. Nothing. He looked behind him at his friends in the fields. They were dug in well enough he thought, their heads bobbing around above the earth as they got in position.

Peter and Jancsi spotted two vehicles travelling along the road towards Nandi. Definitely the enemy, they were travelling at great speed. They turned to warn Nandi but he wasn't there.

"Where's Nandi?"

They all turned and looked.

"He's gone. Must have taken cover somewhere."

It only took a few minutes for three men in the two vehicles to pick their spot. They screeched to a fierce stop on the number 3 road. They all watched through binoculars above high mounds of earth. The men were shouting to each other and all ran to the back of the vehicles and wrenched out what appeared to be two, fairly large, green heavy cannons on short sturdy legs. They easily positioned them at the edges of the field and pointed them towards the dugouts.

"Christ they're loading them with shells. We've stirred a hornet's nest now; everyone, take up aim and take them out quickly before they fire those things."

As they fired, simultaneously the three men stepped back behind a large tree, but they still managed to load a shell into each mortar through the muzzle.

" FIRE!" One of them called out.

This was the beginning of a heavy bombardment. When the first shell hit, there was a dull thud, they felt the ground shake, and with a noise more like a hiss than anything, a huge sheet of white flame poured towards the sky accompanied by smoke and great volumes of earth that erupted 90 metres into the air. It lasted only a few seconds and before it subsided, they all opened fire in force. Some fired at the three soldiers and others into the air towards the falling dirt and shrapnel. The noise was deafening, a barrage of bullets and shells made a ceiling of rushing steel above their heads. They were forced to lie low and cover their heads allowing the three men virtually a freehand. When they realised that they had rattled the teenagers and their shots were virtually non existent or ineffective, the three men confidently began firing and slamming their projectiles at their target one after another. Some of the shells sounded like they were lopsided as they hit all around the trenches and ramparts. Many of them were exploding in the air before they hit the ground. Peter lay with his nose buried in the dirt and wondered if this was death; he covered his ears as clumps of dirt struck him hard across his lower back. He dared himself to check on his friends and as he turned and stared through a haze of smoke, machine gun bullets clipped the ground all around him. He sensed something and in a moment of madness, he took his pistol from its holster and scrambled to the top of the fortification that protected him. One of the Avo was crawling towards them firing

his machine gun intermittently whilst the other two continued to reload and fire the mortar cannon.
Peter fired one after another at the intruder until he emptied the chamber. As the last bullet whizzed from the barrel, Peter rolled head over heals and kept rolling until he fell into a deep shell hole. He wasn't sure if he'd killed him but was certain he at least wounded him. He panted copiously sucking in and swallowing particles of mud. He felt giddy and sick. Steadying himself by pressing two hands against the walls of the crater helped. At last, he was able to look up at the smoke filled sky. Confused, Peter waited for another explosion or gunfire. He poked both ears with his fingers to check he hadn't lost his hearing.

"They've cease fired." Bela let everyone know.

"Why?" Peter inquired from the shell hole.

"It's too dusty. A strong wind is whipping the smoke and dust into the air. I can't see a thing. A shell has hit the car too; it's in flames." Adam was peering through his binoculars trying to give an account of what he could see when Peter interrupted.

"Nobody move I'm coming up."

He clawed his way next to Jancsi and relieved him of his binoculars.

"Mine have smashed; let me see."

Clouds of gun smoke filled the air. They all strained their eyes hard to watch for the enemy's next move. Suddenly a gust of wind cleared the way. Something in the distance made them all twitch for their weapons. A loud chink echoed as they did.
 The figure of a tall man with his hands raised marched through the heat and black smoke billowing from the burning car. It was

difficult to make him out as his outline quivered caused by the intense heat from the smouldering metal rising at an angle from the molten car.

"Hold your fire!" Matyas instructed.

His strides and mannerisms became more familiar as the shimmering heat became the scenery behind him. Laszi and Jancsi smiled at each other as the battle scene photograph stood out. He ambled on closer allowing them to make him out more clearly with his black parachute boots, torn, black, bloodied shirt and his long dark blue coat.
"It's Nandi, it's Nandi." Dinyi screamed out.

"Can I lower my hands or what?" Nandi remarked sarcastically.

"**Yesss!**" They all cheered together and stormed from their trenches patting and embracing him.

Someone threw him half a bed sheet from their rucksack after they'd noticed he was covered in fresh blood.

"Is it your blood have you been shot?"

"No it's from those Communist bastards." Nandi began wiping away the blood from his neck and hands.

"So, have you killed them?"

"Well my father once told me as I'm sure you're all aware of; ambush is the art of capture. But, he also told me to use my brain."

"So, what did you do?"

"One of you killed the first. Him there." Nandi pointed

"That was me." Peter boasted.

"No. It was me." Bela jokingly contradicted.

"What about the two that were firing the shells Nandi? What happened?"

"Forget it….They're dead aren't they?" Nandi threw the bloodstained bed sheet towards the burning car and began walking away from them.

"C'mon let's get back to the college it's time to re-group and get a progress report from Budapest. We must grab what we can from this field, we won't be able to come back and it won't be long before this whole area gets searched and they'll probably bury landmines all over."

"Good point." Janos acknowledged and then began to pick up as many weapons as he could followed by the others.

Peter frowned to himself and curiosity persuaded him to investigate how Nandi had managed to terminate the enemy. "I'll get the dead Avo' men's weapons and take a look." He said to himself.

One of them lay face down in the dirt but somehow his back was arched. The other was sat leaning against a tree facing the road. Only his right arm and his boots could be seen but it was enough to make out how he was slumped.

"Nandi must have sat him there like that." Peter thought.

October 29th 1956

The reason for the arched back became evident when Peter turned the body over with his foot. He tightened the muscles around his eyes when he looked at the gruesome sight. A pickaxe jammed into the solar plexus and the oozing blood caused him to squint but he needed to see the other corpse before concluding. Nandi had left an axe buried into the centre of his forehead, ripped his shirt open and wrote a name in blood across the man's chest. *"Sándor Petőfi."*

Sándor Petőfi; a Historical Hungarian poet, inspired generations of Hungarians with his calls to be a free nation. Peter understood the message as it was intended and knew then the reason to position the Avo facing the road.

"It's a message. A statement to the enemy. A Hungarian would just spit on him if they passed by. But Nandi knows the Communists will read that. But how did Nandi manage to kill two heavily armed, well trained soldiers with woodcutters tools?"

As he questioned it to himself, a flapping bird swooping inside the hole of a nearby tree distracted him. Puzzled, Peter decided to inspect the tree. At first, he couldn't make out the image before him. The bottom half of the tree looked three dimensional, as if the trunk had a symmetrical reflection in front of it. But then, as he reached out and touched the bark, a large section of the tree fell to one side.

"What the hell is this?"

The inside of the trunk was dark and hollow and when Peter popped his head in and looked around the inner shell, he smirked aloud and shook his head.

"The crafty bastard hid in here…And he's used that section as a doorway to conceal himself."

Just then, Peter jumped and screamed out. Trying to reach for his gun wasn't an option; he just continued to throw punches at

October 29th 1956

whatever was attacking him and screeching it's high pitched squawk as it did so. The others had immediately heard the disturbance and they darted over to his aid. Peter managed to silence his screams even when the claws of a barn owl had sank into his forearm. Keeping calm and holding his arm out straight slowly convinced the frightened owl to finish flapping its feathery wings. When it did so Peter called out to his rescuers as they approached,

"Stay where you are. Whatever you do don't come any closer. It's calm now and if any of you excite it, it's liable to get angry and whilst its fucking claws are buried into my skin, I'd rather it didn't get excited."

The lads stopped immediately in a straight line, Nandi was the first to burst out laughing and at once, they were all giggling uncontrollably.

"What's so fucking funny you bastards?" Peter snapped.

The owl had settled and sat very still on Peter's arm, it blinked a few times and every so often, it turned its heart-shaped face towards him as a reminder that his claws were still stuck in his arm. It only added to the comical moment, that, and the dusty mottled brown feathers that had floated to the ground around Peter's feet, remnants of the fight between man and bird.

"Peter." Nandi began in between breaths. "We have rifles, Tommie guns, grenades, petrol bombs, bullets and knives to fight an invincible opponent. And, we are winning. But we begin to lose, to an owl." The laughter increased in volume and Matyas added,

"Ask the owl if it's a communist; if it is I will blow its head off for you."

October 29th 1956

Peter nodded vigorously.

"Good idea, shoot it! Shoot it!"

"No don't shoot it; what were you doing to it?" Adam asked.

"I was just checking out Nandi's homemade air aid shelter and it came from nowhere."

"Of course it will attack you. It's only a mother protecting its babies. Probably got eggs in the tree." Nandi surmised.

"Uncanny don't you think? That's what this revolution is all about; protecting our families, protecting our homes from an invading enemy? Securing the future for our children." Adam commented seriously and managed to pause the laughter while they all reflected on the contrastive parallel for a second.
It took Laszi and Nandi several minutes to tug the claws of the owl from his forearm. They didn't have time to clean the wound or examine the severity, but they were glad it hadn't ripped the flesh even though the claws had pierced deep. Conscious they could be easily detected in the open air field and the smoke would draw attention to their presence, hurrying back to their college was welcomed.

Monday Evening October 29th 1956.

There was an added zest to this particular evening. The mood, the moment was gratifying, terrific. Hearts jumped for joy and it was hard not to be complacent. Every college classroom, dormitory, hallway was heaving with excited students and lecturers. They'd formed their own group discussions and were piecing together events from Budapest and all over the country. Spread out across, desks, tables, and even the floors were pages and pages of that

October 29th 1956

days newspaper stories. There were now half a dozen of Nandi's illegal makeshift radios, cloned by others, set up in various areas of the college. Wine and beer flowed amongst the swollen college and from outside, the atmosphere and loud voices bellowed.

Stalin Street was renamed 'The Street of Hungarian youth.' Stalin square will now be called Gyorgy Dozsa and to Nandi's personal delight, it was announced that Stalin Bridge was now Arpad Bridge. Radio Miskolc announced the red army had been fought to a standstill and Soviet Troops were withdrawing from Hungarian soil. Pockets of resistance remained in Budapest and heavy fighting continues, particularly at the Kilian Barracks.

Hungary was doing the impossible; it was winning. The Russian tanks had been called upon to put down the uprising and found they were faced with a well-organised, fearless populace, which improvised with amazing bravery. The Hungarian weapon against an almighty iron fist was an overpowering common impulse, spirit and emotion, which suddenly united all classes to stand up, eyeball to eyeball, and crush the enemy. They now needed to show a political sense. Parties needed to be set up and a structure was required to show to the whole world that Hungary could not only survive but could function adequately on its own. Relations with the west needed immediate attention, but more importantly, western troops were required to keep the peace and dissuade Russia from any form of revenge attacks.

Amid the celebrations, Nandi and the others sidled away to the river in groups of two's and three's. In the freezing water, they bathed and cleaned their wounds. Nandi's shoulder pained him slightly but he decided not to shift the bandage. A small fire was lit at the side of the river fuelled to begin with by Nandi's shredded blood tarnished clothes. It was best they all did the same to conceal evidence or proof that they'd had any participation in the fighting. Even though the mood of Hungary looked promising the fear that it would blow up in their faces, still loomed.

As the evening grew dark, Nandi and the others sat guzzling some homemade wine talking and staring out of their windows across at the horizon. Celebrations were still ripe all over the college grounds. They sang the National Anthem over and over with more honour and passion each time. It was a melody that every proud Hungarian wanted to fall asleep to.

Nandi's eyes grew heavy, but he felt clean, cosy and safe and he let a half empty bottle of wine slip from his hand when he bedded down and pulled his quilt up to his nose. The others had done the same. Nandi knew he'd be a sleep in seconds but reminded everyone,

"When we wake up tomorrow pray we see tanks travelling in the opposite direction. Then we can be sure they're leaving our land."

Nandi slept in a hot and cold sleep for almost 36 hours. His restless heart pumped his warm Hungarian blood around his body. His deep sleep felt as if he'd drifted in and out of a coma, certain times lifeless, still, without hardly breathing. Other times restive filled with nightmares and unease.

Hungary's history pealed open like a prize grapefruit. These last days in October exposed the true inner core of a nation. The nation had defended its honour; it had cracked the outer tough coconut skin that the Russians created, chipped away the rough edges and now left a pure white nucleus. Its job was now to enhance what it had achieved, embrace it, and repair all structures politically, industrially and mentally. Nandi recuperated for 36 hours, he had thrown all muscle, energy and paid homage to his persecuted country. He had awoken to an historical moment that had not been repeated. This was a country whose chronological past was littered with a common fate in the form of the Turkish, Roman, Austrian and Russian empires. A country left alone, stranded, ambushed from all corners for a thousand years, had now stood up to and defeated an almighty power. With a ramshackle army of men, it defeated the aggressor while the whole world had stood and watched. For Nandi, his efforts were being rewarded and he opened his eyes to a new Hungarian government executing his country's reforms. It was a time like no other. Soviet tanks were rumbling out of Budapest and soon it was promised out of the country forever. On the banks of the Danube, Russian diplomats and their families packed their belongings and on their way out of Hungary. The two highest politburo men were leaving Hungary, it had been said that they'd finally accepted that were no longer wanted in Hungary.

A new political spring was underway, new parties were emerging. Tildy called for the Smallholders Party. Ferenc Erdei appeals for the non-communist Peasant Party and the recall of the Hungarian representative Peter Kos to the United Nations was announced. The new non-communist executive committee was formed in the Independent Smallholders Party and resumed control of its former newspaper 'Kis Ujsag' The Hungarian Social Democratic Party was reorganised and the newspaper 'Nepszava became its official publication. Now, a population starved of truth was being sated with new pamphlets and newspapers. Censorship was abolished. Hungary was alive.

Everything improved quickly in a natural methodical fashion. A new Army Chief of Staff, a new First Deputy Defence Minister, a new Military Commander of the capital. The newly formed Trans-Danubian National Council put forward to the United Nations and requested their support in the evacuation of the Soviet Troops, repudiation of the Warsaw pact, and declared Hungary's neutrality. The UN had put the Hungarian question on its agenda for Friday night. Hungarians felt a sense of pride and knew the eyes of the entire world were upon them. The implication was that they could not be robbed in broad daylight of a course that was under such close scrutiny. They were even more uplifted and reassured when Henry Cabot Lodge, the United States delegate to the UN stated firmly "The United Nations cannot remain a passive spectator to the events in Hungary."

Industries, factories, re-launched their production without being governed by bureaucratic, communist nonsense. All professions from Professors to shopkeepers to café owners, knew how to begin the running of their business, their country. With the removal of the artificial, unnecessary, dogmatic, communist structure, life in Hungary was becoming unbelievably free and happy. The streets in major cities were full of farmers bringing in and distributing food. Truck loads of potatoes; carrots were being offloaded freely to the people on every street corner, shouts of joy and happiness from the farmers and the common people alike. People were standing in crowds, groups, talking, laughing. Everyone in Hungary, every city, town and village stood in unity. The country was one relative.

Prisoners of the years of oppression were at last set free. Over five and a half thousand detainees were let out into the newly formed Hungary. Among them was Cardinal Mindszenty.

Now, the commanders of the militia were chosen, their task, to keep order in Budapest. Mixed patrols circulated throughout the city, they were examining papers of motorists, pedestrians, disarming anyone who was unable to show membership of the National Guard, militia or the police force. Order and security was re-establishing itself in its own euphoria.

Nandi couldn't believe it was midday on October 31st 'My God I've actually missed a day.' He groaned to himself. "Ouch." He yelped quietly when his stiff knees cracked the moment he bent his legs to get out of his bed. With swollen eyelids, the prodding from his finger helped to shift the sleep from his eyes but the light from the window hurt them making them water. For an hour, he had lay awake but had kept his eyes closed whilst he listened to the radio that had been set up in the dormitory. Elated but weary from the long sleep, the radio had been talking to him, ringing out the joyous news like a loud bell filling the air with tremendous applause. The occasion for Nandi had lifted a huge weight from around his neck he couldn't think of anything else but to go home to Mogyoroska to his parents and family. The aches and pains couldn't loosen and ease quick enough even after a few stretching exercises to relieve the stiff tension. Suddenly a radio station burst into a jolly violin verse followed by a few more announcements…

"Major Nemes the Avo secret police chief has been arrested today and imprisoned in the city Police HQ. Some people are screaming for his execution. Meanwhile Budapest has been receiving a supply of food from the village of Biraj and people from all over are helping with the slow restoration of the country's capital. Tractors, horses and bare hands are the tools of the city cleaning up broken glass, abolished buildings, stones and vehicles. Thousands and thousands of Forints have been donated in collection boxes for the dead. The poorest of people are throwing in all they have, a few coins even. Cardinal Mindszenty who was freed yesterday will arrive in Budapest it is said this afternoon."

Attila, Jancsi and Peter entered the dormitory together as Nandi was stretching the neck of his grey pullover over his head.

"Need some help with that?" Attila offered.

He wrenched it over his face with a little difficulty hindered by his throbbing shoulder.

"I'm okay Attila. But I will need to change this bandage soon and have a look at the wound."

"Ohhh, it's your injury that's preventing you from putting on your pullover. I thought it was the size of your head."

"Piss off chubby." Nandi joked back.

"Suppose you've heard about developments?" Jancsi asked Nandi sensing he had by the grins and smiles breaking out across his face.

"Sure have guys. Now all as we need is the west to inject some pressure onto the situation get their arses over here and it's all over. We are actually free."

"I feel a great sense of making history." Peter said proudly of which Nandi replied.

"We have made history. We've shown resilience, power. We have probably changed the future for millions around the world just by demanding to be free. I've got mixed feelings at the moment one of foreboding and another of sheer fulfilment. Like if a doctor had been told not to operate on a young child because it was going to die of pneumonia and there wasn't anything he could do. But against all odds, he operated anyway and he cured him, saved his life. That's how I feel. Yes! I'm going home to share my feelings with my family."

Nandi brushed away a dirty stain from off the front of the bible and pushed it into the pocket of his trousers that was sprawled across his bed.

"And I mustn't forget this; it's protected me until now."

Suddenly Nandi was packed and ready for a visit home. The friends embraced each other and almost cried aloud. There wasn't any need for words. They had fought together, almost died together, adapted to horrific circumstances and they had seen and heard events that would scar and wound them forever. They had a dream for the future of Hungary; they now had a chance to live it. It was over and for Nandi it was now time to share this freedom with those who had taught him to have a vision of how his country should be, to never give up and to put Hungary first.

CHAPTER 11

October 31st 1956

Margit stoked the cast iron stove with broken sticks and twigs in order to boost up the temperature for the freshly plucked chicken she'd only just placed into a pot of water. The flames roared and after she'd gathered the potato and carrot peel, she threw them into the flames also. Vegetable peel roasting, the aroma of chicken, danced and hung in the air. Satisfied, she closed the tiny square oven door and leant a long lean log against it to hold it shut. Blackie carefully listened to her chunters from the limestone veranda.

"How many times do I have to ask Janos to fix the hinge on that oven door?" She murmured to herself.

Blackie lifted is head from under his paw and watched her scurry into the bedroom and his ears pricked up as if it was important for him to ensure he knew what she was doing. When he heard her open the cottage windows, as if satisfied, he replaced his head lethargically back under his paw. Inhaling deeply, his eyelids closed driven by the scent of a raw cut onion placed on a wooden chopping board close to the kitchen door. Something alarmed the dog instantaneously. He didn't feel tired anymore, sensing something he sat up with his back straight and his nose in the air. He yelped aloud twice and then waited. Curious, Blackie made his way to the closed garden gate. It excited him so he stood on his back legs and front paws against the fence. He studied hard at a gathering of people lower down the bank at the water well and then showed his concern by barking repeatedly sending his voice bouncing off the surrounding mountains. Margit covered her ears with her black cotton head square then tied it under her chin before investigating Blackie's concerns. She shuffled along the veranda towards the front gate, stopped and stood on her tiptoes to try and look beyond the bare branches of the front ornamental apple tree that charmed the front corner of the garden. To her

October 31st 1956

right, Feri's six cows lumbered clumsily down the slippery bank signalling their approach by a large bell tied around their neck. Margit could just make out Feri's flat cap peaking above the cows from beyond.

"Feri." She called out. Feri moved a cow aside with the handle of his spade. "Good day Margit." He replied.

"What's going on down there?"

Feri could hardly hear Margit owing to the shouts of laughter and the ringing from the cow's bells. Blackie's barks weren't helping either so Feri stroked him briskly through the fence to calm him.

"What **is** happening down there?" Feri turned and looked to see if he could make out what was causing the commotion.

Suddenly, he realised what was initiating the excitement. Grinning cheekily, he checked Margit's expression. She hadn't realised yet, so Feri decided to prolong the moment and began dropping a few hints.

" Uncle Imre, Uncle Istvan, Aunty Terezia, my mother, Aunty Ilona, cousin Jeno, cousin Jolan, Magdolna, Bela and the neighbours are all congratulating and welcoming someone. They look rather excited. Perhaps he's royalty or maybe Rakoczi himself has come back from the dead." Feri looked towards Margit from the corner of his eye.

"Why would all our family be so interested in a visitor?" Margit replied naively.

Feri wore a broad smile and then began to chuckle loudly. Margit frowned at him at first and then her large, wide-spaced watery green eyes engorged followed by a chuffed smile.

October 31st 1956

"Oh my good Lord, it's Nandi, it's my son. He's okay, he's okay. Quick Feri, Janos is around the back please go and fetch him."

Margit quickly opened the front gate to let Feri through and herself out. She lifted up her long black dress to her knees and ran as quick as she could towards the crowd. They hadn't seen her approaching yet and with each stride, she repeated under her breath. "Thank you God for keeping him safe from the Communists."

When she was within a few metres, she stopped and gazed for a moment. The family noticed her before Nandi did but the glorious welcoming, the kisses, the hugs, slowly stopped and Nandi looked across at his mother. From the look in her face, Nandi was certain that his father had been unable to persuade her that he wasn't involved in the revolution. She had the look of a relieved mother. Biting her lip until it almost bled she slowly moved towards him. As she approached, her hands touched his lean cheeks in an attempt to convince herself it was not a dream, and a choking sob rose in her throat as she flung her arms about him and buried her tear-wet face against his warm throat. Nandi squeezed around her back, rubbed and patted her shoulder blades reassuringly. The surrounding audience either cried, clapped or punched the air above with both fists, a certain sign of splendour and triumph. They linked each other leading a thrilled and jovial dynasty of people towards their home. The overwhelming warmth that was making Nandi beam uncontrollably elevated even more when he saw his father hurdle the garden fence with Blackie alongside him. They both landed with awkward elegance but then Janos gripped his son with both hands locking them around the bottom of his back and swung him around 360 degrees cheering, laughing and calling out.

"My son, my son, the hero has come home after freeing us from a national dungeon."

October 31st 1956

"Steady on Papa. You'll have people thinking I've beaten the Russians single-handedly."

"To me you did! Isn't that right everyone?"

All the family cheered and agreed with Janos.

"You see son. We wouldn't be able to insult the Russian regime if it wasn't for you. Yesterday I spit on a picture of Stalin. It felt great; I could do that because of you."

Nandi tried to answer but then thought better of it. Janos stopped walking with the stamping of both feet, one after another, and pointed a finger at the castle."

"Look!" He demanded in his deep bellowing voice.

The intrigued crowd remained smiling but silenced instantly as if a headmaster from a school had spoken out.

Janos continued,

"We are standing on Rakoczi Road, looking at Rakoczi's castle. Rakoczi has blessed my son. As he fought for Hungary's freedom from Austro-Hungary, my son has fought for freedom from Russia. But my son has won. Now it's celebration time, Feri go and get my barrel of wine from around back. I am the mayor of this village and I say we all get drunk."

With that, everyone laughed and applauded so Nandi released his grip from his mother and father, kissed and hugged Blackie then sprinted into the garden with his dog. Soon after, the party was rampant with festivity. All the family and friends from around the village joined the merriment and flooded their house and land with a flamboyant mood. Someone had lit a fire outside and donated chunks of smoked bacon. Feri junior had volunteered to sharpen as many short wooden spears as he could taken from

October 31st 1956

many bare branches from around the garden. Nandi helped to pierce the thick chunky bacon sliding the slimy meat a few inches along the spears. After they'd prepared about a dozen, Feri junior announced that the barbecue was ready to be cooked. In true

Hungarian style, everyone hung the bacon over the hot flames. The fire hissed as the sizzling bacon dripped and drenched the blaze. Margit passed around plates of bread and with expertise; the barbecue masters soaked the bread with juices from the meat, which tasted divine and even better when swilled with goblets of the homemade wine. There was an added zestful appetite to the frame of mind of everybody to this evening; it lit up the atmosphere like a thousand exploding fireworks. A neighbour had brought an old violin and as the barbecue roasted, he played and sang while he danced around the fire encouraged by rhythmic clapping from all attending Nandi's homecoming party.

It wasn't just the mood in Mogyoroska it was the flavour of Hungary. The entire country were enjoying and experiencing their achievements of freedom. The fear that was living inside their hearts had vanished. The fear that one careless statement could have done away with you, could have got you killed, had been lifted. The nervousness amongst a people, like everyone were not actually freely talking to each other had now eased, passed. The lonely chilling atmosphere was to be no more; they were free and deserved it.

"How old are you now Feri?" Nandi asked Feri Junior.
"I'm seven years old in two weeks time."
"Seven years old and your father lets you use a knife."
"Oh yes, my Dad has taught me how to skin a rabbit."
"Has he really?"
"Yes, and he says he's going to teach me how to kill a boar."
"Nandi can show you how to catch a boar young Feri." Janos interrupted as he approached to fill his mug with wine from a bottle.

October 31st 1956

"Eh papa, please pour me a drink. And I need to speak to you in private when you find a minute."
"Sure son. Here drink this." He passed Nandi his mug and poured himself another.

"Have I just heard you talking about boar catching?" Feri senior joined in ruffling the hair of his son at the same time.
"Yeah. Uncle Janos says Nandi can show me how to catch a boar."
"Ho, ho, ho, that he can son, when he wasn't much older than you he dared to attack one single-handedly."
"I wasn't exactly alone Feri. Blackie did help me." Blackie heard his name and brushed Nandi's leg with his fur encouraging him to throw a lump of smoked bacon into his mouth, which he caught gracefully between his teeth.
"To catch a menace the art is, ambush. That's how we deal with wild animals, set a trap, then, pounce." Nandi winked at Feri junior as his words of wisdom flowed.

Janos listened to Nandi's advice with a proud and fulfilling sensation.
"So, is that how we entrap a boar? Is that what you did?" Feri junior asked.
"Oh I apologise, when I said wild animals I was referring to the Russians."
The joke took a few seconds to register, but when the penny dropped, fits of laughter added to the spice of the party. Nandi took the opportunity to beckon his father out of the way of the family.
"What is it son? What's wrong?"
"I don't want mother to find out so keep it to yourself okay."
"Okay, okay, what is it?"
"I've been stabbed."
Janos gasped. "Christ, where? Show me quickly."

October 31st 1956

"Don't panic, I've been to the hospital they've stitched and bandaged me a few days ago but I haven't inspected the wound since then."
"Where were you stabbed?"

"Here at the front of my shoulder." Nandi touched the area with the flat of his hand.

Janos carefully lifted the pullover over his head, pulled out his recently sharpened penknife and began slicing through the bandage from around the back and then under the armpit. He pulled and loosened the bandage letting parts of it drop to the floor leaving a square piece just covering the wounded area. It was dark so Nandi struck a match while Janos carefully tugged the bandage away. It was held on by crusty dark red blood and Nandi flinched as it ripped away from the lesion. Janos studied the stitching and how it was healing and after he'd brushed away the bits of bandage and dried blood he was satisfied it wasn't septic and looked like it was adequately healing.

"What do you think Papa?"

Janos's eyes flickered into his son's eyes.

"You'll live. It's fine. Avu?"

"Yes."

"What happened to him?"

"Dead. I think."

"Good lad. You will need to give it a good wash. There's a bucket of water in the kitchen, go and clean it up, I'll keep your mother occupied. Tomorrow I'll remove your stitches."

"Are you qualified?"

"Of course I am. I've unstitched and stitched enough leather shoes in my life. This is a piece of cake."

The celebrations went deep into the evening and nobody really wanted the night to end. This was a day Hungary had been waiting for for a thousand years and to be a part of it was an honour, to actually witness their nations release after so many years of torture and depression uplifted their spirits like never before. The

October 31st 1956

feeling was unfamiliar but felt glorious almost like 100,000 people were giving a sigh of joy at the same time. Everyone at the party found it difficult to go home, several times they tried but Janos dragged them back for one reason or another, just searching for excuse after excuse to toast freedom. Eventually only Feri and young Feri junior remained, the others had left for home their songs of freedom still ripe and hung in the air as they ventured to their houses in the village.

As they threw remnants of bread and bacon onto the smouldering flames, the four of them silenced and gazed into the fire.
After a while Feri remembered something and asked Janos,

" You once told me that we are prisoners and there isn't anybody who is willing to listen.". Feri paused for a few seconds allowing enough time for Janos to recollect. Nandi looked at his father waiting for his reaction but Feri continued.

"Do you have the same view today?"
Janos looked back towards Nandi before he answered and studied the glowing flickering flame shadows that brightened all their faces.

"We should enjoy today as it is intended. Tomorrow we find out if anybody has been willing to listen, if they haven't, then God help us because the Russians have been humiliated in the face of the world and they would take any opportunity to clap the chains back onto us."

They all shuddered at the thought of such a possibility and then shook themselves back to reality when Nandi spoke out.

"We must end the night on a high; the truth is none of that is going to happen, we are being scrutinised by the west and soon they will be here to support us. So, tell me father, what is in that large wooden barrel over against the shed?"

October 31st 1956

Nandi pointed in its direction illuminated by the blaze.

Janos laughed out loud. "Aha, now that is something special."

Feri laughed too and couldn't wait to show Nandi what was inside. They surrounded the barrel and Janos opened the lid slowly and the stench was strong and wafted in their faces as he did so causing them all to turn their noses until they got used to the strength of it.

Nandi struck a match and held it inside the shadows of the barrel to reveal, ¾ full, a large mixture of fermented mashed up fruit.

"What's that? What's it for? As if I didn't know."

"Son; it's mostly plums, but there are cherries, apricots and peaches in there also."

"You usually make wine from the grapes don't you?"

"Oh no it isn't going to be wine. It will be Palinka. Tomorrow Feri, you and I are going to distil our very own brandy."

The three men smirked at each other cheekily while Feri junior stood on his tiptoes to enable him to see into the barrel at all the interest. They all burst into a bellowing laughter and the night ended as it had began. Joyous, celebratory and a happy look to the future, for tomorrow, was Palinka day.

November 1ˢᵗ 1956

Nandi and his father overloaded the stove with chopped sticks to ensure a roaring fire. It had just turned 6:15a.m, Janos checked that Margit was still sleeping while Nandi borrowed his father's

heavy overcoat and buttoned it to the neck over his naked chest. They had decided to meet Feri at the village pub to have an early morning drink before they were to set up their makeshift distillery. Nandi and his father stood side-by-side blocking the pub doorway sipping a discoloured Palinka and inhaling deeply the smell of sweet countryside. As Janos chatted, and generally talked about anything unimportant, Nandi smirked at Blackie over the rim of his whittled glass. His dog stood eagerly, panting and glaring at Nandi's beverage.

"Hey father!" Nandi interrupted. "You been feeding my dog Palinka?"

Janos paused and then dipped his thick thumb into the spirit. Blackie was alert and as soon as Janos offered his dripping wet fist to him, he lapped up the mess and slurped at the hot alcohol. Nandi found it incredibly amusing and began teasing Blackie by flicking small droplets at him towards his mouth. Blackie added to the amusement by occasionally panting for breath when the hot flavour coated the back of his throat.

" I can remember when you were a young boy and you threw a snowball at the Avu's car from this very spot and Blackie came to warn me. And then that bastard slapped your face."

Nandi remembered Captain Nistor instantly. He felt his neck burn while his face clouded. He wondered if his father had noticed his nervousness as he contemplated revealing the fate of Captain Nistor. Nandi opened his mouth to speak and as he did, his eyes fearfully widened too. Suddenly, Janos jumped, bellowed and sent Blackie chasing after Feri, who had appeared on the brow of the hill on the road alongside the church. Turning his head, relieved, Nandi smiled when the silhouette of a man wearing a flat cap, baggy dungarees, carrying a scythe and a pitchfork strolled towards them.

November 1ˢᵗ 1956

"I'll get him a drink." Nandi volunteered in an attempt to diffuse the idea to tell his father. As Feri's drink was poured, Nandi toyed with his guilt and then shook himself deciding it was better his father knew nothing of his battles. 'Hungary was not out of the woods yet.' He whispered to himself.

Feri was full of high spirits as he gleefully chuckled deeply when he leaned his farming tools against the pub wall so he could receive the Palinka from Nandi. His rosy cheeks glowed brighter when he poured the full glass into his mouth until the last drop dripped onto his tongue. The three men laughed together cheerfully and Janos decided they were to have another round of drinks and so insisted the landlord brings them out to them. He too joined in the jolly mood and brought out an extra full glass of Palinka for himself and toasted to Hungary's success. They all exchanged the brightest of conversations, joking, laughing, and Miklos the landlord shared some dark red paprika salami and a crust of bread with them all.

"There's nothing better for a Hungarian than Palinka, bread and salami for breakfast. And as my father has always told me 'a good breakfast means you'll have a good day.' Isn't that true father?" Nandi smiled when he asked Janos.

"Bloody is true son. Okay Pekar's, time we opened our very own distillery; then we won't need to drink this crap that Miklos serves in ere."

Feri burst out into a loud squealing laughter and Nandi sniggered raucously as Miklos looked dismayed for a brief second but then took the joke as it was intended along with the others.

"Eh now Mr. Janos Pekar, even the mayor of Mogyoroska can get barred you know?"

November 1st 1956

Janos joined in the laughter and then promised to give Miklos a bottle of the homemade Palinka if he promised to save Feri's tools for him so that they could get on their way.

Nandi couldn't decide if what they were setting up in their kitchen and out on the veranda was panning out to be a distillery or a chemistry lab. All types of equipment came out of the cupboards, rubber tubes, glass bowls of all sizes, pipettes, test tubes, prongs, tweezers, an hourglass and countless cutting implements such as knives or scissors. Janos was excited and laughed deeply when Margit pretended to hit him with a large wooden spoon for 'trashing' her kitchen. Blackie yelped and joined in the atmosphere but Margit decided to walk him across the land, which, Blackie took advantage to chase the hens around, through and under the hen huts.

Nandi and Feri stood at either side of Janos as he demonstrated the set up to the art of distilling pure Palinka. The fermented fruit had been tipped into a large metal bucket and now Janos was heating it up on the stove over a low but hot flame. Every now and then, the fruit spat, trailing a silver steam cloud that spiralled out of the bucket. It glowed and hissed like lava from a volcano forcing Janos to douse the flame slightly to reduce the temperature. Feri knew what to do next; he cut two short lengths of string, rustled through a pile of pots and pans until he found a circular, small but deep metal bowl. He inspected the diameter and then lowered it into the bucket just to ensure it was the right size.

"Looks perfect Feri! Diameter about two inches less than the bucket, great."

Feri then removed it when they were sure it would be adequate for the job and began looping the string through two holes at opposite sides of the bowl. He could now hang the bowl inside the bucket by attaching the other ends of the string to the hinges on the rim of the bucket. He did it carefully and Nandi wore a chuffed smile when he sussed out the purpose for the free hanging bowl inside the bucket about half way between the fruit and the top of the pail.

"Quick Nandi you know what we need next." Feri encouraged.

Nandi filled a large glass bowl full to the rim with cold water while Janos lined the lip of the bucket with two woollen tea towels. Janos could now slowly wedge the glass bowl full of cold water into the mouth of the bucket. He turned it and pressed it down until it was tight and snug, he stood back, combed his hair with his hands and then with a satisfied tone explained,

"The steam will rise from the fermented fruit…"

"Hit the cold glass bowl at the top, turn to liquid and drip into the bowl hanging in between." Nandi interrupted and then Feri continued. "And that is the Palinka caught in the hanging bowl. Wonderful, marvellous and hey presto."

The three men burst open three bottles of beer and supped at them while they waited for the alcohol to collect.

The fumes were strong engulfing the kitchen and the small windowpanes in the front door slowly began to saturate with hot condensation. Nandi wrote something against the glass and then wondered, shuddering as he thought, 'What would happen to this country if the west refused to help.' And then he began the conversation with his father and Feri.

" Poland would help us papa don't you think? You know if nobody else did? After all, General Joseph Bem was Polish and his army fought with us in 1848 for independence; isn't this the same thing?"

November 1st 1956

Feri stroked the bristles on his chin and didn't look as sure as Nandi sounded.

Janos spotted his own reflection in the glass bowl of water straining to see how much Palinka had collected inside. He stared at himself for a second or two then decided to express his doubts.

"Lajos Kossuth! Lajos Kossuth! We all know him as the symbol of Hungarian resistance to foreign rule. He is the reason we Hungarians feel the way we do today, he is probably the reason you Nandi, and thousands of others have fought for freedom today. In 1847, Kossuth advanced his liberal views in a series of brilliant speeches demanding a constitution not only for Hungary, but for Austria as well. His campaign was successful in winning a separate constitution for Hungary. Not everybody was happy with it though and anyway, eventually Kossuth called the Hungarians to arms to defend their independence. With the help of the Polish General Joseph Bem, we won victory after victory because of Kossuth's desire to be free and Bem's assistance because he truly believed in what we were doing."

Janos paused as he collected his thoughts. Nandi waited for a while and then said,

"So, would Poland do the same again with us?"

Feri decided to remind them of the outcome of the 1848 revolution.

"Yes Janos, and we would have still been free now if the bastard Russians hadn't decided to intervene on the side of the Austrians. But yes, I think the Polish would take up arms with us again in this revolution. After all, they have met with the same fate as us what with the Germans then the Russians. If we

November 1st 1956

stick together like we did over one hundred years ago we would all be free, including the Poles."

"Yes that's true father isn't it? We've done the hard bit; we have been the first to stand up to Russia since the Second World War."

Janos had a worried look in his face. Nandi and Feri sensed it so Janos explained his fears.

"I don't know lads. I have my doubts. We need the British and French. I remember during the Second World War when Bela was in hospital dying of pneumonia, a wounded Polish soldier was being treated by the doctors and nurses. The soldier waffled about the horrors of the German and Russian attack on his country. He had been in Warsaw holding off the German air raids when he had a call to retreat to the East immediately as the Russians were advancing. He cursed and swore, complaining all the time how these two countries had persecuted and tortured an innocent race of people inflicting their Nazi and Communist laws on to them. The soldier thanked the Hungarians for their support. But I remember thinking at the time; had Hungary really supported them in their hour of need? There they were being attacked by two of History's most violent nations and we didn't help them. If I can think like that and I am a Hungarian, what must they think?"

The kitchen fell silent while Nandi reflected and then said,

"But it was the British that declared war on Germany after their invasion of Poland but didn't even fire a shot in their defence."

Janos shrugged his shoulders and thought it better not to continue a conversation that he felt the outcome was looming very near and it was just a matter of a short time ahead that would reveal all. Instead, he diverted their attentions onto their fruity distilling alcohol.

November 1st 1956

"Look gentlemen you can see through the shimmering water
in the glass bowl."

The three leaned forward and could see large oval liquid bubbles,
gathering, slipping and sliding against the wet base of the bowl.
As they watched, each bubble seemed to quiver, fizz up slightly
and then drip a soaking rainfall into the free hanging dish beneath.

"Only a short time now before all the fruit has evaporated then we
can taste our homemade firewater." Janos revealed excitedly.

The three of them worked all morning in the kitchen boiling,
simmering, emptying and refilling the slushy fruit to finally
produce two litres of clear, pure Palinka. It tasted divine even
though still very warm and Nandi had to be as drunk as he was to
cope with his father attempting some homemade surgery.
"C'mon ere son place your elbow on the table so I can have a
clear view of the stitches."

Nandi did it and bravely allowed his father to snip away at the
thread and tug it from the wound. It had begun to heal soundly but
still felt very sore when Janos pulled the stitching away from his
skin. Finally, Janos soaked a clean cloth with their freshly made
Palinka and cleaned around the wounded area. When he'd
finished, the scar had knitted neatly but still glowed, however
Janos was happy it had been cleaned up now and sterilised with
alcohol.

That evening Nandi had made the decision to venture back to the
college, so he could have a good sleep and be ready for lessons
the next morning. During the afternoon, Nandi and his parents had
sat around a roaring cast iron stove and told stories. Not epic
stories but tales of their families and friends, an oral history of a
place and its people.

November 1st 1956

Nandi had packed a few things to eat and drink including salami, bread and a small bottle of Palinka squeezed into his briefcase. He embraced his mother and father with an added passion and, as he stood on the veranda in front of the kitchen door, Blackie had been accidentally shut inside the house. He made the mistake known by jumping up against the kitchen door windowpanes, panting and barking profusely. Nandi laughed as if to apologise and opened the kitchen door to allow him to show his affection by licking Nandi's face.

Janos looked at the glass in the kitchen door and noticed something where Blackie had been breathing and steamed up the pane. A word he thought and when his intrigue forced him to look more closely. The poets name had been inscribed there "*Sándor Petöfi*" Janos remembered he had seen Nandi writing something on the window earlier that day.

Father, son and Blackie walked to the village bus stop and while they stood waiting for the bus, Janos decided he would recite a poem from Sándor Petöfi.

"Son, have you still got the bible I gave to you?"
"I carry it everywhere with me father. And, I want to share my freedom with others."
"Is that why you have written Sándor Petöfi on our kitchen door."
Nandi looked happily into his father's eyes and they read each other's thoughts. Janos began and then Nandi joined in.
"On Your Feet, Hungarian! *Rise up, Magyar, the country calls! It's 'now or never' what fate befalls... Shall we live as slaves or free men? That's the question - choose your 'Amen"! God of Hungarians, we swear unto Thee, We swear unto Thee - that slaves we shall no longer be! For up till now we lived like slaves. Damned lie our forefathers in their graves. They, who lived and died in freedom, cannot rest in dusts of thraldom. God of Hungarians, we swear unto Thee, We swear unto Thee - that slaves we shall no longer be!*"

November 1st 1956

Nandi gestured a thumbs up salute to his father through the bus window as it droned out of Mogyoroska. Janos returned the motion and mimed the words clear and defined in order that Nandi could easily lip read, "On Your Feet, Hungarian!"

It was understood by Nandi as it was intended and in the smoky confined space on the old rickety bus, he rested his right hand on the bible in his pocket, winked at the church of Mogyoroska, closed his eyes and drifted into a restful nap before he returned to the rigours of boarding school in Szanto.

CHAPTER 12

November 2nd 1956

Nandi slammed his briefcase onto a circular table that stood in the middle of the college hall.

"So what are you actually saying Mr. Horvath?" They stood alone. His voice echoed in the empty hall and boomed even louder as his tone was raised and angry too.

"I'm saying the British and French have sent their troops to Egypt."

"What the hell is happening in Egypt that could be more important than this?"

"It's all to do with the Suez Canal the lifeline of Europe. The president of Egypt has seized control of it; Britain and France are the main stockholders."

"But it still doesn't make sense. Don't they know we are doomed if they do this."

"The canal represents the only direct means of travel from the Mediterranean to the Indian Ocean, making it vital to the flow of trade between Asia, the Middle East and Europe."

"Aha now I understand." Nandi snapped his fingers at the frightening truth dawning on him in an instant.

"Oil! Oil! Oil! Oil is regarded as much more valuable than the blood of thousands of Hungarian lives. What is the price of a young life compared to the market value of oil? We are naïve fools; we have listened to Radio Free Europe who have been very brave with their broadcasts into Russia's territory sending messages implying they would support us in our quest for freedom. We have believed them. For a thousand years we have

November 2nd 1956

looked for someone to be our friend and for a thousand years we have been betrayed."

Nandi's voice sounded gloomy and sullen. With his head bowed, he lifted his briefcase off the table and slowly strolled out of the hall. No words were spoken. The teacher and student were in total shock … The dashing of all their dreams.

November 3rd 1956 Budapest

Soviet troops slowly manoeuvred surreptitiously encircling major cities, railway lines, airports, strategic targets and the uranium mines in the city of Pecs. One hundred and fifty thousand fresh Russian troops, 5,000 tanks, hundreds of Tupolev Tu2 heavily armed medium bomber warplanes were stationed at the borders on standby ready to fill Hungarian airspace. Hungary's victory, Russia's promise to evacuate, now on a precarious knife-edge.

In the morning, tens of thousands of people hastened towards their places of work. Not all of them had to go by foot because the streetcars had started to run along those lines where the rails had not been torn up and where the tram wires were still intact. It was a pleasure for the people of Budapest to be able to climb aboard the steps of the lumbering yellow trams paying their fares cheerfully. Many factories sent out trucks to fetch their workers. The future was now uncertain with the news of the Suez Crisis but the people of Hungary lived in hope and were treating the day like any other and set about rebuilding their hearts as well as their buildings and livelihoods. If there were many who did not go back to work today, it was not because they were still on strike, but because it was Saturday and it hardly seemed worthwhile. By Monday, all the factories and offices would be running full steam ahead. There was a bustle

November 3rd 1956

around the train stations. The first commuter trains bringing workers from the suburbs were running. The first train bringing medicines arrived at the East Station, coming from the west. The big railroad yards at all major Hungarian Cities announced that traffic had been completely re-established. All food stores, corner shops, clothes shops all now completely open. Queues of shoppers lengthened along the Budapest high streets, waiting to buy bread and potatoes, the housewives certain for the first time they would not return home empty handed. In the espresso shops, there was already black coffee to be had, and some were even able to serve patisserie. On the street corners, chestnut-sellers offered paper cones of warm nuts, which were welcomed in the November crisp chill. The threat of famine in Hungary had vanished; it was free, self sufficient and strengthening through the will and determination of a people. Post Offices had now resumed delivery of mail; glaziers were probably the busiest not just in Budapest. Before anything else, they had been replacing broken windows at the hospitals and now were working elsewhere. The Budapest bakers hadn't stop working through the entire fighting and during their victory week, even though exhausted they continued to work today but were looking forward to a day of rest on Sunday.

That evening the darkness fell over Budapest rapidly. Gaslights and lanterns were lit around craters and bomb holes in the roads and pavements to warn the pedestrian or motorist. But in the deep darkness around Budapest, there was complete silence. Beneath the pines and camouflage netting the Russian guns were lined up for mile after mile and stepped back calibre after calibre. The mortars were in front. Behind them were tanks, their long rifles elevated. Next, came self-propelled guns and following these, batteries of light and heavy artillery. Along the rear were hundreds of multi barrelled rocket launchers capable of firing sixteen projectiles simultaneously. Where the Danube entered the outskirts of the city, the riverbank was jammed with men and equipment.

November 4th 1956 Budapest

Early Morning

The city of Budapest was buzzing with people very early. Shops were closed but there was other work to be done in the main streets, side streets and parks. The unity brought out scores of people in large groups of dozens and more. Enthusiastic people were gossiping and exchanging sparkling conversations until; a low keening sound approached from somewhere off in the distance. It rose rapidly to a terrible piercing scream. For an instant, the crowds seemed mesmerised. Then suddenly the lines of people broke and scattered. But it was too late. Artillery shells burst all over Budapest. Bits of bodies splashed against the boarded up store front. Men and women lay in the street screaming and writhing in agony. Budapest was now Russia's front line. From the outskirts, the ambush of Budapest progressed. With ear-splitting and earthshaking roars, buildings erupted in flame. More than twenty thousand guns of all calibres poured a storm of fire onto the Hungarian freedom fighters positions. Pinned in the merciless glare of the Russian searchlights the Hungarian city seemed to disappear before a rolling wall of bursting shells. Earth, concrete, steel, parts of trees spewed into the air and huge buildings blazed from within. Dusted twilight obliterated the daylight, and to the north and south of Budapest gun flashes stabbed the darkness. Pinpoints of light like deadly firecrackers, winked in rapid succession as tons of shells slammed into their targets. Budapest was suffering a hurricane of explosives so intense that an atmospheric disturbance was created. A fierce hot wind blew hard through

November 4th 1956

the streets and alleyways, there was no hiding place it seemed as the Russian tactic became obvious. They were determined to crush the revolution and show no mercy taking the city block by

396

block if they had to. Everywhere, the Hungarian freedom fighters were firing whatever weapons they had even though they could see no target. The violent thunder of the guns created a concussion so tremendous that defenders of Budapest and their equipment alike shook uncontrollably from the shock. This time with weapons immeasurably superior to the Hungarians, they methodically chopped paths several hundred metres wide like rolling barrages of fiery scythes into the freedom fighter's and civilians alike.

November 4th 1956 Szanto College

Evening

"This is Hungary calling! This is Hungary calling! The last remaining nation, call to the United Nations. Early this morning the Soviet Troops launched a general attack on Hungary. We are requesting you to send us immediate aid. For the sake of God and freedom, help Hungary."

Nandi and his friends had listened to the panic stricken pleas on the radio all afternoon. Begs for assistance had been broadcast to the west in all languages, English, French, German... Nandi's eyes were red and his nose blocked. He felt like he had been crying for hours but now decided that his tears had to stop. The others shared his view as they tucked away their soaked handkerchiefs.

"What time is it?" Nandi asked anyone.

Jancsi checked his watch. "It's half past six almost."

November 4th 1956

Nandi opened his briefcase on the bed. With a penknife, he pulled the back compartment from the inside of the lid to reveal a secret section.

"Anyone who is planning to go to Budapest stay in the room, the rest of you, leave now."

They stared at Nandi hard.

"You have to be crazy to attempt such a thing." Laszi said surprised at Nandi's suggestion.

"Anyone else share Laszi's view?"

Nobody answered.

"Don't be ashamed. I wouldn't blame any of you. This is something I must do and the less anyone knows about my intentions the safer I will be. So, please leave, leave now quickly."

One by one, they shook hands and hugged Nandi as they left the dormitory. He instructed each one in turn to confirm his story that he was ill and was going back home.

Peter reassured Nandi as he left the room, "You know it's not too late. The British and French maybe planning their surprise attack on the Soviets any time now."

Nandi nodded his head vigorously in agreement. "I'm sure they are. I bloody hope they are."

Jancsi was the only one that remained in the room.

"You coming with me Jancsi?"

"No Nandi, my mother is ill and I have to stay with her and…."

"It's okay Jancsi there's no need to explain." Nandi filled his pistol with bullets and slotted it in the secret compartment of the briefcase and dropped about a dozen loose bullets aside it. He

November 4th 1956

sealed the inside of the lid secure. From a drawer at the side of his bed he pulled out a chunk of salami and bread, placed them in his briefcase next to his bible, made the sign of the cross before closing it.

"Nandi you do realise the Russians will not stop. They will be prepared to throw all that they have got at the revolution to ensure a swift defeat. Even if the west are preparing to send help, by the time they've assembled any troops the Russians will have flattened most of Budapest."

Nandi breathed deeply before answering.

"I will be catching the last train to Budapest at 7:17p.m"

"Nandi maybe it's over for us."

There was a silent pause.

"It's over."

Nandi retaliated quickly.

"It is NOT over! For you it's over. For me, it isn't. The west maybe abandoning Budapest, I will not."

Jancsi shook his head prompting Nandi to continue.

"If I don't do this I will not be able to live with myself. Years from now I will be praying for this moment to present itself to me again. But then it will be too late. If I die I will die with no regrets."

"Nandi it will be like committing suicide."

"I am not afraid of committing suicide provided I can die with some honour."

Jancsi was moved at Nandi's passionate emotion. He faltered and then grabbed the forearm of his companion firmly.

November 4th 1956

"You are one brave Hungarian."

Nandi grinned and clutched Jancsi's knuckles.

Jancsi winked encouragingly at Nandi and said "I feel sorry for those Russians when you arrive in Budapest."

"Bastards think they've mastered the art of ambush, wait 'til they get a load of me."

"I have something for you."

Jancsi pulled a piece of paper from his pocket with an address written on it.

"What's this?"

"My cousin Maria and my uncle Paul live here. It's a cottage at Nagytarcsa just outside Budapest. They know of you, I've told them many stories, in fact it wasn't too long ago before the fighting started I told them we might be going to Budapest and may need to take refuge. They're great people, Paul is getting old now but he's a true Hungarian worker. If you need any help or if you are in trouble, go there, they will look after you."

"Thank you Jancsi"

✳✳✳

For once, the train was on time and Nandi boarded the empty carriage with an unfilled feeling at the pit of his stomach. He slid his briefcase under his seat then transfixed a firm glare at his college through a smoke stained window until it disappeared out of sight. Would he return? Would he ever see his parents or Mogyoroska again? What fate lay before him he had no idea. In this cyclonic emotion, he felt somehow content with his decision almost like this was his intended destiny. As he wrestled with his emotions, his eyes grew weary. Pictures of death, war and destruction haunted his light sleep. Images flashed before his eyes,

November 4th 1956

explosions, and bridges collapsing into the river Danube. Sweat coated the frown across his forehead and his head shook from side to side caused by a frightful scene in his nightmare. Nandi was sprinting across the Arpad Bridge that was crumbling behind him. With each stride, the concrete road beneath his feet poured into the river below. He screamed and stretched out an arm to his father waiting, beckoning from the Pest side of the bridge. Janos was shouting to Nandi,

"Promise me something son, that whatever happens in your life, whatever happens in our future, you will always do the right thing, you must always follow your heart and above all, you will be free. And promise you will never leave your family. If you can promise me these things, I will make a pledge to you of my own, I'm going to teach you all I know and more, I'm going to teach you how to use your brain, how to use your hands, how to fend for yourself and to fight for freedom."

A voice from the past echoed over and over in his head, his legs grew tired and his long stretched sprint went into slow motion. His arm remained out-stretched, parallel to the ground; all fingers splayed wide apart desperately trying to reach his father.

Nandi jumped from his sleep instantly before he reached his father in the dream. Something had woken him. For a moment, he was confused and checked all around him. A one-legged beggar was sitting opposite him with a wooden crutch at his side. His face was emaciated, ravaged by tuberculosis Nandi thought. His head hung down in a sleep, undisturbed by the flickering lights in the carriage and the screeching brakes from the train wheels. Nandi pushed his face against the window and cupped his hand around his temple in order to shade a reflection. A signpost whizzed passed the window 'Kistarcsa' and Nandi rubbed his eyes with both thumbs realising Budapest was the next stop.

"Wait a minute. Why are we stopping here? This train supposed to be going straight to the City centre I'm sure. Don't be a clod Nandi, there's fighting in Budapest. We probably can't get through." Still confused he tried to fathom out his situation. The ticket inspector slid open the carriage door roughly and shouted.

November 4th 1956

"Everyone remain seated!" As he passed, Nandi grabbed his arm.
"What's happening?"
"Russian soldiers have stopped the train here at Kistarcsa."

"How many Russian soldiers?"

"Looks like about a dozen or more with machine guns."

The ticket inspector continued towards the back of the train and Nandi's heart began to thump harder. He stared hard once again outside towards the front of the train and to his horror five soldiers began to climb aboard. He grabbed his briefcase from under the seat, stood up and then snatched the wooden crutch from the old man and ran to the toilet bolting the door behind him. The window slid open easily. Carefully he popped his head outside. All was clear this side, dark, aided by another stationary train alongside. He managed swiftly to lean out and throw his briefcase onto the train roof. He blew a sigh of relief as he glanced at himself in a broken mirror, but thought it better to return to his seat when he heard a deep Russian voice from within the carriage. As he opened the door, he checked both connecting carriages. One soldier in each seemed to be checking papers. He gingerly made his way back to his seat and the soldier was shouting to the one-legged man to wake up and get up. The soldier hadn't noticed Nandi approaching until Nandi held out the crutch in front of him with both hands.

"He can't get up without this."

He turned his head sharply, the crutch only a few centimetres from his face. There was a second or two pause as their eyes met. Sensing danger, the soldier began to turn his machine gun towards Nandi. Before the gun became a threat, the soldier felt a sharp whack to his windpipe. Nandi had jabbed the crutch forcefully and the soldier gasped for air. Without hesitation, a violent blow followed the jab to the back of his neck. He collapsed over the seat behind the one-legged man and Nandi knew he'd broken his neck. A quick momentary look confirmed it. He was out of sight for the moment but Nandi needed to move quickly. He replaced

November 4th 1956

the crutch alongside the old man and darted back to the toilet. This time he didn't lock it behind him but climbed out of the window and scrambled onto the roof of the train. He only had a few minutes and it didn't take him that long to retrieve his gun and throw his briefcase beyond the opposite train into what he thought were bushes encompassing a field. He kept his head low but checked the soldier's positions on the Kistarcsa platform. With no time to waste, he leapt to the rocky floor and rolled under the opposite train.

Two soldiers entered Nandi's carriage from opposite sides. Only the one-legged man sat in his seat as they could see.
"Where's Ivan?" One called to the other.
"He should be in here."
They simultaneously scanned the carriage. Their machine guns pointed in front of them slowly walking towards each other.
"Oh Christ he's here."
One of them checked his pulse immediately.
"He's dead. Who the fuck did this?"
The other soldier jammed his machine gun into the side of the one-legged man's head.
"Was it you? I said was it you, you fucking cripple?"
"Don't be stupid it isn't him. Quick raise the alarm now."
They both popped their heads out of the window and blew hard on a whistle encouraging the other soldiers to rush over.
"It's Ivan, it's Ivan. Somebody's killed him and he's on this train."
"Right, every soldier off this train, off this train, now!"
The sergeant major screamed and screamed until all soldiers stood in a line along the Kistarcsa platform. The train driver and the ticket inspector called out to them. "What's happening? We have 100 hundred passengers on board what shall we do?"
With their machine guns raised high they all coolly looked at the sergeant major for instructions.
"Fuck 'em! Blow this last train to Budapest to hell."

November 4th 1956

The machine gun fire and grenades took about five minutes to totally annihilate the seven carriages. All carriages were ablaze. Some had derailed and turned over on their side in the explosions.

Glass from the windows splintered and rained a terrifying
sheet over the offending soldiers. The intense heat forced them to
retreat further away still launching gunshot after gunshot into the
train.

But Nandi was long gone by now. He scrambled through the
muddy field, briefcase in his left hand, pistol in the other. Behind
him was the blazing train illuminating the black sky. To his right,
white and red flashes of light boomed and shone unsteadily on the
horizon. The hammering of guns, less than twenty-five miles
away, was like the sullen thunder of a far-off storm. This was
Budapest.

Nandi had been jogging for about thirty minutes when the vast
area around seemed to swallow him up. He stopped and checked
his breath. The darkness seemed to suffocate him and for a
moment, he was unsure which direction to follow. He sat down on
the floor opened his briefcase and bit a lump out of his salami
stick. After he spat the skin onto the floor, he thought it safe
enough to light a cigarette. He lay back, using his briefcase as a
pillow and tried to ignore the freezing ground beneath him. His
thoughts were blank. For ten minutes in a hypnotic state, he
smoked his cigarette and stared aimlessly at the cloudy night
skies.

"I'll wait until dawn and then I'll move." Nandi whispered to
himself.

After a few hours, he was unsure if he'd been to sleep. He hadn't
moved a muscle he knew that; but it seemed like he'd watched the
sky go from black to a dark grey. He knew one thing for sure,
whether he had been sleeping or staring, there was a new attack on
Budapest and it was coming from the air. As he watched, still not

November 5th 1956

flinching, in tight V-formations, the Russian fighter planes banked
and headed for the city centre. Nandi sat up and could see the

planes getting lower and lower. As they were mere dots, from somewhere on the fringes of Budapest, bursts of bright pink flak and streams of red, yellow and white tracer bullets tried to shoot down the planes. In response, the planes poured out dense clouds of white smoke and within minutes they had laid a thick, fluffy blanket that obscured not only the anti aircraft barrage, but the whole of the east side of Budapest it seemed. Nandi watched the Russian tactic with intrigue, what came next was a bombardment from the air. The pilots couldn't see what they were hitting, nor did they care. The tactic was obvious, as the attack and the smoke screen confused Budapest, reinforcement tanks moved in closer with a free hand, without confrontation.

A farmhouse came into view in the distance. There weren't any roads or narrow lanes leading to it, which, somehow made the farmhouse seem a safe bet to approach. He replaced the pistol back into his briefcase and then began trudging towards the house. It was a fair distance away yet but in the shadows of the dusky morning, an old man was pottering around the farmyard at the front. A single low flying aircraft flew passed; the trees trembled under the breath of wind coming from it. A little fox terrier raced along the field at the back of the house as if he were late for an important dinner. Then above Nandi's head, high up in the now bluish, dark grey sky, a hawk soared, chasing pigeons.
The man noticed him approaching and called out.
"Who's there?"
Nandi answered quickly.
"Excuse me sir, but I'm looking for Nagytarcsa and I got a little lost in the dark last night."
"You are in Nagytarcsa."
"Aha, then you will know Paul and Maria."
"Who are you?"

November 5th 1956

"My name is Nandi, Nandor Pekar." He offered the old man his hand to shake and he returned the gesture with a frail, bloodless hand. He didn't let go.

"Nandi. Where is Jancsi?"

"You are Paul? Oh, that's fantastic. Jancsi is safe; he isn't as stupid as me he has stayed at home."

"What are you doing here Nandi?"

"I want to go to Budapest and help."

"It's a lost cause I think. Brave young men like you getting killed now by the thousands."

"Can you help me Paul? I don't want to put you in any danger, but Jancsi said you would help me."

"Of course I will do what I can. Come in, come in, first you must eat some breakfast and meet my daughter Maria."

As he said that, Maria appeared in the doorway and had been listening from the kitchen. Nandi stopped and stared as she approached rapidly. Her brown silky dress moulded itself to the girl's figure as a sail moulds itself to the mast under a soft gentle breeze. She had thrown her shoulders back a little, and the outline of her breasts were delicately suggested. At each step, the soft skirt clung to her legs, and almost every line of her body was gloriously revealed by her swift, rhythmic gait.

She held out her tiny hand and introduced herself as Nandi kissed both of her cheeks.

"I have heard a lot about you Nandi."

"Only good things hopefully. And you are as pretty as Jancsi suggested."

They sat around the breakfast table with a single light bulb hanging from the ceiling casting a yellowy glow over the table. Maria placed a plate of chicken wings in the centre of the table and a jug of water. She gestured for Nandi to help his self as she pulled up a chair to join them.

"So, how is my cousin Jancsi?" Maria inquired.

"He's fine. Exams went well for him."

November 5th 1956

"And what about fighting with the Russians, have you got caught up in it over there?" Paul needed to know.

"Let's say… We fired a few shots."

"There's more than a few shots being fired now. This is Budapest not Szanto." Paul warned.

Maria leaned on the table with her elbows.

"What are your intentions now Nandi?"

"Me. I want to join the Freedom Fighters. Do you know where I should go?"

Maria answered quickly.

"The Corvin Brigade! It was a growing army and operate in the centre at the Corvin cinema so we last heard."

Nandi paused.

"The Corvin Brigade. Then I will be their next recruit."

Paul stared at Nandi and then Maria and said,

"Nandi, are you brave or just angry?"

"I believe we should be free. I believe good always conquers evil. I have a bible in my pocket to prove that. I still think the west may come to help therefore we need to continue the struggle. And for sure, if the Russians regain control, our lives will not be worth living; and I want my children to grow up in a free country, so, that alone is worth fighting for."

Maria fluttered her eyes before she said,

"But, is it worth dying for?"

Nandi stared hard into Maria's eyes and answered positively.

"When the British landed on the French beaches in June 1944, thousands were slaughtered. They didn't die for nothing. Their country is free. If it meant that my country could be free then I am willing to die for that."

"I'm impressed." Maria smiled when she answered.

"Are you really?" Nandi returned the smile. "So, Maria. What about you? How do you feel?"

"Feel about what?"

"Feel about the future."

Maria was faint in her conversation and as she spoke, Nandi examined every detail of her face to its finest subtleties. Her

November 5th 1956

eyebrows were delicate and their arch was narrow. The left was marked by a small scar, which, though plainly visible, did not mar her beauty; this was rather curious. The large eyes, he didn't know exactly whether they were blue or deep green, were shaded by long lashes. The mouth was large, but the lips were delicate and the corners of her mouth were capable of expressing the sensitive play of her emotions in a thousand shades. She had two types of smiles that made her face look expressive and piquant.

As the morning almost ended, Paul had fell into a silent sleep in his chair but Maria and Nandi talked and talked as if they'd known each other forever. While he slept, she took the opportunity to lead Nandi outside to a nearby barn.

She pulled the large door open only to reveal shelves full of paint, tins of axle-grease, various tools and jars of rusty nails.

Nandi frowned and walked inside.

"What are you showing me?"

"Look over there in those tin barrels."

Nandi removed the lid. They were full of gunpowder, dynamite, knives, grenades and about a dozen handguns.

"Christ, where have these come from?"

"About a week ago during the fighting some young men attacked a convoy of Russian military vehicles. They killed them all, seized their weapons and hid them in here."

"Where are these young men now?"

"They live here in Nagytarcsa."

Nandi stroked his unshaven chin as he thought.

"Can I meet these guys?"

"I can get word to them. Why, what's on your mind?

✳✳✳

Before they arrived Nandi laid out all the weapons across the floor. Maria listened attentively as Nandi explained his plan. That afternoon, ten of the young men arrived at Maria's barn to meet up with Nandi. They were aged between 15 and 20 and were curious to understand Nandi's intentions.

November 5th 1956

"Maria. Why do you let this man have our weapons?" An older one called out.

Maria answered. "Well what do you lot intend to do with them?"

"We are waiting for the right moment."

"And when is the right moment." Nandi asked.

"When the west arrive."

"But that might be too late. Or never."

Nandi let them all ponder as he strutted around the weapons and then said.

"Listen. We are at war. A just war for freedom. What is freedom? What does it mean? I'll tell you. It means we can live peacefully, it means we can have the right to speak out and feel okay to disagree with the government. It means we can eat and drink as free people. It means our children can be happy and prosper. It means our country will get some respect. I'll tell you what I would do with my freedom. I would raise a family of Pekar's, strong and healthy, build a home of my own have grandchildren, great grandchildren. But to get that, to have that privilege is not easy. An ugly great monster stands in our way. It's called Russians. We are in the business of war and our reward is a free nation. To run this business, this trade, the tools of our trade are these weapons. To get what we deserve to help our companions in Budapest we must eliminate the enemy…"

"Okay. But how?"

"There's only one way to win a war. Ambush!"

The ten lads stepped closer towards Nandi. The oldest one spoke to Nandi curiously.

"Where did you come from?"

Nandi grinned and replied.

"From the last train to Budapest."

They all laughed together and introduced themselves to Nandi. Paul brought out 15 small glasses of Palinka whilst Nandi went over his plan.

"I have noticed a large mass of trees about two kilometres from here at the roadside. This looks to be a decisive route into Budapest. We must block off this route, but here we can ambush the tanks or whatever. We can hide in the trees and fields and hit them with grenades, petrol bombs etc…"

"We haven't got any petrol. The Russians confiscated our supplies a couple of days ago."

"Okay it's not a problem."
"Of course it's a problem." Maria told Nandi.
"No, we need to improvise. Paul, would you fetch me as many pairs of woollen socks as you can spare please."
"Socks?" Queried one of the lads.
"Yeah socks. I'll explain in a minute. Does anyone have an update of the war?"
One of the lads knew something and so revealed,
"Unofficially I have heard the Russians have taken Buda Castle. But at Pecs, there is a Hungarian army who are fighting from the hills. They are winning so the rumour has it; they are calling themselves 'The Invisible' or something like that."
"Brilliant!" Nandi replied. "I like that, The Invisible"
Paul entered the barn with about half a dozen pairs of black woollen socks in his arms. He dropped them amongst the weaponry and smiled at the gang. Nandi looked at him as if looking over the rim of spectacles.
"I hope they are clean Paul." He said jokingly.
Maria joined in. "If they weren't we be in with a shout to kill all of the Soviet army just from the smell of my father's feet."
Paul laughed along with the others and waved a fist at Maria.
"You cheeky monkey you."

Maria found herself laughing and actually feeling some kind of happiness and fulfil ness about what they were doing. Amongst her overwhelming pleasure, she looked at Nandi from the corner of her eye and felt there was something special about him. In a short time, he had captured the hearts and the spirits of a few, and as she glanced around the barn, she was not alone with these feelings. Before she finished laughing at the jokes she accidentally found herself cuddling Nandi around his waste and he responded and clutched her to his chest. They looked each other in the eyes and before they got carried away, they released each other instantaneously and Nandi began explaining what to do with the socks.

"Okay, first cram them full with demolition, some TNT and composition B. like this." He had picked up a sock and began to demonstrate. "Then Rig up a long fuse and spread axle grease all over the sock."

After smearing the grease all over the wool, it then became clear to the others and he continued to explain. "At the right moment we light the fuse, sneak up at the sides of the tanks and stick our homemade bombs between the wheel and their tracks. Always hit them in the tracks! The explosion will blow the tracks right off the wheels thus immobilising the tank…Any questions?" Nandi held the homemade bomb outstretched in his hand with the grease dripping to the floor. "Okay, no questions so please, there's 11 more to make can we all muck in?"

Maria picked the remaining socks and threw them one by one to each of them. Eagerly they grabbed at the demolition powder and began preparing the bomb.

Paul shouted up. "Err Nandi. If we don't use the bombs can I have my socks back?"

"Yes Paul. But do you want me to wash them first?"

"No. My boots are too small for me maybe I will be able to get them on a little easier with all that grease."

Maria added. "But don't forget to remove the TNT. Wouldn't want you to have a little accident."

Amid the laughter, two of the lads heard something outside and ran over to the barn door to see. The others followed and could see in the distance, tanks and other military vehicles heading towards Budapest along the road.

"That's it." Nandi's heart pumped faster. "We can make to those trees before they can. No time to lose let's go." With the grease from his hands, he smothered his face for camouflage, picked up what weapons he could and led the way across field. "Everyone, heads down and spread out." He ordered.

They made it to the trees well before the convoy of about 6 tanks and two cars. They were well hidden all around. The rumbling and vibrations rippling through the ground around was terrifying when the tanks were almost on top of them. Nandi was the first to pull the pin from a grenade with his teeth. Suddenly, all hell broke loose. They intended to blow out the first and last tank but the Russians had grown wise to this. They immediately broke their long line and raced into the fields either side of the road. Machine gun fire, explosions, rained from either side. In seconds there were fires ablaze, blood and smoke hurled into the air together. One explosion forced a tree to come crashing down into the road. Mud, metal, branches, dust and bricks became a cocktail of eruptions. The Russians dared to open the hatch and fire relentlessly at the Hungarians creating a wall of bullets thudding into the areas around them.

The smoke cleared slightly by a sudden gust of wind. Nandi had a better view.

"Shit. No more grenades, just my handgun and one sock."

He risked it anyway; he rolled and rolled across the floor until he lay beneath a menacing tank that was blasting its way through. He lit the fuse of his grease bomb and splat it onto the tracks. He knew he had to get away before friendly fire, or the explosion killed him. He did it quickly rolling back into the field. He aimed his gun at the hatch. The bomb exploded and the tank couldn't move. It tried, but the smell of metal burning soon convinced the tanks occupants that they'd been hit. As they tried to scramble out of the hatch, Nandi fired one shot after another at them. He was sure he'd hit them but his attentions were distracted when he saw a single aircraft approaching.

"Oh bollocks."

The lads were winning he thought as shots from the Russians deteriorated. He looked up and scrambled over to one of them. "Quick, give me a sock." He passed it to him immediately. Sharply, Nandi looked over his shoulder. The aircraft skimmed the road behind only a few feet off the ground. It started to spit bullets like a made hornet. He could see and feel them ricocheting all around. Rising to his feet with the bomb in one hand, he had managed to light the fuse and furiously ran like a mad man screaming, sprinting to the right, away from the roadside. The aircraft followed.

"Get down!" Someone cried

Nandi clearly caught the face of the pilot through the blur of the propeller. The guns had stopped, but there was no doubt that Nandi was a target. The Russian pilot nosed up just slightly, aiming to sever Nandi's head with the propeller. Nandi vaulted face first into a ditch, a bare instant before the craft roared passed. He leapt to his feet with only about three centimetres of fuse left to burn, incredibly he ran after the ascending plane; in an instant he was in Szanto town centre and everything had stopped. He stared all around him, he could see Irinka, his friends Jancsi, Laszi, Peter, and crowds of the Szanto gypsies including Irinka's Uncle Joe. He looked at his hands and could see he was holding an old boot. Strangely, everyone had frozen still, no movement. Old ladies, a horse and cart stopped dead like a photograph. Suddenly he could here a slow beat drum roll. All eyes were on Nandi. He gripped the boot tight in his right fist and grit his teeth tight until he felt his jaw crack. The muscles in his lean cheeks pumped and flexed hard until, like someone had released the top off a shaken up bottle of pop, Nandi turned sharply ran to the front of the box, swung his right arm with all of his might and felt his shoulder jolt as he released and hurled the boot. "**Ahhhhhhh**" He shouted out as he watched the boot climb higher. The Szanto gypsies sucked in their breath and watched in amazement as the boot cleared the first set of pegs, then the next, until finally gravity got the better of it and the boot came hurtling to the ground.

His senses came flooding back in a second. The flashback hadn't affected his aim. He stood coolly watching the plane climb towards the crest of a hill. Suddenly, there was a loud crack, and a trail of smoke followed from out of the side of the plane. It began to plummet, its fate unknown as it disappeared behind the hill.

Abruptly, the guns behind him ceased. He turned sharply to see. The scene of carnage was favourable. All tanks were burning, out of action. The Russians lay dead in the road or slumped over the tanks and the two cars. He marched over checking for their own casualties. He counted them all. Nobody was missing. Injuries were rife though. Some had bullet wounds in their arms, legs and shoulders. Others, a few burns and abrasions.

After they'd decided what to do with the wounded, Nandi informed them he would be heading for Budapest in the morning to join up with the Corvin Brigade. Anybody wishing to join him were to meet at this spot at 5a.m.

He entered the cottage only to find Maria leaning over Paul in his bed. He panicked when he saw Maria's hands and arms soaked with blood and she was crying.

"What has happened?"

"Quick Nandi, he was in the garden when a low flying plane fired at him. He's been hit in the stomach."

Nandi rushed over and checked the wound. The bullet had pierced his side and exited through the back.

"Get me some Palinka and gunpowder immediately."

She hurried and fetched them and Nandi poured the alcohol all over the gunshot wound front and back, wiping the area dry with a cotton cloth.

"Get him something to bite onto."

Maria fumbled through the drawer.

"What are you going to do Nandi?" Paul asked.

"This may hurt so bare with me."

Paul managed to sit forward and pull Nandi closer so as he could whisper into his ear. " You are a brave lad. My prayers are with you. Do not fail Nandi you will not get another chance, so take it. I cannot tell you what to do but I imagine sometimes, what if I could turn into an un-noticed door into a hidden garden and find there my past, ready to be lived again. How would I change things? And one other thing Nandi, I think my daughter likes you."

Maria passed Nandi a thin sharpening stone.

"Here bite this."

Paul bit hard and screamed as Nandi coated the two bullet holes with gunpowder and lit it. It was a few minutes later when it was apparent that igniting the gunpowder had melted the skin fusing and sealing the holes.

Maria poured cold water all over the burnt area to douse the pain and control Paul's screams. It was a fair while later when Paul complained that Nandi had wasted his Palinka.

"And what about my socks?" He asked

Maria and Nandi smiled when they informed him they'd all been used in a good cause and one had even took out the plane that had shot him.

Nandi sent word to the lads that there had been a change of plan and he wouldn't be joining the Corvin Brigade just yet in light of Paul's injury. He felt compelled to stay with the old man until he'd recovered. Maria didn't seem to mind, but tried to contain her relieved feeling of safety if Nandi stayed.

When Paul's pain sort of eased Maria lay a cold damp cloth against his forehead. He sighed as she did and it wasn't long before he sank into a deep sleep.

Maria poured Nandi a glass of Palinka and herself wine and they sat at the table under the dim light.

"It seems strange doesn't it?" Nandi broke the silence.

"What's strange?"

"How we sit here almost calmly while Budapest is under siege."

As he said it, there was a couple of dull booms in the distance and the single bulb flickered rapidly.

Maria was startled at first but then breathed deeply almost used to the sounds of war around her.

"Your words to my friends earlier. So sincere, did you mean all of it?"

"I certainly did. It's more important to me than anything; that my children, grandchildren grow up in a free world. You and I, we will never be free even if the Russians were to leave right now. We've already witnessed and lived through torturous times and it's because of this, it's important that my next generation live to be free."

"Who has taught you to be this way?"

"My father I suppose."

"What's he like?"

"Oh he's a solid man with good family values."

"Look I'll show you something."

Nandi pulled his bible from his pocket, opened it and read his fathers words.

"King Herrod asked John the Baptist 'if I gave you your freedom, what would you do with it?' John answered 'I would follow the one who I have made the way for.'
Nandi, if you were in chains as was John the Baptist and you were asked the same question, what would be your answer?
To find your true answer you must search your soul.

Son, to handle yourself use your head. To find the courage to seek freedom and confront others, use your heart.
Time and space will never divide
Or keep my son from my side"

Maria arranged her thoughts before commenting.
"That's beautiful." She remarked admirably
Nandi opened another page and a single stem of a Lilly of the Valley flower fell onto the table followed by a firmly pressed white rose.

"And what is this?" She pointed to the Lilly of the Valley.

"It is my father's favourite flower."
"And the other?"
Nandi paused as if too difficult to answer. She looked into his moist eyes and sensed pain.
"This is Irinka's flower."
"And who is Irinka?"

"She was my only love."

"You say, was"

"Yes was. They murdered her, you know, the Avo."

"Why?"

Nandi's voice slightly increased in volume.

"Who really knows why? Maybe I wouldn't be here today if they hadn't."

Nandi spent almost all night opening up to this beautiful, sensitive woman. She was attentive and it seemed intending to know everything about Nandi. In almost 24 hours, she had learned everything there was to know about him and warmed to his quiet but strong nature by the minute. By the morning, Nandi had bedded down on the small sofa and Maria had covered him with shawls.

The next 24 hours had been restless for them all but constant care for Paul had eventually seemed to improve his wound. That night Nandi had vowed to leave for Budapest the next morning. Little news had trickled through to them they had limited knowledge of Budapest's fate but Nandi was still determined to continue on to the city.

It was early on November 7th when Nandi awoke and filled his briefcase once again with few supplies. Paul still slept and he could hear Maria rummaging around in her bedroom. He knocked quietly on her door as she whispered for him to enter.

"I'm almost ready to go now Maria."

She didn't look at him but answered

"Yes I know."

Nandi thought he sensed a little hostility

"What's the matter?"

She turned her back paused and said,

"You know you don't have to go. You could stay here until it's all over. Maybe we are destined to be slaves and maybe **we** have a destiny. You know, you and I."

"Maria. If I get through this I will come for you."

"Oh my God don't; don't make empty promises that you know you will not keep."

"Okay, then is it okay for me to tell you that I love you."

There was a long silence. Nothing could be heard but the tiny music of flames floating in from the kitchen through the ajar bedroom door.

Maria raised her eyes slowly and cautiously to Nandi, but when their glances met, she turned her head away abruptly.

He seized her hand and, after a short struggle, held it prisoner in his own. Then he carried it to his lips, and pressed his mouth into her soft palm. Maria turned her back but did not withdraw her hand. Nandi kissed it again sending a burning sensation tingling through to her shoulder. She drew her hand away gently and said, "Father might hear us, come in and spank us"

The threat sounded so implausible that she smiled at herself. She strained, however, to hear something towards the door.

Nandi caught hold of Maria's hand again; she resisted feebly. He tried to draw her towards him, but Maria clung with the other hand to the wardrobe door handle. She held it tight and he could not draw her away.

"I am strong..." Maria said, her cheeks flushed and her eyes sparkling, filled with eagerness for this new and fascinating game. Nandi took advantage of this moment and decided to challenge Maria's strength and tugged at her with so sudden and sharp a jerk that she released the door handle, lost her balance and all but fell onto him. He held her in his two strong arms, so that she could not move. He pressed his mouth against her lips. At first, she kept her lips tightly closed to protect herself from the kiss, but soon her lips relaxed, melted, and for the first time in her life, she experienced a rapturous tantalising kiss. Now her hand clung tight to the nape of Nandi's neck and her shoulders quivered with this fiery, new delight.

Nandi held her, trembling, in his arms. He was acutely conscious of the contours of her body that pressed itself against him and its two tender, burning breasts. Their kisses grew more passionate with every slow and tender mouth movement until Nandi slowly unbuttoned the back of her dress. As he undid the last button, she pushed him away gently, took the straps from her shoulders and let the dress slither to the floor about her feet. She stepped away from it; naked body exposed and nervously told Nandi,

"I am a virgin."

"Don't worry." He answered kindly. "I'll be okay."

CHAPTER 13

November 8th 1956

"Are you leaving for Budapest?" Paul asked Nandi, when he entered the kitchen.

"Yes I am." He answered, gently squeezing Paul's right shoulder careful not to knock his arm whilst he ladled a spoonful of pea soup into his mouth.

Maria held Nandi a dark grey short woollen jacket open. "Here try this on, it belonged to Jancsi's father, it should fit, he was as big as you."

Nandi slid the jacket on over his thin pullover, right arm first and then the left. "Perfect." Maria delighted and began buttoning up the front pulling him a little closer as she got higher towards the neck.

"You see Nandi. It's a thick jacket so if a bullet with your name on it strikes you, it will not pierce your body. Then, you have to keep your promise to me." Nandi smiled reassuringly into her eye's attempting to comfort her as the words got stuck in her throat. She dropped her eyes to the floor when she felt her cheeks burn, and tentatively moved away from Nandi then unassumingly made her way outside into the back fields facing Budapest. Nandi attempted to follow, but Paul grabbed his arm and persuaded him to sit next to him.

"How's your bullet wound this morning?"

"Oh sod it; the Nazi's did worse than that to me?"

"Hegyeshalom!"

"It's the border between Hungary and Austria." Nandi commented, slightly sarcastic.

"The No.10 road leads you there. 2 km from Hegyshalom in a large field elevated on a slight hilly mound there is a red tiled

November 8th 1956

roof cottage, its front door and porch face Austria. There, lives a man, a little younger than me, he's known as Gyorgy. I don't know if it's an alias.

During the war, he and I smuggled microfilm to the west. After the war, I lost contact with him, but I hear he's been working with the west against the commie's. The point is, you may need him."

"Why would I?"

Paul shrugged his shoulders, didn't answer just continued to spoon up his soup; and then he remembered something else.

"Here, I have something for you." Paul lifted up his whittled soup dish and passed Nandi a small key.

"What is it for?" Nandi took it and looked at its slender point and jagged edge.

"Beneath the hay in my barn covered with a large Hessian bag, you will find a Méray 500 motorcycle. Take it, it's yours. Transport to Budapest."

"What about fuel?"

"It's full." Paul winked as he answered. "The Russians didn't find it and I had a feeling it may come in handy. Question is, can you ride a motorcycle?"

"I can give it a try, can't I? Thank you very much."

Outside, Maria stood motionless, arms folded across her tiny shoulders. Her outline pressed against a half land and half sky horizon. Her hair blew away from her face in a northerly direction and stood out against the glowing flames from Budapest.

Nandi walked behind her but remained a few steps back peering with her at the disturbing sight. She knew he was there but remained static. After a few moments, Nandi pulled the bible from his pocket and began flicking through the Old Testament pages until he found a passage that he was looking for. He cleared his throat before reading it.

" Ecclesiastes 4:9-12. Two are better than one, because they have a good return for their toil. For if they fall, one will lift up his fellow; but woe to him who is alone when he falls and has not another to lift him up."

He closed the bible and replaced it into his pocket.

"I will come back Maria."

Without any more words, she turned and clung on to Nandi. They kissed repeatedly and Maria found it comforting when he kissed the tears from her cheeks and eyes. Paul found the energy to peak through a small window and was sure he would remember the silhouetted sight of their lips entwined with a background of orange explosions behind, from the Budapest raids.

It took Nandi and Maria almost an hour to bring the old motorcycle to life. They choked when it spluttered and backfired, Paul, even though

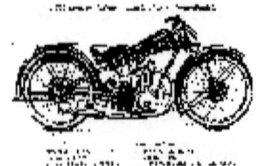

limping, joined them outside to congratulate 'Nandi the mechanic' he joked.

Nandi kept the 4 stroke engine revving whilst Maria used an old belt of Paul's to strap his briefcase to his back. Paul took the accelerator from Nandi so he had the opportunity to embrace Maria once again. Amid the ear piercing, high pitched sound from the motorcycle, it didn't take him too long to find the page from the bible he'd just read.

"Here." He said to Maria tearing the flimsy page in two vertically. "You save that half of the page and when I return, we can repair it as we repair our hearts."

She took the half page, folded it four times, clenched her hand and kissed her fist.

Nandi sat onto the springy seat, revved it high and sped off towards the road. Maria followed as far as she could across the field, waving all the time, until he disappeared over the crest of the uneven road towards Budapest.

It was hard to control at first, but after only a few kilometres, the gears began to shift more easily and the stiff steering seamed to loosen allowing him to increase his speed. From a distance, he trailed a long tail of smoke and dust that took its time to clear. Growing aware that he maybe drawing attention to his entrance into the city, he slammed on the brakes and steered into the skid before he stopped engulfing himself in a cloud of dusted smoke. When the gritty blur shifted, he could hear but not see, the activities and sounds of men's voices approaching from beyond the bend in the road ahead. Aware they were only a short distance ahead he veered of the road slowly into the dry mud of the field alongside the road into a position where he could observe them. He crouched low behind a mound of earth, turned off the motorcycle, lay it down beside and watched. A dejecting sight confronted him. With heads bowed down, seven Hungarian men streaked with blood and dirt all over their faces, clothes torn and shredded, lumbered lethargically back along the road. Assessed safe to do so, Nandi released his briefcase from his back and approached them.

"Excuse me gentlemen."

They didn't answer, just continued to walk forward in their hypnotic state.

"Please; talk to me, what is happening?"

He deliberately shouldered and nudged them as they passed attempting to snap them out of it. Eventually two of them stopped while the others carried on away. One of them decided to explain.

"The battle is one sided and bloody. Budapest is a heap of rubble. Our defences are disorganised, confused. They are slaughtering everything in their path. We have been wiped out; this is all that is left from a unit of over 100 men."

"Where are you going?"

"We don't know. Away. Home I suppose."

"We haven't got a home if they win." Nandi reminded.

Suddenly, a loud whistle from a distant train echoed and carried through the air. Nandi turned in its direction only to see the steam from a train hitched to one carriage, standing stationary on the horizon only a few kilometres away. One of the men looked at the other, nodded and said.

"That'll be them."

He nodded back and they both brushed Nandi's shoulders either side as they walked on.

"Wait!" He pulled one of them back and the other stopped walking too.

"What do you mean that'll be them?"

"We heard yesterday that the Russians were bringing into Budapest by train, more supplies, heavy artillery. Our mission was to guard the railway lines and prevent it from entering Budapest. Our positions were attacked though, we were struck hard, and we dispersed."

"Right!" Nandi ran to his motorcycle. One of the men shouted to him.

"What are you going to do?"

"Keep your ears open men. Keep your ears open, your mission has not yet failed."

Nandi kick-started the bike with furious venom and zoomed in a diagonal parallel to the railway lines. His back wheel spun, and slipped sending plumes of burnt rubber into the air. He stopped at a suitable distance from the track and opened his briefcase. He armed himself with the pistol ensuring the chamber was full. He pulled out a single bottle of beer, bit the top off between his teeth, took three mouthfuls and poured the rest over the floor. After checking how much petrol was in the tank, he repeatedly struck it with the but of his gun near to the top until he had punctured a tiny hole. The fuel began to pour out and he held the mouth of the bottle to it. He hardly spilled any and when it was almost full, he stood the bottle up against the bike. He had just started to tear a piece out of his pullover when he heard another whistle coming from the train that was now in transit. Sweating all over, he bit his top lip hard as he stuffed a piece of his pullover right down into the neck of the bottle until it dipped into the fuel. When the Molotov cocktail was ready, he stuffed it tight into his jacket pocket, held his pistol in his left hand, got on the bike and raced towards the railway crossing on the road in an attempt to cut the train off. When he arrived there, he dismounted the bike on the Budapest side of the track, faced the railway crossing and waited. Behind him, he hadn't noticed two Russian soldiers standing by a boarded up shop looking at him suspiciously. The train picked up speed. Nandi's heart raced. It got closer. He pulled the bottle from his pocket and held it patiently in front of him. The train was almost there.

"Oy! Comrade"

He recognised the accent.

"Fuck!" He said to himself but didn't turn around.

The soldiers slowly began walking towards him.

The train began its crossing, passed the signal that was now ringing out its alarm.

He caught site of the driver. A soldier dressed in full Russian military uniform.

No hesitation. He pushed the pistol in his trousers, struck a match and lit the fuse. Bang! A shot was fired from behind him. It must have hit his leg as he felt the right one buckle at the knee and found himself kneeling on the ground. He threw the petrol bomb into the engine cab of the train and wasted no more time, rolling away from the scene. He had managed to retrieve his gun in the confusion and fired frantically towards the two soldiers still rolling away. Expecting nothing but death, the burning train hurtled away and Nandi was targeted with a barrage of bullets. He pushed his nose deep down in the dirt and covered his head. Suddenly the gunshots ceased. 'Am I dead?' He thought. He dared himself to look up. He could see the two soldiers lying sprawled across the road only a few metres away. He tried to stand. "Ouch!" He cried out as a sharp pain shot up his leg towards his groin. He managed it, but walked back to the road with a severe limp. He stared down at the soldiers. They were dead alright. Bullets wound, dozens of them around their heads.

"What the fuck…" He checked the chamber of his gun. "I've only fired 5 shots."

"Oy! Brave man. Over hear."

Nandi looked across the track to the other side. He breathed a sigh of relief when he realised. The two dejected Hungarian men had followed. They hid behind a tree on the opposite side of the railway line and took out the Russian soldiers. Nandi waved an appreciative wave. As he did, the ground shook. He turned in the direction of the targeted train only to watch it exploding with furious velocity and derailing instantaneously. The ammunition aboard the single carriage caused a hurricane of blasts in succession setting alight the bare trees that perimetered the railway line. The explosions finished after a short while leaving an inferno to mark

Nandi's attack. He picked up the bike noticing that the petrol was still leaking from the tank. He struggled to mount it, but did it anyway. He turned it towards Budapest. Kick starting it was easy.

"Where are you going?" One of them called out.

Nandi stopped when he heard another train whistle. He looked.

"It's got to be another carriage full of ammunition." The signals once again sounded, announcing the arrival of the other oncoming train.

"Great! It's going to plough right into the other one. Two birds with one stone."

He waved again to the lads and shouted,

"I'm off to Budapest."

"He's fucking crazy."

They said to each other.

Nandi sped off towards Budapest. He only travelled about 100 metres when he was forced to stop.

Three Russian tanks turned the corner approaching him head on.

"Oh bollocks!"

In a panic, he turned sharply, pulled back the throttle and sped back towards the level crossing. At top speed he hurried. The signal rang out its alarm. The train was hurtling. It got closer. Nandi was inches away from the level crossing. So was the train. He closed his eyes and screamed.

The train walloped his back wheel as he crossed sending him hurling into the air whilst the motorcycle spun like a spinning top. He somersaulted head over heels landing awkwardly in a ditch on the side of his head. He slumped in a heap. There was no movement.

CHAPTER 14

December 7th 1956

A white-hot pain shot through his head as he tried to open his eyes. He moaned as the pain spread to his neck, down his arms then through his back. The light hurt his eyes, making them water, leaving his vision distorted. He blinked, clearing his eyes but wished he'd kept them shut. He was in a familiar room but couldn't decide where. He realised that he wasn't alone. There was someone asleep in a chair beside his bed. A woman. He tried to sit up and move his legs but a searing pain in his leg made him cry out. 'What was going on?' Nandi thought. The woman awoke and immediately called out to Paul. She leaned over to him with tears in her eyes. She spoke with muted tones as if she were afraid the sound of her voice would break him somehow.

"So, you're finally awake. You gave me an almighty scare you know. How are you feeling?" Her voice was strangely comforting.

"I can't move without something hurting. What happened? What am I doing here?"

"The motorcycle was hit by a train. You were riding it. Don't you remember? You've been unconscious since they brought you here nearly 4 weeks ago. You have a severe gash to your head with a hairline-fractured skull, and a bullet wound at the back of your right leg. They are both healing quite nicely though."

He tried to remember and took a deep breath but was met only by a sharp pain in his head causing him to grimace. As it subsided, a few thoughts flooded back.

"Who brought me back here…?" He faltered for a few seconds then continued…"Maria." In an instant, she was recalled with affection.

"Two men. You met them on your way to Budapest. They explained everything, how you blew two trains full of ammunition. And, how they shot the two soldiers who were shooting at you. You tried to escape three Russian tanks, crossed the railway line, but got struck by the second oncoming train. Anyway, the second train slowed before it smashed into the first train, leaving a long row of train carriages between you and the tanks, giving enough time for them to whisk you away on a horse and cart."

"Why here?"

"They found this address in your pocket. Jancsi must have given it to you. It was his handwriting."

"Oh God, where's my briefcase?"

"They didn't bring it with them."

"That's why God prevented me from getting to Budapest. Because I didn't have my briefcase. It brings me luck; you know it was given to me by…"

"Your doctor after your brother Bela died." Maria interrupted.

"How do you know that?"

"In your comatose state; you talk a lot."

Paul shuffled into the bedroom.

"Well son. You've blown up my socks, used up all my Palinka, demolished my motorcycle and stolen my daughter's heart." Nandi laughed through his pain and caught hold of Maria's hand. "Glad you're okay son." Paul put his hand over the top of theirs.

Nandi remembered something else.

"Four bloody weeks. Have you sent message to my parents?"

Paul stalled before he answered,

"No Nandi, we dare not risk that. The Russians are arresting anybody who they deem suspicious."

"The Russians? What's happened?"

"Bastards have won. The revolution is over. Freedom is lost. Now they are rampaging over Hungary. Killing, arresting, only yesterday a queue of people waiting for bread at the bakery were machine gunned to death."

Nandi's eyes filled with tears.

"And the west? English? French? America?"

Paul shook his head and looked down at the floor. Nandi grit his teeth and turned his head the opposite way towards the wall.

Maria decided to diffuse the depression and offered Nandi a mug of water and some food.

Mogyoroska. The same day

Janos entered the kitchen with Jancsi close behind. He carried on into the bedroom and beckoned Margit to follow with his eyes. Eager for news the three of them sat down at the table in the centre of the room.

"Have you heard anything?" Margit encouraged a quick answer.

Janos sighed heavily. "Jancsi has finally come clean with all that he knows."

Jancsi nervously looked into Margit's worried eyes.

"You must understand Mrs. Pekar, the Russians would have killed me if I let on anything, and I was concerned for Nandi's safety."

"So tell me quickly, where is Nandi?"

Blackie, who was under the table, slid out, stood on his hind legs, placed his paws on the table and pricked up his ears as if he understood the question and was waiting impatiently for the answer.

"I don't know where he is. But, I can tell you he stubbornly head off to Budapest to join up with the resistance after I tried to persuade him not to. He's a brave lad and would always tell us that if we wanted freedom, we had to put Hungary first before everything even our families."

Janos bowed his head toward the floor.

"So, he could be dead or arrested or anything?" Margit fearfully stated.

"I don't know. But, if it's any hope at all, I gave him an address of my uncle, a safe house. I told him to go there if he got into danger. But, for the safety of my family, we mustn't get in touch with him."

"We understand that Jancsi. But if you do hear something…"

"You will be the first to know." Jancsi reassured.

Janos's head still bowed toward the floor; held his lips tightly shut but couldn't hold back a tearful wail. He watched, eyes wide open, a stream of tears dripping from his eyes onto the green lino covered floor. Margit thanked Jancsi and then led him out and bid him goodbye.

When she returned to the kitchen Jancsi stood up and embraced Margit and cried like an uncontrollable baby on her shoulder. Blackie curled up next to them on the floor, covered his eyes with a paw and whimpered too adding to the sadness. Through his tears, he repeated over and over, "It's my fault, it's my fault I told him to put Hungary first."

"No Janos no. I'm proud of you and I'm proud of our son. He's done something that many brave Hungarian men have done over a thousand years. Jancsi didn't do it, nor did any of the others."

Janos stopped his crying and with a tear-wet face, he gaped into the decipherable glazed eyes of his wife and said.

"So you don't blame me?"

"How could I blame you? You have taught him well. It's because of his upbringing; it's because of your teachings that will keep him alive. Yes alive, he's a survivor, and he's a survivor because of you. He's alive our boy is, I feel it in my heart."

Janos smiled joyfully and responded.

"Yes he is Margit. Yes he is!"

Blackie joined in immediately and jumped onto Janos's chest.

"Nandi's alive Blackie. Go find him boy, go and find him."

As if he understood every word Blackie ran outside, through the outside gate and down the bank into the village.

Margit released her husband and followed Blackie. She stood alone outside the garden gate and stared aimlessly at the skyline towards Budapest. She made the sign of the cross on her chest and pressed her hands together. A strong breeze blew from the Rakoczi castle and sent a chill through her spine and she whispered,

"Nandi, wherever you are tonight…Listen to the wind. Your mother sends you her blessings."

Nagytarcsa. Late that evening.

Nandi awoke suddenly in the middle of a restless sleep. His body was soaked with sweat even though a frozen chill swept across country. Maria had been disturbed by Nandi's nightmares and entered the bedroom and sat beside him on the bed.

"What is it Nandi?"

"I've been dreaming."

"You've been doing a lot of that. I'm getting used to you talking in your sleep; I think you've narrated the whole of your life to me since you were born through your nightmares. What was it about this time my dear?" She asked with a concerning tone as she shuffled along the bed a little closer to his face allowing him to answer quietly so not to disturb her father.

"Outside my house in Mogyoroska is the Rakoczi castle, it stands proudly on top of high mountain. I've climbed it many times, on one occasion me and my father climbed it. It was this time in my dream, only this time I was falling from the top. My father was holding on to me frantically, screaming 'don't fall, don't fall.' Eventually I lost my grip and began floating. All the time I was gazing up at my father's face and I was shouting to him, I'm sorry father, I tried my best, I tried to hang on to my freedom but I've couldn't hang on any longer. I've failed."

Nandi choked and then said; "And then you walked in."

Maria, noticing that Nandi was soaked all over, walked to the tiny bedroom window and opened it. A gust of wind swooped into the room, brushed Nandi's face, and cooled the room instantly. The comforting breeze reduced his temperature immediately and he lay still for a moment. Maria threw back the quilt and lay down beside him and placed her right hand against his beating heart. Nandi smiled and she noticed him looking content.

"What's the matter Nandi?" She questioned curiously.

"My mother is with me tonight Maria. And, I know now what to do."

December 8th 1956 5:a.m.

Maria awoke only to find she was alone in Nandi's bed. Through the open window the pounding of an axe repeatedly chopping logs softened into melody like a regular drum beat. She leapt out of bed and wrapped a long coat around her shoulders and continued outside. Nandi stood, shirtless, swinging Paul's large axe at a few logs. The morning was dark, the night skies clear and Nandi had already chopped up a large pile of wood. Even though her presence was evident, feeling her eyes piercing into his sweaty back, he continued to hack away at the wooded, sawn-off tree trunks unaffected by her loom. With each hew, the sharp steel axe head struck the wood and sent a flurry a thin sharp splinters hurtling upwards that made the scene look like Nandi was amongst a tiny firework display enhanced by the hot steam rising off his body into the cool air.

"Nandi." She called out to him softly.

He didn't respond and the axe was forced to continue its duty.

Realising his probable intent, she sighed deeply, closed her eyes for a second and took a few steps closer to him.

"If you are intending to do what I think you are intending. You should stop and think twice. There's no more war. It's finished.

436

December 8th 1956

The dream has gone. Before, there was a purpose a, a, course.
Now. Now there isn't anything to fight for. Before there were
reasons but this, this is meaningless. There isn't anywhere to go.
There isn't anybody to help you. The freedom fighters have either
been killed, arrested or have fled the country. You should go
home to see your mother and father; they will be in a glorious
mood when you arrive home to see their only son still alive.
They've lost one son I'm sure they do not want to lose another.
There is future here, I know it looks grim for the moment but if
we can learn to live together with the Russians, maybe you can
raise a family of your own, and when the time is right, we can
leave and maybe travel the world. There must be some hope for
us. Nandi please listen." She stepped a little closer to him
encouraged to do so when he stopped swinging the axe. She ran a
finger down his greasy spine and fought to hold back her tears.
Nandi dropped the axe to the floor and turned to her and caught
hold of her finger. His determined glare spoke volumes and she
knew what would follow was to be a final decision whether full of
bravery or stupidity.

"Maria. Would you rather live in a country run by another nation
where your souls and children's souls are owned and manipulated
by another? Or, fight against it and maybe die a horrible death?
You could lie couldn't you? Say you'd do one thing but do
another?"

Maria gazed up decoding his face. The image of him would be
firmly fixed into the deepest part of her memory. She memorised
every line and curve. Her eyes lowered and stared towards his
soaked windpipe. She opened her mouth to say more but thought
it hopeless. She now knew his soul, his mind, his burning
determination. He had to complete what he'd set out to do and
there wouldn't be an army in the world to stop him. He had made
his decision and was a man of his word, he would never break a
promise, not even to himself and she knew it. She put her hand

inside the coat pocket and pulled out the half torn bible page and placed into his left hand.

"Keep this Nandi, I do not think it will ever be fused back together if you leave…But, I do understand you…I'll go get your things…"

Maria released their clasp and left Nandi standing holding the half a bible page in his hand.

It was almost an hour later when he returned to the house. Maria had laid out across the bed his clean clothes and had added a pair of gloves and a scarf to his attire. Salami, bread, his gun, a penknife, a few coins and a half smoked packet of cigarettes and matches were also amongst his supplies.

"You only have one bullet in your gun. And the doctor from the village will be here in a couple of hours I hope to God that you will wait to see him, because together we have nursed you, cleaned your wounds, removed your stitches, shaved your face, bathed you, so you have to let him check you over, he would like to see you up and around I'm sure."

As her words tumbled over each other, he pulled her to him and offered her his mouth. At first, she resisted turning her face slightly away, but then turned back and pressed a firm kiss against his eager lips. She was forced to accept his decision and for the next few hours, she ensured they would be memorable. She would smile at him every time he looked at her or spoke to her. She kissed him on the cheek and he her when they passed each other.

The doctor arrived and they exchanged interesting conversations while being examined. The wound across his head was healing and the doctor explained how the parietal bone had got a small hairline crack. He was confident that it had mended itself too as there was little pain when he pressed hard against it. Maria was almost sad to see the doctor leave and felt a little guilty when she realised that she was disappointed at the doctor's positive analysis.

Paul gripped his large shoulders and then made his way outside to wait to see him off. After a long kiss, Maria decided she couldn't bear to watch him walking away, so she turned her back and rested her forehead in the palm of her hand. Nandi didn't say a word, but he quietly pulled out their bible page, opened it, and left it face up in the middle of the kitchen table, held in place by a butter knife. One last glance over to Maria he couldn't resist before closing the front door firmly behind him.

December 8th. Entering Budapest.

A bitter chill enveloped the once magnificent city. It was a cold so cold, that it was visible. Visible in the shape of a white coloured wind. Icicles hanging from every roof-top, enhanced by a shiny winter sunshine strongly emitting a kind of cold burning through a hazy stretch of cloud. This wasn't the Budapest that Nandi knew and loved. The city had been shaken to the core. Buildings gashed by flying debris. Shattered stumps are all that remain. Budapest was a ghost city. Roads were torn up.

Pavement stones and cobblestones had been piled into barricades at the junction of every road or street. Great buildings had been reduced to rubble and here and there fires still burned. Nandi struggled to find one single pain of glass in any building that wasn't either smashed or cracked.

For the first time during the whole conflict, Nandi was afraid. He was glad that he'd been to fetch his briefcase from the field after leaving Maria and Paul, and he gripped it tight holding it firm to his heart. Street after street the horrific sight of Budapest emerged, each building more battered and scarred than the other. Telephone wires were down coiled up in the gutters. Where the pavements weren't torn up, they were littered with glass and stained with blood. Nandi's heart was shattered, a once beautiful city all around him, battered, bludgeoned, smashed and evidence that it had bled into submission. Beneath his feet, he tried to clamber over rubble and glass. Here and there, his pathway was lined with spent cartridges and shell cases under his feet, remnants of an unquenchable Hungarian fighting spirit. Despite the catastrophe that overlooked him, there was proof all around that the people of Budapest had put up a desperate, gallant resistance to the Russian onslaught.

But Nandi was distraught, lost, alone. For the first time, his panic filled mind couldn't comprehend; he thought he was going out of his mind as he struggled to collect his thoughts. He knew what to do. He had to find a secluded alleyway and fast. He ran in a blind panic, tripping and stumbling as he went. At one point he grew so dizzy he couldn't prevent himself from falling into the wall of a building, then a bent lamppost. He even knocked a frightened old man down to the floor. Scared and unsure, Nandi left him there. A few people looked on, but had an understandable façade that seemed to accept this kind of behaviour as an intrinsic part of the Hungarian life.

At last, he found an isolated alleyway. He picked up the briefcase with his two hands and held it in front of his face. His hands were shaking vigorously and he tried to focus and concentrate in order to control them. Instead, his vision became distorted and he thought he'd gone deaf. He tried desperately to regain his hearing but he couldn't hear anything except his own heavy breathing, the

eerie sound like a gasping mountaineer, the kind they would
endure at high altitudes.

He did it; he managed to regain his hearing and sight. He put his
briefcase on the floor and checked his hands. The shaking had
stopped. Now he could do what he came here to do. He sat down
on the briefcase, put his face into his hands and began to cry. He
squeezed his mouth tight but his loud whimpers still burst
through. His tears flowed all over his hands and face and after a
while, he repeatedly began to smack himself across the forehead
with both hands.

"No, no, no, no, no. Why lord? Why, why, why. Surely we are the
good guys."

He noticed something in the shadows of the alley a few metres
away. A filthy, blood stained Hungarian flag, crumpled up in a
heap. He knew it was there but at first, he didn't react. He was
crying and knew he had to finish. It was a while later when he felt
that he might have let all his emotions burst free. He sniffed a few
times and wiped his face dry with his dirty hand. His lip was still
quivering but he dragged himself over to the flag. He pulled it but
it was stuck on something so he yanked it free and exposed a hard
gruesome sight lying sprawled beneath the flag. An old man of
about seventy lay dead, spattered with machine gun holes. Nandi
tried to turn him over but his body was stiff. As the whole body
moved, the posture of the murdered man clearly was holding
something under his arm. He knelt down closer to see a loaf of
bread half eaten by rats.

Nandi couldn't do anything but scream. **"No!"** The shout was
long and lingering and echoed off the walls of the alleyway. He
thought he was in some kind of a nightmare and tried to wake
himself up. He backed away from the corpse and continued to
walk backwards staring at it as he went. The alleyway grew duller
as he stepped slowly further away. When far enough so as he

couldn't make out the body, he pressed his back against the wall, pushed his knuckles against his closed eyes and slid down until he was sitting down and rested his elbows on his knees. Frenziedly, he continued crying to himself in a desperate attempt to relieve his cancerous tension.

He didn't know how long he had been in a trance, but when focusing was apparent again, he was far away from the alleyway where he'd found the corpse. Wandering through the streets of Budapest in a meaningless way without any point of direction in mind was somehow insane. He had yet to find an undamaged building amongst the images of a ceaseless barrage. The people walking the streets trudging in all directions had drawn, cadaver faces, grey and lost looking. Somehow, the middle of huge high street was suffocating, but it indicated the city centre. The road was very straight and very wide and stretched for at least five kilometres. He fancied that the Danube must be at the other end and was intrigued to find out which bridge would emerge when he reached there. The road before him had been blitzed. Huge craters in no set pattern were dangerously spaced out on both sides and down the middle. The Russians had lay a few flat planks of wood across them but looked perilous and confirmation of an invading army's ruthless disrespect for Hungarian civilian safety. Buildings that spanned either side of this road had been totally chopped in half shedding their materials in heaped stony piles at their feet that spilled out into the road. A more ghastly sight emerged from the bombed buildings when Nandi studied each floor level and could make out a bedroom, bathroom or kitchen. They were homes of people, crushed, demolished.

He was careful not to fall down a hole dodging them all, stepping or leaping over fallen lampposts and any obstacle scattered around him. The centre was growing more rampant with the Russian military. Tanks and military cars manoeuvred in front of him. On every corner, black shirted Avo with sub-machine guns guarded groups of terrified civilians; sobbing women, children, young and old men. They didn't seem to pay any attention to Nandi making his way to the river. But he suddenly grew very afraid aware he had a pistol hidden inside his briefcase. They would arrest him and kill him for sure. Over to his right down another street, he noticed, a few blocks beyond, thick black smoke pouring between the apexes of a distant rooftop. He turned off the main street sharply and hoped he'd avoided suspicion. After a few steps along the echoic street, he glanced over his shoulder to be sure that he hadn't been followed.

Finally, he reached the burning building. It was a church that was blazing from within and Nandi felt horrified to know that the Russians were prepared to let it burn to the ground. The restoration of this historic city was close to impossible and Nandi's mortified heart sank even further when he entered the churchyard to find a wooded statue of Christ burning alone on the floor next to a stone grave. He stared at the flickering flames for a few moments until a noise from around the back distracted him.

He hid behind the tall gravestone, checked all around him and without thinking he opened up his briefcase. Fumbling slightly he pulled back the secret compartment and checked his pistol was full.

"What the hell are you doing Nandi? He asked himself.

His subconscious mind took over his actions and if the arsonist was there, he was prepared to make him pay. He peeped with one eye around from the stone. He could see someone rummaging around at the side of the church. Before he approached him, he looked around once more; all was clear so he ran towards him keeping his arm stretched out aiming the gun at him as he advanced. The stranger turned quickly when he realised someone was there only to find Nandi holding the pistol into his face and yelling,

"Get down on your knees now!"

An ageing man between 60 and 65 held his arms up in the air immediately and fell to his knees. Nandi circled him without saying another word only tried to decide who he was. When behind him, through a shaky voice the man tried to explain.

"Please sir I was only trying to find some food for my dog. He's ill you see, he has had a bullet wound and..."

"Shut up! Who has set fire to this church?"

"I don't know sir, but the Avo and the Russians have been burning Budapest to the ground since our surrender. Oh, are you anything to do with the Avo?"

"Don't be bloody stupid." Nandi stood in front of him now and deemed it safe to continue but still pointed the gun towards him. "I am with the resistance and I want to find out where the rest of the fighters are and find out what we can do about this occupation."

The man shook his head.

"What's the matter?"

"My daughter was only fourteen years old, she's been captured and they have shot my wife and dog because they tried to prevent them from doing so. My dog has survived but my wife wasn't so lucky."

The man lowered his arms and Nandi let him sob. Eventually Nandi put away his gun and sat beside him on the floor. When he'd regained control of his emotions he continued just as the winter chill was intensified with a light drizzle.

"The revolution has been defeated, it has drowned in blood and buried beneath the rubble. There aren't any more freedom fighters, they are either dead, been arrested imprisoned or shot. And those in prison and are alive, will eventually be executed. We humiliated the might of the Russians in front of the whole world; they will not leave any rebel participant alive. Freedom rose from the ashes of communism, then it blazed before it has been beaten back down."

Nandi was staring at the floor and interrupted.

"We can't just give up."

"We haven't given up. Hundreds of thousands of brave Hungarians have escaped the country and gone off to free countries. They've escaped. The

Russians didn't succeed to capture them. They fought for freedom and have got it."

"It's not the same. We wanted freedom in our own country not in someone else's."

"God works in mysterious ways. I would have gone with them, took my daughter too, but now I have to wait to see if she returns."

"I don't know." Nandi doubted what the man was saying. "I do not know what we've proved, what we've gained, what the hell have we been fighting for, what have we achieved without our freedom?"

"I saw the Hungarian people rip up the streets of Budapest to build barricades, and at night they fought by the light of fires, a lot of them to the death. They have sworn to fight to the end and they did. The Russians threw everything at us apart from the atomic bomb. You want to know what we have achieved, I'll tell you. At this moment, the world is in shock that a country with less population than the city of London has dared to stand up against the Soviet Empire. The hundreds of thousands that have escaped will not be looked on as refugees they will be welcomed as heroes. The revolution has been lost for now but it will prove to be more successful than we think. Now our plight can show the world that communism is not what it claims to be. Because of what we've done the whole world have seen the Russians true character. An evil nation that is holding its territory's by brute force. Any communism in any other country of the world can no longer claim that communism is peaceful and just. Khrushchev can no longer be received in the West as a friend of the Western nations. Now he will be seen as the leader of a huge monster and will never be trusted. This is what our country has achieved. And only time will tell.

As we have been alone, now Russia will be alone. The west will let them destroy themselves. We have defeated Russia; they just don't know it yet."

Nandi felt a certain kind of relief from the man's words and he told him so through a pleasant smile. They talked some more and shared Nandi's salami and the man put a few pieces aside for his dog.

"I'd better put this away." Nandi replaced the gun and locked his briefcase.

"So, you actually think we've beaten the Russians then?"

"In a strange sort of way yeah. I have heard that during this whole conflict, they have had more fatalities than us. How's that then when they've got all the equipment and modern weapons eh? Bows and arrows against the lightening and the bows and arrows come out on top."

"Is that true? We have killed more?"

"They would never admit it ever? But our count revealed over 50,000 of them have been killed. We have lost less than half of that."

Nandi chewed up the last chunk of his salami and then lit a cigarette. He offered one to the man who accepted it delightfully. They smoked them together and somehow Nandi began to feel lifted by the man's enthusiasm and felt constrained to show him his gratitude.

"Which way is it to the Danube through the back streets? I need to avoid the Russians." The man started to explain but Nandi interrupted after the first few directional explanations.

"Which bridge are you leading me towards?"

"It will be the Elizabeth bridge; why?"

"Which one will lead me to Vienna?"

A smirk escaped the man's throat. "Vienna. Are you crazy?"

"No, you said that the heroes have left the country. So, maybe I want to do the same."

"You don't understand do you? That was before."

"Before what?"

"The revolution has been over for almost a month. Back then it was easy. Yugoslavia and Austria were virtually wide open. Everyone for days maybe longer, were just able to stroll out. Now, now it's different."

"Different, how?"

"The whole border stretching from Austria, north, south, you know the perimeter of Hungary. Is completely cut off."

Nandi frowned at the man.

"It's a bloody minefield. There's searchlights, barbed wire, trip wires, hundreds of guards with machine guns patrolling. There are miles of freshly buried mines; you couldn't get through the first 10 metres before you would be blown into oblivion." He warned.

Nandi's face changed colour.

"Yes, my friend, we are well and truly in a national prison now. Nobody can come in; and nobody can go out."

Nandi realised the sudden reality. "So, we are dead if we stay, and dead if we go."

"It seems that way doesn't it?"

Nandi felt dizzy once more, stood, picking up his briefcase as he rose.

"What are you going to do?"

"I haven't a clue...C'mon take me to the Danube please."

The man's knees cracked as Nandi helped him to his feet. They walked silently through the streets dodging and weaving passed suspicious looking people or vehicles. When only a short distance from the river, Nandi thanked the man, shook his hand and continued on his lonely trek to the riverbank.

The sight of the Danube was breathtaking. He leaned on the oval stonewall that protected the steep slope to the waters edge. The Elizabeth Bridge was in front of him to the left and he studied the movement of traffic and people over the Buda side. He couldn't move from this spot, only tried to concentrate and memorise the view. A movement above caught his eye and he looked up to see murky, black clouds moving to reveal a dark blue sky. The stars looked like bright penlights dotted here and there. As his eyes

leapt from one star to another, the frown he sported deepened as
he searched his mind for solutions. He squinted a few times, the
strain of fighting back a frustrating, sombre pain showed in every
line and every move of his face. Eventually, he licked his lips like
a lion that had spotted his prey.

"I'm going to get out of Hungary." He said it to himself, stern and
with conviction. "I have to beat the Russians for the last time.
They think they've beaten me, they think they can do what they
want to my country and me. My next mission; to prove them
wrong. I will get through their wall of steel. Minefields or not, I'm
going to beat them."

Determined to cross the Danube undetected, he checked all
corners thoroughly. There were patrolling tanks and vehicles on
the Buda side he could see from where he stood. Around him were
the Avo a distance away on the street corners mainly. High up in
the bomb riddled buildings snipers with long rifles stood, with
feet wide apart, on show for all to see, prepared to pick off any
suspect. Even army patrol boats sailed in both directions in
clusters of three and fours armed to the teeth with all kinds of
guns of all calibres. It was dangerous; but driven by an
overwhelming desire to defeat the impossible and to be free; he
scrupulously strolled towards the main road that led over the
Elizabeth Bridge. There was much hustle and bustle as he
approached, the crossroads was being held up and vehicles
directed by a Russian soldier who seemed to have a great feeling
of power as he relentlessly blew his whistle and waved his arms at
the traffic. Nandi took advantage of the bumper-to-bumper
vehicles and made his way between them quickly. He'd noticed an
opened backed lorry creeping through the traffic his intentions to
stow away in the back. But, by a sudden impulse he realised if one
of the snipers saw him hopping on the back, they would surely
open fire, or at least radio through to a checkpoint on the Buda
side. Thinking quickly, without looking up, Nandi slid his body
alongside the lorry and knocked on the window. A man with a

bearded face wound his window down and Nandi asked him if this was the Elizabeth Bridge, he responded nodding his head and Nandi threw him a cigarette. The scene from the snipers positions would take away all suspicions that Nandi was a stow away. Unobtrusively, Nandi threw his briefcase aboard and climbed in the back of the empty trailer; the driver unaware he'd done so.

He sat in the corner towards the front of the trailer deep in the shadows. At first, the lorry was stop, start, the engine rumbling and the airbrakes screeching. The next few moments were tense, not knowing if he'd been seen or whether the Russians would stop the lorry for a routine check. Nandi could only stare out of the back of the lorry as, like a scene from a black and white film, the images of Budapest, the Danube, and the Elizabeth Bridge, fuzzy and unstable, disappeared out of sight as the lorry climbed the hilly roads of Buda. Nandi felt it safe to slide his bottom to the back and check the direction the lorry was travelling. Looking at the lanes and road signs, through obstacles and a fair distance, Nandi caught a two second glimpse of a bronze statue of a huge bird with wings outstretched both soaring and protective. It stood on the pinnacle of a supporting cast iron tower and as the lorry turned, by a trick of perspective, the bird's head seemed to follow Nandi. The experience was overwhelming and it took a moment to control the cold shudder that rushed his body. He recalled the Hungarian Myth of the Turul Bird with great fondness and decided to repeat the story to himself out loud.

"Attila the King of the Huns over 1,500 years ago, had a son named Ugyek. The legend says that Ugyek's wife had a dream in which the Turul bird appeared to her. In this dream, a crystal-clear stream started to flow from her, and as it moved westward, it grew into a mighty river. This dream represented her symbolic impregnation by the Turul, and meant that she would give birth to a line of great rulers. Ugyek's wife later gave birth to Almos, who was the father of Arpad. Arpad, probably the greatest Hungarian ever lived. The founder of Hungary. The fucking Russians dared to replace the name of our Arpad Bridge with that bastard Stalin. We have showed them not to interfere with our History. The Turul Bird, I can't believe I've just seen it. It must be a sign of some kind."

Nandi was content with the obvious direction that the lorry was travelling. It had to be the next city Gyor; the main road didn't lead to anywhere else. Budapest was a mere distant sight with a smoky haze projecting above it when Nandi closed his eyes to rest. He squeezed his knees to his chest and placed his forehead onto them and could almost hear himself snore amid the droning diesel engine chugging and straining.

CHAPTER 15

December 8th 1956. 10p.m

The horizon in front of him was black and a wavy line outlining surrounding hills and the Hegyshalom border was in complete silence. The sky was a lighter shade of black than the ground but where they met each other defined a long stretch of military activity. Vehicles were in constant movement, headlights were coming and going, swooping, evidence of them travelling in all directions along the border. A hundred watchtowers stood out in a long line against the sky sporadically lit up by each other's swivelling searchlight. Nandi was only about 4 kilometres away. He stood, briefcase in one hand, with the other tucked away in his pocket. His poise saw him standing, slightly leaning on his left leg, staring and studying the fortress before him. He took a left off the roadside deep into the shadows of the wooded fields and started to jog into the darkness, he hoped in the right direction.

He was about 2km from the border when he spotted what he was looking for. In the middle of the large field elevated on a hill stood a red tiled roof cottage. It faced the border as Nandi was approaching the back. There weren't any windows at the rear but the radiant glow of a hanging lantern flickered at the side of the house. It acted as a guide and Nandi followed it.

A light tap on the front door encouraged a deep shout from within.

"Who the hell is that knocking at this time of night?"

The light from another room turned on and cascaded onto the front porch.

"My name is Nandi and I am need to speak to Gyorgy please."

December 8th 1956

There was a silence for a few seconds.

"He's not here. What do you want him for?" The answer was gruff but not convincing.

"Erm… Paul has sent me from Nagytarcsa. You now sir it's a little difficult talking to a door."

Silence fell once again, a little longer this time until the sound of a chair dragging across a tiled floor, followed by the sharp unlocking of the bolted door. A lean, tall man of about 67 years old, bald on top with tufts of white hair above his ears, swung open the front door.

Startled, Nandi stepped back.

"How do you know Paul?" He asked with a low but slightly aggressive tone.

"He's, he's going to be my father-in-law."

"My God is Maria old enough to get married. How time flies."

"You know him then, Paul?"

"Yeah I know him. But what do you want Gyorgy for?"

"I need to get out of Hungary and he said Gyorgy may be able to help."

"Are fucking mad? What are you saying lad?"

The man stepped outside and pushed Nandi to one side and looked all around into the dark field behind him.

"I hope you haven't been followed, you'll have me shot saying things like that."

He walked back into the doorway and studied Nandi's face and fondled his chin as he looked.

Nandi shrugged his shoulders and waited for a reply.

December 8th 1956

"Listen. What did you say your name was?"

"Nandi, my name is Nandi."

The man lowered his voice to a whisper.

"Listen Nandi, I am Gyorgy. And yes, it was true I have helped some few to get out. But that was weeks ago. Nobody can get through there now. You've left it too late. So, go, go back to Maria and give up, there's no way out now."

Gyorgy attempted to close the door but Nandi blocked it with his foot.

"Wait! I am going through the border whether you help me or not. It is not over; it's not too late. Nothing is impossible. Now listen, I have travelled all the way from the other side of Hungary from a small village close to the Czechoslovakia border; I am not about to tuck tail and run just because of a few landmines. So, please whatever help you can give me."

Gyorgy looked into Nandi's desperate eyes. When Nandi finished talking he stared at his boot wedging the door open. Nandi moved his foot away and swallowed.

He continued once more.

"Look, I know you don't know me and I haven't any money to pay you. But you see this briefcase, it's real leather, it's probably worth more money on the black market. You can have it, it's yours, but please, please take it."

Gyorgy relented and opened the door wide and beckoned for Nandi to come in. He closed the door behind them and pulled up a chair at the kitchen table and offered it to Nandi.

"Are you hungry Nandi?" His voice was now lower in tone somewhat pitiful.

"I feel too sick to be hungry."

December 8th 1956

Gyorgy placed some wine and a block of cheese on the table. "Eat and drink it son, you can sleep on the sofa. And tomorrow we will talk about your escape."

"Thank you sir; thank you."

"Don't thank me you fool. I'm probably leading you to your death. May God forgive me!"

December 9th 1956. 7:00a.m

Gyorgy carried a bucket of milk still warm from his cow, into the kitchen and plonked it into the centre of the table spilling a little as he did. Nandi had slept well but had been awake for the last hour so sat up sprightly, pushed the large cushions and pillows that had kept him warm all night to one side, and leaned forward to wipe away the spilled milk with the palm of his hand.

"Nandi, that's your breakfast. Freshly milked 10 minutes ago so grab that beaker and scoop it out."

Nandi was careful to move away the layer of skin that had formed on the surface before dunking the beaker into the milk until it filled. He swallowed it hungrily but waited politely until Gyorgy offered him some more.

Gyorgy began tidying the kitchen but kept one eye keenly observing Nandi.

"Are you still determined to get out? You know attempt the impossible?"

Without looking at Gyorgy he answered confidently. "Absolutely, absolutely."

"And what are you going to do if you get through?"

Nandi now had to look at Gyorgy.

December 9th 1956

"Do?"

"Yes do"

"Well I'll be free of course. That's what this has all been about, freedom. Only God knows what I will do with that freedom. And only God will decide if I deserve it."

Gyorgy smile admirably and said.

"You will be free with the westerners; you know the one's that didn't help us in our hour of need."

Nandi scowled hard and looked back into his mug of milk. "I will have to live with them to understand why they didn't help us. You never know maybe they still have plans to help us; it took them almost 5 years to rescue France from Hitler."

Gyorgy threw a farmers cap with long earflaps at Nandi. "Put that on, put your coat on and come outside I want to show you something."

They both walked out into the freezing winter's morning, it was still dark but day was breaking over Austria.

Gyorgy led the way across the frozen mud towards his barn.

"The Commander of the Freedom fighters army, a guy called Pongrasz, in the midst of the heavy fighting continued to send word to me asking me of any news from the west. Is there any news from the west? They had promised a lot, they said they were going to send us supplies, and Pongrasz was eager for it."

Gyorgy paused whilst he pulled open the large heavy wooden doors to his barn. He walked inside and asked Nandi to pull the doors closed behind him. Gyorgy struck a match and fumbled about in the corner. The match burnt out scolding his finger as it did so he passed the box to Nandi and asked him to light up the way. After removing some gardening tools and a loose bail of

December 9th 1956

hay, he revealed about 20 wooden boxes, heavily labelled 'UK' or 'USA' but most were marked up 'NATO.'

Nandi gasped and lit another match quickly.

"My God NATO, Russia's biggest enemy. What's inside?"

"Take a look Nandi, be my guest. But be careful, remember the west want us to defeat communism."

Excitedly, Nandi reached for the crowbar on an opposite shelf and began levering off the nailed down lids. He removed the lids from 3 or 4 boxes before checking inside and then everywhere went dark. He waited patiently for Gyorgy to strike another match. He did it and Nandi pulled back a black cover that was hiding the contents of the boxes. He couldn't believe it. He checked all through that box and then the next. Throwing the objects over his head Gyorgy called out.

"It's no good searching through everything; it's all the same I've checked."

Nandi stopped rummaging and slammed the lid of one of the boxes down hard and stormed over towards Gyorgy.

"And what the fuck were we supposed to do with chocolate? Is this their idea of a joke? Are they taking the piss? Perhaps they wanted us to hit the Russian army with the blocks of chocolate instead of our homemade petrol bombs. Hey maybe they are laced with cyanide or maybe there's an atomic bomb hidden under the wrappers or something? The FUCKIN BASTARDS"

"All your ranting and raving won't do anything Nandi. I know because I've tried. I know because I've cried. They were supposed to drop these in over Budapest by a supply plane. But not only did they drop in this crap, they were about 100 km short. They fell here in my field and on the roadside. Immediately I collected them in my car, rounding them up one by one on my back seat and in my boot, risking my life for bars of chocolate. I was excited and before I opened the boxes, I sent a coded message to Pongrasz telling him his supplies were here. I wanted to lift his morale, to urge him on to keep battling, c'mon guys' help is coming, help is coming…But, there wasn't any help. Only this. 20 lousy boxes of chocolate." Gyorgy's eyes were full of tears and Nandi comforted him.

"If it's any help at all Gyorgy, I will get through this Russian barricade and I will at least tell our story to the west. At least."

"Good lad, good lad. And while you are there would you ram a bar of this chocolate down President Eisenhower's throat?"

"Will do!" Nandi smirked as he answered.

For the rest of the day Gyorgy went over the plan, drawing a detailed map of Hegyshalom on a large sheet of paper. He sketched out all their positions to the best of his knowledge and pointed out the areas that he knew where the landmines lay. There were mines, barbed wire, deep trenches, tripwires, patrols, patrol dogs, searchlights and not to mention enough firepower from the Russian army to invade Austria. The task, unattainable. But the determination, tremendous. By late afternoon, they had gone over the plan 100 times. Nandi, nervous but not deterred, checked the time and now only had to wait one hour after nightfall before his fate began.

First, there was checkpoint area on the road towards the border. Gyorgy was certain if he drove Nandi passed there they would be safe because the guards there had gotten used to Gyorgy as he drove passed them on a regular basis to get paraffin from a border garage further on. However, before he got to the garage there was a second checkpoint area, these guards were never the same few and were changed on an hourly basis. They always searched Gyorgy's car. Gyorgy explained that he would take him passed the first checkpoint and when he gave the signal,

Gyorgy wouldn't slow down, Nandi must dive out of the boot of his car and roll into the fields. Then, he would be on his own.

He stood outside staring frostily over to the west blowing the smoke from his cigarette towards Hegyshalom. The sight before him was darkening slowly and the vast terrain looked falsely calm, full of danger and maybe death. He drew the last drag on his cigarette until the smouldering ash from it almost burnt his lips. After flicking it away, he fastened the earflaps from his black hat under his chin. In one pocket, he checked for the long pointed dagger given to him from Gyorgy and in the other, he had his revolver. The scarf was pulled snug around his neck and before he buttoned up his dark grey short woollen jacket he patted the bible tucked away in the inside pocket. He would carry nothing more; he left his cigarettes, matches, some loose coins, his penknife and leather briefcase with Gyorgy. He breathed deeply through his nose, took one last look at Hungary behind him, then turned, winked and made the sign of the cross on his chest at Austria before pulling his gloves on over his hands to the wrist. He opened the kitchen door and Gyorgy was warming his hands against the log filled oven but turned sharply to see Nandi, leaned towards a tin of black boot polish on the table and slid it to Nandi. He dipped his fingers into it and smeared a clump around his face leaving a small area free around the eyes.

"I'm ready. Let's do it!"

***

Nandi held the boot lid down from inside and after Gyorgy seemed to drive over a high ramp causing his car to bounce and Nandi to hold the boot lid firm, he shouted out to Nandi.

"GO, GO NOW!"

Without hesitation, he crawled out of the boot onto the roadside and just managed to put a hand to the lid closing it firmly. He didn't bother to look around, as planned, he rolled into the grassy bank, scrambled to the top of the slight eminence and slid down the other side on his back until he reached the bottom. His feet were deep in freezing slush but he had to leave them there until the searchlight swooped passed. As it did, he curled into a ball and pushed his nose into his knees. It passed, and Nandi was able to scuttle like a crab on all fours into a small cluster of trees. He crouched down, observing all around him. It was here he started to breath again, he was sure he'd held his breath until now. His heart raced and he almost choked as his body gasped for oxygen. It was at least ten minutes before he'd calmed and was able to secrete saliva. He licked his lips and sighed when he was certain his strong palpitations and exaltation feeling had calmed.

Nandi knew now that phase one of his escape from captivity was so far so good. He hadn't been seen and it was obvious by now that Gyorgy hadn't created any suspicions or there would have been some lively movement or something from the roadside. As it was, everything remained as it was half an hour earlier. Peering through the spiky branches, he observed all around into the blackness. The sky above was littered with an array of tiny stars and a full moon was half covered with black clouds. In front, the spiked watchtowers rising high up, cast long shadows over the surrounding fields. From here, the land in front looked as large as the Goby desert except the sand was black. Large, circular and very white searchlights crossed and interchanged, glowing a frightening pattern sweeping the path before him. It was these lights coupled with the moonlight that caused a creepy sight of shifting shadows bringing the vast topography to the fore, alive with fear.

He counted the number of times the lights crossed each other and he measured the distance in front to the minefield. From here to the minefield was complete open land, bumpy, grassy in places with frozen puddles and rock hard mud. There was a barbed wire fence before the landmines that occasionally glinted when the beams of light struck them. Calculating, about 400 metres away on foot over rough terrain would take about 10 or 15 minutes to walk. But, he was going to have to crawl and avoid been seen.

He began. Lying flat on his stomach with his face down he dragged himself slowly across the field with very slow movements. He moved only a few centimetres at a time using his knees and elbows but counted at sixty second intervals. Then he stopped dead and waited for the two searchlights to pass. The first minute was okay because they missed him but the next sixty seconds was the one that he knew would light him up. Question was, was he dark enough to blend in with the ground? Slowly, but with strength and true grit, he forced his body behind a raised clump and stopped. Through gritted teeth and a fast beating heart he pushed the top of his head against the mud and counted 56..57..58..59..He almost felt the light burn his legs. He waited expecting nothing but death. He didn't breath until forced to do so. No alarms, no warning signal, he hadn't been seen. "Must continue." He whispered to himself. He'd barely travelled halfway when the freezing ground almost burned his body. Uncontrollably, he began shivering and almost couldn't stop his teeth from his bottom and top jaw chattering. His knees and elbows had numbed, he couldn't feel them but he wasn't sure if it was the cold or he'd broke through a pain barrier. He was certain they were bleeding but ignored the fact and remained constant, pushing, forcing himself through the treacherous conditions. The focus was on a part of the barbed wire fence that didn't seem to have been scanned by the lights at all. Staring over at it, his vision distorted when his eyes began watering. Desperately, he rubbed them and as he moved his arms up, the bone in his elbow cracked.

He was feeling very dizzy and sick.

"Oh Christ I'm not going to make it."

A compelling feeling overcame him, a voice shouted in his head. **"Get up and run, run, run to the fence."**

Struggling to move he stared up at the sky. Suddenly it was day, the sky was blue and the sun shining a blistering heat. He was in the fields by his college with his friends. There smiling faces stared at him and Nandi could hear himself talking to them.

"Okay listen. I know it sounds ridiculous in this heat, but in a few hours it will start to go dark. We have already lost some supplies, if needs be we can refuel our water supplies at the well just outside that farmhouse. We are going to need to set up camp in a suitable area and we are going to have to light a campfire. And if none of you have realised it, we haven't any matches. I can light a fire but only in daylight, I cannot do it when the sun goes down."

"Some kind of a magician are you Nandi?" Istvan joked.

Nandi smiled with his eyes but then seriously continued,

"Please trust me. And, you want to win don't you?"

Nandi could see himself running with his friends and remembered his thoughts as he ran. 'He was in the middle of a war zone being bombed by enemy aircraft from above. He dodged the bullets raining all around him and hurdled the anthills imagined them to be hidden mines. Nandi condemned himself to death as he accidentally crushed an anthill with his right boot.'

For some reason in his delirious state, this time when he stood on an anthill imagining it to be a landmine brought him back to his senses.

He shook his head and brought himself back to reality.

462

"No, if I run I will die. Keep moving Nandi, keep moving, must outwit the Russians."

From somewhere he found strength. He squeezed the last drop of energy from his muscles and bones. He made it. Cut, bleeding, freezing, he now sat leaning against a wooden post that had rows and rows of barbed wire nailed to it and spanned for miles either side of him probably the whole perimeter of Hungary he thought. He was breathing heavy and sat flexing his arms, bending his legs at the knees and wiggling his toes and fingers. He knew he must get the blood circulating again but he was safe for now from the searchlights.

Mogyoroska

The fear rose in Janos's eyes when a member of the secret police entered their house without permission. Janos pushed his chair back with his feet and stood up face to face with him.

"Where is Mrs. Pekar?"

"She's at the church praying for our son."

"I hope she's praying very hard."

"Why?"

"I have some news for you."

"What news? Tell me quickly."

"Your son took the last train to Budapest on November 4th."

"Yes we know that already."

"The train didn't make it to Budapest. It was stopped outside Budapest as Kistarcsa. Reports have it that there was some freedom fighters aboard the train and they opened fire on the Russian soldiers. It was only because of the soldier's excellent training that kept them alive and from being injured. Consequently, they had no choice but to engage the train after they ensured the civilians were safe. The last train to Budapest with your son on it was blown up."

"His body, did you find his body?"

"All bodies found on the train were unidentifiable."

Janos fell back into his chair.

"I trust you will let your wife know of this news…I'll see myself out"

He left leaving Janos shocked and without emotion. "That doesn't mean anything, that doesn't mean he's dead."

Janos laced up his boots and ran down into the village into the overcrowded church. He pushed his way to the front, acknowledged the priest with a nod and kneeled beside Margit. He gripped both of her hands and they both stared at the large painting of the crucifixion, the twisted body of Christ looking down at them. The congregation silenced and they let all members of the family to the front to sit around Janos and Margit.

It was after a few minutes when Janos stood up and asked the priest if he could say a few words.

"A policeman has just informed me that the last train to Budapest on November 4th had been blown up by the Russian soldiers. There wasn't any survivors and as you all know, Nandi was on that train. They haven't found his body but they fear the worst." The whole church gasped at the same time.

"But don't you believe any of it. Because I don't. I know my wife doesn't believe it. He's alive and do you know how I know that. Because I told him never to leave me. Long ago I said to my son, I said 'Promise me something son, that whatever happens in your life, whatever happens in our future, you will always do the right thing, you must always follow your heart and above all, you will be free. And promise you will never leave your family. If you can promise me these things, I will make a pledge to you of my own, I'm going to teach you all I know and more, I'm going to teach you how to use your brain, how to use your hands, how to fend for yourself and to fight for freedom.' Now I kept my promise to him, most of you know that, and Pekar's always keep their promise. So, my wife and I are going to leave now and we are going home to wait for our son."

The congregation tearfully watched Janos and Margit leave the church.

As they entered their home Margit asked Janos if there had been any sign of Blackie yet.

"No nothing. He has gone off to search for Nandi and he wont come back until Nandi does."

As they turned out the light Janos prayed one more time.

"Please lord. Take good care of our son."

Hegyeshalom

Stretching his arm in between the barbed wire, he poked the dagger carefully into the soil. It was difficult and his hand trembled with each prod. He moved along and kept piercing the soil deep enough to make contact with anything. Suddenly he felt it. He froze and stared wide eyed with fear. On his knees, he slowly pulled back the dagger. He prodded again on the other side just to be sure. It was there. A landmine. He slowly pushed away the soil to reveal it. There wasn't many searchlights that beamed across the minefield, why should they? Nobody would be foolish enough to go into it, and if they did, the explosion would be enough to attract the attentions of the guards. Nandi had timed it, one light every five minutes started at one end of the field and flashed across in a vertical straight line up and down. He knew it was due near to him at any second. Then it came. He crouched down low and waited as it lit up the field in front only to reveal the imprints of a thousand tramping boots.

"Footprints from the fleeing Hungarians before the mines were laid."

Luckily, he now knew the position of the first landmine. According to Gyorgy, they had been buried 3 metres apart in diagonal lines. All he needed to do now was get in there. Using the dagger he began sawing through the thick, spiked wire, the task was hindered by his cold fingers that he tried to rectify it by blowing hot air into his palms. It took almost an hour to cut through three strands of wire but now he could bend it back to allow enough room for him to crawl through. He squeezed through the small hole with relative ease into the outskirts of a furious den of hidden bombs, and then decided this time he would crawl through on his back. This way he could see all around and could monitor what was going on. He prayed Gyorgy was correct and so guessed at 3 metres. He felt it, the second landmine. Precisely diagonal to the other and precisely 3 metres. He pushed his body around it and continued on to the next. He was in the centre of the minefield when he had to stop. Even though he was chilled to the bone, his face was soaked with sweat and dirt. "I must stop my hands from trembling."

The cold and his nerves together were a lethal combination and he knew if he prodded at a mine too vigorously, it would explode in his face.

466

Ten landmines later, Nandi lay directly in between two watchtowers. To his left it was about 50 metres away, and similar to his right. He lay dead centre and had an amusing

thought. 'If I was to lie here with my bare arse in the air, I wonder if they'd see me. Probably would, but it would be a comical way to die.'

The crackling interference from their transmitter radio's broke the night silence and although he couldn't make out what the guards were saying, he felt somehow reassured that if they were talking to someone on the radio, then their attentions couldn't be on guarding the minefield. He battled on, prodding, feeling, skirting around the limb removing bombs.

Suddenly, there was nothing. He pushed the dagger in further. Still nothing. 4 metres, 5 metres, 6 metres. There appeared to be no more landmines. His heart beat hard like a drum pounding against his ribs. "Mustn't get too carried away. Maybe they've changed direction." He was on his knees now and walked a little quicker still prodding all the time. He'd done it. He was passed the mines. He wanted to jump for joy but couldn't. Instead, he pressed his head against the ground and whispered out loud.

"Thank God."

But, something caught his attention. In the darkness in front of him, he heard something. He looked up but couldn't make it out but something was moving, rustling around in the grass. He pulled his pistol from his pocket and aimed it in front but not before he checked the watchtowers. Startled, he jumped when he caught the eyes of a fox staring at him.

"Oh shit. Go away you pest, go away."

The fox didn't move for a minute it just stared. Nandi shuffled forward and then almost slipped down a very deep manmade trench. He looked down and tried to make out how deep it was.

Then, he saw the reflection of the moon in the frosty water at the bottom. The fox yelped and moved a few feet away and then stopped again. That was it. The guards had heard something and began turning the searchlights this way. Panicking he threw

December 9th 1956

himself into the trench and lay face up in the freezing water. It wasn't too deep, but the water covered his body, only his black face remained above the surface. Eventually, there were three searchlights scanning the whole area. A thousand needles seemed to be stabbing into Nandi's body as the cold water tortured him. He wanted to scream out and give up but something prevented him from doing so. The large round light moved closer and closer to Nandi. He closed his eyes tight imagining the light may reflect against the whites of his eyes. The trench was wide, deep and very, very long stretching for mile after mile. He wasn't sure where the searchlight was so he opened one eye slowly. Shivering, his lips had turned blue and he couldn't prevent the hot steamy breath bellowing out of his mouth and rising into the air. The Russians were certain to spot him now and then he heard it. A single shot was fired from the watchtower. "If they've shot me I didn't feel a thing. But then I'm so cold maybe I wouldn't feel it." He opened both of his eyes fully and gazed into the night skies. Without lifting his head out of the water, he rolled his eyes around in order to see what was going on. The three beams of light lit up an area above and he saw the hind legs of the fox hanging over the trench. It was lifeless and appeared to be smeared with blood. Then, through sounds travelling underwater, he could laughter from the watchtowers.

Waiting just five minutes in freezing water was like walking through the fires of hell. Without hesitation, he scrambled out of the water as soon as the lights moved away and continued their regular repeating search patterns towards the East.

He shivered and shuddered and wanted to remove his wet clothes but knew he couldn't, he needed to stay camouflaged.

"Oh God. Hypothermia I'm going to die of Hypothermia."

He clawed his way to the top of the trench and was met by a clear field, landmine free. He started to jog into the blackness

December 9th 1956

knowing he was free from spotlights for at least a hundred metres. His waterlogged clothes dragged him down and seemed to get heavier with each step he took. Eventually, they grew so heavy they pulled him to the floor and he rolled head over heels across the ground. But he didn't stop, determined and with a forceful crawl, driven only by courage and rage, he continued his journey on his hands and knees. Now the next obstacle greeted him. A 6 metre high rounded wall of barbed wire. There was no way over it, no way under it, only through it.

"Oh God what next?"

He remained on his knees while he caught his breath. The freezing water had stopped his knees and elbows from bleeding for now as he checked his wounds.

After a while, he grew impatient with himself. He knew he would pass out soon so battling on wasn't an option. He didn't have many choices now if he stayed he would die. If he gave himself up, he would die. If he goes on, he might die. This was the only option. He staggered when he levitated to his feet. With both hands, he tried to twist and pull a gap in the barbed wire. It slashed holes in his gloves, cut through his coat, tore into his legs and pressed hard into his head and hair. He was in the middle of this steel rose bush, tangled and trapped. He couldn't move. He went limp and dropped down but the barbed wire held him upright. His eyes closed, his eyeballs rolled around until he could see the image of Christ in the church at his home in Mogyoroska. He was walking down the centre of the aisle in the church. He could see the large painting of the crucifixion on the far wall to

the left, it was eerily compelling, he walked further forward
along the centre aisle, still gazing at Jesus. His twisted body
seemed to turn towards him, Nandi focused on the image of pain;
Christ's knotted muscles standing out from the arms, as they bore
the weight of the body, the head bowed it appeared, in defeat.
Jesus had the thorns of the rose bush pressed into his temple. The

December 9th 1956

flashback grew more real when Nandi stood outside himself in the
middle of the barbed wire.
The image of Christ in the painting at his village church, and
himself hanging there, head bowed, in defeat surrounded by
Russians as Jesus was surrounded by Romans.

His own stance caught up in the sharp steel
needles, identically resembled the painting of Jesus in the church
hanging there, nailed to the cross. He then could hear his fathers
voice 'I'm going to teach you how to use your brain, how to use
your hands, how to fend for yourself and to fight for freedom. So
c'mon Nandi, you must never leave your family. Never give up.
Now get up Nandi, get up now, your mother and I are waiting for
you, don't leave us.'
Suddenly, his eyes flickered open. He frowned hard. Relentlessly
he pulled his tangled arm away from the spikes. He then yanked
his leg free.
"C'mon." He ordered himself.
Without fear, without feeling the pain he squeezed himself
through the remainder of the wire. It pulled him, cut him, but this
time he treated it without any respect and he was rewarded for it
when he jumped free to the other side.
"Yes you bastard I've made it through."
He ducked instantly when he noticed just in time a searchlight
travelling quickly at head height.

"Forgot about that one he said to himself. Now, where the hell am I?"

He wasn't sure whether to walk or crawl. For now, he risked it and marched on ignoring the trickles of blood rolling off him from all angles.

Then he saw the next Russian box of tricks. Trip wires. They were positioned at different heights with about two metres of space between each of them.

December 9th 1956

"Oh my God." They stretched as far as the eye could see. "Do they go all the way to France?"

Attached to the tripwires were flares. If the wires were struck, the flare nearest to, shot up into the sky and lit up the whole area. Nandi knew if he caught one, it would be all over for him.

"How can I get through with all these drenched clothes on weighing me down."

He did it anyway. By slow strides. One after another he stepped over them. The different heights of wire were confusing. At first, he didn't understand the reasoning for it but now he was in the middle of this great field of tripwires and flares, he felt disorientated and somewhat claustrophobic. One mistake and the wire would shake and boom he was dead.

He couldn't stand up any longer it had been over thirty minutes since he began clambering over them. He sat down once again and stared towards Austria.

"Dear God am I ever going to make it?"

Five minutes rest and he was on his way again. This time he held his pistol in his right hand and started to jog and hurdle the trip wire. After about twenty or more tripwires his jog turned into more like a sprint. He was anxious and his anxiety took over his mind. He felt the muscles in his cheekbones pump as he sped up faster and faster. The darkness enveloped him and in a dizzy state, he couldn't see the wires any more. He wasn't sure if he'd gone passed them.

It cut deep into his shinbone and skittled him tossing him into the air. The pistol flew from his hand and as he stretched his arm out for it, he plunged into the following tripwire. The whoosh from the flares screamed passed his ears. The piercing sound was so loud Nandi had to cover both ears relieved to feel they were both still attached to his head. He couldn't keep his eyes open; the flash was so bright it seemed like day. The pupils in his eyes dilated so fast, he was blinded for an instant. He lay on the floor helpless awaiting his fate. The sounds of men shouting and the clunking of

December 9th 1956

weapons arming themselves drew nearer. He was doomed and the barks from several German Shepherds drowned out the words from the patrol guards.

They were moving closer and Nandi had given up. "God doesn't want me to escape. This is as far as I can go. I am ready to give my life to the Russians here and now."

He smiled to himself and floated off to the past once again.

"We've caught the boar, we've caught the boar."
Driven only by courage and anger from the events of the day he shuffled himself out along the branch. He found himself having a birds-eye view of his dog and the boar battling with each other through sides of the enclosure, oblivious to Nandi overhead surveying his prey like a predator. It was now for Nandi that the whole world went quiet and in slow motion. He couldn't hear the barking of his dog, the grunts from the boar, nor could he hear his approaching father, closely followed by Feri Pekar shouting,
" No Nandi, no."
He had one thing in mind, defeat the enemy; it's now or never. He poised himself for attack, now sitting with both legs on the same side of the branch slightly apart, gripping the spear with both hands pointing the spike towards the ground between his feet.

472

Waiting the auspicious moment, until it came; his heart missed a beat as his aim became perfect, the boar had galloped and stopped directly beneath the spike. Nandi could see the back of the boar's neck was exposed and vulnerable; he clenched the spear tight in his hands and leapt from the tree, he could hear the wind whistling passed his ears as he plummeted towards the animal,

" I mustn't blink." He thought. His eyes remained wide and transfixed onto the neck of the boar. With a jolt, a thud and a rough tumble, Nandi had vaulted into the corner of the enclosure

December 9th 1956

somehow upside down with his legs ledged against the fence. He seemed to be in this position for ages until he came to his senses, "Where is the boar? Where is my spear?" He said to himself. "Must get up off the floor."
Now he could hear his father and Feri,

"Nandi get up, quickly, quickly, run, run,"

Nandi made himself stand up, his legs were a little shaky and his head dizzy, but after brushing himself down he soon pulled his senses back together.

"I'm not even hurt." He reassured himself.
He looked across at his victim. The boar lay curled up with its back facing Nandi, the spear stood firm and erect clearly exposing the area of penetration, deep into the neck of the boar. Nandi smiled nervously at his cousin and father who were together holding open the trap door, still beckoning and calling to their triumphant young protégé.

"C'mon Nandi, get out of there it isn't dead." His father called out to him. He was right; seconds after Nandi had brushed himself off the boar began stirring. At first Nandi didn't move, only watched the boar struggle to his feet. It grunted, shook its head from side to side and then squealed as it broke of the spear with

*its right hoof. A trickle of blood oozed from the open wound
and then it caught sight of the culprit. As Nandi and the wild
animal made eye contact, panic and the realisation that the
animal would attack, engulfed Nandi's thoughts.*

*"Shit, run." He told himself and he did. Run that is, as he did
manage to keep control of his bodily functions...just about.
He darted in a flash towards the exit; the boar was alert and
galloped towards the exit itself in an attempt to block off any
escape route. Nandi knew he must get there first; the race for the*

December 9th 1956

*door seemed a long one and as he got closer, so did the boar.
Now almost side by side, both with heads down, Nandi just one or
two strides ahead, the finish line was approaching. Nandi shouted
out loud as he could feel the hot breath of the pig against his
ankle. He raced through the exit with such speed as he felt a sharp
ripping pain cut through his shinbone which sent him hurtling
head over heels landing face down in the snow. He had tripped
over the trap door wire, the very thing that had caught the animal,
had now hindered Nandi's escape, expecting nothing but attack
from an angry pig, Nandi's life passed before his eyes. In a
second he looked behind him to see his attacker, visibility was
poor owing to the exploding snow dust which had erupted around
him amidst the mayhem. As if in a strange dream, Nandi was
looking down to earth from a cloud, he could see his country
being swallowed by a huge wild animal, he could see himself
hurtling spear after spear at this wild animal.*

He turned his head and looked for the boar. Instead, six German
Shepherds were approaching held on a lead by six guards. They
shouted something to him. He strained hard to understand. Then
he realised. The language was unfamiliar. Not Hungarian, not
Russian. It was German.
He sat up straight immediately. They surrounded him with smiling
faces. Two of them helped him to his feet. They were talking all
of the time and Nandi began smiling when the German language

was so comforting to hear. He started to laugh, then the
laughter turned to tears and he fell to his knees and held on to the
legs of one of the guards.
"You have made it young man. Only God knows how, nobody has
escaped from Hungary for weeks. It's a miracle. Your safe now
son, your in Austria, you've made it to the west. You are free."
The Austrian guard spoke good Hungarian.

Nandi couldn't remember being rolled onto a stretcher but when
he came to, he was being carried across the field towards a large
lit up building. His shivering body was the only movement from

December 9th 1956

him, apart from his eyes that stared and searched hard towards
Hungary.
He was lifted onto a soft bed and quickly stripped from his wet
frozen clothes and a clean, warm quilt was thrown over him.
There were more guards inside, all busy, all doing something or
another seemingly excited by their unexpected visitor. Nandi
listened hard to their ramblings and tuned his brain in to the
sergeant's voice, coloured, as it was, with mock gravity. He was
ordering them all about, that was obvious, and Nandi was certain
he'd sent for a doctor. Lethargically but observantly, he studied
the room and their activities. Opposite the bed on the far wall was
a log fire; to his left the doorway to the outside, in the right hand
corner was a discoloured gas cooker. The oven door had been left
open revealing decomposed flakes of paint on the inside leaving a
black ash coating on the oven walls. As he watched, a guard put a
saucepan full of something on the top and lit it with a match.
Another guard knelt down by the log fire and began piling on
more chopped sticks and logs. He blew into the smouldering ash
underneath and suddenly the intense heat ignited the sticks and
logs sending the flames leaping up into the chimney. Even though
the outside door had blown open with an increased wintry wind
from outside, the room increased in temperature instantly with the
light from the smoky spitting logs. There was a large, bright, light
bulb in the centre of the ceiling that swung around from the drafty

doorway throwing shadows around the room. Nandi watched
its movement fading in and out of its hazy focus. His shivering
grew less vigorous and he pulled the quilt up to his nose
defending his face from the increasing rapid winds, which now
added the spatter of rain to its forlorn soundtrack. The sergeant
crossed the room towards the door, his bulk defying the wind.
After slamming it shut, he dragged a low wooden stool across the
floor next to Nandi and sat on it.
He spoke Hungarian with a strong German accent.
"Hi son. My name is Sergeant Klein, Sergeant Istvan Klein. Yes I
have a Hungarian Christian name with an Austrian surname."

December 9th 1956

Nandi frowned. "It's a long story but my grandfather was
Hungarian, hence the reason I can speak your lingo a little."
He looked across the room at the guard by the cooker and noticed
he was pouring the hot drink. When he caught his eye, he
beckoned him over quickly.
"Here, a steaming drink of hot chocolate. Can you sit up?"
Nandi grimaced as he pulled his legs around to sit on the edge of
the bed gripping the quilt tight around him. He was still shivering
slightly so he moved off the bed and settled down on the floor in
the pool of swaying light thrown out by the fire.
Sergeant Klein passed him the hot mug of chocolate. He cupped it
with two hands, didn't drink it at first, just let the piping hot,
sticky steam burn all around his dirty bloodstained face.
"What's you name then young man? I see you don't have any
identification papers on you except for your bible; which I have
put in that drawer over there."
Nandi checked for the drawer.
He tried to answer him as he battled for control of his dry and
swollen tongue.
"Pekar; Nandor Pekar." His voice was coarse so he began sipping
the hot chocolate. His face lit up slightly as he swallowed it.
"Never drank hot chocolate before then Nandor?"

"Please, call me Nandi. No, it's extremely tasty."

"Get it down you son, you need to warm everything up, get everything working again. I can see you have a lot of nasty cuts and bruises, I have sent for a doctor, but I don't think there's anything to worry about, it's just a precaution. How long did it take you to get through that hell hole?"

"What time is it now?"
Sergeant Klein checked his watch.

"It's nearly twenty to five."

December 9th 1956

"Since about 7 o'clock last night."

"How did you get passed the landmines?"

"I crawled around them."

"I tell you what Nandi, you've got more guts than anybody I've ever known."

"It's not guts Sergeant Klein. It's a need. A simple need to be free. Asked whether I'd rather live under the control of communism or crawl through a mine field on a freezing cold night...Well, here's your answer."

The sergeant smiled proudly at Nandi, patted his right shoulder, stood up and asked if could eat some hot boiled chicken legs. Nandi thought about it for a second and answered,

"Yes I could. Thank you."

The sergeant made his way towards a door at the side of the log fire and stopped before he opened it.

"For the moment you must rest here and when you wake up I will have you transferred to our refugee safe house in Nickelsdorf. There, they will take care of you and there are other Hungarians for you to get together with."

"What is happening to us? What will happen to me?"

Sergeant Klein had opened the other door and walked into the other room when he started to answer Nandi but his voice had trailed off and Nandi couldn't make out what he was saying for a moment, before he emerged in a clearing of steam from the kitchen with a plate of boiled chicken legs.

December 9th 1956

"I'm sorry Sergeant. I didn't quite catch what you said."

"We have lists of places you can go. Western countries all over the world are accepting you, greeting you with open arms. You have a choice of places, you decide and we will arrange your transport. Anyway, no more talking. I can see the doctor through the window getting out of his van. After you've finished your chocolate, eaten your chicken, and after the doctor has cleaned you up, dressed your wounds, you must sleep. All these guards will be patrolling this area, if you need something, shout them. You will be quite safe here."

The doctor flung open the door and closed it behind him quickly. He was wearing a white coat and carrying a large leather medical bag, his broad face beaming as he came in from the cold. He took a visual examination of Nandi. "Can one of you run him a hot bath please? Quickly."

Two guards tended to the doctor's request and entered the small bathroom through a door to the far right of the bed.

Within an hour he had soaked his frozen bones in a tub of hot water, his cuts had been cleaned with antiseptic, the deeper more severe ones dressed with bandage, his stomach filled with hot drinks and hot chicken. Hardly believing what was happening, Nandi lay covered with a warm quilt in front of an open log fire in an Austrian border guardhouse, being guarded by Austrian patrols. The Geneva Convention and NATO protecting him, preventing the untouchable, unbeatable communisms from stealing him away even though they were a cock-stride from him. For the first time he felt safe. Nervously, he smiled to himself and let his tired eyes and body sink into the deepest sleep without objection.

December 10th 1956. 1:30p.m

They had given Nandi some old but clean blue dungarees and a high necked black thick woollen jumper to replace his own shredded and soaked attire. He was fully dressed and had just finished a hot mug of coffee when he stepped outside to be greeted by a wintry blue sky. The sun was very high above the horizon, its orb an amazing shade of violet, hazy, as Nandi had to squint to allow for the sudden increase of brightness from being inside a dull room. He widened his eyes eventually to have his first look at a free country in the daytime staring towards the west in the direction of Vienna. The landscape looked bleached and friendly.

A young border guard approached Nandi and offered him a cigarette. He lit it eagerly and was happy he could also speak some Hungarian.

"I speak some Russian too." He told Nandi.

"It's no use to me. I don't speak a word of Russian and never have any intentions of doing." Nandi replied cockily.

"Eisenhower has made a statement today something to do with today being Human Rights day; I have caught some of it on the radio, he mentions about the sufferings of the Hungarian people."

"Oh did he?" Nandi snapped. "Fantastic to hear his words, but we didn't want words we wanted action, he promised us, they all did, and what did they send us? Chocolate, bars of bloody chocolate.."

"I think they were afraid of starting another world war."

"The Russians are afraid of America and the entire western world. All as NATO had to do was park their air force in Budapest and that would have been it, 'goodnight Vienna' excuse the pun, okay goodnight Moscow. And they promised it, we heard it in Hungary,

December 10th 1956

that Henry Cabot Lodge, the United States delegate, had said firmly: 'The United Nations cannot remain a passive spectator to the events in Hungary.' Now that to me and to any civilized human being, meant that action and support from them would be imminent."

"Yes, we know he said that. But did you know what was printed in the New York Times on the same day? It was all over the news on every radio station."

Nandi's face remained blank and waited for the guard to continue.

"It said something like that the big western powers appear to have decided to keep the Hungarian question to one side for the moment, until such time it becomes clear that the freedom fighters have attained their objective."

Nandi stepped away from the guard in the direction towards Hungary. He took three successive drags on his cigarette, stared gloomily into his country and then, letting the smoke from his

480

final pull on the cigarette find its own way out of his mouth
and into the breeze, he muttered quietly to himself.

"The future of Hungary was in our own hands. It is better to live fighting for
what you believe in than to die regretting what you could have done. The
loneliness of Hungary is a source of strength, an oasis in the European desert.
Our fate was in our hands, we are a people that have been tragically left on our
own between east and west."

Nandi remembered the words from the old man at Szikszo
hospital from several weeks before. He felt quite afraid and alone;
he had understood the History of Hungary that they had a past of
being abandoned by the rest of the world. But now, he had
witnessed it, he was living through it, he was feeling the empty
sick pain of abandonment and now knew how Hungarian heroes
of the past must have felt. Hungary, for a thousand years had lived
with the same repeating consistencies and now the burning
sensation inside the pit of his stomach, for a second, made him

December 10th 1956

feel he wanted to go back into Hungary, gather an army and fight
to the death.
"What else could a good patriot of Hungary do?" He said to
himself before he threw his burnt out cigarette to the floor.

His depression was interrupted when Sergeant Klein's vehicle
droned its arrival. He stepped out with another man and with
beaming smiles they marched over to Nandi. Before Sergeant
Klein could introduce him, the other man couldn't restrain his
excitement and began shaking Nandi's hand and patting him on
both shoulders with two hands.

"Fantastic, fantastic, this is wonderful. I am Tibor, Tibor Szabo, I
have been appointed by Austrians foreign minister Mr. Kurt
Waldheim, he is the ambassador to Canada. I have been appointed
to help all refugees but I was so sad because some have tried to
get through but have been arrested or shot. I haven't seen anybody
for weeks. I was here on business when the revolt broke out and
since the middle of November; I have been assisting the

evacuation. But I had given up hope of any more escapees and now you turn up. I couldn't wait to see you, the one, the brave one that got through the bloody Russian blockade, well done! Well done!"

Once again, he began patting and hugging Nandi.

"Shall you be taking me to Nickelsdorf?"

"Yes, yes, we must fill out some documents, answer some questions, have a look at the options around the world. You aren't alone; there are six others at the moment all waiting for deportation to Canada and America. A few left a day before yesterday to England…Have you got family in Hungary?"

"Yes my parents."

December 10th 1956

"Do they know you are here?"

"No they know nothing of my fight against the Russians or my plans to escape. They probably think I'm dead."

"When you get to your destination. That is the time to inform them that you are alive and well."

"Are we leaving for Nickelsdorf now?"

"Yes now, it's very close."

"I'm just going to get my bible and then I will be ready."

✳ ✳ ✳

That evening the darkness fell rapidly over Austria. Nandi had just finished filling out the relevant documents and had been introduced to the other six refugees and shown to his sleeping quarters. It was a fairly long room with bunk beds down either side. Nandi was underneath a 30 year old man named Aaron who had already shared some yellow pepper and salami with him. Nandi, tired and exhausted, sat on his bed and checked the condition of the bible. It was dirty, bent and creased, but on the whole, it had survived a gruelling battle for freedom. He read the words from his father, checked the pressed rose and Lilly of the Valley and the half torn page that bore a reminder of Maria and a promise he must keep.

"Will I ever go back to my home? Will I ever see Hungary again?" He asked himself.

"None of us will." Aaron had leaned his head from the top bunk and looked down towards Nandi. "We'll never eat goulash again,

December 10th 1956

we'll never be able drip our bacon over an open fire and we'll never taste Palinka or enjoy our wine the fruits of the vine." Aaron chuckled after he'd said it and then carried on as Nandi was imagining the scenery of Mogyoroska.
"So I've heard, in America, if you go to the butchers shop, they actually throw away the feet and the head from a chicken. Imagine that, what a waste."

Nandi grinned at Aaron's comments and then asked him,

"Where are you from?"

"I'm from a small village near to Csorna. Do you know it?"

"Yes. It's western Hungary, in fact it isn't too far from the border is it?"

"That's right, not too far."

"Was there much military action there?"

"Oh yes from all over. But, when I thought it was over, when all the fighting stopped, the Russians and the Avu, they kept coming back rampaging over the town. I live just outside amid luscious vineyards. The scenery is enchanting. As far as the eye can see there are rolling vineyards and vine-covered hills. The succulent red grapes are so juicy; a walk through the fields could leave you feeling light-headed, warmed by the sun and exhilarated by the fragrance. The combination of sunlight with the pleasant aroma of wine, made life bearable when the Avu attacked and tried to destroy our human sensibility and self esteem, sucking our pride and honour."

"Yes, but that is why we stood up to them and we actually beat them didn't we?"

December 10th 1956

Aaron looked sad as he answered Nandi.

"It is the one's we have left behind that I feel sorry for. They are the one's that are going to suffer now more than ever before. That's why I left. It was a few days after the Russians had taken control of Budapest. A large group of Russian soldiers were in our village intoxicated by wine. They tore down everything in sight, rampaging, maniacally massacring hundreds of people destroying their property. I saw our narrow alleys streaming with a mixture of blood and wine, the victims' cries piercing the air. After they'd gone and the savages had worn themselves out, my friends and neighbours worked together to wash the blood away and the bodies were buried in their forefathers graves at the edge of town…So, I decided to leave, I'm lucky I suppose, I have no family, there's just me to take care of. How about you Nandi, where are you from?"

"Mogyoroska. It's to the East in the Zemplen mountains'. I'm seeing it now; the Rakoczi castle staring down at me. It stands on a huge mountain opposite my house. It's a magical place, full of mysterious new corners to discover and storylines to live out. Full of spirit. My father's a farmer, we have animals, he collects hay in the summer for the winter. It's, it's my home; and I'm leaving it, I'm going to start a new life somewhere else."

"Have you decided where you are going to go yet Nandi?"

"Yes, yes I have, I've told him."

"And where are you going?"

"England, I'm going to England. I considered Canada, but he doesn't think I can get there for another few weeks, but I can go to England within a couple of days. So, no point in messing around,

December 10th 1956

he says there's plenty of work there or I could even continue my college education."

"How will you communicate with the English?"

"I'm going to learn their language of course and the way to do that perfectly, is to forget your own language and to think in English. If I can do that, I will learn it perfectly and then I can get a job and begin a new life. And also if I can speak English perfectly, I can perfectly take the piss out of their football team reminding them that we beat them 6-3 at Wembley and 7-1 in Budapest."

CHAPTER 16

December 16th 1956. 8:30a.m

"Look Nandi Look."

Laszi, another refugee he'd met on the way to England banged on the porthole window from outside. He sat with four other Hungarians eating his first ever English breakfast. It was an unusual flavour, the bacon was un-smoked and lean, a fried egg and beans in some kind of orangey tomatoey red sauce. The five of them couldn't make up their minds if they were enjoying the peculiar taste made more unusual by the strange combinations of dairy food, meat and vegetables. They made fun of the very white flimsy thin sliced bread but even though it was extraordinary to taste foreign food for the first time, the un-spicy tang was strangely persuasive and Nandi was working hard to clean the entire plate. He forked a slice of bacon into his mouth and shouted back to Laszi.

"What's the matter?"

"Over there in the distance. Great big white rocks."

"We'll be out in a second."

Nandi was the first to finish and he swept the bread around the remaining bean sauce and swallowed it.

"Well, I certainly hope I can get used to this crap food or I'll be writing to Khrushchev in Moscow and telling him it's his fault I've got to eat food without paprika so he can bloody well post me a box full of spices and smoked bacon."

The others laughed and agreed as Nandi stood up and wiped his lips on a paper napkin and then said as he strained to look out of the window.

December 16th 1956

"C'mon hurry up guys; I'm going out on deck to check out the famous White Cliffs of Dover."

The outside was blustery and the sky was completely white with a few shades of grey. The cliffs rose high from the sea in their calm majesty and Nandi was elated, gazing at the picturesque solid chalk rocks of Dover in their extreme. The ship added to the glory swaying gently as it drove on full throttle to the free land. One by one, the newly formed group of Hungarian friends lined the safety barrier at the bow of the ship. Peter was the last one to join them after he'd swilled his last piece of bread down with a mouthful of black coffee. A semblance of light forced its way through a hole in the clouds and actually formed a bright glow behind the black smoke that poured from the ship's funnel. Nandi studied the rocky coastline and transfixed a gaze on a line of waves of low pressure that were evidently fuelling the sea water closest to the cliffs creating stronger waves that crashed against the shoreline menacingly and battered against the white rocks.

"It's beautiful." Someone said; and then Nandi reminded everyone.

"We'll be docking in less than half an hour… England. Freedom. What is in store for us?"

He thought hard about his family back home in his village and wandered if he'd ever see them again. A small tear filled the lower lid of his right eye as memories of his parents, cousins, aunties and uncles flooded his thoughts. It felt incredible and hard to comprehend what was happening at this moment. For the whole of Nandi's life, he had spent fighting a communist system. Struggling to keep hold of the only thing left that could have been free that the communists couldn't seize. Freedom of thought. As long as he had his mind, he would be free. Until they even tried to control the thoughts of a nation and then the

December 16th 1956

national prisoner rebelled; and now this. Heading towards England, the free country that wouldn't help Hungary in their hour of need but now offered Nandi a home, a future. Would he ever come to terms with these heterogeneous feelings?

"So Nandi, where are you going after we have docked in Dover?"

"A place called Blackpool. So they say, this is where I'm to learn English."

CHAPTER 17
(Over 30 years later)

MAY 13th 1987

Stoke-on-Trent (England) 9:30a.m

Nandor Pekar had taken his wife to work earlier, helped his daughter
with her four-year-old twin boys and taken them to school with her
before dropping Gayna (his daughter) off to his wife at Hanley market
where they worked together.
He drew his old Morris Marina discoloured off-white van to a standstill
outside his home in Portland Street, Hanley. For the moment, he just
wrenched the handbrake as high and as hard as he could, then, just
stared through the windscreen to the top of the street. He found it

difficult to move for a while and almost afraid to look at his home.
He knew he had to, but for the time being, he just listened to the voices
echoing in his head.
Richard (his son) had left to work this morning at 8:00a.m without his
keys to the house he was sure. The voices he could hear in his head were
that of the conversation shared with Richard that morning.

"Are you planning to come home for your dinner today Rich?"

Richard was clipping the press-studs of his blue overall jacket and when
he reached the breast pocket, which scrolled the name of the garage
where he worked *TYRESERVICES*, he stopped and left the neck part
open and then answered his father.

"No not today Dad I'll be staying at work, probably get some chips or
something."

May 13th 1987

Nandi stared at the Tyreservices sign and flashed back to a sickening
moment from over thirty years before. Just for a second he had a vision,
a ghost from his forgotten past. He could see the body of a dead soldier
with a woodcutters axe buried into the centre of his forehead, his shirt
was ripped open and the name "*Sándor Petöfi*." had been scrolled
across the dead soldiers' chest in blood.
The flashback subsided and disappeared completely after he blinked
hard two or three times.

"Are you okay Dad?" Richard asked when he saw his father struggling
to focus.

"Yeah, yes son. Just a bit of a headache coming on that's all. I was just
checking you weren't coming home for dinner because you haven't got
a key to the house and I didn't fancy leaving the house unlocked, as I
won't be in. I've got a lot of work on today and I plan to have this house

I'm doing fully completed by tonight. Just got the stairs and living room to wallpaper and a bit of glossing and that's it, finished. So, I won't be coming home until it's all done."

"No problem Dad. I'll see you tonight."

These last words from his son echoed a few times in his head and then he was certain that nobody had access to the house only himself.

He fumbled for the door latch and then needed to shoulder the door open before climbing out of his van and slammed the door closed. Standing on the pavement in front of his house, he stopped and admired the front view. The beautiful contours of a typical English town house that stood out against the others in the row. The outer layer painting at the top front, a brilliant diamond white, and his bedroom window, large with about 30 or 40 smaller

May 13th 1987

rectangle panes to make up the whole window. The artificial shutters on either side of the bedroom window a chocolate brown gloss that added a European look to its character. And the large downstairs living room bay window that bowed outwards, that too was filled with double the amount of rectangle panes than the upstairs.

But Nandi admired the front garden, its look a minute version of his childhood home far away deep in the wilderness of the Zemplen mountains in Eastern Hungary. The crimson red rose trees, one either side of his garden, and the white roses blended together to form a beautiful array of colours brightening up the front enhanced by an ornamental cherry tree further over to the left.

He imagined it how it was, how it had looked so old and tatty when they'd first moved there in 1974. 'How much work I've done to transform it from that into this modern but somehow antique looking home.' He thought to himself, breathing deeply a sigh of satisfaction. Someone walked passed him and brushed passed his shoulder shaking him from his trance encouraging him to open the cream coloured wrought iron gate and enter his front garden onto the concrete walkway that led to the dark solid oak front door. Before he slotted the key in the lock, he smoothed his hand against the wooden door number 33, and then over his brown plastic advertisement and read it out to himself in his mind. 'First Class Painter & Decorator, Satisfaction Guaranteed.'

"How did I end up here? From Mogyoroska, Hungary to Stoke-on-Trent, England as a painter and decorator" he asked himself and then unlocked the front door and walked inside.

The living room and kitchen had been knocked into one many years ago. Before he proceeded into the kitchen to make a coffee, he put his favourite love song on the turntable of the record player next to the television, placed the stylus at the beginning and sat down on the sofa to listen to 'All the Love in The World' by Dionne Warwick.

Soothed by the melody, Nandi drifted off to the past many years before.

He remembered docking at Dover docks as a Hungarian refugee over 30 years ago in the winter of 1956. It was the end of a bitter fight for freedom against the Russians and their communist system. Lost and unsure, he was surrounded by other refugees he'd met on his journey from Austria. Their names had been read off a list; documents and applications filled out and stamped at customs before a further haul to the seaside resort of Blackpool.

"Blackpool." He said to himself. "Christ I was exhausted and confused by the time I got there. All as they wanted to do was check us into the hostel and all as I wanted to do was buy and write out a postcard to my parents. I did it anyway and felt a great relief when I posted it at the post office the next morning."

'All The Love in The World' faded and then stopped with a sudden swift retraction from the arm of the record player and back to its starting point, announcing its arrival by a loud click. The impetuous silence that fell across the room was, for a while, rudely disappointing, but Nandi used the interruption from his reminiscences to pour himself a strong, black coffee. He sat down with it after restarting the song again.
He whispered, reminding himself of when he first met his English wife.

" When I first saw Gwen she was barely fifteen. Even though totally English, she had the qualities of a European princess, a shapely body and a pure heart that once touched, simply melted my own .I fell in love with her at first sight. Me, a foreigner from overseas trying to take the heart of a young English girl who's father had been a sergeant major in world war two and wore his long curly military moustache and stood with a stature that demanded respect. I was up against it. He, a decorated soldier with medals for bravery pinned to his chest, recognised for it by his own government. And me, in his eyes, a rebel from other parts of the world who had fought against his own government Probably thought I was a Nazi spy or something."

Nandi was correct. He was up against it in those days. But Jack Evans (Gwen's father) had not met the likes of Nandi before. Nandi's tall, broad shoulders, dark hair to go with his tanned complexion and large handsome pale green eyes were only the exterior that in itself, turned heads from every female, and even male. But Nandi, who, inside, had the heart of a lion and the nature of a butterfly, soon overwhelmed Jack.

It was 1958 when he first laid eyes on Gwen, 3 months and 3 days before his 20th birthday. They were married two years later and were blessed with their first baby daughter, Gayna, one year after that.

Nandi was remembering the delight and excitement, the feeling that you've created a human being. As the feeling reoccurred for a few minutes, he smiled while he sipped and swallowed his black coffee. Enjoying the unfamiliar feeling, he relaxed further back into the sofa and remembered some more.

"Gayna was beautiful, she had a fiery auburn tinge to her hair and oh my God her eyes, she had Pekar eyes like my father and me, large but more green than my own."

Then, he stopped smiling. He remembered the gut wrenching nausea. Hugging Gayna when she was one day old wandering if he would ever be allowed to enter Hungary again. He loved his Hungarian and English mixed daughter and he wanted his parents to share the love. A tear dripped from his cheek onto Gayna's chin knowing how her Hungarian grandparents would dote on her and how they would be praying at the village church to catch a glimpse of their first grandchild and praying they could hold her some day.

494

Margit and Janos (Nandi's mother and father) received his post card from Blackpool late January 1957. They had been praying for his life since November of 1956 when he was reported missing. They'd heard nothing of his whereabouts for two months, then, suddenly it arrived. Nandi could see his mother now dancing around the kitchen kissing the postcard and then onto the veranda, shouting and crying, "Thank you lord, thank you, thank you."

Janos (his father) was at his Mayor's office in the village and Margit could hardly stay on balance as she ran down the snowy bank to show him that their son was alive and well living in England. His father cried for a whole week until he couldn't cry any more.

"I was the talk of every village for miles around. Everyone knew of me, I was a kind of hero. My mother invited the whole village to church for a celebration that day, then back home for chicken paprika. My father, oh my God my father, at first he was bewildered and probably angry with me, but after the initial shock he was so proud; to most people, I was a hero, to him, I was more like a God."

Nandi spent years trying to describe his forbidden home in Hungary to his English wife and daughter. A solid provider for his family he landed a secure job at the beginning of 1962 at the Michelin Tyre factory in Stoke and promised that with his increased salary that somehow he would save enough money to take his proudly found family back to his roots in Mogyoroska.

Alas, he wasn't allowed back. If he did, he would have been arrested for crimes against the state and hanged. For now, the grandparents of Gayna could only settle for the odd letter and photograph.

Once again, his song finished playing on the record player. Carrying the remnants of his coffee into the kitchen, he caught himself in the gold-framed mirror on the chimneybreast above the gas-fire and approached it with a serious composure.

"Well Nandi." He said to himself. "You are 48 years old, have a full thick, black head of hair with a few sprays of grey; are you tough enough to go through with it?" He stared himself in the eyes as if waiting for the reflection to answer. Then he smirked when he saw himself in a pub brawl back in 1961 at the Railway Inn across Vale Place.

Darts was an English pub game that Nandi enjoyed playing occasionally with Vic, Gwen's brother. His new English family of in-laws had a clear picture of the Hungarian way of life and Nandi's struggle against communism and his tough battle to escape the clutches of the Soviet Union. They were all having a family evening at the Railway Tavern when two youths interrupted and sat beside the family. Loud and foulmouthed they were asked on several occasions to relax. Nandi had clocked them and studied their body language discretely. Suddenly, the two youths split up; one dragged a chair and sat under the dartboard in front of the glowing coal fire, and the other beside Nandi's mother-in-law. Gwen hadn't seen Nandi's face change in this way before.

"Are you okay Nandi?" She asked him.

The muscles in his cheekbones pumped and then he answered,

"When I was a boy in Hungary a member of the hated communist secret police slapped my face. I learned to fight because of him."

Gwen frowned heavily and then listened to Vic talking to the man under the dartboard.

"C'mon mate. If you sit there you are liable to get a dart in your eye."

"And if he does." The other one interrupted. "You'll get this glass in your face."

"What did you say?" Vic raised his voice.

Then Vic's aging mother tried to diffuse the situation.

"Excuse me young man, but that's my son you're speaking to."

"Is it really? Then this glass will be for you also."

Nandi turned over the large, heavy, round; pub table full of half drank glasses of beer and whiskey onto the man's chest. Pandemonium erupted.
Trying extremely hard to remember where Gwen had gone, still looking at himself in the mirror, he decided not to bother and continue with the memories of the fight.

"I quickly began firing my best punches hoping to gain the advantage in the early going. However, at first, my best shots seemed only to have the effect of further infuriating him. Get his eyes, get his eyes, I reminded myself. My experience from my fighting in the revolution would payoff, the willingness to fight for your country, this, a pub brawl, had to be a synch. Consequently, my experience and quickness allowed me to hold my own and though I hadn't caught him with a knockout punch yet, I was stinging him with punches and kicks. And then, in his frustration that he hadn't hit me yet because I'd been dodging around, he tries to Rugby tackle me around my waste. I stepped back as he came and kicked his lowered head and, to his misfortune, I struck him with brute force in his left eye. Now, my opponent was cut and bleeding and couldn't see. My tactics from the beginning. Next, had to help my brother-in-law. The other guy was over him and Vic was on his back."

Respect from Gwen's family grew and grew for Nandi after his loyalty prevailed. Nandi rescued Vic when he immobilised the second bully with several sharp rabbit punches.
Recalling that moment, he grinned once again at himself in the mirror hearing the voices from his mother-in-law.

"Stop it Nandi, stop it! You'll kill him! You'll kill him!"

'So what?' I thought. 'I've killed before.'

And then, when the police came they asked Nandi and Vic what weapon they'd used to hit them.

"Nothing only my fists I told him."

By now, Nandi was re-enacting the fight scene in the kitchen mirror shadow boxing against his own reflected image. Then, he remembered the question he'd asked himself which triggered off the memory of his pub fight from 1961.

"Are you tough enough to go through with it?"
He paused and looked at himself again straight-laced and firm.

"Yes. I am."

He walked over to the sink and filled a small white vase full of water and left it flowerless in the kitchen window. The backdoor key had always been difficult to turn, but he unlocked it today with ease and went outside into his large back garden that started with a yellow and red flag-stoned yard with a wooden shed over in the left corner. Steps lead to the second tear, flowers, trees and shrubs to the left and to the right, a concrete base suitable for sun-beds and deck chairs on summer days. Finally, the top part was larger with cabbages and carrots in the vegetable patch and higher up, a homemade greenhouse and a beautiful rockery homing the finest of plants and flowers of all colours. It was here Nandi ventured until he cut six stems from his favourite flowers the Lilly of the Valley, that were blooming beautifully. Their white round and small bell-shaped petals stood away from the stems pert and erect. He smelled them gently before cupping them together in his right hand.

By the backdoor he didn't go inside yet, he decided to lay the flowers on the garden table and smoke a Hamlet cigar that he had retrieved from his shirt breast pocket. The time it took him to smoke the whole length hadn't gone anywhere. For him, one second he was lighting it, the next he was stubbing it out in an ashtray on the table. He remained there for ten minutes, motionless and dumb, listening to the beating of his own heart. For him those ten minutes were very long but he snapped himself away from the trance, picked the flowers up off the table, went back inside and planted them into the small white vase. Whilst he admired them turning it around in his hand, he remembered that the next day was Gwen's birthday and the conversation shared with Gayna before dropping the twins off at school.

"It's your mothers' birthday tomorrow."

"Yes I know. What have you got for her, Dad?"
"Oh, something unusual."

The sun burst through a fluffy white cloud, penetrated the thin net curtains in the kitchen window, and onto the Lilly of the Valley flowers distracting his attention away from the unusual gift he was giving his wife for her birthday the next day. He narrowed his eyes to protect them from the sun and placed the vase down beside the teapot on the worktop, and then decided it was time to restart 'All The Love in The World.' As he did, he turned up the volume so he could here it from every room of the house. The hot water was hot enough now so he began filling the bathtub and proceeding upstairs to fetch himself a clean and smart attire. He chose almost brand new underwear, pants and socks he'd only worn once before he recalled.

"Now then?" He wanted to ask himself something before he got into the bath. "How did Richard tell me, how my record player can play a record twice?" He loomed over the turntable.
"Aha, I remember now. Hold the switch down on auto and do not release the switch until the needle has almost landed on the vinyl." He did it as he commentated, and now the Dionne Warwick classic would automatically start again for a second time while he bathed. The beginning of the song prompted him to run into the bathroom, strip off his clothes and soak in the hot, full bathtub where memories of his past invaded his mind once again.

It was around 1965 when he'd heard of a few Hungarians venturing back home to visit their family. Gwen and Nandi, excited at the prospect of visiting his much talked about home, began enquiring. The Soviets had agreed to a certain few going behind the iron curtain without restrictions. Leaders of the resistance from Budapest were blacklisted and their acts had been regarded as treason and death was the penalty for that crime. Letters passed to and from Mogyoroska to Stoke-on-Trent. Nandi's father knew of Nandi's active role in the revolution, but did the authorities? After a while, Janos had confirmation that Nandi hadn't been blacklisted. Nervous and uncertain, knowing his own personal involvement in the atrocities, knowing he was responsible for the death of Avu and Russian lives he thought wise to become British. To obtain a British passport, this surely would protect him against arrest or imprisonment. After all, he wouldn't be Hungarian.

"How do you feel Nandi about been naturalised as a British Citizen?" He remembered Gwen asking him.

"If being English allows me a chance to see my home, my parents, and allows me to take my daughter to see where I have come from, then English I must be. I would call it another victory for me. I beat them in battles, they tried to kill me but I defied them, they tried to imprison me in my own country, I defied that too, and now, they are trying to keep me out. I'm going to beat that also."

"Do you know Nandi; I've never actually heard you speak in Hungarian. I hope you can remember how to do it." Gwen was smiling as the excitement to go and visit this dream of a country that had never seemed possible before, the thought of Nandi conversing in a language she wouldn't understand sent a thrilling sensation through her body.

"Somehow, I have trained my mind to think in English. I think in English, I talk in English. I really don't know if I could think in Hungarian again. This has been troubling me for a while, but then I have realised. It doesn't affect who I am, I may have an English mind, but I have a Hungarian heart. This is the most important."

Nandi was naturalised as a citizen of the United Kingdom in October of 1966.

As he scrubbed his neck and ears with scented soapsuds, an occasional shiver travelled the length of his spine. In his mind, he was travelling back to Hungary for the first time in the summer of 1967 with his wife and daughter.
Europe seemed so old then. No motorways, two-way roads only. Dirt tracks, hills and winding lanes that pierced mainstream Europe heading for this far away Eastern land.

He rinsed away the soap from his eyes and launched into his memory blurting it out loud.

"Fancy driving all the way to Hungary, 1 ½ thousand miles away, in a borrowed Mini Traveller. Christ I owed a lot to my brother-in-law Michael that year. He leant me that car just so I could get home to see my family that I hadn't seen for over 11 years. Even though we had 8 punctures on the way, I still owed him a lot."

The tears and the joy when Nandi reached Mogyoroska that summer. He remembered the road through the mountainous countryside. The fields surrounded them on all sides; they were of gold's, yellows and pale greens. As Mogyoroska approached, Nandi quietened and steadily forced the Mini Traveller through the tiresome jaunt, into an emotional mixture of tranquil beauty, mystery, excitement, flooding them internally with a powerful exaltation sensation, which grew as they travelled deeper and deeper into the picturesque mountainous countryside of what could be a remote and forgotten land. The roads were narrow and carried the scent of dust, twisting and turning with humps and bumps, surrounded by fields, and high mountains behind the fields, forming a sloping, green line against a cloudless, deep blue sky. The route had taken them higher and higher into the sky; closer to Nandi's childhood home. The narrow, dusty, uneven lanes were very long and would suddenly, rather rudely, twist sharply to the left, then sharply to the right, gradually getting steeper, gradually getting higher. Every few miles, the uninhabited country roads were intervened by small residential villages, easily identified by its graveyard and church, signalling a village was approaching.

But Nandi's home seemed to be at the end of the world. It was the last house in the last village, aside the last mountain. Nandi, his mother and father held each other in their front garden and sobbed, wailing aloud. In fact, Nandi remembered the soreness in his throat before he dived out of the Mini Traveller, as a consequence of holding back his tears for the final ten miles of the journey. They just couldn't release the grip on each other; they just couldn't stop their tears. Nandi's father had promised himself that he was never going to let him go and it seemed he never was. They pressed their cheeks firmly into each others letting their tears mix and become one. After a while when they thought they had control, Nandi tried to introduce them to his wife and

502

daughter but couldn't find the words. And it didn't matter, Gwen's Mother-in-Law, Father-in-law and Gayna's grandparents didn't need and introduction, they didn't need a language. The emotion was their language, they spent almost forever it seemed, hugging them and kissing them.

This reunited moment echoed and bounced of every corner of Nandi's mind as he lay down again in the bath. The celebrations that day went well into the night and enhanced when every aunt, uncle, cousin, jammed the garden and cottage and flourished the land. They chair lifted him and drowned him with wine and questions.

An hour later, Nandi was dressed in a beige pair of cotton trousers and a blue and pale green summer shirt. He smelled fresh and clean of Brut deodorant and his clean-shaven face smarted from Aramis aftershave. He laid out some unpaid bills across the bedroom dressing table and unscrewed the lid of a whiskey bottle and poured himself a decent measure in a cut-glass tumbler. Swallowing it slowly, he decisively made up his mind to walk down to his local pub The Portland Inn at the bottom of the street and have a beer and a cigar. He checked his watch.

"Ten to twelve. Just in time."

"Hi Lou." Lou was the Landlord at The Portland Inn.

"Ay up Nand! What can I get you?"

"A pint of Skol please. Oh, and a light for my cigar, I've forgotten my lighter."

He smoked the cigar and drank the lager slowly taking a swig of it after each drag. Lou was busy doing the last minute chores before the gang came in from Century Oils, the oil company only a short distance away on Century Street. He hardly exchanged much more conversation with Nandi and after he'd prepared a few sandwiches and placed them at the end of the bar and returned to the lounge, Nandi had left leaving the froth from his lager lightly coating the inside of his empty glass on the bar.

Before he went back inside his house, he started up his Morris Marina van and parked it around the corner on Stansgate Place out of sight. He ensured the backdoors were locked as well as the front before he left it parked there. In the house, he opened the back kitchen window but pulled it to so it seemed closed.

"Right then." He started to do his security checks around the downstairs. "The backdoor and front doors are locked. Must just close the bathroom door," He closed it. "The kitchen window is closed but can be opened. Now, I will put the needle onto the beginning of my favourite song in the whole world, but switch off the record player, and then the next time it is switched on the song will just begin to play. Oh, I think it's better if I take the phone off the hook, I don't want any interruptions this afternoon."

He carried the vase with the Lilly of the Valley flowers up into his bedroom and placed them on the long dressing table at the side of their king size double bed. It was time to take his medication so he poured three tablets into his hand from the bottle and swallowed them down with a mouthful of whiskey. It stung the back of his throat and he sucked in his breath to soothe the sensation, then, dried his lips with the back of his hand. He wanted to draw the curtains and before he did he switched on the bedroom light, bolted the bedroom door, and then stood in front of the bedroom window gazing through one of the rectangular panes, waiting there motionless as a sentinel at his post. He held his arms outstretched and grabbed both curtains in his hands, he didn't close them at first he remembered the painting of Christ in his church at Mogyoroska on the wall and for the moment he

simulated the painting with his arms out and he bowed his head as if
defeated.
After dragging the curtains tightly together, he opened a gap in the
curtain with a constricted hand in order for him to peer through it. He
didn't know why or what he was looking for but found himself straining
to see if anybody was coming through the entry from the adjacent street,
Winifred Street. His daughter and mother-in-law lived in Winifred
Street and for some reason he felt compelled to check.

He left Blackpool for Stoke-on-Trent in 1957 simply because this
English city offered potential. It had coalmines, steel works, pot banks,
the Michelin and his first rented accommodation was in Winifred Street.
What history that street possessed, this was where he met his wife
Gwen. And this was where Gwen had lived with her parents, four sisters
and one brother. Nandi remembered the history of Winifred Street as he
stared through the gap in the curtains.
"Since then I've got married, I am the father of two children, I have
three grandsons, I've owned a pub, a chip shop, done almost 23 years
for the Michelin and am now a self employed painter and decorator."

A depressed expression still impregnated his grey façade even after
reminding himself of his relatively content and successful outcomes.
This time a full glass of whiskey may help. He poured it, sat at the end
of the bed opposite the large oval dressing table mirror, and then,
watched himself supping away at it. His mirror image changed and he
could see someone else. He knew the person but it still took a whole lot
of thought for him to realise it was a younger look of himself. A mere
replica of the past. His mind was teasing him, constantly playing tricks.
The sudden raise of blood pressure had caused the alcohol to go straight
to his head. He saw his younger version (18 yrs old) give a military
salute followed by the sign of the cross against his chest and held in his
hand a Huzagol 35 M. rifle. Nandi watched as the reflection of

himself in the mirror held the rifle up in front of his face giving it a visual inspection and checked the integral charger and box magazine. He could see himself preparing the rifle, physically unlocking the rotating lugs on the detachable bolt head that went into the receiver. His vision vanished when he looked away from the mirror towards the bottle of Temazepam tablets. Shaking weak hands still managed to unscrew the lid once more and empty out another three anti-depressants. He downed them with his whiskey and started to feel very relaxed and for once he was happy with the situation he'd built about him. The feeling triggered off further memories. The birth of his son Richard, on December 7th 1968.

"I kept my promise to my father. He insisted I carried on our surname. My son was six months old when I took him to Mogyoroska. The closer I got to my village the more proud I became, knowing I had fathered my dad's first grandson, to carry on the family name. By the time I reached the door, I thought I was going to explode with anticipation. It was only my second time home to Hungary in the summer of 1969 and now I had my second child to brag about. My father was ecstatic, another Pekar, another Pekar, he shouted and celebrated." Nandi breathed deeply through his nostrils before taking another sip of whiskey and then decided to talk more of the past to himself. "God knows I've tried my best with him. I've tried to instil in him brains and brawn like my father had done with me in those early tough years under soviet rule in Hungary. I don't know if I've managed it. The brawn is there that's for sure. He's as tall as me, probably slightly broader. He definitely has my eyes, large, bluer though, but the same shape. Hungarian heart, I don't know? The brains to ambush an enemy in a battle for freedom, I just don't know? Jeans, denim jackets, blockhead haircut, dog chains and the willingness to fight for any reason, seems to be his way of life." Nandi smirked, chuckled, shook his head and then continued on about his son. "Girls and gangs. I shouldn't be too hard on him; he's 18 years of age. Growing up as we all have to. He thinks he's a man, well,

May 13ᵗʰ 1987

we'll see how much of a man he is. The bible, my bible, it was given to me by my father; it survived countless incursions during my fight for freedom. It protected me. Now where is it?"

Suspecting the bottom drawer, he dropped to his knees in front of it and rummaged around. He found it, and with a proud decorum, he knew exactly what he wanted to do. First, he read the words written to him by his father way back in 1956 and then, he turned over the page, picked up a pen and began writing a note to his son.

' *To Richard Sándor Pekar, from your loving Dad 13/05/1987.*'

After he'd written it, he turned back a page to the words from his father and then let his eyes blur with tears before flicking through the pages to find what he was looking for, a pressed white rose and pressed Lilly of the Valley stems. Two, once silky white flowers now charred and smeared with a hint of brown caused with age. He let a single tear drip onto them and then ran his finger along the ripped page of the bible. This page was sacred to him and his heart missed a beat recalling the reason to press the flowers on that particular torn-out page.
He closed it and placed it on the dressing table next to the vase with the fresh Lilly of the Valley.

Gwen's birthday card was large and colourful and the gold lettered words on the front stood out against the coloured bouquet of flowers '*To my Darling Wife, Happy Birthday.*'
He spent the next hour writing on the inside page. He needed to say so much and he'd began the first paragraph the day before; but now continued to finalise the unusual gift he'd got for her. During the essay of love and devotion he'd wrote to his wife he continued to intermittently sip away at the whiskey. At the end of the birthday card he filled the glass almost to the rim once more. His hand shook but he managed not to spill any. Noticing the whiskey

bottle was down to the last third, it encouraged him to stand up and reach inside his trouser pocket and empty all of his coins onto the dressing table and added a final line to the birthday card. He read it out loud to himself as he wrote each word.

"Have, a, last, drink, on, me."

Encouraged to do so by a sudden sharp pain in his forehead, Nandi took two strong paracetamol tablets and swallowed them with a mouthful of whiskey. With the birthday card in his hand, he sat back down on the bed and pushed his back against the wall behind the headboard, then read back the words he'd written to his wife.

My Dearest Gwen!

I don't even know how to start. It would have been better if I decided not to say anything just go. After all the pain I have had until now I think I can stand a bit more. The hardest thing is about all of this that I love you so much. I cannot bear to leave you alone. But, it will turn out all right for you. I feel useless in your life anymore. Physically tired and mentally exhausted. I have not gone mad, just frail. I have been called for. Sorry about your birthday present, I wish I had plenty of money I would have given you anything. I haven't the money so I offer you my life. It has been yours and only yours as long as I have been with you. Do not blame yourself or anybody else. No one can even think how I felt. It would have needed a miracle, all constant supervision on your part, which I could not ask for. I have always put you first and I am doing it now, I cannot give you anything else so I let you go free. I only ask you to remember me sometimes. I have loved you so much that I cannot say.

Nandi.

We should have kissed this morning at the market for the last time. Oh how much I love you isn't the life.

I love you

I love you

I love you

I lived for you.

If there is an after life which I think there is I will watch over all of you.

Have a last drink on me.

508

He shuffled across the bed back to the dressing table to pick up his pen and added a few more words at the end.

Sorry I left you no drink.

He dropped the pen back down and this time mixed a few painkillers with more Temazepam in his hand and swallowed them one at a time with his whiskey. The middle drawer contained all of his life insurance policies prepared and compiled days before. He pulled them out and laid them neatly on the dressing table at the other end. He still hadn't finished. Perfectly organised, and well thought out, his suicide plan was falling together as he had intended. The next phase was to ensure that his final thoughts were relayed to his children whom he loved dearly. He tore out a page from his lined papered notebook, leaned on his insurance policy book and began to scribble words from his heart.

My Dear Son,

We have not had the time to get close because you have become a young man before I new it. It makes no difference I have loved you and I hope I can watch over you even longer. Please look after your mother; she is the best in the world. She will need a lot of help in the future. I am not even trying to tell you how I feel it would not make any sense to you. Just ask you to forgive me.
The bible was my father's, your grandfather's. My father died in 1977 as you well know and yours now in 1987. He made me; he gave me a soul to be proud of. This bible has been a guide for me. When you can, I will need you to find a woman name Maria Arany. Her address was 9 Jozsef Utca, Nagytarcsa. Show her the torn out page in the bible.
Sorry I cannot write anymore it's breaking my heart.
Your Loving Dad

With his recently sharpened penknife, he cut the paper to an exact size beneath the last sentence. He folded the note carefully twice so as it fitted snug inside a pale yellow envelope. He licked it and then addressed the front to: *Rich.* He made a neat pile for him. At the bottom, the bible, on top of that, the envelope. He then unclipped his gold watch and opened the strap to lie face up followed by his thick gold wedding ring that slid off his finger relatively easily due to the sweat that was running from his arms around his wrist and onto his fingers. He emptied his glass of whiskey and then filled it with the final third from the bottle and let the empty bottle drop to the floor. He hurried to prepare more paper for Gayna and set about to write her his farewells also.

My Dear Gay,

This is the last letter of three. I cannot even see what I writing. I must ask you to forgive me for stepping on one side. I think it will be better for all. Even me. As I said to Rich, you must look after your mother. She is great. Something else, please visit my grave sometimes it will be very lonely without you all.
Your Loving Dad.

As with Richard's note, he cut it out neatly, folded it twice and slotted into an identical pale yellow envelope, sealed it and addressed it: *To Gay.* The scene on the dressing room table was a breathtaking and disturbing sight. He checked it all. Flowers in a vase, bills, insurance policy, suicide notes, birthday card, bible, watch and his wedding ring. He stood up and wobbled as he did, then, with a steady stature he unhooked the clasp of his necklace from around his neck, kissed it and dropped it in a heap on Gayna's letter. The stage was set. He'd done it all except for one more thing. His photograph, his favourite photograph. He tried hard to remember its whereabouts. With his vision blurring rapidly he threw his head from side to side searching every nook and cranny, every shelf top and then he saw it. It was above the fireplace on the other side of the room. He steadied his quivering trudge across the room by leaning his left hand onto the mattress. The picture meant the world to him so he pressed it against his heart and then kissed it. He was sat on a wall staring into Gwen's

510

May 13th 1987

eyes with his left arm wrapped around her back and waste. Behind him,
the River Danube and The Arpad Bridge that spanned over the river
from Buda to Pest. The Arpad bridge was by far his favourite and it
hadn't been intended that day in 1980 to have his photograph taken with
it behind his beloved wife and him. But by an act of fate, the bridge
appeared on a photograph. He knew that it was this bridge that had
played a part in his decisions to fight for freedom.

He gently laid it on the pillow. He thought it best to write one note on
the unpaid household bills. So he did: *Bills sorry.*
After that, there wasn't anything left to do but to fall asleep. He
swallowed a further helping of Temazepam, painkillers and finished the
whiskey. Peacefully, he took off his glasses and placed them on the
floor. He kicked of his shoes and then pulled back the covers and the
room span when he climbed into bed and pulled the covers up to his
chin. He was curled and lay as a baby lies in its mother's womb.

"I'm free." He said in a voice scarcely intelligible.

His eyes closed firmly as he felt a sharp stitch in his left side; so sharp
he caught his breath in half inspirations, two or three times, before
venturing on a full inflation of the lungs. Then, there was nausea, and an
uncomfortable tightness across his chest.